History Matters

History Matters

A Festschrift in Honor of Stuart Macdonald

Edited by
JOHN A. VISSERS
and ERNEST VAN ECK

PICKWICK *Publications* • Eugene, Oregon

HISTORY MATTERS
A Festschrift in Honor of Stuart Macdonald

Pickwick Publications
An Imprint of Wipf and Stock Publishers
199 W. 8th Ave., Suite 3
Eugene, OR 97401

www.wipfandstock.com

PAPERBACK ISBN: 979-8-3852-7616-5
HARDCOVER ISBN: 979-8-3852-7617-2
EBOOK ISBN: 979-8-3852-7618-9

Cataloging-in-Publication data:

Names: Vissers, John A., editor. | Van Eck, Ernest, editor.

Title: History matters : a festschrift in honor of Stuart Macdonald / edited by John A. Vissers and Ernest van Eck.

Description: Eugene, OR: Pickwick Publications, 2026. | Includes bibliographical references.

Identifiers: ISBN: 979-8-3852-7616-5 (paperback). | ISBN: 979-8-3852-7617-2 (hardcover). | ISBN: 979-8-3852-7618-9 (ebook).

Subjects: LCSH: Christianity—Canada. | Christianity—Scotland. | Macdonald, Stuart. | Presbyterian Church—Canada. | Church history. | Theology.

Classification: BR570 H23 2026 (print). | BR570 (ebook).

VERSION NUMBER 041026

Contents

Preface

John A. Vissers
Winter 2026

This Festschrift is presented to the Rev. Stuart Macdonald, BA, MA, MDiv, PhD, in recognition of his retirement on June 30, 2025, after 40 years of service to The Presbyterian Church in Canada, including 29 years at Knox College and the Toronto School of Theology.

BIOGRAPHY

Stuart Macdonald was born in Toronto in May 1957, the second son of a Scottish father and a Canadian mother of deep Christian faith. The family moved to Orillia when Stuart was a child, where the family attended Orillia-St. Andrew's Presbyterian Church, a large, active Protestant congregation in town immortalized in the writings of Canadian author Stephen Leacock. During Stuart's childhood and youth, the congregation was led by the Rev. Dr. Eric Beggs, an Irish Presbyterian who immigrated to Canada. Orillia St. Andrew's under Beggs's leadership represented a broadly evangelical and Reformed Canadian mainline small-town flourishing church. As a teenager, Stuart was active in the Presbyterian Young People's Society (PYPS) and as a counsellor at Huron Feathers (Sauble Beach) and at one of the synod's camps, Camp Iona. This was the 1970s, when Canadian Presbyterian youth participated in the broader spiritual movements of the time, such as the Jesus movement and the neo-Pentecostal charismatic movement. In the late 1970s, Stuart studied Scottish history at the University of Guelph, where he completed an undergraduate degree (with one year taken at St. Andrews University, Scotland) and a master's degree. This was followed by studies in theology at Knox College, from which he graduated with his Master of Divinity in 1985. During his theological studies, he worked under the supervision of the Rev. Dr. William Adamson at St. Giles Kingsway Presbyterian Church in West Toronto and at St. Andrew's Cobourg under the supervision of the Rev. Dr. Stephen Hayes. Thus began a very distinguished forty-year career as a minister and theological educator in the Presbyterian Church in Canada.

Following ordination in 1985, Stuart was appointed as the minister of a small two-point charge in the Presbytery of Lindsay-Peterborough. In 1988, he succeeded Stephen Hayes as the minister of the Presbyterian Church in Cobourg, Ontario. During this time, Stuart also successfully completed a doctorate in Scottish history at the University of Guelph with a thesis on the Scottish witch hunts, an area of study within which he is a leading expert.

In 1996, after more than a decade as a congregational pastor, he was appointed as Assistant Professor of Church and Society, Director of Basic Degree Studies, and Director of Field Education at Knox College. He served at Knox for the next 29 years, until his retirement in 2025, during which time he was active as a teacher, administrator, and minister. Over the years, he was promoted to Associate Professor, received tenure in 2008, and later became a Full Professor. In addition to his teaching and research, he has made significant contributions to the life of the college. Stuart has served in multiple roles at Knox College, including terms as Dean, Vice-Principal, and Acting Principal.

In retirement, Stuart continues to be active in teaching and graduate supervision. Family has always been and remains important. Stuart has a daughter, Meaghan, a son-in-law, Joe, a grandson, Levon, and a son, Brendan. Stuart is married to the Rev. Gale Macdonald, with whom he shares a love of travel, hiking, spending time with friends, and time together at their cottage on Lake Huron.

Beyond Knox College, Prof. Macdonald has been a dedicated and influential scholar, making significant contributions to the academic community. His research has advanced the fields of Scottish history, Reformation studies, and Canadian Presbyterianism, leaving a lasting impact on academia. Through his work, he has inspired generations of students and researchers. A longstanding member of the Canadian Society of Presbyterian History, he served as its president from 2019 to 2024 and has also been an active member and president (one-year term) of the Canadian Society of Church History.

Over the years, Stuart has authored numerous articles and books, further cementing his reputation as a leading historian. Among his noteworthy publications are *The Witches of Fife: Witch-hunting in a Scottish*

Shire, 1560–1710 (John Tuckwell Publishers, 2002) and *Leaving Christianity: Changing Allegiance in Canada since 1945* (McGill-Queen's University Press, 2017), coauthored with Brian Clarke, and his latest book, *Tradition and Tension: The Presbyterian Church in Canada, 1945–1985*, also published by McGill-Queen's University Press.

Colleagues and friends express their gratitude to Prof. Macdonald for his dedication and many contributions to Knox College. The church and the academy have been enriched by his presence, benefiting from his vast knowledge, experience, and unwavering commitment. We have enjoyed his sense of humor and been uplifted by his singing and guitar playing at services and events. His wisdom, steady guidance, thoughtfulness, and caring presence will be deeply missed. A mentor to many colleagues, he has modelled both ethical scholarship and faithful servanthood.

CONVERSATION AND REFLECTIONS

1. **Stuart, you have been a minister of the PCC for forty years and a professor and administrator at Knox College for almost thirty years. What do you consider the most critical aspects of these roles? How did they differ? How did they overlap?**

I have always tried to keep these roles distinct, while recognizing they do overlap.

As a minister, one is responsible for leading a Christian community by what one says and by the example one offers. I loved preaching, leading others in prayer, and performing various important pastoral acts.

As a professor, one needs to teach the subjects considered important for those preparing for ministry. What is it that students need to know and understand? In my case, those subjects have been aspects of congregational ministry and the history of Christianity.

As an administrator, it is your responsibility to structure the environment so that students are most likely to succeed and faculty can do their jobs effectively. The goal was (and is) to produce better ministers, counsellors, and a more educated laity. It's easy, given the committees, meetings, details, and emails that take up so much of the workday, to lose sight of this. I always tried to stay focused on students and my colleagues.

In whatever role I found myself (sometimes more than one role at the same time) I tried to keep clarity about that specific role: What is it I'm here to do? What am I called to do? How do I keep these roles distinct? At times, it was challenging. What I tried to do in each of these roles was do the tasks with integrity, but also with compassion.

2. **How has the church changed over your time as a minister and teacher?**

Hugely, sometimes more than I can even imagine. When I graduated from Knox with my M.Div. in 1985 and went out into ministry, there was a hope that we could make the church grow by better preaching, better pastoral care, and by attending to all kinds of important small things that would make people feel welcome. When I came to Knox as a faculty member in 1996, we still thought this, though we knew things were in more serious shape than we had imagined in the 1980s. Intentional, competent ministry was still what we tried to speak about—and let me be apparent, however much else has changed, I still believe this is absolutely vital to any success. It is now clear that we are in a completely different landscape. Growth is not an issue; adapting and transforming for this new reality is the issue. That has now become clear.

Trying to understand the changes we were experiencing was something I did both as a minister and after I joined the faculty. I still remember writing a sermon about Reginald Bibby's *Fragmented Gods* when it first came out in 1987 and sharing it not only with my congregation but also with several others when I was invited to be a guest preacher. Like so many of my colleagues, I was reading widely, trying to find a solution or a response to the situation. And this was one key element that led me to begin working with my colleague Brian Clarke to understand the reality of Christianity's changing place in Canada. Sometimes you hope you've got something wrong with your research: unfortunately, I don't believe we did. The data we uncovered showing that the 1960s were a key moment in Canadian history, when religious allegiances fundamentally changed, and Canada became a country where more people had no religious identity, has only been confirmed by subsequent studies.

We now have a much clearer picture of what has happened in Canada. I am proud to have been part of the research that has helped to generate that clarity. At the same time, what remains disappointing is the level of denial in so many denominations, including our own, that we are in a different context from the one we were in until very recently. We are dealing with a major, fundamental change, and we continue to treat it as if buying better coffee or doing minor things will somehow, almost magically, return us to the golden days of yore. We keep being told it's our theology that's wrong. As *Tradition and Tension* showed, the Presbyterian Church in Canada was still a very conservative denomination, culturally and theologically, in the 1960s when these changes began. We had a creed from the seventeenth century and used a hymn book from the early twentieth. Yet we continue to look inside our denomination for the cause of our decline rather than take seriously the cultural shift that is all too evident, or we simply pretend it has not happened.

I have always tried to be realistic with our students about these changes. I've appreciated how open they have been and how open Knox College has been to talk about these changes. I have not felt like a "voice crying in the wilderness" at Knox College, but I have heard from my colleagues and our students that this was important information. In other church contexts, though, it has too often felt like this was not crucial information or, as noted above, that people have denied it without producing any facts to challenge the current findings.

The church did not bury its head in the sand in 1966 when membership first declined, nor did we do so in later years as we looked at the state of the church and changes in its place in society. I worry that we now do. We are ignoring the challenges, hoping they will go away. They will not.

3. **How has theological education changed over your time at Knox College?**

Theological Education has also changed, though perhaps not as dramatically. We have become less church-focused and more focused on the University and its requirements. This is completely understandable and not without its benefits. Indeed, when I was serving as a minister, I was concerned that our denominational college faculty would publish more and share their knowledge more widely. This is something I'm pleased to say has been a reality in my time at Knox. It has been wonderful to see the program offerings at Knox diversify. Knox is very different now from when I began.

In graduate education (the Th.M., M.A., and Ph.D.) the change has become even more dramatic. I continue to be disappointed that we have not been able to sustain or recreate a robust graduate program focused on congregational issues, as the DMin did in its heyday. I worry that our current Ph.D. focuses too much on the discipline of "theology" and not enough on the other disciplines that I consider part of theological education (Biblical studies, historical studies, preaching, congregational studies, worship, church music, and pastoral theology). I worry that academics — not only in theological colleges but across the university — are more concerned with speaking to other academics than with communicating their insights to the public at large.

All these changes are understandable. There are these strong forces, exerting something like a gravitational pull in these directions. There is a certain understanding of what an academic environment should be. Some of these changes are certainly improvements. At the same time, I believe that theological colleges need to work, and work hard, to communicate with the church and with the broadest possible audience.

4. **Your research interests have included Scottish history, Canadian Presbyterianism, Christianity in Canada, and Congregational Leadership. Please describe these areas of research, how they overlap, and how they have shaped your approach to teaching and leadership, and what you believe your most important contributions are.**

Teaching shapes research. This has been very true in my case.

When I began at Knox, I was still completing my Doctoral thesis, which dealt with seventeenth-century Scotland. It was assumed that because I was a historian, I must know a great deal about the history of the Presbyterian Church in Canada. My knowledge was much more limited than was supposed! I had the experience of being a congregational minister for over 10 years and was familiar with some of the recent literature. So, teaching courses related to ministry also made sense, even though I had a great deal to learn here as well.

It was the experience of teaching and reading the subject at hand and then trying to communicate it effectively to the students in the class that really shifted my research away from seventeenth-century Scotland to a wide variety of other topics. There are those moments when you are more or less repeating what the textbook and the secondary literature state is true, when you suddenly ask yourself, "Is this true?" What actually is the social gospel? I'm describing the temperance movement. Is that all there was to the social gospel, or what else was it? Or, you are teaching about the 16th-century Reformation, and you tell your students that John Knox believed the mass was dangerous and idolatrous, but you are not sure why. Or, you say something about how Presbyterians established new congregations in the 1950s, and some of your students (who are from those congregations) suggest a different understanding entirely. Each of these experiences, and many similar ones, has led me to read more, consider new questions, and then try to share those thoughts through class lectures, presentations, and sometimes publications.

The end result was that I have written in these different fields, as is evident in my C.V. It may look scattered, but I think what unites my research is its connection to teaching and the clear use of the historical method. I have approached each topic, trying to ask, "what happened?" and only once there is clarity on what happened has the crucial question of "why?" been addressed. What I have truly appreciated at Knox College has been the support of this kind of curiosity! When Brian Clarke and I began work on religious demographics in Canada, it wasn't clear how important this work would be, nor how many years it would take to adequately research and publish on such a complicated and vital topic. When I headed off to a conference on John Knox, no one questioned how this related to the work I had been doing on Canada. I truly appreciate the support and the trust I was given.

In terms of the details and what I think I have written that was important:

I am immensely proud of *Leaving Christianity*, and I believe it is crucial to our understanding of religion in Canada today. *Tradition and Tension* only confirms those findings and shows even more thoroughly how dramatically different the situation is today from the golden age of the 1950s, when I was born.

My research on the witch-hunt in Scotland has raised significant questions, questions that challenge the conventional understandings in important ways. I would note the article on John Knox's contribution to the origins of what we know and think of as the Scottish witch-hunt.

The article on Presbyterians (and other Reformed Christians) and ethnicity would be another publication that I believe made a significant contribution.

There are also some new articles that grew out of the research on *Tradition and Tension* that I think are very interesting.

In everything I have written, I have tried to share something I believed mattered and tried to communicate it so that anyone who was interested could understand and respond.

5. **What are the most important lessons you learned from congregants and students over the years, and how has that shaped your ministry and scholarship?**

Congregants and students have genuine concerns. They are all trying, in their own ways, to be disciples and fulfill their various callings.

Taking this seriously has shaped everything I've done. At the same time, as I became more and more aware of our shifting context, I found myself thinking and rethinking things.

As noted already, these are what have really shaped my ministry and the academic work I've done.

6. **Who do you consider the most influential in shaping your Christian journey, and what have you learned from them?**

My parents. They were gentle, thoughtful people of deep faith. They were by no means perfect, and we had our challenges (particularly when I was a teenager!), but through it all, I came to appreciate how much they expressed their faith in all they said and in how they lived their lives.

I had some great mentors: Eric Beggs (my home minister in Orillia), Ron Archer (my youth minister), and Bill Adamson and Stephen Hayes (during my studies at Knox). They were very different, but those differences helped me see that one didn't have to fit a particular mould to be an effective minister. That encouraged me to find my own voice, one that was distinct from each of them.

Friends were also key. They shaped my faith when I was young, those I worked with at Huron Feathers and Camp Iona in particular, and more broadly within the networks of the Presbyterian Young People's Society at the time. Friends have remained very important.

More recently, I have experienced what it is like to be a minister's spouse. Gale has been a great model of effective leadership in a congregation. She has modelled how to navigate effectively so many challenges in congregational life today. She has also supported my work while inviting me to be part of a congregation in meaningful ways for me.

Alongside those inside the church, it's been my friends outside of the church who have been very important. Having music as a hobby and playing open mics means you get to know, often at a surprisingly deep level, people who are not in your congregation or workplace. Some of them have a Christian faith. Some of them have a different faith. Some of them would not identify with any faith. Becoming friends and hearing their concerns has been an incredible gift. Being exposed to a variety of people outside of a religious context certainly forces you to think differently. Too often, churches can become bubbles, and ministers can find themselves without time to get to know people outside those bubbles.

I have been so fortunate to have great friends. They put up with me. They are themselves and let me be myself. They accept me, even if they don't always agree.

7. **What have been the most important things you have tried to instill in your students?**

Love people. Respect them. Treat them as you would like to be treated. (Hopefully that rings some bells for everyone in terms of Scripture, but it's not just something in the Bible; it's how we are called to live.) Be humble. Listen. You (and I) always have something to learn.

Be disciples. Know who you follow and continue to follow Christ. For those in leadership, there is a responsibility to lead. Don't be afraid to lead. Just remember to try to follow the example of Jesus in how he led others.

If you remember these things, that's what matters. The individual facts and dates that we spend so much time talking about in class, these matter. But you can always look these up. It's who you are that's most important.

PUBLICATION LIST

Books

Macdonald, Stuart, and Brian Clarke. *Leaving Christianity: Changing Allegiance in Canada since 1945*. Montreal and Kingston: McGill-Queen's University Press, 2017.

Macdonald, Stuart. *The Witches of Fife: Witch-Hunting in a Scottish Shire, 1560–1710.* East Linton: Tuckwell Press, 2002. E-book ed., Edinburgh: Birlinn, 2014.

Macdonald, Stuart, and Daniel MacLeod, eds. *Keeping the Kirk: Scottish Religion at Home and in the Diaspora.* Guelph series in Scottish Studies 3. Guelph: Centre for Scottish Studies, 2014.

Macdonald, Stuart. *Tradition and Tensions: The Presbyterian Church in Canada, 1945–1985*. Montreal and Kingston: McGill-Queen's University Press, 2025.

Peer-Reviewed Articles

Macdonald, Stuart. "Crofter Colonisation in Canada, 1886–1892: The Scottish Political Background." *Northern Scotland* 7 (1986) 47–59.

Macdonald, Stuart. "Torture and the Scottish Witch-Hunt: A Re-examination." *Scottish Tradition* 27 (2002) 95–114.

Macdonald, Stuart. "Enemies of God Revisited: Recent Publications on Scottish Witch-Hunting." *Scottish Economic and Social History* 23 (2003) 65–84.

Macdonald, Stuart, and Brian Clarke. "Simply 'Christian': Canada's Newest Major Religious Denomination." *Toronto Journal of Theology* 23 (2007) 109–25.

Macdonald, Stuart, and Brian Clarke. "How Are Canada's Five Largest Protestant Denominations Faring? A Look at the 2001 Census." *Studies in Religion / Sciences Religieuses* 40 (2012) 511–34.

Macdonald, Stuart. "The Changed (and Changing) Face of Church History." *Toronto Journal of Theology*, Supplement 1 (2015) 29–42.

Macdonald, Stuart. "John Knox, the Scottish Church, and Witchcraft Accusations." *Sixteenth Century Journal* 48 (2017) 635–50.

Macdonald, Stuart. "Counting Witches: Illuminating and Distorting the Shape of Witchcraft Accusations in Scotland." *Journal of Scottish Historical Studies* 37 (2017) 1–18.

Macdonald, Stuart. "Interesting Times Indeed: Reflections on the Last Decade at the Toronto School of Theology." *Toronto Journal of Theology* 37 (2021) 14–22.

Chapters in Multi-Author Volumes

Macdonald, Stuart. "In Search of the Devil in Fife Witchcraft Cases, 1560–1705." In *The Scottish Witch-Hunt in Context*, edited by Julian Goodare, 33–50. Manchester: Manchester University Press, 2002.

Macdonald, Stuart. "Theological Field Education and Leaving Christendom: Initial Reflections." In *Theological Reflection from a Protestant Canadian Context*, edited by Abigail Johnson. Toronto: Association for Theological Field Education, 2002. Reprinted in *Journal of Supervision and Training in Ministry* 23 (2003) 84–94.

Macdonald, Stuart. "Presbyterian and Reformed Christians and Ethnicity." In *Christianity and Ethnicity in Canada*, edited by Paul Bramadat and David Seljak, 168–203. Toronto: University of Toronto Press, 2008.

Macdonald, Stuart. "Religion and Secularization in Canada: Education and the Impact on Mission." In *Christian Mission and Education in Modern China, Japan, and Korea: Historical Studies*, edited by Jan A. B. Jongeneel et al., 27–42. New York: Peter Lang, 2009.

Macdonald, Stuart. "Canadian Presbyterians and Vatican II: A Silent Revolution." In *Vatican II: Expériences canadiennes – Canadian Experiences*, edited by Michael Attridge, Catherine E. Clifford, and Gilles Routhier, 78–105. Ottawa: University of Ottawa Press, 2011.

Macdonald, Stuart. "For Empire and God: Canadian Presbyterians and the Great War." In *Canadian Churches and the First World War*, edited by Gordon L. Heath, 133–51. Eugene, OR: Pickwick Publications, 2014.

Macdonald, Stuart. "Loss of Memory in the Diaspora: The Debate around the Relocation of the Statue of Margaret Wilson at Knox College, Toronto." In *Keeping the Kirk: Scottish Religion at Home and in the Diaspora*, edited by Daniel MacLeod and Stuart Macdonald, 225–50. Guelph: University of Guelph, 2014.

Macdonald, Stuart. "A Different Kind of Congress: The Congress of Concern, 1968." In *Do No Harm: A Festschrift in Honor of Charles Fensham*, edited by Ernest van Eck and George R. Hunsberger, 129–48. Eugene, OR: Pickwick Publications, 2025.

Macdonald, Stuart, and Clarke Brown. "No Need to Turn Out the Lights: Anglicans in Canada in the Twentieth and Twenty-First Centuries." In *Reformation Worlds: Antecedents and Legacies in the Anglican Tradition*, edited by Sean A. Otto and Thomas Powers, 199–212. New York: Peter Lang, 2016.

Forthcoming

Macdonald, Stuart. "Beyond Church Courts: The Evolution of Structures and Polity in the Presbyterian Church in Canada." In an edited collection by Sarah Travis and Robert Revington. Forthcoming.

Macdonald, Stuart. "A New Kind of Conflict? Debating the Program to Combat Racism in the Anglican Church of Canada." Forthcoming.

Contributors

Dr. Phyllis D. Airhart, Professor Emerita of the History of Christianity, Emmanuel College, Toronto School of Theology, University of Toronto

Rev. Dr. Lee Beach, Associate Professor of Christian Ministry and Director of Ministry Formation, McMaster Divinity College, Hamilton, ON

Rev. Dr. Roland J. De Vries, Principal, The Presbyterian College, Montreal

Dr Elizabeth Ewan, Professor Emerita of Scottish Studies and History, University of Guelph

Rev. Dr. Charles Fensham, Professor Emeritus, Knox College, Toronto School of Theology, University of Toronto

Dr James R. Ginther, Professor of Medieval Theology, Regis St. Michael's Faculty of Theology, University of St Michael's College, and Interim Director, Centre for Medieval Studies, University of Toronto

Michael F. Graham, Emeritus Professor of History, University of Akron

Rev. Canon Dr. Alan L. Hayes, Professor Emeritus of the History of Christianity, Wycliffe College, Toronto School of Theology, University of Toronto

Rev. Dr. Gordon L. Heath, FRHistS, Professor of Christian History and Centenary Chair in World Christianity, McMaster Divinity College

Rev. Dr. Joon Won Kim, Associate Pastor, Choonghyun Presbyterian Church, Seoul, South Korea

Rev. Dr. Ross A. Lockhart, Dean of St. Andrew's Hall, Vancouver

Dr. Amanda Pullan, Sessional Lecturer, Knox College, Toronto School of Theology, University of Toronto

Dr. Robert Revington, Research Fellow, McMaster Divinity College, Hamilton, ON

Rev. Dr. Ernest van Eck, Principal and Professor of New Testament at Knox College, Toronto School of Theology, University of Toronto

Rev. Dr. John A. Vissers, Professor of Systematic Theology at Knox College, Toronto School of Theology, University of Toronto

Introduction

Ernest van Eck and John A. Vissers

HISTORY MATTERS

History matters because it reveals the concealed architecture of the present. The institutions, convictions, conflicts, and compromises that shape contemporary religious life did not emerge spontaneously; they are the outcomes of decisions made, paths chosen, and alternatives rejected across generations. To understand why Canadian churches find themselves navigating post-Christendom realities—declining membership, eroded social capital, contested identities, and uncertain futures—requires looking backward with rigor and honesty. History exposes not only what happened, but why it happened, illuminating the structures of belief, power, and belonging that once seemed permanent and now appear fragile. It challenges assumptions, complicates narratives of triumph or decline, and demands accountability for the ways past actions continue to shape present possibilities.

History matters also because it allows us to see the trajectories, tensions, and transformations that shape both the church and society. By examining the past, we gain insight into how decisions, beliefs, and practices were formed, contested, and reinterpreted over time, revealing patterns that can inform present action and future discernment. Historical study cultivates perspective, reminding us that contemporary challenges—whether in ministry, mission, or ecclesial identity—are not new, but part of ongoing human and theological narratives. It also fosters humility: by situating our own context within centuries of struggle, creativity, and reflection, we are reminded that our decisions, while significant, are part of a larger story that transcends any single generation. In short, history matters because it shapes understanding, guides ethical reflection, and sustains a sense of continuity and responsibility across time.

The contributors to this Festschrift explore diverse historical moments and contexts, yet their work converges around shared themes: the formation and fragmentation of Christian identity, the negotiation of power and authority in ecclesial and civic life, the encounter between tradition and transformation, and the persistent question of what it means to bear witness in a pluralistic world. The essays gathered in this volume also demonstrate that historical inquiry is never neutral. It is shaped by the questions historians ask, the sources they privilege, and the interpretive frameworks they bring to their work. Whether examining witch trials in sixteenth-century Scotland, demonological debates in seventeenth-century England, moral reasoning surrounding wartime bombing, or the theological formation of medieval church leaders, these studies reveal the past as a contested and complex terrain. History matters precisely because it refuses to yield easy answers. Instead, it draws readers into ambiguity, tension, and unfinished human experience.

Taken together, the essays collected in *History Matters* exemplify why historical study remains indispensable for thoughtful theological reflection and responsible engagement with the challenges of the present.

ESSAYS IN CELEBRATION

Phyllis Airhart, in her essay titled *Ecumenism and Denominational Identity in a Pluralistic World: Canadian Protestant Responses*, argues that the postwar crisis of Canadian Protestant ecumenism and denominational identity is inseparable from the decline and transformation of the foreign missionary enterprise in a rapidly pluralizing world. Building on Stuart Macdonald's insight that strategies effective in the 1950s ceased to work after the 1960s, she contends that missions functioned as a hidden fifth pillar shaping denominational purpose, finances, governance, and ecumenical cooperation. Modern ecumenism emerged from missionary collaboration, most notably the 1910 Edinburgh Conference, and initially assumed the universality of Christianity within a Christendom framework tied to Western culture and colonial expansion.

After the Second World War, however, anticolonial movements, the expulsion of missionaries, and the growing identification of missions with imperialism undermined both missionary enthusiasm and ecumenical confidence. As Christianity encountered religious pluralism more directly, figures such as Wilfred Cantwell Smith warned that traditional proselytizing evangelism was theologically and practically unsustainable. In response, ecumenical Protestantism redefined mission from "missions" to a holistic "mission to the world," emphasizing Christian presence, social engagement, and interfaith openness rather than conversion.

This shift, embodied in developments such as the merger of the International Missionary Council into the World Council of Churches and denominational reports like the United Church's 1966 World Mission statement and the Presbyterian LAMP report, intensified divisions between ecumenical leaders and conservative evangelicals, who saw these changes as a repudiation of the gospel and a threat to confessional identity. Airhart shows how these theological debates had concrete institutional consequences: denominational structures built to support expansive missionary enterprises struggled once missions contracted, budgets shrank, and governance models shifted from corporate confidence to regulatory management of decline. For Presbyterians in particular, ecumenism revived unresolved anxieties from the failed 1925 church union, with fears that cooperation would lead to the erosion or death of denominational identity. Efforts to reorganize the church around a "mission to the world" provoked resistance, sharpened internal conflict, and ultimately failed to produce either renewed unity or effective adaptation.

In her conclusion, Airhart situates these struggles within a broader cultural shift toward individualism, de-institutionalization, and congregational rather than denominational loyalty. While ecumenical dreams of organic unity faded, new forms of cooperation, networks, and shared spaces emerged amid ongoing pluralism. Denominational identity, once sustained by missions and opposition to rivals, has become increasingly thin, as many Canadian Protestants care less about labels and more about credible witness in a post-Christian, post-Christendom society.

Lee Beach's chapter, *The Church in Canada: Responding to Post-Christendom*, engages the empirical analysis of decline offered by Clarke and Macdonald in *Leaving Christianity* and turns to the question of how the Canadian church might respond faithfully in a post-Christendom context. Accepting that secularization is neither temporary nor reversible, Beach argues that decline must be understood within broader cultural transformations that have reshaped the plausibility of Christian belief. Drawing on Charles Taylor, he describes secularization as the shift from a society in which belief in God was assumed to one in which faith is merely one option among many, increasingly relegated to the private sphere. This change has been reinforced by rationalism, consumerism, individualization, and the "immanent frame," within which transcendence is no longer experienced as a taken-for-granted reality.

Beach identifies several implications of this shift for the church's life and ministry. First, the erosion of a shared Christian vocabulary means that churches can no longer assume even basic familiarity with the gospel, while historical and contemporary scandals have deepened public mistrust. Second, the rise of individualism has relocated authority from communal tradition to the autonomous self, fostering forms of spirituality that prize authenticity and personal meaning over belonging and doctrinal coherence. Third, the dominance of the immanent frame has weakened confidence in a God who speaks and acts in the world, rendering public expressions of faith socially awkward or intellectually suspect. Together, these dynamics challenge not only church attendance but the church's theological confidence and imagination.

Rather than offering managerial solutions or strategies for institutional recovery, Beach situates the church in a liminal moment akin to biblical periods of waiting, such as Israel's exile or the disciples' waiting for the Spirit. He characterizes this posture as "waiting as mission," an active and discerning stance that resists premature action and attends carefully to signs of God's presence. This waiting is not passive resignation but a commitment to depth over growth, formation over performance, and theological attentiveness over pragmatic efficiency.

Within this framework, Beach highlights three practices that remain essential even amid decline: sustained spiritual discernment rooted in theology, ongoing missional engagement shaped by local context, and faithful corporate worship that bears witness to the mystery and otherness of God. In conclusion, Beach offers a hopeful counterpoint to narratives of despair. While acknowledging the gravity of institutional decline, he argues that the church's future lies not in reclaiming cultural authority or replicating past models, but in humble, patient participation in God's work from the margins of a post-Christendom society.

In *Pastoral Ministry as Unfinished*, Roland J. De Vries offers a theologically rich and pastorally honest reflection on the open-ended nature of ministry. Beginning with an autobiographical account of his relationship with his grandfather, Gerrit Baak, De Vries introduces "unfinishedness" as a defining feature of human life. His grandfather's life story, partially recorded but never completed, becomes a metaphor for relationships, vocations, and meanings that resist closure. This personal narrative sets the stage for a broader theological exploration of pastoral ministry as work that is inherently incomplete.

De Vries argues that pastoral ministry is unfinished in two distinct but related senses. First, it is unfinished because there is always more to do. As long as life continues with its cycles of birth, growth, suffering, and death, pastoral work remains ongoing. Second, and more profoundly, pastoral ministry is unfinished because pastors are inserted mid-narrative into the lives of individuals, congregations, and institutions that preceded them and will continue after their departure. Pastors rarely see the final outcome of their labor, whether in the spiritual growth of individuals, the long-term impact of preaching, or the future of congregational initiatives begun under their leadership.

This sense of incompletion is intensified in the contemporary context of mainline Protestant decline. Pastors increasingly serve congregations whose long-term survival is uncertain, raising existential questions about the meaning of ministry undertaken in fragile or transitional settings. De Vries insists that this uncertainty is not a pastoral failure but an unavoidable condition of ministry itself.

To deepen this claim, De Vries turns to the Gospel of Mark and its famously abrupt ending. Drawing on Matthew Larsen's work, he suggests that Mark was not originally understood as a finished literary product but as *hypomnēmata*, provisional notes intended for ongoing interpretation and completion by others. Just as Matthew builds upon and reshapes Mark's narrative, pastoral ministry participates in a tradition of faithful incompleteness, trusting the Spirit to carry forward what individual ministers cannot finish.

Finally, De Vries draws on Karl Barth's theology of time to frame limitation as a gift rather than a deficit. Human life, including pastoral vocation, is a "unique opportunity" precisely because it is finite. In Christ, God has embraced temporal limitation, affirming unfinished human lives as meaningful and beloved. Pastoral ministry, therefore, is not about achieving closure or measurable success, but about faithful presence, gift-giving, and trust in God's work beyond visible outcomes. To live pastorally is to embrace unfinishedness not as failure, but as a form of obedience, gratitude, and hope.

Elizabeth Ewan's chapter, *Maintaining a Godly Society: Offences and Forgiveness in the St. Andrews Burgh Court in the Later Sixteenth Century*, examines how municipal authorities in post-Reformation St. Andrews sought to create and maintain a "godly society" through the regulation of interpersonal conduct. Drawing on surviving burgh court records from 1589–1592, Ewan situates the court's activity within the broader context of the Scottish Reformation, where ecclesiastical and secular authorities collaborated to enforce moral discipline and social order. Cases ranged from verbal insults to physical assaults, often reflecting deeper tensions within the community, as exemplified by the 1572 witchcraft case in which a woman's refusal to forgive her offender contributed to her conviction.

The St. Andrews burgh court combined punishment with ritualized reconciliation. Offenders were frequently required to seek forgiveness from their victims, sometimes kneeling at the site of the offence, in the court itself, or at the market cross—the symbolic heart of the town. These rituals served multiple purposes: they publicly restored the victim's reputation, demonstrated the authorities' commitment to justice, reinforced social hierarchies, and provided a visible reminder to the community and to God that moral order was upheld. In some cases, the court also required symbolic acts, such as handing over weapons used in assaults, to reinforce dependence on the mercy of the injured party and the authority of the magistrates.

Although corporal punishments like the cuckstool, jougs, and stocks were rarely employed, the threat of their use, together with financial penalties, underscored the magistrates' capacity to enforce conformity. Monetary fines often went toward communal projects, including repairs to the harbor or town gates, reflecting a practical as well as moral dimension to punishment: breaches of personal conduct could be transformed into contributions to the common good.

Ewan emphasizes the importance of forgiveness in maintaining the godly community. Over 80% of verbal and physical assault cases required public acts of contrition, demonstrating that social cohesion relied not solely on punishment but on the ritual repair of relationships. The court's insistence on public forgiveness echoes practices in the Reformed Kirk, linking civic and ecclesiastical authority in the moral governance of the town.

Despite these efforts, the chapter highlights the limitations of such initiatives. Resistance by offenders, persistent family feuds, and later municipal unrest illustrate the difficulty of fully realizing the ideal of a godly society. Nevertheless, the St. Andrews authorities' combination of ritualized reconciliation, targeted sanctions, and civic oversight reflects a deliberate attempt to govern both behavior and conscience, striving to embody Reformed ideals even in an imperfect and often resistant community.

In "*What to Make of History in the Study of Mission*," Charles Fensham reflects on the complex relationship between mission history, theological reflection, and the present. Drawing inspiration from Virginia Burrus, he underscores that the study of history is never neutral: historians are inevitably shaped by their own context, experiences, and biases. Mission history, therefore, is both descriptive—telling the story of the church's engagement across cultures and frontiers—and normative, inviting theological and ethical reflection on how the gospel has been interpreted and enacted.

Fensham illustrates this interplay through his early experience with the Māòhi church in French Polynesia, highlighting how colonial missionary practices imposed Western homophobic norms, suppressing recognition of

Maāhuū, two-spirited individuals with socially valued roles. His encounter demonstrates how the lived experience of mission intersects with cultural interpretation, ethical reflection, and historical narrative. It also raises the critical question of whose perspectives are included or excluded in historical accounts and how such exclusions reflect theological and cultural biases.

The essay situates mission history within broader debates in historiography and theology. Fensham traces the historical development of church history—from Eusebius' universal vision of the "people of God," to early typologies of church eras, to modern concepts of salvation history and the integration of social sciences. He emphasizes that church and mission history are invariably shaped by theological frameworks, such as the notion of the ideal early church or paradigms of decline and reform, as well as by the historian's cultural and personal standpoint. Even critical methodologies, including Schleiermacher's advocacy for theology as a "historical and empirical science," cannot entirely escape bias.

Fensham extends this argument to the study of sexuality and gender in church and mission history. He notes the historical silences around the persecution or marginalization of sexual and gender diverse individuals, the lacunae in mainstream church historiography, and the tendency to conflate historical practice with theological normativity. His own research—particularly on the treatment of the Ma[set macron over a]hu[set macron over u] and engagement with African theologians—reveals both the colonial origins of homophobia in churches and the ways secular historical scholarship can illuminate neglected dimensions of mission history.

Ultimately, Fensham argues that mission historians and missiologists must engage openly with their biases while striving for historical and ethical integrity. The descriptive task of recording mission history is inseparable from normative reflection on Scripture, ethics, and theological paradigms. Exemplars such as David Bosch, J.H. Bavinck, and Bevans and Schroeder demonstrate the necessity of ordering historical narratives using interpretive frameworks, while acknowledging that choices in selection, emphasis, and interpretation reflect the historian's perspective. Fensham concludes that critical, self-reflective engagement with history is essential for Missiology, enabling scholars to learn from past successes and failures, confront silences, and apply lessons ethically in contemporary mission contexts.

In *The Formation of Pastoral Leaders in the Twelfth Century: The Genesis Commentary of Stephen Langton in Context*, James Ginther examines how Langton (ca. 1150–1228), Archbishop of Canterbury and a master at the University of Paris, used biblical exegesis to shape the formation of Christian leaders, particularly prelates. Ginther situates this inquiry within multiple contexts: institutional, educational, exegetical, and liturgical, revealing how medieval theological pedagogy aimed to cultivate both intellectual and moral capacities necessary for pastoral leadership.

Langton's commentary on Genesis illustrates a sophisticated interpretive strategy that intertwined literal, allegorical, tropological, and occasionally anagogical readings. Central to his method was the concept that Scripture could instruct on leadership: prelates were depicted as figures who exercized both the power of order—authority to bind, loose, and administer sacraments—and jurisdictional power—responsibility over the faithful and their temporal resources. Twelfth-century bishops were often political as well as spiritual leaders, managing diocesan land, finances, and personnel, yet Langton emphasized that temporalities existed to serve spiritual ends.

Ginther highlights Langton's reliance on historical models, particularly Gregory the Great's *Regula pastoralis*, which provided a detailed account of episcopal virtues, pastoral duties, and self-care. Similarly, Bernard of Clairvaux's *De moribus et officio episcoporum* offered guidance connecting monastic virtue to episcopal conduct, particularly humility, charity, and chastity. Langton's commentaries functioned as complementary texts to these earlier works, embedding principles of prelacy within exegetical instruction.

A crucial aspect of Langton's pedagogy was medieval spiritual exegesis. Following Augustine's guidance, Langton sought to ensure that moral and spiritual readings of Scripture—though flexible—were rooted in the literal text and advanced Christian charity. Classical rhetoric informed his teaching, especially memory techniques that allowed students to recall theological and moral concepts through biblical narratives. For example, his inaugural sermon used the Exodus plagues to illustrate moral obstacles and social challenges relevant to leadership, linking the study of Scripture to practical virtues required of future pastors and bishops.

Langton's Genesis commentary also emphasizes the ethical and social dimensions of leadership. Human beings, created in God's image and likeness, were called to exercize dominion responsibly; prelates, as intermediaries between God and laity, had to ensure that temporal goods served the vulnerable and poor rather than the powerful. Through repeated biblical references and the integration of liturgical readings, Langton cultivated habits of mind and moral awareness that prepared his students to navigate the complexities of ecclesial authority and pastoral care.

Ginther's study demonstrates that the formation of prelates in the twelfth century was not achieved through specialized schools but through rigorous theological education embedded in biblical exegesis, classical pedagogy, and liturgical practice. Langton's commentary illustrates how intellectual rigor, moral formation, and practical reflection on leadership were interwoven, providing a model for understanding medieval approaches to pastoral formation and the ethical responsibilities of ecclesial office.

In *Reading Reginald Scot in Scotland*, Michael Graham examines the reception of Reginald Scot's *Discoverie of Witchcraft* (1584) among Scottish readers, situating it within the broader context of Scottish and English witchcraft beliefs and demonological debates. Scot, writing in England, was radically skeptical, denying the possibility of witchcraft and questioning the role of the Devil in human misfortune. He framed much of his critique in terms of divine providence, arguing that attributing misfortune to witches displaced God from the central role in creation. Though Scot made only brief references to Scottish witchcraft practices—such as the putative accusation boxes used in kirk sessions—these references, often based on secondary sources like Jean Bodin, reinforced English perceptions of Scotland as primitive and legally lax, rather than providing accurate ethnographic insight.

Graham traces how Scottish readers engaged with Scot's work. The most famous was King James VI, who, while criticizing Scot for skepticism, nonetheless incorporated elements of Scot's interpretation into his own *Daemonologie* (1597), particularly in the character of Philomathes, who voiced doubt about witchcraft, and in nuanced readings of biblical passages like the Witch of Endor. In this way, Scot indirectly shaped Scottish demonological discourse, even among those who rejected his central thesis. Other Scottish readers, such as Robert Gordon of Straloch, engaged critically with Scot's arguments, noting errors or questioning his conclusions, often returning to more credulous sources like King James' text.

Graham highlights the long-term trajectory of Scot's reception in Scotland. By the late seventeenth century, Scottish skepticism toward witchcraft remained limited, as demonstrated by George Sinclair's *Satan's Invisible World Discovered* (1685), which associated disbelief in witches with atheism and rejected Scot's skepticism outright. Similarly, legal authorities such as Sir George Mackenzie of Rosehaugh drew on continental demonological sources while ignoring Scot, though some of Scot's ideas may have influenced Dutch translations circulating in Scotland.

Finally, Graham examines the intellectual afterlife of Scot in the eighteenth and nineteenth centuries. Figures like William Annand and Sir Walter Scott collected and read Scot's work, but often misinterpreted it or valued it for its folkloric and magical curiosities rather than its skeptical arguments. Scot's book, Graham argues, was consistently read according to the interests and biases of its readers rather than as Scot intended, highlighting the complex and mediated transmission of ideas across cultural and temporal contexts.

Overall, the essay underscores that while Scot's skepticism had little immediate impact on Scottish witchcraft belief, his *Discoverie of Witchcraft* remained a touchstone for debate, annotation, and intellectual curiosity, illustrating the uneven reception of radical thought across national and temporal boundaries.

In *Leaving Christianity Revisited*, Alan Hayes builds on Stuart Macdonald and Brian Clarke's *Leaving Christianity: Changing Allegiances in Canada since 1945*, applying their methodology to the Anglican Church of Canada (ACC). Macdonald and Clarke demonstrated that the decline of Canadian Christianity was a complex, decades-long phenomenon, best understood through statistical analysis of census data, denominational returns, and social surveys. They highlighted trends across denominations, noting peaks in the early 1960s followed by gradual and accelerating declines in membership, baptisms, Sunday school enrolment, and attendance, influenced by broader social and cultural shifts in postwar Canada.

Hayes confirms these trends for the ACC using updated census (2021) and denominational (2022–2023) data, revealing a 78% collapse in membership from 1961 to 2023, and corresponding declines in attendance, parish rolls, and identifiable givers. He observes that the decline was largely cohort-driven: fewer baptisms in the 1960s and 1970s led to fewer young Anglicans, creating a snowball effect that persisted into subsequent generations. Parish consolidation and the closure of congregations exacerbated losses, as surviving churches often failed to retain former members.

Beyond statistics, Hayes emphasizes mundane, everyday reasons for leaving: demographic changes, competing leisure opportunities, parish conflicts, and dissatisfaction with church culture. Disputes over the place of LGBTQ+ persons, ordination of women, and liturgical reforms contributed to some departures, but he notes that ideological positions alone do not account for most of the decline. Many left simply due to fatigue, dissatisfaction, or the slow erosion of "social capital" that had previously supported robust church engagement.

Hayes also highlights structural factors unique to the ACC: small congregations limit programmatic diversity and growth potential, and clergy-to-laity ratios are high, resulting in part-time ministry and reduced resources for outreach. External factors, such as the residential school legacy, sexual abuse scandals, and COVID-19 church closures, further diminished attraction and retention. Yet, he notes periods of renewal, particularly in the 1970s and 1980s, when the ACC embraced inclusivity, social justice initiatives, and ecumenical engagement, demonstrating an ability to respond to cultural shifts, albeit inconsistently.

Ultimately, Hayes presents a nuanced picture: the decline of the ACC reflects a combination of historical cohort effects, cultural change, internal disputes, structural limitations, and everyday parish realities. While macro trends illuminate broad patterns of Canadian Christian disaffiliation, Hayes's granular focus on the ACC underscores the complex interplay of personal, institutional, and societal factors driving both departures and the persistent challenge of attracting new adherents.

Gordon Heath's chapter, *"Between Evil and Less Evil": Canadian Churches and Area Bombing in World War Two*, examines the complex moral responses of Canadian Protestant churches to the Allied bombing campaigns over Germany and Japan. By the end of the war, cities in both countries had been devastated, with hundreds of thousands of civilian deaths, while the Allies lost some 81,000 airmen. The chapter does not aim to resolve the moral question of whether bombing was justified or effective but instead focuses on how Canadian churches navigated the ethical dilemmas of area and carpet bombing, which deliberately targeted civilian populations.

Canadian Protestant churches—comprising roughly 60 percent of the population—were internally diverse, ranging from major denominations such as the United Church of Canada (UCC), Anglicans, Presbyterians, and Baptists to smaller ethnic or pacifist communities, including Mennonites and Pentecostals. Heath's research draws primarily on denominational periodicals, which offered a mix of news, editorials, prayers, and commentary on international affairs. These sources reveal both official denominational positions and the nuances of public discussion, though they are limited in capturing private congregational opinions.

Initially, churches expressed general trust in the Allied command, believing that leaders would exercize bombing with restraint and strategic purpose. Early commentary even supported targeting German urban centers, framing it as a justified response to prior German aggression. Yet, as the war progressed and the human cost of indiscriminate bombing became clearer, church commentary increasingly reflected tension and moral unease. Clergy and periodicals wrestled with the just war tradition, particularly the principle of non-combatant immunity, which area bombing violated. The dilemma was articulated as choosing "between evil and less evil," reflecting the churches' struggle to reconcile the need for victory with ethical convictions.

Some voices, such as UCC minister R. Edis Fairbairn, condemned the Allied bombing campaigns as morally corrosive, arguing that they reduced the Allies to the level of the very militarists they opposed. Other commentary emphasized repentance, restraint, and moral reflection, urging that even in acts of war, soldiers and civilians should maintain charity and avoid hatred. Statements from Canadian churches, particularly following the destruction of Dresden and the atomic bombings of Hiroshima and Nagasaki, acknowledged the moral ambiguity of these actions while asserting that, in the absence of alternatives, continued bombing might be necessary to avert a greater evil.

Postwar reflections emphasized a dual recognition: rejoicing in victory while maintaining humility and moral accountability. The churches stressed that the moral lessons of modern warfare—including mass destruction and dehumanization—demanded vigilance, ethical reflection, and a role for Christianity in shaping the emerging atomic age. The Mennonite and Lutheran communities, in particular, highlighted the need for moral clarity and restraint, warning against uncritical acceptance of military necessity.

Heath concludes that Canadian Protestant churches navigated a paradoxical moral landscape: supporting the war against fascism while struggling with the ethical compromises inherent in area bombing. Their responses, characterized by reticence, critique, repentance, and a reluctant acknowledgment of necessity, illustrate that wartime churches were neither unconditionally patriotic nor morally unengaged. They framed the Allied bombing campaigns as a troubling "case of moral slippage," often necessary yet deeply problematic, reflecting the enduring tension between ethical principles and wartime exigencies.

Joon Won Kim's essay, *Two Calvinists' Understandings of the Scripture and Administration of the Biblical Ceremonies and Missional Implications*, explores the differing approaches of Richard Hooker and John Knox to Scripture, liturgy, and the administration of worship, particularly in relation to the Book of Common Prayer (BCP), and draws missional lessons for contemporary churches. While both reformers were influenced by Calvin, neither adhered strictly to his theology, and their interpretations of Scripture led to contrasting liturgical applications.

The essay situates Hooker and Knox in the sixteenth-century Reformation context. In England, debates over the BCP focused less on theology and more on ceremony, with disputes over adiaphora—practices considered non-essential to faith. Knox rejected the BCP, criticizing elements he deemed superstitious, such as kneeling at the altar, while Hooker defended the liturgy in his *Lawes Ecclesiastical Politie*, emphasizing the reasoned and rational application of Scripture to public worship. These disputes extended across England and the European continent, influencing the formation of Scottish Presbyterian worship and the defense of Anglican liturgy.

Both reformers acknowledged the authority of Scripture and the importance of the Holy Spirit in interpretation, yet their hermeneutics diverged. Hooker integrated Scripture with reason and tradition, allowing flexibility in liturgical practice when Scripture was silent on specific details. For him, kneeling at the Lord's Supper was an expression of piety, justified through Scripture, reason, and the voice of the Church. Knox, in contrast, emphasized the literal authority and omnicompetence of Scripture, interpreting ceremonies strictly according to biblical prescription. He opposed kneeling at the altar, seeing it as a superstitious innovation incompatible with Scripture. This strict literalism reflected Knox's commitment to purging idolatrous practices and restoring biblical worship.

Kim highlights that these historical differences offer missional insights. Hooker's approach exemplifies cultural contextualization, showing how worship can remain faithful to Scripture while engaging with local traditions and reason. Knox's rigor demonstrates the necessity of maintaining biblical fidelity, particularly when cultural practices distort the gospel. Using the frameworks of Flemming's contextualization theory and Bauckham's missional hermeneutics, Kim suggests that contemporary churches can draw lessons from both approaches: balancing respect for cultural context with commitment to the essence of the gospel. Examples include Asian and African contexts, where adaptation of local rituals to Christian worship requires discernment.

In conclusion, Hooker and Knox can be seen as representing two strands of Calvinist thought—Hookerian Calvinism and Knoxian Calvinism—reflecting different applications of Scripture to liturgy. Their divergent approaches to the BCP and eucharistic practice reveal the theological underpinnings of worship and illustrate how historical debates inform contemporary missional practice. By examining these historical cases through a missional lens, Kim argues that the church today can navigate the tension between cultural engagement and scriptural fidelity, ensuring that worship and mission remain both biblically grounded and contextually relevant.

Ross Lockhart, in his chapter titled *Evangelism in a Quiet Voice: A historical reflection on the emphasis on Active Evangelism in the FLAMES initiative of the Presbyterian Church in Canada* examines the historical and theological roots of evangelism within the Presbyterian Church in Canada (PCC), focusing on the FLAMES initiative of 1999–2005, and especially the year dedicated to "Active Evangelism." Lockhart opens with a pastoral anecdote illustrating the discomfort many Presbyterians feel in speaking about their faith, reflecting a wider cultural hesitancy toward overt evangelism. The chapter situates this reluctance within a historical trajectory, highlighting how the PCC has continually sought to encourage members to articulate and live out the gospel.

Lockhart traces the denomination's evangelistic efforts from the mid-20th century. Stuart Macdonald's scholarship notes that from 1945 to 1985, boards such as the Board of Evangelism and Social Action encouraged Presbyterians to share their faith with conviction rooted in Scripture and personal experience. The church responded to membership decline in the 1960s and 1970s with renewed emphasis on proclamation and teaching, culminating in ambitious initiatives like "Double in the Eighties," which aimed to expand membership while equipping laity for evangelism. This effort was reinforced by the publication of *Living Faith*, whose ninth section codified mission and evangelism as central to Presbyterian identity, emphasizing both proclamation and service as inseparable dimensions of Christian witness.

The FLAMES initiative—an acronym for Focus on Children, Teens and Young Adults; Laity Equipping; Active Evangelism; Mission; Education; and Spirituality—sought to continue this trajectory into the 21st century. Lockhart examines the 2002–2003 "Year of Active Evangelism," designed to amplify what the General Assembly noted was typically a "quiet voice" in Presbyterian witness. Preceding the year, a two-day conference at Knox College provided historical, theological, and practical foundations, emphasizing relational evangelism modelled on Jesus' approach: one-on-one engagement and disciple-making, rather than large-scale programs.

Lockhart highlights how the initiative was reflected in *The Presbyterian Record*, which offered monthly columns from leaders and guest contributors. Moderator Mark Lewis emphasized that evangelism is both verbal and enacted, encouraging members to witness through deeds, hospitality, and service. Contributors such as Jim Czegledi, Rick Horst, and Carey Nieuwhof provided practical strategies, including relational faith-sharing, contemporary worship services designed for newcomers, and new church-planting efforts. Leadership was consistently highlighted as essential for fostering a culture of evangelism, alongside attention to congregational adaptation and technological innovation.

The chapter also reflects on critiques and tensions, including concerns that new evangelistic methods might alienate longstanding members. Nevertheless, the initiative underscored the PCC's commitment to active participation by all members, situating evangelism as both a communal and individual calling.

Lockhart concludes by connecting the FLAMES initiative to broader missiological conversations. Drawing on contemporary scholars such as Rick Osmer, Priscilla Pope-Levison, and Andy Root, he emphasizes that evangelism today is best understood relationally, sacramentally, and contextually, integrating hospitality, integrity, message-bearing, and church-rootedness.

Even a "quiet voice," Lockhart argues, can serve as a meaningful witness in a world seeking hope, beauty, and truth, reaffirming evangelism as a vital, ongoing practice in the life of the PCC.

In a chapter titled *Ishmael as Insult: Presbyterians, Quakers, and Scriptural Polemics in 1650s England,* Amanda Pullan investigates the striking prominence of the Genesis story of Hagar and Ishmael in seventeenth-century England, particularly in the 1650s, and explains its unusual popularity in printed texts and domestic embroidery. Pullan's interest was initially sparked by the appearance of the Expulsion of Hagar and Ishmael in needlework, a choice that seemed morally ambiguous and atypical compared with other Genesis narratives. She situates this story within the Protestant Reformation tradition, noting that Reformers often used Genesis for household instruction, as Old Testament stories were seen as safer exemplars than the life of Christ. However, this did not fully explain the story's mid-seventeenth-century resonance, which Pullan investigates using corpus analysis of Early English Books Online, a digital collection of printed texts from 1475–1700.

Her findings reveal a remarkable spike in mentions of "Ishmael" during the 1650s, a trend that exceeds all other decades of the century. Close reading of these texts shows that the term was employed as a pointed insult, primarily by Quakers, directed at Presbyterian and Independent ministers aligned with Cromwell's national church. The insult drew on the longstanding allegorical interpretation of Ishmael as a persecutor of the true believers, derived from Paul's exposition in Galatians 4, in which Hagar and Ishmael represent the old covenant and those antagonistic to the children of promise.

Pullan traces the allegorical use of the story through history, from early Christian exegesis, medieval iconography, and Reformation commentaries by Luther and Calvin, to sixteenth-century biblical annotations in the Geneva Bible, Douai-Rheims, and the Authorized Version. Across these centuries, Ishmael consistently symbolized opposition to God's promise and persecution of the true church. This symbolism became a potent rhetorical tool for the Quakers in the politically and religiously chaotic 1650s, when sects proliferated amid the English Civil Wars and the Interregnum, creating a "religious marketplace" of competing claims to authority.

Pullan highlights key pamphlet debates, including Christopher Atkinson's *Ishmael and his mother cast out into the wilderness* (1655), written from prison, which applied the allegory to attack conforming ministers like Samuel Townsend, who mocked and imprisoned Quakers. Similarly, John Whitehead's *The Enmitie Between the Two Seeds* identifies persecuting ministers as "sons of Ishmael," drawing parallels to biblical persecution of Isaac.

In contrast, Presbyterian ministers such as William Kaye engaged in these disputes without invoking Ishmael, underscoring the Quakers' strategic use of biblical allegory as a weapon in public controversy.

The study demonstrates that this rhetoric was more than a theological polemic; it reflected a battle for religious authority and scriptural expertise in the public sphere. The use of Ishmael symbolized both moral condemnation and a display of learned engagement with scripture, appealing to lay audiences fascinated by public debate and clerical contests. The story's popularity, Pullan argues, was tied to its allegorical resonance in a period when discerning the true church was a pressing social and spiritual concern.

Pullan concludes that the 1650s saw a unique interplay of scriptural knowledge, public performance, and sectarian conflict. The Quakers' use of Ishmael exemplifies how biblical literacy, allegorical interpretation, and rhetorical skill could serve as tools for establishing authority and critiquing opponents, leaving a lasting impression on print culture and religious discourse in England. The decade reveals a Reformed church where knowledge, debate, and the ability to wield scripture were central to power, visibility, and legitimacy.

Robert Revington, in his chapter titled Death of Christian Canada? Does Arthur Leonard Griffith's Testimony Support Stuart Macdonald and Brian Clarke's Theory of Canadian Church Decline in the 1960s? examines the testimony of Arthur Leonard Griffith, a Canadian minister and later professor, to assess whether it supports Stuart Macdonald and Brian Clarke's thesis in *Leaving Christianity: Changing Allegiances in Canada since 1945* regarding the decline of Canadian churches in the 1960s. Griffith's uniquely long ministry—from his ordination in 1945 until his retirement in 1986, with continued preaching well into the 2010s—positions him as a rare first-hand witness whose career aligns closely with the period analyzed by Macdonald and Clarke. Unlike many clergy whose perceptions of church decline were often unreliable, Griffith provides a balanced account, noting both the growth of Canadian churches in the postwar era and their sharp decline beginning in the 1960s.

Revington outlines Griffith's career, highlighting key postings: early ministry in smaller Ontario churches, Chalmers United Church in Ottawa during the 1950s, City Temple in London in the early 1960s, Deer Park United Church in Toronto, and later St. Paul's Bloor Street in the Anglican Church. Griffith's autobiography records extraordinary church growth in the 1950s, including rising memberships, Sunday School enrolments, new church buildings, and active ministerial recruitment. His reflections corroborate statistical data showing that Canadian Protestant churches experienced exceptional growth until the early 1960s, after which decline was rapid—a pattern consistent with the "short and sharp cultural revolution" identified by Callum G. Brown in Britain and mirrored in Canada by Macdonald and Clarke.

The essay situates Griffith's observations alongside Macdonald and Clarke's scholarship. Macdonald had already noted the unreliability of clergy testimony in general, yet Griffith's account stands out for its accuracy and historical perspective. Griffith confirms that by the mid-to-late 1960s, the church's influence had waned, attendance was falling, Sunday School enrolments were dropping, and congregations were struggling to maintain vitality. These observations align closely with Clarke and Macdonald's statistical analysis, including census and baptismal data, which show a pronounced decline in Christian affiliation from the 1960s onward, alongside a simultaneous postwar growth period in the 1950s that is often overlooked in secularization narratives.

Revington emphasizes that Griffith's reflections are particularly valuable because they provide a human, experiential lens on trends documented statistically. Griffith attributes the decline to factors such as increasing leisure and affluence, changing cultural priorities, and a shift in societal values, echoing broader analyses of postwar secularization and the cultural upheavals of the 1960s. His firsthand perspective also offers insight into how clergy and congregants perceived and responded to these changes.

In conclusion, Griffith's testimony strongly corroborates the trajectory outlined by Macdonald and Clarke: Canadian churches thrived in the postwar 1950s but faced sudden decline in the 1960s, a pattern that continues to shape contemporary religious life. Revington argues that Griffith provides a rare, reliable narrative that complements the statistical research, bridging personal experience with historical data, and highlighting the importance of understanding both the successes and challenges of Canadian churches in the twentieth century. His account affirms that recognizing the 1950s growth is as important as documenting the 1960s decline, offering context for both historical scholarship and contemporary ecclesial reflection.

John A. Vissers' essay, *Reformulating the Faith*, explores the nature and development of doctrine within The Presbyterian Church in Canada (PCC) from its formation in 1875 through the mid-1980s, focusing particularly on the period covered in Stuart Macdonald's *Tradition and Tension: The Presbyterian Church in Canada, 1945–1985*. Vissers begins with the 1970 Preamble to the Ordination Questions, which affirms that the PCC is bound only to Jesus Christ as the Church's King and Head, with Holy Scripture as the canon of all doctrine. The preamble establishes subordinate standards—the Westminster Confession of Faith, the Declaration of Faith Concerning Church and Nation, and *Living Faith*—while allowing for future doctrinal reformulation under the guidance of the Holy Spirit. This formulation frames doctrine as Christologically grounded, biblically normative, historically continuous, and open-ended, signalling a shift from a closed confessional posture to one permitting ongoing development.

Vissers traces the historical foundations of this approach back to the 1875 Basis of Union, which unified four Presbyterian bodies in Canada. The Westminster Confession of Faith and the Larger and Shorter Catechisms were adopted as subordinate standards, but with interpretive clauses allowing "liberty of conscience" on issues such as church-state relations. The Basis of Union aimed primarily at creating a strong, unified Protestant church in Canada, not at reformulating doctrine. Subsequent adjustments, such as the 1889 clarification on marriage and divorce, reflected interpretive flexibility rather than doctrinal reformulation.

Church union in 1925 with the Methodist and Congregationalist churches created further doctrinal tension. The minority of "continuing Presbyterians" rejected the Basis of Union for legal, doctrinal, and ecclesiastical reasons, insisting on adherence to the Westminster Standards. This conflict underscored that doctrine was central to denominational identity and that unity required negotiated confessional agreement. The continuing Presbyterians reconstituted the General Assembly at Knox Church in Toronto at the precise moment the United Church of Canada was legally formed, affirming both their continuity with historic Presbyterianism and the ongoing uncertainty about confessional authority.

From 1945 to 1985, the PCC engaged deeply with the question of doctrine in practice. Key developments included the Declaration of Faith Concerning Church and Nation (1955), recognition of several Reformed confessions as parallel standards (1962), and the ordination of women as elders and ministers (1966). The 1970 Preamble clarified that such changes were part of the church's continuing function of reformulating the faith. While the ordination of women initially provoked confusion and dissent, the preamble established that doctrine was now both grounded in subordinate standards and open to guided development, resolving earlier ambiguities about authority and continuity.

Vissers concludes that Canadian Presbyterians have historically balanced fidelity to Scripture, confessional heritage, and responsiveness to changing contexts. Doctrine is simultaneously a testimony to historic truth, a framework for instruction and governance, and a living expression of the church's witness. The 1970 Preamble and subsequent developments formalized a dynamic understanding of doctrine, emphasizing the church's vocation to confess, interpret, and reformulate its faith under Christ's lordship.

THE CONTRIBUTION OF STUART MACDONALD

Across these essays, Stuart Macdonald's scholarship emerges as a consistent point of reference and orientation. His work on Canadian Presbyterianism demonstrates how careful empirical research and disciplined historical analysis can illuminate the complexities of denominational life, secularization, and ecclesial identity. By integrating meticulous archival study with quantitative and demographic data, Macdonald has shown that history is never merely descriptive. Attention to patterns of membership, belief, and institutional change carries ethical and theological weight, equipping churches to discern more faithfully how to respond to contemporary challenges.

Stuart's scholarly career embodies the conviction that history matters not as an abstract academic pursuit, but as essential groundwork for understanding the present. His work spans an unusually wide range, from witch-hunting in early modern Scotland to the decline of Canadian Christianity in the late twentieth century. Despite this breadth, his scholarship is unified by methodological rigor, theological attentiveness, and a consistent refusal to accept simplistic explanations. Whether examining judicial procedures in Scottish witch trials, using quantitative methods to uncover patterns hidden by narrative sources, or collaborating with Brian Clarke to chart the statistical contours of church decline in Canada, Macdonald has insisted that historical claims must be tested against evidence and that inherited narratives must be interrogated rather than assumed.

This approach is exemplified in *Leaving Christianity: Changing Allegiances in Canada since 1945*, co-authored with Clarke. Through careful demographic and statistical analysis, the study challenged prevailing explanations that located church decline primarily in the cultural upheavals of the 1960s. Instead, it revealed a more complex trajectory marked by postwar growth, followed by decline shaped by cohort effects, failures of generational transmission, and broader social transformations. The book has had a lasting impact on scholarly and ecclesial discussions, reshaping how the recent history of Canadian Christianity is understood. A similar attentiveness to complexity characterizes T*radition and Tension: The Presbyterian Church in Canada, 1945–1985*, which offers a nuanced institutional and theological portrait of a denomination negotiating continuity and change, doctrinal commitment and ecumenical engagement, resistance and adaptation. Macdonald's understated conclusion, "Things worked. Until they no longer did," captures both the contingency of institutional success and the necessity of honest historical reckoning.

Macdonald's contributions extend well beyond his major monographs. His work on witch-hunting, particularly in *The Witches of Fife*, demonstrated that local context, legal practice, and economic conditions were as decisive as demonological belief in shaping prosecutions. His articles range widely, addressing topics such as the theological assumptions underlying witchcraft accusations, Presbyterian responses to Vatican II, church involvement in the Great War, and contested questions of memory and symbolism, including the relocation of a statue at Knox College. In each case, his research illustrates how historical inquiry can illuminate contemporary debates about authority, identity, and mission without being reduced to advocacy.

Taken together, Stuart Macdonald's scholarship reminds us that history matters because it teaches discernment, cultivates humility, and resists the twin temptations of nostalgia and amnesia. Understanding what happened and why is indispensable for navigating what comes next. This volume honors his legacy by continuing that work: asking difficult questions, attending carefully to complexity, and trusting that rigorous historical inquiry can serve the church's ongoing vocation of faithful witness in a changing world.

Abbreviations

OLD TESTAMENT

Exod	Exodus
Gen	Genesis
Jer	Jeremiah
1 Sam	1 Samuel

NEW TESTAMENT

Acts	Acts
1 Cor	1 Corinthians
Eph	Ephesians
Gal	Galatians

OTHER

AV	Authorized Version (King James Bible)
DR	Douai-Rheims Bible
EEBO	Early English Books Online
GV	Geneva Bible
NSRV	New Revised Standard Version

1

Ecumenism and Denominational Identity in a Pluralistic World

Canadian Protestant Responses

PHYLLIS AIRHART

INTRODUCTION

TRADITION AND TENSION, STUART Macdonald's in-depth study of the Presbyterian Church in Canada between 1945 and 1985, ends with these words: "Things worked. Until they no longer did. Adapting to a different Canada, one that is post-Christian and post-Christendom, remains a challenge."[1] The book tells the story of the denomination during four critical decades, identifying how the 1960s were a turning point in four key areas: church extension, denominational identity, the place of women, and theology and worship. Building on these four themes, he demonstrates how strategies that had been successful in the 1950s and early 1960s no longer produced the same results.

However, during the "golden years" of the 1950s some astute observers spotted signs of trouble in a once flourishing initiative that Macdonald says might have been considered as a fifth theme: the foreign missionary

1. Macdonald, *Tension and Tradition*, 244.

enterprise.[2] It is likely that most people would not associate the loss of missionary enthusiasm with the challenges that Canadian Protestant churches faced in the decades that followed. But a closer look suggests that the changing fortunes of foreign missions as they adjusted to the pluralistic world that replaced Christendom after the second world war contributed to the ecumenical malaise that followed. Ironically the missionary impulse that had sparked the modern ecumenical movement in 1910 later disrupted the denominational ecosystem that comprised it.

The Presbyterian Church in Canada and the United Church of Canada experienced these changing dynamics of missions and ecumenism in a rapidly changing world. While embracing their national identity as denominations "in" and "of" Canada, their networks extended beyond Canada because of their prominent role in the missionary movement. They had enough in common to have once considered an organic union. Yet the resistance to the founding of the United Church in 1925 left bad feelings that lingered for decades and shaped the identity of the continuing Presbyterian Church. While both remained connected to the ecumenical movement with missions as a common concern, postwar pluralism created new tensions both within and between them.

MODERN ECUMENISM AS A MISSIONARY INITIATIVE

The modern ecumenical movement grew out of what was primarily a gathering of missionary societies. In 1910, thousands of delegates and observers left the historic World Missionary Conference in Edinburgh, committed to co-operation in evangelizing the world and extending the influence of Christian civilization. Denominational bureaucracies combined with local missionary societies to fund missionaries whose travels around the world tailed the routes of nineteenth-century colonial expansion.

The old watchword of "evangelization of the world in this generation" that inspired those at Edinburgh raised different questions after the First World War ended in 1918. The hostilities roused in China, Japan, and Korea by the treaty negotiations in 1919 had repercussions for missions. Many missionaries attempted to obliterate or at least transcend racial and ethnic differences under the banner of "world friendship" by focusing on social service as well as evangelism.[3] Robert Wright found that Canadian churches played a key role in these initiatives with programs that were

2. Macdonald, *Tension and Tradition*, 5.

3. Robert, *Christian Mission*, 65–67.

"recast as vehicles for the realization of a worldwide Christian fellowship."[4] But this more expansive approach to missions drew controversy in some circles by defining evangelism as any activity that delivered the message of Jesus Christ, whether preaching, teaching, or healing.[5]

On the eve of the Second World War, other denominational leaders might well have agreed with how United Church executive Jesse Arnup summed up the task facing his denomination in 1937: "Of set purpose it aims to make Canada wholly Christian; but its ultimate objective is nothing less than the fulfillment of God's purpose for the whole world."[6] But that aspiration was connected to the success of its missionary enterprise: "You cannot think of God except as a missionary God," he advised. "So it is with the Church. Rob it of its missionary purpose and passion and you remove both its right and its power to carry on."[7]

But world events were about to imperil the enthusiasm for world missions and the hopes for Christian internationalism that it had fostered. The aftermath of the Second World War disclosed the practical limitations of the Christian message as an inclusive and universal basis for world harmony. The spread of anticolonial and liberation movements disrupted the missionary enterprise in many countries, and the uncoupling of Christianity and culture that marked the end of Christendom altered the course of Protestant advance around the world, including Canada. Missionaries whose calling had once been considered noble came to be viewed as pawns of Western colonialism, creating not only a vocational crisis for them but an identity crisis for denominations that had derived a sense of purpose by supporting their work. It was also a blow to the ambitions of modern ecumenism as the demands of ministry in a pluralistic world subdued the calls for evangelization.

MISSIONS, ECUMENISM, AND THE POSTWAR NEW WORLD ORDER

The aftermath of the war changed the map of the world and with it the ecclesial landscape of global Christianity. What was for Protestant denominations in Canada a time of confidence and growth was in other places a period of loss. Former mission fields disappeared as collateral damage in

4. Wright, *World Mission*, 37.

5. Patterson, "Loss of a Protestant Missionary Consensus," 84–91, and Wacker, "Second Thoughts," 282–300.

6. Arnup, *New Church Faces*, 77.

7. Arnup, *New Church Faces*, 236.

places affected by the "revolt against the West." As liberation movements swept across areas of the world that had been targeted for evangelization, church leaders observed "closing doors" for missions, and "Westerners" were no longer welcome. With the rejection of European and North American Christendom and its ideals of Christian internationalism, secular ideologies took hold. Foreign missionaries were expelled in many places, and their schools and hospitals were confiscated. In secular circles in the West, "the missionary became a whipping boy for failed colonial practices."[8] The future of Christianity in many places now rested with the local leaders they had nurtured.

Writing in 1956, John Webster Grant described the emergence of a concept of "world Christianity" that challenged "denominational frameworks" by demanding that newer leaders be considered equal contributors—an idea some older missionaries found difficult to accept. Complicating matters further was that missionaries had often been funded by what Grant described as "that useful but defective institution, the missionary society," that still thought in terms of "foreign fields," whereas their converts wanted to be treated as partnering churches.[9] He credited another ecumenical organization, the International Missionary Council (IMC), formed in 1921, for highlighting a vision of the church "as having one missionary task in all parts of the world," rather than seeing Christianity and paganism in "geographical terms." Rather than focusing on issues of faith and order commonly regarded as ecumenical, he saw the IMC as excelling in "practical ecumenicity."[10]

It was in this context that international ecumenism saw the culmination of negotiations that had momentous consequences for global Christianity: the amalgamation of two major ecumenical organizations, both tracing their origins to the missionary movement. The World Council of Churches (WCC) held its first assembly in 1948. At the New Delhi assembly in 1961, the IMC became the WCC's Division of World Mission and Evangelism. Five years later, the United Church's Commission on World Mission would declare this to have been a turning point: it "underscored the place of mission in the whole life of the World Council of Churches and so gave that body a new direction and significance."[11]

8. Robert, *Christian Mission*, 67–68.

9. Grant, *World Church*, 21. See also Grant, *Ship Under the Cross*, a succinct study of the ecumenical movement from the time of the early church.

10. Grant, *World Church*, 22, 29.

11. "World Mission," *Record of Proceedings*, 327.

While the IMC adopted the name of the WCC after the merger, it is arguable that the agenda of the former did more to shape ecumenism as time went on. Their union became a flashpoint by drawing attention to the double meaning of "world mission" that they had adopted: global in geographical reach but also concerned with programs to reach the world outside the church. Norman Goodall, the British missionary credited with guiding the merger to completion, recalled resistance to it from evangelicals who were critical of the new approach. He recounted his experience of meeting church leaders in Scandinavia who complained that the ecumenical movement had become "less congenial and more suspect." They equated the word ecumenical with theological liberalism and the movement itself as "the product of doctrinal indifference."[12]

Ecumenical initiatives designed to bring churches into closer cooperation by emphasizing their common task instead created divisions over *how* to be the church in the world. The idea that God's mission could not be separated from other aspects of the church's life and teaching deepened the divide between ecumenical enthusiasts and conservative evangelicals. Critics of ecumenism detected a repudiation of past efforts to convert the world to Christ in the rhetorical move from "world missions" to the church's "mission to the world."[13] At the second assembly of the WCC in Evanston in 1954, there were hints of concern about the conversion of those of other faiths as the goal of evangelism. The term "proselytism" cropped up with negative connotations that were more explicit by the time the WCC met for its third assembly in 1961. A statement on "Christian Witness, Proselytism and Religious Liberty in the Setting of the World Council of Churches" was prepared after the Evanston assembly and revised twice by the Central Committee (1956 and 1960) before being received by the assembly in New Delhi the following year.

THE CHALLENGE OF PLURALISM FOR EVANGELISM

An early warning of the difficulties ahead for hopes of evangelizing the world came from a Canadian historian of comparative religions. Wilfred Cantwell Smith had been ordained and sent in 1940 as a missionary to teach in Lahore (in what was then India and later Pakistan) with support from Knox Presbyterian Church in Toronto, the congregation in which he was

12. Goodall, "'Evangelicals," 210–11.

13. For an analysis of the paradigm shift in ecclesiology and the role of missionary conferences in reshaping how churches saw their "mission to the world" during the 1950s and 1960s, see Bosch, *Transforming Mission*, 368–93.

raised. In an article published in 1960 in the ecumenical Protestant *Christian Century* magazine, he cautioned that Christian thought was about to face a massive challenge, the third in its history and akin to its early encounter with Greek philosophy and centuries later with science: how to discover and proclaim its message in today's "cosmopolitan world" where everyone was becoming a "minority in a complexity of diverse groups." Smith feared that Christianity was theologically unequipped to accept other religions and foresaw that the new question needing a theological response would be this: "how is it possible to hold a firm, deep, vibrant Christian faith, wholehearted and committed, without knowing that God meets other men in other ways?" His own response was that Christians would "not go far wrong if we insist that loyalty to Christ impels us to love our new neighbours of other faiths as we do ourselves."[14]

A year later, Smith delivered a lecture that was published as a section of his groundbreaking book *The Faith of Other Men*. He expanded on the challenge to Christianity that he saw happening on the mission field as the ecumenical movement confronted other religious traditions. His conclusion was stated, as he put it, bluntly and vigorously: "the missionary movement is in profound and fundamental crisis." In some places, it had come to an end, with missionaries unwelcome in places like China, Angola, India, and the Arab world. Recruitment was also a problem. Smith warned that religious history was taking a turn that he predicted would end the phase of "proselytizing evangelism"; what would follow had not yet been worked out.[15]

Somewhat counterintuitively, ecumenical Protestantism responded to the contraction of "world missions" in the postwar period with an expansion of its "mission to the world" that pushed churches to reconsider what mission to their *own* context entailed. The United Church responded with the lengthy report of the Commission on World Mission (over 100 pages) prepared for the 1966 General Council. Its sixteen recommendations formed the basis for a new direction in the United Church's mission policy. The eleventh signaled a then-controversial openness to other faiths that differed from past approaches to missions and evangelism: "The church should recognize that God is creatively and redemptively at work in the religious life of all mankind."[16]

C. Douglas Jay, a professor at Emmanuel College who served as secretary of the commission and was instrumental in drafting its report,

14. Smith, "Christianity's Third Great Challenge," 505–8.

15. Smith, *Faith of Other Men*, 114–20. The second part of the book is identified as a lecture given to a joint meeting in Montreal in 1961 of three organizations then referred to as the "Learned Societies."

16. "World Mission," *Record of Proceedings*, 435.

recognized its significance for the missionary work of the church. Invited to give the R.P. MacKay Memorial Lectures in 1967, Jay described how the ecumenical task had shifted from focusing on missionary enterprises—"missions"—to making "an effective Christian presence in the world." In current ecumenical thinking, he explained, the boundary was no longer between home and foreign missions, but between the church and the world. This was, he suggested, "a more acceptable theological and strategic approach in an age when proselytism (which the report had defined in its glossary as the practice of making converts) had been called into question.[17] He warned that the Western missionary movement was facing important changes in "its strategy, organization and spirit" as it came to terms with the end of its expansion and former dominance.[18] Reflecting on the report thirty years later, Jay astutely assessed its impact: "the United Church pioneered in the establishment of an interfaith dialogue portfolio" that was ahead of similar initiatives in the World Council of Churches by several years.[19]

The Presbyterian Church also recast its approach to mission. For example, the "Life and Mission Projects" (LAMP) report identified the challenges facing the church in ecumenical terms similar to the United Church's "World Mission" report. A section on "the world we live in" noted that in a short period of time half the world's population had moved from "colonialism into post-colonial nationalism," and older approaches to mission were being "adjusted to fit the movements towards nationalism."[20] The report spoke in terms of a "mission to the world" where "God is at work in and through all that is happening."[21] and acknowledged the tension between those who wanted to focus on evangelism and others on social action.[22] It also made a detailed proposal for restructuring congregational life and national structures.[23]

The idea that God's mission could not be separated from other aspects of the church's life and teaching generated controversy as ecumenical and denominational gatherings around the world explored its implications. The temperature of the debates shot up when what was thought of as traditional

17. Jay, *World Mission*, 2–4. For the definition of proselytism, see "World Mission," *Record of Proceedings*, 303.

18. Jay, *World Mission*, 11–12.

19. Jay, "Missiological Implications," 278.

20. Committee on Life and Mission Projects (LAMP), "Into the '70s in Life and Mission," 11. For an analysis of the LAMP report, see Macdonald, *Tension and Tradition*, 142–46.

21. LAMP, 12.

22. LAMP, 25.

23. LAMP, 29–38; 56–60.

evangelism was castigated as a distortion of the church's true mission. At the World Student Christian Federation in 1964 a case was made for redefining evangelism as Christian *presence*, rather than *proclamation*: the church's witness at times needed to be silent.[24] Meanwhile the growing polarization of ecumenical and evangelical Protestants was evident at the first World Congress on Evangelism that met in Berlin in the fall of 1966. According to one United Church observer, rather than "listening to the world," evangelicals were preparing to speak to it in a new way. For instance, World Vision, a relief organization supported by evangelicals, was urging churches to make use of computers and other technological advances in promoting evangelism.[25]

The deepening divide within Protestantism was on display as the WCC celebrated its twentieth anniversary at Uppsala in 1968. Union Seminary professor Johannes Hoekendijk raised hackles when he condemned the traditional approach to evangelism as heretical. Dismissing the "introverted" parish system as a medieval invention, he questioned whether converts should join existing congregations. Instead, he proposed direct action in society, a model of church organization that he dubbed "go-structures."[26]

Missiology expanded moral and social issues familiar to Western Christianity by placing them alongside questions about how to relate to the sometimes hostile non-Western world. Racial issues were particularly complicated, perhaps one of the reasons why the Programme to Combat Racism became such a lightning rod when it was launched in 1969. WCC statements on racial justice resonated in different ways depending on whether the context was apartheid in Rhodesia and South Africa, civil rights in the US, or residential schools for Indigenous children in Canada. For instance, calls for active support for the anti-apartheid movement replaced the older ecumenical model of producing studies with recommendations based on shared principles.[27] A new generation of leaders called instead for clear-cut policies on pressing social issues and even political partisanship.

Ironically, involvement in the ecumenical movement divided Christian communities between those for and against its mission to the world. Both sides tacitly acknowledged that Christendom was gone. The former aimed to adjust to postwar pluralism by expanding its mission to "the

24. Hutchison, "Americans in World Mission," 159.

25. Somerville, "World's Evangelicals Look at Themselves," 14–15.

26. Hutchison, "Americans in World Mission," 160–1, who remarks that these provocative positions were presented with Hoekendijk's "characteristic acerbity."

27. "Racism, Discrimination and Xenophobia," https://www.oikoumene.org/what-we-do/racism-discrimination-and-xenophobia, connects the WCC's current program on dealing with diversity to its 1948 origins.

world," while the latter saw opportunities for building global Christianity with a message that echoed the aims expressed after 1910 for the "evangelization of the world."

ECUMENISM AND DENOMINATIONAL IDENTITY

Despite their past differences, the Presbyterian Church and the United Church followed a trajectory similar to what Craig Dykstra and James Hudnut-Beumler observed in their study of Protestant denominations in the US. They suggest that in the 1960s, there was a shift from a "corporate" to "regulatory agency" model of governance, related in part to undertaking the church's "mission to the world." One of the pressure points was "the first-world chauvinism present in so much of the churches' own historical mission activities."[28] Past efforts to bring mission and service activities under central control were not only designed to avoid fundraising competition between them but to take charge of the foreign mission income, "which was considerable and much easier to raise than monies for domestic mission activities."[29]

Decisions facing the once successful missionary enterprise were not always popular; as Dykstra and Hudnut-Beumler put it in marketing terms, "the national churches were divesting themselves of some of their most popular products."[30] Combined with a slow economy and declining membership, the budgetary impact was a blow to their programs. Much of the denominational "machinery" had been designed to run the missionary operation. Now, the old corporate model and the consensus supporting it began to crumble, giving way to being more akin to a regulatory agency to "adjudicate the distribution of dwindling resources."[31] Financial challenges set the leaders of ecumenical Protestants on a search for more effective ways to organize that included renewed calls for organic union.

The case of how the Presbyterian Church navigated the tensions created by the new approach to world mission offers clues to the mystery of why "things no longer worked" for them and denominations with similar structures. Macdonald drops tantalizing hints, noting the ties of foreign

28. Dykstra and Hudnut-Beumler, "National Organizational Structures," 318. For an analysis of this paradigm shift on the national structures of denominations (and the concomitant shift of energy to the congregational level), see Roozen, "National Denominational Structures," 596–98.

29. Dykstra and Hudnut-Beumler, 317.

30. Dykstra and Hudnut-Beumler, 319.

31. Dykstra and Hudnut-Beumler, 321.

missions to other aspects of denominational oversight. For instance, he notes that the traditional Presbyterian system of church courts had been set up to handle discipline, not growth and missionary activity: "It was not a system designed to raise money." Missions, both home and foreign, were connected to its fundraising, leadership, and perhaps most importantly, its sense of purpose.[32]

The links between foreign missions and ecumenism raised questions about denominational identity as well as financial viability. The Presbyterian Church was in a unique position, shaped in part by what it was *not*: the United Church of Canada. The specter of 1925 and the threat of organic union still hung over interchurch discussions. There was opposition in some circles to the Presbyterian Church's involvement in ecumenical ventures such as the formation of the Canadian Council of Churches in 1944 and especially the WCC in 1948.[33] Tensions heightened after the New Delhi assembly in 1961, with suspicion not only of the merger with the IMC but also of openness to Eastern Orthodox participation.

Given the ties between missions and Christian unity, it is not surprising that Presbyterians were drawn into what John Moir calls "a civil war" within the denomination, with support for missionary cooperation equated with theological modernism.[34] The work of the Presbyterian Church's Committee on Inter-Church Relations, set up by the General Assembly in 1960 "to study the distinctive Presbyterian witness to Christian unity and the catholicity of the Church," was one flashpoint. The study material for the church's courts and congregations that circulated as a pamphlet in 1961 credited the WCC and the World Presbyterian Alliance for shaping a new approach to mission. The foreword to the pamphlet warned readers to expect ideas that were "probably provocative, possibly instructive and challenging" to engage the church in a "complex and disturbing dialogue."[35]

And it was indeed provocative. The pamphlet quoted the WCC: ecumenism was "*everything that relates to the whole task of the whole Church to bring the whole Gospel to the whole world*."[36] It drew attention to the statement from the WCC's Evanston assembly, signed by their own Presbyterian representatives, which conjectured that "inherited forms of life" might need

32. Macdonald, *Tension and Tradition*, 51–52.

33. Moir, *Enduring Witness*, 242, 251–52.

34. Moir, *Enduring Witness*, 252.

35. Presbyterian Church in Canada (PCC), "Church Catholic," Foreword. The pamphlet refers to the action of the 1960 General Assembly in describing the committee's aims.

36. PCC, "Church Catholic," 31–32, para. 150; underlining in the original typescript.

to die to avoid the dividing power of sin.[37] One of the discussion questions put it bluntly: "Is it possible, in your opinion, that God may be desiring the death of The Presbyterian Church in Canada in the sense and for the purpose set forth in [paragraph] 169?"[38] A working paper published the next year again linked mission with ecumenism, arguing that past inter-church dialogue had disregarded the "fundamental element of mission": the "deep relation between the church and the world."[39] Rather than an attitude of hostility and opposition, encountering the world involved "radical identification."[40] The influence of international ecumenism was again evident in frequent references to the WCC and its "mission to the world," including the recent New Delhi assembly.[41]

ORGANIZING FOR A "MISSION TO THE WORLD": RESISTING AND RESTRUCTURING

Perhaps it was sentiments like those that provoked W. Stanford Reid to edit a pamphlet the following year that countered the claims of the ecumenical movement. He saw its logic as a demand for one to "declare whether or not they believe it a sin to be a Presbyterian."[42] The organic unity promoted by some ecumenists would mean "the submerging of our identity as a Presbyterian Church in a great 'universal' church" that might even eventually include Roman Catholics. He added, "A good many Presbyterians feel that we fought the church union battle in 1925 and now need have no more fear. The fact is, however, that we face an infinitely greater threat" that he identified as being "forced into another church union."[43] Reid was particularly concerned about the implications for missions, cautioning that it was "most of all in our overseas work" that the "church unionist emphasis" was strong.[44] He remained adamant in his opposition in years to come, retorting

37. PCC, "Church Catholic," 34, paras. 168–69.

38. PCC, "Church Catholic," 44, para. 218.

39. PCC, "Church Catholic: Working Paper," Foreword.

40. PCC, "Church Catholic: Working Paper," 22, paras. 89–90.

41. PCC, "Church Catholic: Working Paper," 22–23, paras. 96–103.

42. Reid, "Whither the Presbyterian Church in Canada," 21. Anti-ecumenism is a persistent theme in *Tradition and Tension* and Reid features as a recurring critic of cooperative initiatives. Moir also highlights Reid's leadership, noting that he "soon assumed the role of spokesman for the anti-ecumenists." Moir, *Enduring Witness*, 253. See also MacLeod, *W. Stanford Reid*.

43. Reid, "Whither the Presbyterian Church in Canada," 23–24.

44. Reid, "Whither the Presbyterian Church in Canada," 22.

an objection to an article in the *Presbyterian Record* in a letter to the editor: "We must now face the issue of whether we wish to continue as Presbyterians," Reid retorted, "or whether we are prepared to accept a revolutionary position which will largely eliminate our specifically reformed witness in favour of something much more general, in preparation for the next big church union movement."[45]

Reid's ire had been raised on that occasion by one of the leaders who promoted the new approach to mission. McGill University theologian Joseph McLelland was a member of the Committee on Inter-Church Relations and was described as having made a "substantial" contribution to its publications.[46] His warnings in the 1960s about his denomination's insularity from the world and his call for a new blueprint for mission[47] triggered clashes not unlike what other North American denominations experienced. He challenged the claim that "evangelicalism" entailed "the separation of God and the world," insisting rather that "the direction or orientation of the Christian, of the church, is toward the world."[48] Alluding to what he called "the classic words of Evanston" (a reference to the WCC assembly held there), he contended that to evangelize is to participate in Christ's life and ministry to the world.[49]

McLelland cautioned that denominationalism was a danger, not because it prevented unity, but because it hindered the mission of the church. In 1965, as Presbyterians celebrated the 40th anniversary of their resistance to church union, he complained that his church had wandered in the wilderness for those forty years, using the memory of the controversy in a futile attempt to create a confessional church mystique and an evangelical ethos—and raising doubts thereby about the United Church's pedigree. "When," he asked in 1965, "have we discussed church extension in our church courts without being conscious of the shadow of the United Church as our rival and threat?"[50] But the United Church was not without criticism; he con-

45. Reid, "McLelland's Blueprint," 9.

46. Stuart Coles, then the secretary for Lay Studies, is identified in the Foreword to both the 1961 and 1962 pamphlets as the main author. He had recently chaired the committee that produced the Confession of Faith concerning Church and Nation (1955).

47. McLelland, "Blueprint for a New Model," 10–17.

48. McLelland, "Why Our Pond Is Lukewarm," addresses to the Toronto and Kingston Synod, October 1965, 11. His title linked his theme to similar concerns in the United Church by playing off the publicity generated by the latter's *Why the Sea Is Boiling Hot*.

49. McLelland, "Why Our Pond Is Lukewarm," 13.

50. McLelland, "Why Our Pond Is Lukewarm," 12.

sidered the Canadian experience of church both "a warning and a guide: how not to do it."[51] One aspect of his analysis was his interest in reconsidering the "federation" model that had been rejected during the church union controversy.[52]

McCelland was among those who were open to a restructuring of church and ministry that challenged denominational identity. He detailed his views on ecumenism in 1967 with his restructuring proposal that was "radical" in "the sense of one who is rooted."[53] Talk of "reunion" had reached an impasse, he argued in *Toward a Radical Church*, creating disunity and "alienating those who are committed to traditional evangelism." McLelland acknowledged the problem of organic union for Reid and other anti-ecumenists: it called for denominations to commit "ecclesiastical suicide."[54] Yet his presentation of a "radical" alternative, such as conciliar unity, tended to focus more on the deficiencies of other ecumenical models without spelling out its features.[55]

The outcome of such calls for radical restructuring mostly fell short of the hopes of a younger generation of activists who were coming on the scene. Presenting a bold new venture that was grounded in sociology as well as theology, they billed ministry for the sake of the world as a strategy for facing new social realities. As pluralism replaced a disappearing Christendom and rapid social change set in, Ray Hord insisted that the United Church's most urgent task was "to prepare and train her members to be a part of the church of the dispersion" that was "scattered in a pluralistic culture." The church would only continue to influence the world if it discovered "forms of fellowship and service that are more congenial to current experience."[56]

There were similar proposals in the Presbyterian Church. Stuart Coles previewed his concerns in 1968 in an article titled "Crisis = Danger + Opportunity," pondering whether anyone would notice if the Presbyterian Church simply disappeared from Canadian and overseas communities. Rather than "fixing our eyes on what God has done in the ancient past," he called for a new reformation to end "the foolish and unnecessary bondages

51. McLelland, *Toward a Radical Church*, 134.

52. McLelland, *Toward a Radical Church*, 131–32.

53. McLelland, *Toward a Radical Church*, 79.

54. McLelland, *Toward a Radical Church*, 2.

55. See chapter 8 on "Conciliar Unity," in McClelland, *Toward a Radical Church*, 72–88. For a critique of his lack of a model despite his use of the term, see Macdonald, *Tension and Tradition*, 137–38.

56. Hord, "It is Later Than We Think," 11–12. For analysis of this new approach to mission on the United Church, see the chapter on "Listening to the World" in Airhart, *Church with the Soul of a Nation*, 225–54.

to outworn structures."[57] Later that year, he was among the Presbyterians who organized a "Congress of Concern" that issued a "Declaration of Concern" aimed at shaking up the church from top to bottom.[58] Their views were dismissed as a mere quest for "relevancy" by those who "were at first amused, then confused and finally angered by their words and actions."[59]

There were indications that both churches were moving beyond the bitter controversy of 1925, yet that "next big church union" did not happen; events were to show that anti-union sentiment was still strong in influential circles fifty years later. An open letter signed by some of the most recognizable names in the two churches was published in June 1975 on the occasion of the 100th anniversary of the Presbyterian Church in Canada and the 50th anniversary of the founding of the United Church. It called for reconciliation and urged that a committee be set up to study "the possibility of closer relations."[60] Two years later, the *Presbyterian Record* reported on promising proposals for mutual recognition of ministries that had gone forward for discussion by each denomination.[61] But less than a year later, an editorial titled "Backward Christian Soldiers" announced the disappointing result: the General Assembly failed to move forward with the recommendations, despite the United Church's willingness to do so. The editorial blamed those opposed to it for picking at "old scar tissue" and "dragging old biases and fears" out of the cellar, "like rusty relics from past battles", and displayed like "trophies."[62]

The new approach to "mission" met a chilly reception among evangelicals in both denominations who saw its emphasis on Christian presence and openness to other faiths as a repudiation of efforts to convert the world to Christ: what was *evangelism* to them had been redefined as *proselytism* and disparaged as such. They joined other conservative evangelicals, some of whom thought of themselves as nondenominational or trans-denominational, rather than ecumenical, a word they deplored. "A unity is being cultivated among Christian believers, unlike the current ecumenism which seems to superimpose a pseudo-unity on organizational structure," enthused United Church minister Berkley Reynolds as he heralded the founding of the United Church Renewal Fellowship as evidence of a new day dawning

57. Coles, "Crisis = Danger + Opportunity," 10–11.

58. "The Congress of Concern" (dated 4–5 June 1968) was an eight-page memo setting out the group's recommendations for "renewal and action"; see General Correspondence, Stuart Bowyer Coles fonds, box 1–7.

59. Moir, *Enduring Witness*, 260.

60. "A Call for Reconciliation," 2.

61. Rayner, "Our Talks with the United Church," 3.

62. "Backward Christian Soldiers," 4; editorial.

for Canadian evangelicals. He also drew attention to the Canadian Anglican Evangelical Fellowship and the Evangelical Fellowship of Canada (comparing the latter to the National Association of Evangelicals in the US) as signs of an evangelical revival. He credited the Berlin Congress, along with the Billy Graham and Leighton Ford crusades, for bringing evangelicals from different denominations together.[63] In the Presbyterian Church, the debate over liberty of conscience after the decision to ordain women soon fueled the formation of Renewal Fellowship to represent evangelicals.[64]

Macdonald finds that there was no consensus in the Presbyterian Church on how to relate to other Protestant denominations at home and overseas. There was initially "a fear bordering on paranoia" of winding up in a church union of some sort. Hindrance of "any given line of missionary effort" was among the objections to cooperation. Anti-ecumenists warned that cooperation in home and foreign missions might lead to the "emasculation and obliteration of our Doctrinal Standards" and undermine their denomination's "spirituality and power." There was particular suspicion of interchurch initiatives involving the United Church, with strict conditions on even observing that denomination's negotiations with the Anglican Church.[65]

The United Church met with less resistance in experimenting with different ecumenical arrangements. Katharine Hockin, among the missionaries expelled from China in 1951, described her "pilgrimage in mission" from growing up as a child born in 1910 to missionary parents, to working in Toronto for the United Church as it implemented the "mission to/in six continents" after the New Delhi assembly, then attending the 1980 assembly of the WCC in Vancouver as a registered visitor. There she observed what she described as "a shift from traditional exclusivism to more inclusive celebration" that included not only the leadership of many women from the "third world" but presentations by guests from the major world religions.[66]

CONCLUSION: WHITHER DENOMINATIONAL IDENTITY?

As he observed the ecumenical situation in 1968, American historian Sidney Mead was concerned that its leaders were still dealing with the problem of the previous century, where denominational differences were top of mind.

63. Reynolds, "Evangelical Renaissance," 10.
64. Macdonald, *Tension and Tradition*, 210.
65. Macdonald, *Tension and Tradition*, 65–66.
66. Hockin, "My Pilgrimage in Mission," 30.

He pithily described them as "sleepwalking" in their efforts to achieve unity before confronting the challenge of pluralism posed by encountering the world's religions. "In the dark, it is said, all cats are grey—and in the darkness gathering about the church of Christ, all Christians look about alike."[67] Yet one might now wonder if the cats can be seen at all. Individualism and de-institutionalization have diminished denominational identity almost to the point of invisibility. There has been a rapid and radical shift from the assumption of the universality of Christian truth—"what is true for all" to expressive individualism—"what is true for me."

A century ago, there were ecumenists who imagined the end of denominations that would come through church unions. Today, Christianity remains fragmented. There are now more denomination-like entities than before 1910, as well as still divided confessional families. There are also alternatives to the familiar forms of denominationalism in the form of cross-denominational experiments as well as nondenominational churches (NDC) that tend to be evangelical and intentionally local rather than national or international. The significant growth of NDCs is again changing the map of global Christianity that was redrawn in the postwar period. Christianity in places that were once "foreign fields" for Western missionaries are perhaps adapting to the realities of pluralism more effectively than the ecumenical Protestants who opened them; the geographical center of Christianity has shifted south and east over the last century.

Meanwhile, the challenge of pluralism to Christianity that Wilfred Cantwell Smith warned of persists and extends to Canada. Pluralism now involves not only encounters between other religious institutions but the implications of a shift of religious toleration from institutions to individuals, where personal faith cannot be disentangled from everyday life. For instance, liberals and conservatives alike are struggling with how to respond to the "secularism bill" passed by the provincial government of Quebec that bans government employees from wearing religious symbols. Strikingly, religious values are contrasted with "Canadian values." As North American society becomes culturally less Christian, are we gradually moving towards a time when freedom *from* religion will shape public policy as much or more than freedom *of* religion did in the past?

The "agency" model has not solved the problems facing national denominational structures. Technology has opened new ways of connecting that have further eroded the old denominational and ecumenical configurations of the twentieth century. The organizational culture in churches (and society) today is much more chaotic; relations are less orderly and more

67. Mead, "Prospects for the Church in America," 24–26.

ephemeral. Yet taskforces, coalitions and networks still bring together diverse points of view and are transforming the corporate structure of what was once the Protestant "mainstream." There are new experiments in ecumenical cooperation underway with formal mergers replaced (often of necessity) by alternatives such as sharing space. For instance, Bloor Street United Church in Toronto, formerly Bloor Street Presbyterian, is the site of a major condo redevelopment that includes a worship area for the congregation, as well as a lease agreement between the Anglican, Presbyterian and United churches to share space for their national offices and archives.[68]

What about the sense of mission and service that was once tied to denominational identity? Andrew Faiz, national editor of the *Presbyterian Record*, a denominational magazine that ceased publication in 2016, now works for *Broadview*, formerly the *United Church Observer*. Growing up in the Presbyterian Church, he recalls hearing "mythic tales of how we once were nearly absorbed into the United Church." He remembers "old, old men expressing acrimony toward the United Church. For them, denominational identity mattered." But it is a rant he says he has not heard decades. "Most of the people I sit with in the pews do not seem so fussed about being Presbyterian. They are much more concerned about how to witness in society."[69]

My own experience suggests that more of us are becoming "congregationalists" for whom the experience of worship and witness—"mission", one might say—is more important than a denominational name on the church's sign. It is an individual rather than "tribal" decision—another aspect of the lived realities of a pluralistic world that reflects the fractured experience of belief and belonging, whether religious or secular.

So again, to quote Macdonald, "Adapting to a different Canada, one that is post-Christian and post-Christendom, remains a challenge."

BIBLIOGRAPHY

Airhart, Phyllis. *A Church with the Soul of a Nation: Making and Remaking the United Church of Canada*. Montreal and Kingston: McGill-Queen's University Press, 2014.

Arnup, Jesse. *A New Church Faces a New World*. Toronto: United Church, 1937.

"Backward Christian Soldiers." *Presbyterian Record*, July/August 1978.

68. Anthony Teles, "Year in Review: Tracking Construction at Cielo Condos in the Annex," *Urban Toronto*, December 20, 2024, https://urbantoronto.ca/news/2024/12/year-review-tracking-construction-cielo-condos-annex.57636.

69. Andrew Faiz, "The Church Union That Was—And Wasn't," *Broadview*, June 5, 2025, https://broadview.org/presbyterian-church-in-canada-union/.

Bosch, David J. *Transforming Mission: Paradigm Shifts in Theology of Mission.* Maryknoll, NY: Orbis, 1993.

"A Call for Reconciliation." *Presbyterian Record*, June 1975.

Coles, Stuart. "Crisis = Danger + Opportunity." *Presbyterian Record*, 1968.

Committee on Life and Mission Projects (LAMP). "Into the '70s in Life and Mission." Toronto: Presbyterian Church in Canada, 1969.

Dykstra, Craig, and James Hudnut-Beumler. "The National Organizational Structures of Protestant Denominations: An Invitation to a Conversation." In *The Organizational Revolution: Presbyterians and American Denominationalism*, edited by Milton J. Coalter et al., 307–31. Louisville: Westminster John Knox, 1992.

Goodall, Norman. "'Evangelicals' and the WCC-IMC." *International Review of Missions* 47.186 (April 1958) 210–11.

Grant, John Webster. *The Ship Under the Cross.* Toronto: Ryerson, 1960.

———. *World Church: Achievement or Hope?* Toronto: Ryerson, 1956.

Hockin, Katharine B. "My Pilgrimage in Mission." In *Voices from the Ecumenical Movement*, edited by the World Council of Churches, 53–58. Geneva: World Council of Churches, 1980.

Hoekendijk, Johannes. *The Church Inside Out.* Philadelphia: Westminster, 1966.

Hord, J. R. "It is Later Than We Think," *The Cutting Edge*, Evangelism and Social Service Annual Report, 1968.

Hutchison, William. "Americans in World Mission: Revision and Realignment." In *Altered Landscapes: Christianity in America, 1935–1985*, edited by David W. Lotz, 155–70. Grand Rapids: Eerdmans, 1989.

Jay, C. Douglas. "Missiological Implications of Christianizing the Social Order with Special Reference to the United Church of Canada." *Toronto Journal of Theology* 12.2 (1996) 275–84.

———. *World Mission and World Civilization.* Toronto: Board of World Mission, United Church of Canada, [1967?].

Macdonald, Stuart. *Tradition and Tension: The Presbyterian Church in Canada, 1945–1985*. Toronto: Presbyterian Publications, 1986.

MacLoed, A. Donald. *W. Stanford Reid: An Evangelical Calvinist in the Academy.* Montreal & Kingston: McGill-Queen's University Press, 2004.

McLelland, Joseph C. "Blueprint for a New Model." *Presbyterian Record*, September 1967.

———. *Toward a Radical Church: New Models for Ecumenical Relations.* Toronto: Ryerson, 1967.

———. "Why Our Pond Is Lukewarm, or Forty Years in the Wilderness." Address to the Toronto and Kingston Synod, October 1965.

Mead, Sidney E. *The Lively Experiment.* New York: Harper & Row, 1963.

———. "Prospects for the Church in America." In *The Future of the American Church*, edited by Philip J. Hefner. Philadelphia: Fortress, 1968.

Moir, John S. *Enduring Witness: A History of the Presbyterian Church in Canada.* Toronto: Presbyterian Publications, 1974.

Patterson, James Alan. "The Loss of a Protestant Missionary Consensus: Foreign Missions and the Fundamentalist-Modernist Conflict." In *Earthen Vessels: American Evangelicals and Foreign Missions, 1880–1980*, edited by Joel A. Carpenter and Wilbert R. Shenk, 73–91. Grand Rapids: Eerdmans, 1990.

Presbyterian Church in Canada (PCC). "Presbyterians and the Church Catholic." General Assembly Committee on Inter-Church Relations, 1961.

———. "Presbyterians and the Church Catholic: A Working Paper." General Assembly Committee on Inter-Church Relations, 1962.

Rayner, Decourcy H. "Our Talks with the United Church." *Presbyterian Record*, October 1977.

Reid, W. Stanford. "McLelland's Blueprint." *Presbyterian Record*, November 1967.

———. "Whither the Presbyterian Church in Canada?" In *In the Unity of Faith: Some Comments on the Position of Presbyterian Church in Canada in the Modern Ecumenical Movement*, edited by W. Stanford Reid. [n.p.], 1962.

Reynolds, J. Berkley. "Evangelical Renaissance." *Small Voice* 1.1 (1967).

Robert, Dana. *Christian Mission: How Christianity Became a World Religion*. Malden, MA: Wiley-Blackwell, 2009.

Roozen, David. "National Denominational Structures' Engagement with Postmodernity: An Integrative Summary from an Organizational Perspective." In *Church, Identity, and Change: Theology and Denominational Structures in Unsettled Times*, edited by David A. Roozen and James R. Nieman. Grand Rapids: Eerdmans, 2005.

Smith, Wilfred Cantwell. "The Christian Mission in a Pluralist Society." *Christian Century* 77 (1960) 1142–46.

———. "Christianity's Third Great Challenge." *Christian Century* (April 27, 1960) 505–8.

———. *The Faith of Other Men*. New York: Harper, 1962.

Somerville, James. "The World's Evangelicals Look at Themselves—and Their Future." *United Church Observer* (January 1, 1967) 14–15.

United Church of Canada. *Report of the Commission on World Mission*. Toronto: United Church, 1966.

Wacker, Grant. "Second Thoughts on the Great Commission: Liberal Protestants and Foreign Missions." In *Earthen Vessels: American Evangelicals and Foreign Missions, 1880–1980*, edited by Joel A. Carpenter and Wilbert R. Shenk, 282–300. Grand Rapids: Eerdmans, 1990.

World Council of Churches. *Christian Witness, Proselytism and Religious Liberty*. Geneva: World Council of Churches, 1961.

———. *The New Delhi Report*. Geneva: World Council of Churches, 1961.

Wright, Robert. *A World Mission: Canadian Protestantism and the Quest for a New International Order 1918–1939*. Montreal and Kingston: McGill-Queen's University Press, 1991.

2

The Church in Canada

Responding to Post-Christendom

Lee Beach

INTRODUCTION

The decline of the church in Canada had been a topic for some time before Stuart Macdonald and his research/writing partner Brian Clarke undertook a massive project that produced the 2017 book *Leaving Christianity: Changing Allegiances in Canada since 1945*. While there were already numerous studies that demonstrate the losses that have occurred across denominational traditions, Clarke and Macdonald's project provides one of the most thorough and insightful resources that the church in Canada could have hoped for. It is a long-term, widespread study that reveals the extent of the decline in almost every area of the church in Canadian society. The evidence of decline that the book displays has not changed much in recent years as the 2021 Canadian census demonstrates,[1] nonetheless the book offers a vivid picture of what is going on in Canadian society and its relationship to Christianity. The book concludes with the question "Quo Vadis Canada?" That is Latin for "Where are you going?" It is the right question in response to the data and analysis that Clarke and Macdonald have provided and it continues to be the key question for the church to answer

1. See Murray, "The End is Nigh?" 9.

as it navigates its way through the realities of a changed religious and social landscape. While the authors of *Leaving Christianity* offer some reflection on this question, this chapter will seek to engage with that conversation and provide, what is intended to be some practical insight into how the church needs to conduct itself if it is to thrive in a time that has been labeled by some as a "Post-Christian" era.[2]

To engage the question "Where are you going?", this essay will explore three key areas. First, the concept of secularism and its pervasive influence on Canadian culture will be briefly considered. This idea has a significant role to play in helping us understand one of the overarching cultural realities that influences contemporary human thinking, especially as it relates to religion and its role in society. Next, we will reflect on some of the implications of secularism on contemporary ministry. From here we will consider the possibility that this is a time for the church to enter into a posture of waiting. This does not mean passivity, rather it is an active waiting that anticipates God's current and future activity but also understands that we are in a time of deep cultural transition and perhaps this calls us to take a posture that forces us to re-think our former practices, expectations and metrics and adopt an active but more patient outlook on how the church can find its footing in today's Canadian (and North American) context.

SECULARIZATION AND THE DECLINE OF CHRISTIAN FAITH AND PRACTICE

Leadership Guru Max DePree taught that the first work of leadership was to "define reality."[3] DePree's wisdom is prescient for the contemporary church as we seek to understand how to effectively be the church in Canada today. Before we can decide where we are going, we need to accurately determine where we are. It is one thing to understand that among Protestant mainline Churches, as Clarke and Macdonald document, there is overall and long-term decline.[4] Or to grasp that, according to the latest 2021 census, the Catholic Church has declined, as have certain evangelical denominations after several decades of growth or at least plateauing.[5] While numbers like

2. For example, see Murray, *Post-Christendom*. See also Hall, *End of Christendom*, and Beach, *Church in Exile*.

3. De Pree, *Leadership Is an Art*, 11.

4. Clarke and Macdonald, *Leaving Christianity*, 29.

5. Murray, "The End Is Nigh?" 9. Murray particularly points out that Pentecostalism declined by 79,680 adherents between 2011–2021 after many years of numerical growth.

these are important because they do tell a story, something more essential is at the heart of a proper understanding of the culture we live in. That is, the role that secularization has played, and continues to play in the overall ethos of Canadian culture. This needs to be understood in order for the church to properly define its current reality. A brief examination of secularism and its influence on Canadian life is necessary if we are to forge a basic understanding of how the church needs to understand itself in the twenty-first century.[6]

In the early years of Canada's nationhood, the forces of secularization were already beginning to encroach on public life.[7] Canada's development as a nation had a strong religious tone to it and was not influenced by secularizing forces in an obvious way, at least until after World War Two. However, upon close scrutiny it is not hard to discern how the secular trends of the West as a whole were echoed in the evolution of Canadian society.

McGill University professor Charles Taylor, who has written extensively on the issue of secularism, identifies the many nuances that mark it as both a philosophy and as a movement. He offers a partial definition when he writes that the shift to secularity consists, among other things, in "a move from a society where belief in God is unchallenged and indeed, unproblematic, to one in which it is understood to be one option among others, and frequently not the easiest to embrace."[8] Similarly, historian Ramsey Cook, in his survey of the secularization of Canada, defines it simply as "the shift from a religious explanation of man's [sic] behaviour to a non-religious one."[9] This shift was increasingly taking place as Canada moved from being a nation that valued religion and Christian religion in particular as a central part of its national identity, to a nation that was no longer inclined to give preference to any one religion.[10] Paul Bramadat identifies

6. It must be noted that secularism, as a philosophy and secularization, as a social movement are multi-faceted and not simply defined. A thorough analysis of these forces in Western culture is beyond the purview of this chapter. What follows here is a brief tracing of the major contours of both as they affected (and continue to affect) Canadian life. For an interesting delineation of these terms, offered by someone writing at the time that Canada was coming to grips with the swirling winds of secularizing forces, see MacGuigan, "Unity in the Secular City," 149–50.

7. This section of this chapter is a summary of a section from my doctoral dissertation, *A Hopeful Demise.*

8. Taylor, *Secular Age*, 3.

9. Cook, *Regenerators*, 4.

10. This is not to insinuate that the idea of religious neutrality was brand new to Canada. Many influential leaders in early Canada were not overly religious or insisted that one religion (or denomination) should never be preferred over another. In certain ways it can be argued that this was the founding view of Canadian society. As Miller

the two broader cultural forces that converge in the secularization process as rationalism (the process of organizing life around scientific and logical principles) and disenchantment (the gradual disempowerment of ideas or institutions associated with magic or religion).[11] The forces that drove secularism were rooted in scientific and religious studies. The growing acceptance of Darwinian evolution provided a scientific explanation for the world that no longer necessitated belief in God or, at least, made belief in God less compelling to those who were disinclined toward belief in the first place. The advent of historical criticism in biblical studies in the nineteenth century, as well as the emerging field of comparative religion, provided a religious critique of long-held Christian beliefs and gave people alternative ways of thinking about Christian faith. In many ways it allowed for a relaxation of those beliefs.[12]

A move away from Christian adherence also allowed for the increase in beliefs and practices that had often been considered taboo by the religious establishment. In certain ways this was epitomized by the move toward consumerism. The consumeristic impulse is a part of any developing society and is accepted as a natural part of life. That said, some, such as historian George Rawlyk, theorize that the movement of secularization in Canada was ultimately more driven by the "internal decay" brought on by consumerism than it was by the "external attacks" delivered by Darwin or the German biblical scholars with the historical criticism that they espoused.[13] Re-iterating this view is sociologist Steve Bruce, who acknowledges that science has certainly undermined Christian faith in the Western world but that the real issue is not science's overt intellectual conflict with religion as much as its empowerment of a rationalistic worldview. Bruce writes,

> I suggest that the primary secularizing effects of science came not from its direct refutation of religious ideas but through the general encouragement to a rationalistic orientation to the world that science has given; the embodiment of that rationalistic

notes in "Unity/Diversity," John A. Macdonald's founding vision was one of "unity in diversity," 71. The prominence of Christian belief came about as a matter of fact, simply because most of the early citizens of Canada were practicing Christians. The valuing of religion then, was more an intrinsic value than one that was legislated. See Marshall, *Secularizing the Faith*, 22–24.

11. Bramadat, "Beyond Christian Canada," 4.

12. For a concise overview of the influence of Darwin and Historical Criticism see Clarke, "English-Speaking Canada," 317–22. Also, Kuffert traces the movement of science and technology in the shaping of the consciousness of Canadian society in chapter 3 of *A Great Duty*.

13. Rawlyk, *Canadian Baptists*, 36–37.

> outlook in bureaucracy as the dominant form of social organization; and the role of technology in increasing our sense of mastery over our own fate.[14]

Whether Rawlyk's and Bruce's analyses are correct or not, they nonetheless remind us that numerous secularizing forces were at work and were slowly but steadily, changing the complexion of Canadian life. A scientific worldview was replacing the Christian one as Canada evolved into an urban-industrial society where there were multiple indications of decline in the moral authority of the churches and in religious commitment among its citizens.[15] This shift developed in a way that led Canadians away from ecclesiastical authority and toward individual authority and the individual's ability to pursue personal fulfillment without regard to any particular set of religious beliefs or codes.

David Marshall, in his study on the church's role in the secularization of Canadian life, observes how this process occurred gradually. He writes that, there "was not a crisis or a serious rupture from a religious past. The process of secularization in Canada, for the most part, was slow and at times imperceptible."[16]

However, as the process unfolded, Marshall further observes how the prospect of a society where religious beliefs and institutions were in decline brought about much consternation for many Canadians, as Christianity had been considered foundational to the nation's moral life and social order.[17] In an article published in the *Presbyterian Record* in 1967, William E. Hume noted the effect of secularization on Presbyterian ministry when he wrote,

> Society is undergoing a process called secularization. God was once considered indigenous to our culture. Today he is being moved out of the culture. He is a sectarian symbol in a pluralistic society. This church, therefore, is feeling the pinch of being just one institution among others attempting to justify its existence.[18]

14. Bruce, *God is Dead,* 73.
15. Marshall, *Secularizing the Faith,* 16.
16. Marshall, *Secularizing the Faith,* 19.
17. Marshall, *Secularizing the Faith,* 4.
18. Hume, "Care of Your Minister," 10, as cited in Miedema, *For Canada's Sake,* 56. It must be noted that the process of secularization in Quebec is a story all its own. While a review of this shift in Quebec society is beyond the scope of this current study see Perin, "French-Speaking Canada"; also Fay, *History of Canadian Catholics,* especially chapter fourteen, and Baum, *Church in Quebec,* especially chapters one and two.

This short historical reflection opens the way for further reflection on how secularism has taken over the worldview of most Canadians. As Taylor points out, in large parts of the world the work of public institutions and public discourse carries on without any reference or seeming need for God.[19] Further, as already noted the conditions for belief are shaped in a way that makes religious faith a tougher option for people to choose because society does not intrinsically affirm it, at least as a public matter.[20] Thus, society as a whole reflects a world where religious belief and experience is allocated to the realm of the private. Faith is fine, but it is best kept private or at most shared among those who believe like you do. The idea that there is a transcendent God who is active in the world is no longer embraced as a given. In fact, the opposite is true, and even if one is spiritual that aspect of your life is usually not invited into the workplace, the local hockey arena, casual social gatherings or personal conversation unless explicitly invited. Life moves on with little overt reference in regular society and day to life to the divine. Practical theologian Andrew Root writes, "We live in a secular age because we can imagine living, and at times do live, as though there is no transcendent quality to life at all."[21]

None of this is meant to insinuate that Canada was at one time a "Christian country" where Christian morality and ethics were devoutly practiced and society was like a quasi heaven on earth. It is to say however, that our society has experienced a significant shift to the degree that in Canada, and other parts of the Global North, we are facing "a religious landscape that we have never seen before."[22] This is a daunting challenge and there are numerous implications that need to be identified. Let us consider three significant ones that affect how the church can proceed in its engagement with contemporary Canadian culture.

IMPLICATIONS FOR MINISTRY

Reference Points

Old Testament theologian Walter Brueggemann puts his finger on the reality of the new religious landscape that the church functions on when he states,

19. Taylor, *Secular Age*, 1–2.
20. Taylor, *Secular Age*, 3.
21. Root, *Churches*, 8.
22. Clarke and Macdonald, *Leaving Christianity*, 26.

> There was a time . . . when a Christian preacher could count on the shared premises of the listening community, reflective of a large theological consensus. There was a time, when the *assumption of God* completely dominated Western imagination, and the holy Catholic Church roughly uttered the shared consensus of all parties. That consensus was rough and perhaps not very healthy, but at least the preacher could work from it.[23]

Brueggemann's point, of course, is that this consensus, as loose as it may have been, no longer holds at all. This is true, at least in part, because the language of Christendom has been lost and the culture at large no longer helps the church inculcate the ideas of Christianity into the wider population.

As a child and a teenager, I did not grow up going to church. My family had some nominal Christian faith, but attending church was not part of our regular practice. I did not receive basic bible teaching from kind Sunday school teachers or long-winded preachers. But, when a high school friend of mine first shared with me about his faith in Jesus and how Jesus had died on a cross for my sins, I had heard that story before. I did not understand that it had implications for my life, but I had a knowledge of the basic contours of the story. How did I obtain that knowledge? Not from the church because apart from attending some weddings, funerals and christenings, I had never had much exposure to the church. I had a basic understanding of the crucifixion story because somehow the culture delivered it to me. Simply by being a kid growing up in Canada in the late-sixties, seventies and early eighties, I had absorbed some of the details of the gospel story. When my friend shared his faith with me, I had enough understanding that I could comprehend the basic message he was trying to communicate. Further, the idea of believing in this message was not implausible to me because, while church attendance may have been in decline, I did not think it preposterous that someone would go to church. It was not my world at that time, but I knew that there were lots of people for whom it was their world.

This is no longer the case. Canadian children grow up not only with no exposure to the church but also with limited, if any, exposure to the basic message of Christianity.[24] This lack of Christian education creates a challenge for the church in terms of where to start sharing the Christian message with people who have no introductory knowledge of it and who live in a world that provides no plausibility structure for Christian belief.

To complicate this further, for some in our culture, there is an inherent bias against the message of Christianity and the church. They have formed

23. Brueggemann, *Deep Memory*, 1.

24. Thiessen, *Meaning*, 135–36.

an impression about the church that is rooted in financial and sexual scandal, residential schools, racism, sexism, homophobia, and many other personal experiences that they or members of their family have had that make them skeptical that the church is a place to go for community, solace and answers to life's questions.[25]

The early church, as depicted in the New Testament, faced the immense challenge of having to communicate the gospel to a culture that did not know its basic content. In this sense, their challenge was even greater than ours in Canada today. Christianity was a whole new philosophy that included many radical claims. How to effectively communicate this message that was so different from anything that had been offered before was an immense challenge for the early church. However, in those early days, the church was not saddled with the same kind of bias against it that we in Canada face today. The message it preached may have seemed strange, but it did not come with a fifteen-hundred-year track record that is spotty at best and scandalous at worst. This is one of the challenges that the current cultural landscape presents.

The Turn to Individualization

A second significant shift that affects the current cultural landscape is the move toward an individualized approach to spirituality that is catalyzed by a rejection of organized religion on one hand but also as a response to the perceived chaos or uncertainty that typifies life in the modern world on the other.[26]

The move away from traditional religious practices to a more individual approach to spirituality is characterized by several things. First, a way of gaining power in a world where one often feels disempowered by the numerous voices that bombard us with information and leave us wondering what voice to listen to. For some, this leads to a search for their own inner voice that will guide them and empower them to make their own decisions about truth and the best path for their life. As Charles Taylor has observed, in the seeming tumult of life in the modern world, people are not defined by passive disengagement, but rather they are defined by "this new power of expressive self-articulation."[27] There is a move toward the inside that gives people power to self-define as opposed to being defined by external forces,

25. Thiessen, *Meaning,* 138–41.

26. See Taylor, *Secular Age,* especially chapter 13, for an overview on the move to a more individualistic society.

27. Taylor, *Sources of Self,* 390.

including institutions that once may have played a larger role in guiding people into embracing a particular worldview that would direct their lives. This move inside becomes the way we understand what it means to be human. We feel strongest when we express ourselves authentically, rather than in the ways defined by older sources of power.[28] This, of course, has consequences for the ministry of the church. It becomes just one of the many competing voices that must be sifted through and ultimately adjudicated by the internal voice of the individual. Joel Thiessen, in his study of people who have departed from organized religion, tells the story of a man named "Larry" who illustrates this kind of inner empowerment as he reflects on certain beliefs from his Anglican heritage. He indicates that he still agrees with some of them but not so much with others. He states, "[S]ometimes you cherry-pick . . . You pick what you like . . . Whereas years ago, it used to be that you couldn't cherry pick. It was all inclusive. You got what you got."[29]

This is the way that people both within and outside of the church are inclined to think these days. Of course, this is not wrong; thinking for ourselves is a sign of maturity and appropriate independence. However, the modern turn to the inner voice is rooted in a basic mistrust of institutions and traditionally authoritative voices. This makes any claim of ultimate truth, which is at the heart of Christianity, a difficult message for people today to swallow. It further erodes the place of religious community. The church is seen as restrictive and intolerant of different views. This empowers people to be guided by their own compass, even if it sometimes violates the accepted views of a given church community. Thus, spiritual beliefs, as they are privatized, do not need an external validation, at least not by a traditional community of faith. The view that there is value in the corporate experience in faith development is eschewed for an attitude that says one can believe without belonging.[30]

Finally, the individual spiritual quest has become as much about self-discovery as it is about finding God. Personal spirituality can be equated with such contemporary catch phrases as "your inner self," "you do you," "my true self," and "my truth." Again, these concepts are not all wrong, but they do demonstrate an emphasis on one's own inner consciousness as being primary when it comes to living an authentic life. For many, the pursuit of spirituality plays an important role in this journey of gaining self-knowledge.

28. Russo, *Shifting Secular Age*, 40–41.

29. Thiessen, *Meaning*, 3–4.

30. Clarke and Macdonald, *Leaving Christianity*, 231.

Robert Fuller, in his work on the modern idea of people identifying as "spiritual but not religious," reflects on theories developed by Carl Jung and notes that in the move away from traditional religion and toward a spirituality that is most often very individual, "[T]here is no line separating psychology and spirituality."[31] The spiritual quest is intertwined with a quest for identity, autonomy and centeredness that provides some kind of grounding for life in this world. Where in the past the church and its teachings may have been seen as a place that provided this, increasingly it is an individual matter.

The turn to individualization presents the church with the challenge of how to present its message in a world filled with messages and with people who are increasingly trusting their own inner voices to discern truth. As Andrew Root writes, "[T]here is no longer any transcendent referent to meaning and purpose that does not begin and end with me. I may be able to find spirituality, but its epicenter will be not outside me but within me."[32]

The Immanent Frame

The third result of secularization that the church finds itself rubbing shoulders with is the prevailing idea of the immanent frame. This term is used by Charles Taylor to describe the idea that we live in a highly rational, structured world that can be explained and experienced without any reference to, or need for, the supernatural. That said, Taylor breaks down the concept of the immanent frame by offering two distinct categories of understanding it. The open frame and the closed frame. The open frame is still largely conditioned by rational and utilitarian forces, but it leaves room for the supernatural to play a role in one's understanding of the world. The closed frame is largely closed to this possibility and works from the assumption that something like God has no real role to play in one's experience in this world. Taylor recognizes that many people feel pulled between the two poles and that there is a cross-pressure that one feels living between them. However, in a functional way, that is, in the reality of day-to-day life in the Western world, given that the immanent frame has developed under the auspices of the modern world and its emphasis on scientism and religious liberalism, Taylor notes that "living within this frame pushes us to the closed perspective."[33]

31. Fuller, *Spiritual, But Not Religious*, 138.

32. Root, *Secular Age*, 142.

33. Taylor, *Secular Age*, 555. For an overview of the idea of the immanent frame see Taylor, *Secular Age*, 542–57.

Even for those who live with an inclination toward a more open perspective, in public one may be tempted to conduct themselves as if the immanent frame that they live in is closed. This has massive ramifications for the practice of faith, both personally and corporately. Reflecting on this reality, Andrew Root observes, "[I]t is easier to conceive of God only as a flat concept—a kind of final contingent relation behind the curtain of all other explanations—than to conceive of God as an acting and speaking agent in this world."[34] This can lead to a form of Deistic theology if not straight out agnosticism or atheism. At minimum, it can lead to a lack of confidence in one's Christian faith and a hesitancy to speak about it freely. As an example, it may seem appropriate to tell someone we are praying for them when we discover they are going through a hard time. However, when we feel like we are living in a place where people are generally skeptical of the idea that God is active and can break through into the experience of life in this world, we are certainly more hesitant to assure people of our prayers. We have a suspicion that they will think our words to be quaint, ridiculously naïve or a platitude that will have absolutely no bearing on their situation.[35] Most modern people in the Western world do not assume that God acts directly in the affairs of the world. In our context, doubt and suspicion are the direct result of living in the immanent frame.[36]

Again, this does not discount the idea that many, if not most, people do believe in God. Rather, it captures the reality that our culture has become highly secular, and the impact of that is much more than just a decline in church attendance. It flows down deep into the roots of human understanding of the way things are, how the world works. Functionally, there is not much room for active belief in a God who is present and moving in the immanent frame in which we live.

All three of these realities contribute to the fact that people are leaving Christianity (as the title of Clarke and Macdonald's book tells us). It also leads us back to the question under consideration in this chapter: how does the church respond?

WE HAVE BEEN HERE BEFORE

It is worth noting that finding ourselves in a time of transition where the future is unclear is not new for God's people. In some ways, it is almost a perpetual state of being; there are some instances in scripture that remind

34. Root, *Churches*, 11.

35. Adapted from an example used by Root, *Churches*, 11.

36. Root, *Churches*, 13.

us of the way that God works when his followers face times of challenge to their future.

In the book of Exodus, Israel is living in slavery in Egypt, and any idea of a prosperous future is a distant one at best. But the biblical text tells us that God is aware of his people's struggles, and he initiates a plan for deliverance (Exod 2:23–25). As the story unfolds, God begins to enact his plan to release Israel from their current situation in Egypt. He is acting, but the unfolding story of his actions makes clear that it is not a nice, straight path to deliverance. In fact immediately after Moses and Aaron visit Pharoah to request that the Israelites be let go to celebrate a special religious festival in the dessert, Pharoah responds by not only denying their request but ordering that their labor be made harder by taking away delivery of much needed straw that helps them make bricks so that they have to gather it themselves, while still maintaining the same quota of bricks each day. God's act of deliverance begins with a decline into more severe work conditions for the Hebrew slaves. Centuries later, the Prophet Jeremiah comes to the Israelites and prophesies that the nation will be exiled to Babylon, however, he also prophesies that deliverance will come. One day they will return to the land (27:22; 30:3). However, before that happens, Jeremiah tells the people that there will be a long period when Israel will live in the land of Babylon. They are to settle in, live their lives, work hard for the good of Babylon because it is their home now too (Jer 29:4–7). Before deliverance comes, there will be a time of waiting.

It seems like God is not hesitant to place his people in a liminal space at certain times in their journey with him in this world. The concept of liminality describes a time when an individual or a group finds itself in between one thing and another thing. "A liminal stage is a stage of transition, a period that is neither one thing nor another."[37] It is a time when something has ended, but what is to come is not yet clear. This was true of the Hebrew people when God began the work of deliverance from Egypt, and when he promised a return to the land from Exile. In many ways, it was the experience of the early church as they moved from a band of travelling disciples to a movement that would ultimately become established as the church. It is also true for the post-Christendom church today.

Liminal times can be times of great stress, but they are also times of tremendous possibility, as they almost always produce new ideas, creativity, and a more cohesive community that is refined and renewed in its life

37. Frost, *Exiles*, 109. Frost is drawing from the work of anthropologist Victor Turner and Arnold van Gennep.

together. If this is to be true for the Canadian church today, what is required of it as it journeys through this time of liminality?

WAITING AS MISSION

The question, "how does the church respond?" implies some kind of activity-based initiatives that will tangibly engage the context in demonstrable ways. While there is a definite place for the church to engage in tangible activities, perhaps the time we find ourselves in also calls for a time of waiting. A time for discernment that will lead toward a response that is in keeping with God's initiatives in the world we inhabit. Such a proposal can seem passive and unproductive. Yet it is in keeping with ways that God has acted in the past, most notably after Jesus' resurrection he instructs his disciples to wait in Jerusalem for the Holy Spirit to come to them so that they can fulfill their mission as his witnesses to the whole earth (Acts 1: 8). It is similar to the Israelite people in Babylon settling in and learning to live there productively, even benefitting their captors. This time of waiting prepared the early church to effectively participate in God's initiative in the work of sending his Spirit and starting his church. It also led Israel to go through a time of refinement that shaped their future. The act of waiting is an act of mission. It is a posture of preparation that anticipates and participates in what God is up to, even if it is not fully clear at this point what that exactly is.

It hardly needs to be said that most of us have a built-in resistance to waiting. Our culture shapes this proclivity toward resisting waiting because it values results. Productivity gets commendations, waiting seems lazy. We also like immediate gratification. If there is a problem, we want it fixed as soon as possible. Waiting for things to be rectified and our having to put up with any inconveniences that are caused by things not going as we expect them to is the ultimate frustration. We want to see things moving along. We want to get positive results as fast as possible.

Added to this is the fact that people will expect leaders to come up with the right ideas and get things done. As the authors of the book *The Practice of Adaptive Leadership* rightly note, "Even if you do not have the foggiest idea of what to do, you have a strong incentive to give in to others' demands that you: 'Do Something!'"[38]

All of these impulses, both internal and external, make the idea of waiting seem unresponsive to the problem. Yet, there are situations when a time for reflection, recalibration and discernment is absolutely necessary. Perhaps this is the case in these post-Christian days that we find ourselves

38. Heifetz et.al., *Adaptive Leadership*, 44.

in. We need to "[R]esist the pressure to do something, and spend more time diagnosing the problem, even if taking that much time feels excruciatingly uncomfortable."[39]

This is not to insinuate that the church simply sits passively. Waiting may be resisted by some because it seems to be unresponsive to the situation, but for others, it is also an act of resistance toward the situation. It is an important and tangible response to the way things are. In this sense, waiting is an active engagement with what is going on, with an understanding that what needs to be said or done, beyond waiting, is not yet completely clear, but it comes with a clear sense that *something* is going to happen. God is going to direct, move, act, and we want to be ready to join in when it happens. This is because waiting is always contingent upon the idea that we are waiting for something. We are waiting for change, or at least some kind of new development that will bring about what we hope will be a positive experience for us. Indeed, something is going to change, but in the meantime, we will wait, not passively but with anticipation of the impending change.[40] This is an important posture for the church to assume in the days of post-Christendom, a posture of waiting that is resistant to the Status Quo and is anticipating that clarity and opportunity will arise as the days ahead unfold.

This kind of waiting puts the emphasis on the concept of *being* before *doing*. It is the activity of cultivating depth before breadth. Encounter with God before the accrual of resources. The two are not mutually exclusive, but one must precede the other, even though at times the *doing* needs to be emphasized and *being* maintained as a catalyst to the doing. There are other times when the need to intentionally emphasize the being side of ministry, typified by a season of waiting, needs to be lifted up as the primary act of ministerial faithfulness. In light of our current challenges, a time of waiting with a view toward reclaiming our identity as the church in post-Christendom is of utmost importance.

But what is it that we are waiting for? The answer is nothing new, but something that we have, at times, in the regular routines of church life and the immediate crises of keeping things afloat, neglected. That is, signs of God's in-breaking. Indications of God's activity in the world around us that, if we were attentive, could open doors to meaningful ministry. This is mission 101, where is God at work, and how can we join him? This question is a guiding light for personal and congregational discernment when it comes to engaging in mission. It is a question that, in order to answer it properly, requires some degree of waiting.

39. Heifetz et.al., *Adaptive Leadership*, 44.

40. Root, *Churches*, 153.

There was a time, and perhaps for some churches this is still the way things are done, when our approach to mission came from a place of privilege. The church had a place in society that commended it as an institution that had answers to life's most important questions. The church could rely on that currency. This seems like a distant memory, but some churches function as if it is still true. Churches existed as places that could attract people, especially if they ran good programs that met felt needs, conducted lively worship services that included decent preaching. The church could work from a diagnostic-prescriptive posture. That is, it believed it could diagnose what was wrong with the world and the people in it, and it could offer the right prescription for how to cure things; the church had the answers. This approach to ministry may have been appropriate in a certain cultural context, and it may have even served to benefit many people. However, it did not require much waiting to discern signs of God's in-breaking. It functioned from a place of well-earned confidence that doing certain things well would yield positive results. As we have already noted, things have changed, and that kind of confidence is terribly misplaced, except in the most exceptional of circumstances.

The approach needed today is one of waiting. An approach that is decidedly humble, local, engaged, and responsive. It is humble in that the church must realize that we no longer have a place of privilege; in fact, our place may be closer to the margins than the center. This should evoke a certain amount of humbleness as we understand that we work from a subordinate position in our overall relationship to the wider society. It is local because there are very few, "one-size-fits-all" solutions anymore. Ministry is local in a climate that is as diverse and fractious as the one we experience in Canada. Our discerning signs of God's in-breaking will be shaped by where we live and how we decide to do ministry and respond to the needs around us, depending on our sense of how the gospel interfaces effectively with our immediate context. It is engaged because often the way we discern God's in-breaking is not by retreating to a cloister (although there is a place for that), but by being with people, laboring in the trenches of human need and experiencing the struggles, lost dreams, and future hopes of real people, living real lives. It is responsive in that it does not come with a clear diagnosis of what is wrong and a prescription for how it can be cured. Rather, we come to listen, to observe and to respond according to what we hear and see. This is how we enter into a time of waiting for God's in-breaking.

This does not assume that God will somehow break into the world in some highly dramatic way that will change everything for everyone. While this is our ultimate eschatological hope, in the meantime, what we are called to discern is a consistent, ongoing pattern of God's activity that we can join in with so that the Kingdom of God can be built up and the good news of the gospel can bring hope and life into the context in which every local church serves. If the church can do this consistently, it will be responding faithfully to the story of decline and decay that has defined it now for decades.

ACTIVITIES OF WAITING

As already stated, the posture of waiting does not mean complete inactivity. It includes some specific activities that must take place in order for this time of waiting to be useful for the church, while at the same time maintaining the church's ministry to the world.

Spiritual Discernment rooted in Theological Reflection

The work of spiritual discernment, at least in part, invites us to ponder the questions "where is God at work?" and "What is the Spirit saying to the church?" These are questions the church should always be asking, but they become even more poignant in liminal times. Fundamental to the work of spiritual discernment for the church is the practice of theological reflection. Spiritual discernment seeks insight; theological reflection is, at its core, what Anselm famously described as "faith seeking understanding."[41] Both practices have as their goal a clearer comprehension of God's purposes. Spiritual discernment is guided by prayerful listening but must be informed by reflection on Biblical ideas, Christian doctrine and other sources that help us to hear God's voice and act faithfully. Theological reflection is the process of carefully reflecting upon our theological convictions by intentionally engaging a variety of sources with the intent of understanding our faith more clearly. This approach can be applied within the life of the church as it seeks to understand its context and how it should act within it. Theological reflection helps to answer the question, "what is the Spirit saying to the church?" In fact, that question cannot be answered without theological reflection.

As the church today seeks to negotiate its way through the changing cultural landscape, spiritual discernment, guided by careful theological reflection drawing from the Bible, the theological tradition of the church, reason, experience, contemporary culture and the collective wisdom that comes from communal conversation must be an ongoing practice for local congregations as they try and find their way forward in faithfully being

41. Dew, Jr., and Campbell, Jr., *Natural Theology*, 4.

the church. Today's church leaders have to learn how to lead their church in spiritual discernment rooted in collective theological reflection so as to appropriately make decisions on what the Spirit is saying to them about meaningful ministry today.

Mission

The church is made for mission. The mission of the church is rooted in the very nature of God.[42] No matter what its context is, at the heart of the church is a call to mission that defines it. Even in times when the context around us has changed and continues to change, there is a need for the local church to figure out how it will engage its community in outreach so as to bring blessing and benefit to the community. This takes spiritual discernment to know the best way to engage our place and time. Each context demands a unique approach. Discerning the way to engage in mission in Canada today takes prayerful listening, but this listening must be strongly linked to the actual practice of mission. There is no better way to figure out how to do a contextually relevant mission than to actually engage in a mission in your context. As a church does this, it will discern the needs of a community, how to best love the people in that community and how to offer the good news to that community in works and words.

No matter how difficult a context may be, and how much the church finds itself in a liminal time, the need for it to stay on mission, even if it is a struggle, is always needed. Added to this is evidence that points to the possibility that among young people in Canada today, there is an openness to established religion, including Christianity.[43] If this is true, then the need for ongoing missional engagement is substantial, as it is imperative that we remember that we never know how God will use our efforts for his purposes.

Worship

Similar to mission, the act of corporate worship is at the heart of the local church, and it is essential to continue this practice even in days when it seems like fewer people are interested in partaking in this type of gathering. For many words, rituals, and cultural peculiarities of a church worship gathering are remote and strange. Perhaps many find it hard to connect to

42. Wright, *Mission of God*, 23.

43. See "Why Gen Z is Leading a Religious Resurgence," https://youtu.be/tHWxNcTxn24?si=U4Jua3rEHy9WIENN, for a CTV national news story on this topic.

their "real" lives. However, these words and rituals (maybe even some of the peculiarities) are defining features of Christian faith. Even if they seem archaic, they are what define our faith tradition. Worship singing, prayers, litanies, preaching, the Lord's supper, passing the peace, all of these are activities that are foreign outside of the church gathered for worship. Yet these acts of worship are a significant part of what we have to offer to the world. The church offers a *strange* word to the world. It offers something that cannot be found elsewhere. It is the mystery of Christ wrapped up in practices that become vehicles for grace and encounter. It does not matter if it always makes sense to a modern mind; it only matters that it is faithfully performed and offered as a way for people to meet God and find the life that only he can provide.

The church responds to a time of decay and decline by persevering in its worship practices, offering the strangeness of Christian faith to its community in faith that God is at work in our world and our gathering bears witness to this fact.

CONCLUSION

I first got to know Stuart Macdonald when we were both pastors in the Southern Ontario town of Cobourg. Stuart was the Pastor of St. Andrews Presbyterian church, and I was the pastor of Cobourg Alliance Church (Christian and Missionary Alliance). Ultimately, we both ended up pursuing academic careers, and as a result, our paths crossed from time to time over the years. It seemed to me that Stuart never lost his pastoral instincts despite his immersion in the academy. He remained a man of faith who understood the central place of the local church and desired to see local churches flourish throughout Canada. Thus, it is no surprise that one of his great contributions from his academic work is a book that informs and challenges the ministry of the church and its leaders, as *Leaving Christianity* does. He and Clarke's volume is a clear and sobering provocation to the Canadian (and North American) church to understand its context and to get busy trying to address it effectively.

Clarke and Macdonald reflect on the idea that in a time of dramatic change, religion can respond with innovation.[44] More specifically, the church need not lose hope. This chapter has attempted to point in the direction of a response that generates hope by inviting the church into a time of discernment without forsaking the ongoing ministry of the church on a weekly basis. As we wait and work for the good of the kingdom, the historic

44. Clarke and Macdonald, *Leaving Christianity*, 19.

innovative impulse of the church will continue to percolate and produce new initiatives that respond effectively to our times. This will allow for the possibility of renewal. What form this renewal takes is yet to be determined but, by faith, we believe it will continue to make the good news of Jesus Christ known and the church a movement that continues to play a positive, needed role in Canadian society.

BIBLIOGRAPHY

Baum, Gregory. *The Church in Quebec*. Ottawa: Novalis, 1991.

Beach, Lee. *The Church in Exile: Living in Hope after Christendom*. Downers Grove, IL: InterVarsity, 2015.

Bramadat, Paul. "Beyond Christian Canada: Religion and Ethnicity in a Multicultural Society." In *Religion and Ethnicity in Canada*, edited by Paul Bramadat and David Seljak, 1–29. Toronto: University of Toronto Press, 2009.

Bruce, Steve. *God is Dead: Secularization in the West*. Religion in the Modern World: From Cathedrals to Cults. Oxford: Oxford University Press, 1996.

Brueggemann, Walter. *Cadences of Home: Preaching among Exiles*. Louisville: Westminster John Knox, 1997.

Brueggemann, Walter, and Patrick D. Miller. *Deep Memory, Exuberant Hope: Contested Truth in a Post-Christian World*. Minneapolis: Fortress, 2000.

Clarke, Brian. "English-Speaking Canada from 1854." In *A Concise History or Christianity in Canada*, edited by Terrence Murphy and Roberto Perin, 317–22. Toronto: Oxford University Press, 1996.

Clarke, Brian, and Stuart Macdonald. *Leaving Christianity: Changing Allegiances in Canada Since 1945*. Montreal and Kingston: McGill-Queen's University Press, 2017.

Cook, Ramsay. *The Regenerators: Social Criticism in Late Victorian English Canada*. Toronto: University of Toronto Press, 1985.

De Pree, Max. *Leadership Is an Art*. New York: Doubleday, 1989.

Dew, James K., Jr., and Ronnie P. Campbell, Jr., eds. *Natural Theology*. Baker, 2024.

Fay, Terrence J. *A History of Canadian Catholics*. Montreal and Kingston: McGill-Queen's University Press, 2002.

Frost, Michael. *Exiles: Living Missionally in a Post Christian Culture*. Baker, 2006

Fuller, Robert C. *Spiritual, But Not Religious: Understanding Unchurched America*. Oxford: Oxford University Press, 2001.

Hall, Douglas J. *The End of Christendom and the Future of Christianity*. 1997. Reprint, Eugene, OR: Wipf & Stock, 2002.

Heifetz, Ronald A., et al. *The Practice of Adaptive Leadership: Tools and Tactics for Changing Your Organization and the World*. Boston: Cambridge: Harvard Business, 2009.

Hume, William E. "The Impact of Secularization on Presbyterian Ministry." *Presbyterian Record*, 1967.

Kuffert, L. B. *A Great Duty: Canadian Responses to Modern Life and Mass Culture, 1939–1967*. Montreal and Kingston: McGill-Queen's University Press, 2003.

MacGuigan, Mark. "Unity in the Secular City." In *One Church, Two Nations?*, edited by Philip Leblanc and Arnold Edinborough. Don Mills, ON: Longmans, 1968.

Marshall, David B. *Secularizing the Faith: Canadian Protestant Clergy and the Crisis of Belief, 1850–1940*. Toronto: University of Toronto Press, 1992.

Miedema, Gary. *For Canada's Sake: Public Religion, Centennial Celebrations, and the Re-making of Canada in the 1960s*. Montreal and Kingston: McGill-Queen's University Press, 2005.

Miller, Kristyan Spelman, and Paull Thompson, eds. *Unity and Diversity in Language Use*. London: Continnuum, 2005.

Murray, Stuart. *Post-Christendom: Church and Mission in a Strange New World*. Eugene, OR: Cascade Books, 2004.

Murray, Taylor. "The End Is Nigh?: Religious Affiliation in Canada's 2021 Census Data." *Post-Christendom Studies* 8 (2023) 6–13.

Perin, Roberto. "French-Speaking Canada." In *A Concise History of Christianity in Canada*, edited by Terrence Murphy and Roberto Perin. Toronto: Oxford University Press, 1996.

Rawlyk, George A., ed. *Canadian Baptists and Christian Higher Education*. Montreal and Kingston: McGill-Queen's University Press, 1988.

Root, Andrew. *Churches and the Crisis of Decline: A Hopeful, Practical Ecclesiology for a Secular Age*. Ministry in a Secular Age. Grand Rapids: Baker, 2022.

———. *The Congregation in a Secular Age: Keeping Sacred Time against the Speed of Modern Life*. Grand Rapids: Baker Academic, 2021.

Ruso, Domenic. *The Bible for a Shifting Secular Age: Hearing the Truth You Need for the Life You Are Meant to Live*. Eugene, OR: Cascade Books, 2025.

Statistics Canada. *Census of Population, 2021*. Ottawa: Government of Canada, 2022.

Taylor, Charles. *A Secular Age*. Cambridge: Belknap of Harvard University Press, 2007.

———. *Sources of the Self: The Making of the Modern Identity*. Cambridge: Harvard University Press, 1992.

Thiessen, Joel. *The Meaning of Sunday: The Practice of Belief in a Secular Age*. Montreal and Kingston: McGill-Queen's University Press, 2015.

Wright, Christopher J. H. *Mission of God: Unlocking the Bible's Grand Narrative*. Downers Grove, IL: InterVarsity, 2006.

3

Pastoral Ministry as Unfinished

Roland J. De Vries

AUTOBIOGRAPHY OF THE UNFINISHED

I remember very well the last time I saw my maternal grandfather. It was in 1988 and I was an awkward and insecure teenager sitting beside him on his hospital bed. I remember the thinness of his legs and arms, his weakness, and my sense that he was fading. There was also a feeling that I didn't fully know Gerrit Baak; that my knowledge of his unique identity and gifting was incomplete. This was a man who was a house painter by trade but also an artist by vocation. His artwork graced the walls of my family home growing up, and he gave the gift of a painting to each of his grandchildren. Grandpa also loved to play checkers (there was no winning against him!), could do three-digit multiplication almost instantaneously in his head, and sang in church with gusto and apparent love for the hymns of our Christian faith. Even knowing all of this and cherishing it, there was much in him that invited deeper understanding and friendship.

From my own experiences with him and stories from the wider family, I know that Gerrit Baak was a profoundly sensitive man and, in some sense, an unhappy person. It is difficult to pin down the exact sources of his sadness, but the fact that he lived through two world wars and then, at midlife, immigrated to a new country must have been contributing factors. He was born in the Netherlands in 1909, which is to say that the first decades of his life were marked by the fear and poverty-inducing reality of two world wars, and by a significant economic depression that hit the Netherlands in the 1920's. Later, after immigrating to Canada in 1951 with his wife Johanna and their children, Gerrit lived his remaining decades in a country where he was never quite at home. He was caught, classically, between two worlds—a first world to which he could not return, and a second to which he felt he never belonged.

It seems that the pain written on the surface of my grandpa's life was also the result of his frustration with the modern world. It was a world he experienced as running away from him; as displacing a simple and beautiful way of life he cherished. A few years before he died in 1988, he wrote a series of vignettes from his life; short narratives and reflections to which he gave the simple title "As I Think Back." One of his vignettes revolves around a simple wooden handpump that was located close to his grandfather's small thatched-roof house and a nearby brook. Gerrit and his friends would play nearby, catching fish in the running stream or bringing water gushing up from the ground by heaving on the levered, wooden arm of the pump. He tells of a time that a minnow made its way from the stream into the well, and later into a pot of tea! On that day they were banished from playing near the pump. As he tells this childhood story, however, he moves into a reflective mode:

> A few years later when [my] Grandpa died and our aunt came to live with us, I can still see the tears in my dad's eyes when he locked the door for the last time. A few years later the little old house was torn down, but the old pump stood there for many more years; it gradually sank a little crooked until one time it too disappeared. Then it was as if, just like the wooden pump, a little part of our youth had also disappeared.[1]

Many of his stories are sadly nostalgic in this way, though certainly not all. He also speaks of the temptation to dip girls' ponytails in the ink-pots on school desks, his love of planting potatoes with his father, and the delight in receiving a checkers board from Sint-Nicolaas as a six-year-old, (which he owned to the end of his life). Reading his reflections, however, you get the feeling he simply could not abide this modern world, in which everything was *snel*, *snel*, *snel* (quick, quick, quick). A world in which local friendship and community were being displaced by the radio and the television and the busyness of scattered lives.

At the head of her translation of my grandpa's reflections (from his native Dutch) my Aunt Annie wrote words that are simple but also significant:

1. Baak, "As I think Back."

"Grandpa started to write his story a few years before his death. Unfortunately, he never did finish it." Similarly, at the end of her translation, she added the following as a postscript: "Unfortunately, Grandpa either lost interest or became too ill to continue his thoughts and stories." In other words, "As I Look Back" is an unfinished work. Gerrit Baak seems not to have had the chance to tell his own story in a complete way, or to give a comprehensive view of what he understood his life to have meant. Certainly, I gain insight into the heart and life of my grandpa through his written reflections. But the abrupt ending of the script means that there is much that remains unexplained, unexplored, and unknown. Time and death have together removed the possibility of knowing anything more, and I have been left with a relationship that seems somehow unfinished.

PASTORAL WORK AS UNFINISHED

"Pastoral work is never finished." Most church leaders will agree with this statement without a moment's hesitation. There is always another sermon to write, a new outreach venture to launch, an important pastoral visit to make, another staff member to hire, or a study program to prepare. There is always more to do. And we aren't just talking here about busy pastors on the edge of burnout, run off their feet trying to meet every personal and congregational need around them. Even pastors who have achieved a healthy life-work balance, who understand that the church is not theirs to build or save, will recognize that pastoral ministry has no endpoint. This is because the work of "building up the saints for the work of ministry" (Eph 4:12) won't conclude this side of the eschaton. As long as the cycle of congregational and family life continues—as long as there is birth, life, and death—so will the work of pastoral leaders continue. The good work of baptizing children, praying with the dying, proclaiming the gospel, and reaching out in the love is never finished.

But there is another quite different sense in which pastoral work is never finished. It is unfinished also in the sense that the work of pastoral ministry involves relationships and tasks that do not have a conclusive endpoint. This is because a pastoral calling involves being set down, mid-script, in the lives of families and institutions. These have had a life prior to the pastor's arrival, and they will continue on after their departure. It is particularly at the pastor's departure that it becomes apparent that many threads have not yet been woven into the tapestry of people's lives. Pastors pursue their work all the while realizing that the impact of this ministry can't be defined in a conclusive sense. A congregational leader may trust that their ministry will produce enduring results and will have an impact for the future, but they can rarely know the full extent or meaning of these. So pastoral ministry is unfinished not only in the sense that there is always more work to do. It is unfinished also in the sense that the people and communities served will continue their lives and stories beyond the point of the pastor's encounter with them.

A simple example to make the point. Consider a hypothetical, congregational mission initiated by a pastor. She has worked with congregation members to imagine a creative project that meets a need in the neighborhood. Over time, with her team of volunteers, she began to see this initiative bear some fruit. It seems to be making a difference in the lives of the neighborhood and is helping the congregation think differently about its own faith and life. It is exciting! But in year four of the project, the personal circumstances of the pastor change. Her spouse has a professional opportunity across the country, and she discerns that God is indeed inviting her into a different context and ministry. At the moment of departure, the pastor will wonder about this mission outreach. Will it survive? Will congregational commitment falter in the absence of her leadership? The truth is, the life of this missional project is not close to being completed. Although she was instrumental in launching it, the pastor will not be around to discern its flourishing or, alternatively, its slow slide into incompletion. The work is unfinished.

This example expresses the "unfinishedness" that attaches to so much of pastoral ministry—so much of congregational leadership has this quality of being open-ended. Will the newly expressed faith of a young woman flourish into maturity? Will the care we extend to a struggling family bear fruit for their healing? Will our preaching change the way that people live, think and worship? The answer to these questions is simply: We cannot know. All of this is a deeply personal issue for a pastor and may also become a challenge for a pastor who must live with the many threads that are left loose and unwoven.

In professions or vocations other than pastoral ministry, it is often easier to achieve a sense of completion. Think of someone in public relations who completes a new marketing campaign, or a physiotherapist who guides a client back to regular physical activity, or a project manager who oversees the launch of a new product line. In so many fields of work, finishing something is integral to a person's vocation. Pastoral ministry, however, rarely provides this kind of conclusive endpoint in relation to which the leader can sit back with satisfaction and say: "Ah, that's finished. It is all good."

It is almost necessary, obligatory to speak about the unfinished nature of much of pastoral ministry. To this, it can be added that the present context of challenge and decline within mainline Protestantism only exacerbates the issues. Pastors invest themselves in the life of local congregations without the confidence that it will survive the coming years, let alone decades. Given the rate of congregational closures among Presbyterian, Anglican, and United churches, and given the post-pandemic exacerbation of decline, there are a significant number of pastoral leaders who can imagine a not-too-distant moment when the doors of the congregation they serve will close permanently. Not only is the pastor offering gifts within ministries that may not endure, but they also serve local congregations that may not endure in anything close to their present shape.

Returning to the autobiographical note that commences this essay, the relationship described there was unfinished in two senses. The written narrative of the life of Gerrit Baak is unfinished—his own account of the meaning of his life has not been completed. More personally, those who loved and knew him also have a sense that there was more of him that has been seen and understood. Lost is the possibility of an ongoing encounter by which his family and friends can gain a deeper understanding of him. The passage of time and the reality of death mean that they can no longer contribute to his life in even a small way. In all of this, there is a living and breathing sense of loss; an awareness that within the confines of one life, there is a perennial incompleteness to reality. To put the matter rather starkly, it can be said that, notwithstanding the "*Tetelestai*" ("It is finished") of Jesus on the cross, there is something always and everywhere unfinished in human life, relationships, and communities.

This is the context in which the pastor serves and prays and preaches and leads. Pastoral work is unfinished in the same way that my grandpa's written life-story was unfinished, and in the same way that my personal relationships with him are unfinished. There is more to be known and understood, and further stories to be traced out into the future. A last visit at a bedside, an offer of pastoral care, an unfolding mission project, and a teaching series are all implicated in this kind of incompletion. In the larger scheme, the pastor also must wonder about the future of the church and of the local congregation where she serves—does this congregation have a life and witness beyond the coming few years or decade? Will those I serve persist in faith within the life of the church, or will they finally walk away from the church? Our purpose here will be to finally say that this pastoral and human vocation within "unfinishedness" is one to be embraced and celebrated; that it is entirely consistent with who we are and are called to be. Yet on our way to that celebration and embrace we acknowledge that living with such incompletion is often experienced as a burden and loss.

This isn't to deny there are moments of clarity, fullness, and joy in life and ministry. Evidently, personal relationships, including with those who knew my grandpa, are full of moments to enjoy and cherish. To speak personally, again, there were genuine moments of encounter—listening to his instructions as I cut the grass at his and grandma's place, or as I painted their front porch; watching grandpa and my uncles playing cards at the dining room table; being shocked again that he could multiply such large figures in his head. He gave me one of his paintings, and every day I see it on the wall above our piano. I have his translated life story in a filing cabinet, to be pulled out and explored again.

In the context of pastoral ministry, there are similar moments of fulfillment. Moments of meaning when pastors pray with those who are struggling, share the promises of God with those who need to hear them, or challenge a way of being that is contrary to the gospel. In the pastor's personal life and in the lives of those served, God's grace and transformative power can be discerned. Nothing that is said here represents a refusal of this. And yet all of this beauty and meaning is against the backdrop of stories unfinished; of narratives whose direction and outcome cannot be known or understood with certainty.

We, humans, long for the experience of completion—it is both a powerful concept and a powerful reality in our lives. In western music, there is almost always a closing chord or note that returns us "home"—there is musical resolution that brings us both relief and satisfaction. In the relationships with friends, there is a desire to see them work through troubles and find themselves on a new path of respect and care. A good novel is perceived as one in which the narrative arc allows relationships or experiences to be interpreted in a complete and meaningful way. The absence of such resolution, or the absence of full meaning, rubs the wrong way. There is something in us that wishes for more conversations; for additional opportunities to learn and become a blessing. In the absence of this, we often feel a kind of woundedness or loss. All of which is simply to repeat that we must acknowledge the tension of the unfinished.

How, then, to face this reality? To answer this question, there is a need to push deeper in terms of cultural and theological understanding, which will be done here in two ways. First, by way of a concrete example of the unfinished in the Christian tradition. Second, by turning to a more explicitly theological set of ideas provides orientation and assurance in the face of the incomplete reality of ministry and of the church.

UNFINISHED GOSPEL

The gospel of Mark for its odd ending(s).[2] The narrative ends abruptly at chapter 16, verse 8, with the women fleeing from the empty tomb. This comment is added: "They said nothing to anyone, because they were afraid." Among the earliest Christians, there were evidently those who wondered about this ending of the story. How could this foundational story of faith and hope end with uncertainty and fear? How could followers of Jesus have a defining narrative that didn't portray him as risen? In view of this apparent frustration, or at least with a desire for completeness, some among the earliest Christians decided to provide a "proper" ending to the story. Among the various manuscript traditions, there is an additional, short ending to the gospel in Mark in which the women report their findings to the other disciples and the risen Jesus commissions his disciples for ministry. There is also a longer, additional ending in which Jesus appears to the disciples, commissions them (including to pick up snakes and drink poison, we note), and then ascends to the right hand of God. The original, uncertain ending of Mark's gospel is intriguing. If the Gospel originally ended with uncertainty and fear, this implies that a neat resolution of every story or situation can't be our goal. It suggests that living with the unfinished is a spiritual practice we can embrace; that tying a bow of completion on every relationship and encounter isn't our calling.

But it turns out that this Gospel is likely unfinished in an even more significant sense. According to Matthew Larsen, the earliest Jesus-followers didn't actually think of Mark's gospel as an authored, completed, and published book.[3] They didn't think of it as "finished." This idea will go against the grain of what many were taught over the years through biblical studies and research. It has been assumed and taught that this narrative was written by someone named Mark (even if we do not know which Mark, exactly), that it gives a particular account of Jesus, and that it was originally circulated as a finished book or text. Expressed differently, this text of Mark was one of four completed and published *gospels* (leaving aside non-canonical texts that also bear the name gospel but which are beyond the scope of this reflection). Larsen points out, however, that this common idea of what a gospel is (an authored, published book) began to develop only in the third

2. Matthew Larsen engages with the endings of Mark's gospel in the context of his discussion of the earliest users of the text, and we are following Larsen here and in the paragraphs that follow. Larsen, *Gospels*.

3. Larsen, *Gospels*, 11.

century. Prior to that time, Mark's text almost certainly wasn't thought of as a gospel/book.[4]

But how, then, was it understood? Larsen argues that the gospel of Mark was thought of as an instance of *hypomnēmata*. Across the ancient Mediterranean world, the label *hypomnēmata* was attached to certain kinds of texts. For example, this label would be attached to the rough draft of a book, to a set of notes, or to the raw material used for writing a more comprehensive text.[5] Referring to both *hypomnēmata* and *commentarii*, Larsen writes that "they are not literature per se, at least not yet. They are inchoate, provisional, and often exist specifically for the creation of other texts. As the root of both words indicates, although they are often textual objects, they relate to memory more than writing. They are skeletons that need the breath of human memory to bring them to life."[6] This would mean that the "gospel of Mark" was not originally understood as a completed book about Jesus. Rather, it was seen as an incomplete collection of thoughts and memories related to Jesus; an organized set of notes sharing parts of Jesus' life. This text of Mark could also have been seen as raw material made available for other writers.[7]

With this in mind, it is not surprising that some thought it reasonable to add different endings to the story—simply adding some details to a collection of rough notes would have been considered normal and appropriate. In the present cultural moment, such an approach to texts would be seen as entirely inappropriate. Adding a new ending to the story is seen as a tampering with someone else's text. In the late modern context, it might be thought of as a betrayal of Mark's intellectual property rights. In other words, it is difficult, today, to think of the Gospel of Mark as raw material for free use by others. But in the first and second century it is almost certain that the Gospel of Mark was thought of in this way.[8] So argues Larsen.

4. Larsen, *Gospels*, 1–9.

5. Larsen, *Gospels*, 100.

6. Larsen, *Gospels*, 11.

7. Larsen, *Gospels*, 100.

8. Larsen explores, for example, the inappropriateness of applying the concept of "forgery" to the additional endings of Mark, and the anachronism that is displayed in doing so. Larsen, *Gospels*, 119. He writes, in conclusion with respect to the multiple endings: "All the new endings of the textual tradition of the Gospel according to Mark may be better understood [as improving an open text which was ambiguous or lacking], because they attempt to rework the text we now call the Gospel according to Mark by adding . . . a much-needed proper ending—complete with a resurrected Jesus and all. Stated simply, adding an ending to an unfinished text would be regarded as a *proper response to such a text*." (italics added)

All of this is also expressed in the relationship of the Gospel of Mark to the Gospel of Matthew, for example. It is widely agreed among Biblical scholars that Matthew took the text of Mark as a foundation for his own work[9]—Matthew built his narrative on the basis of Mark's text. Biblical scholars are also intrigued by the ways that Matthew's particular ideas are expressed in the ways that he changes or makes use of Mark's text, and a good number of pastors have played with these differences in their preaching and teaching. Again, from a modern point of view, this approach of Matthew will likely be seen as objectionable. "Why not write your own gospel instead of modifying someone else's text!?" But if Mark's text is an instance of *hypomnēmata,* as Larsen argues, then a different point of view is possible. Namely, that the earliest Christians understood Mark and Matthew as part of *one* textual tradition, rather than seeing these as two different Gospels.[10] "Ancient readers could well have supposed that the textual tradition we now call the Gospel according to Matthew is the same work—the same gospel—as the one we call the Gospel according to Mark, just with some clarification."[11] Otherwise put, Matthew simply polished the narrative of Mark, offered interpretation, and added missing pieces—the genealogy, birth narratives, events around his death and resurrection, and key teachings. Matthew, in effect, completed the story.[12]

Returning to the practice of pastoral ministry, pastors can do much worse than take the Gospel of Mark as an example. It wasn't Mark's calling to tell the complete story of Jesus. It was not his vocation to write the definitive account of Jesus's life and ministry (Mark may not have known that such a definitive telling was an option for him). Rather, his task was to gather up stories and significant snippets from the astonishing life of this Jesus. His vocation was to make these pieces of narrative available for the continued telling of that story. Mark certainly knew what he was doing as he made choices in the gathering of particular stories and sayings, but he also couldn't know what others would do with them. Perhaps it is not too much of a stretch to say that Mark trusted the Holy Spirit to fulfill his own work through others. Similarly, pastors give themselves to the tasks of ministry not knowing how God might, by His grace, bring it to completion. Pastoral ministry is an example of *hypomnēmata.* It is by definition unfinished and is rather a collection of actions, encounters, experiences, teaching moments, and relationships—each of which ripples out from the life and ministry of

9. For an argument that Matthew in fact precedes Mark, see Powell, *Evolution.*

10. Powell, *Evolution*, 113.

11. Powell, *Evolution*, 113.

12. Powell, *Evolution*, 107.

the pastor, extending into that which cannot be fully known or imagined. The assurance for pastors lies in the assurance that it is Christ who is at work, and it is God in Christ who is giving final form to the lives of individuals, families, and communities. God in Christ sees what we have done. In the broader ecclesial context of decline, the future of congregations—whatever that future may be in individual instances—is similarly in the gracious care of Christ.

It is worth noting that the Apostle Paul would have understood this well. In one of his letters to the church in Corinth, Paul speaks of the various leaders who have ministered there, and asks: "What then is Apollos? What is Paul? Servants through whom you came to believe, as the Lord assigned to each. I planted, Apollos watered, but God gave the growth" (1 Cor 3:5–6, NRSV). Paul focuses on the primacy of what Christ has done in bringing faith to fullness within the church. His own work was unfinished, as was that of Apollos. Paul may have planted the seed, but he could not know what would finally happen as the gospel sprang to life in a given community. Apollos may have come along and watered that seed, but he also could not know whether a subsequent drought would undermine everything he had said and done. That is, there is something decidedly unfinished about the work of Paul and Apollos and the pastoral work of anyone who follows in the same path, even if there is also a call to a deep trust in God's purposes in Christ. Pastors offer themselves prayerfully in service, but rarely get to see the final result; they do not see the fully woven tapestry. In the same way that God in Christ brings faith to life, so it is God who has the privilege of full vision—of seeing the tapestry in its final form.

KARL BARTH AND THE TIME OF OUR LIVES

Within any reflection on the temporal nature of life, and particularly on the limited temporal scope of human lives and ministries, it is worth turning to the theological writings of Karl Barth for further insight. In many cases, readers here may have theological differences with Barth, as with any theologian. Yet his writings can bear fruit in our reflection on the practicalities of pastoral ministry as we have been attending to them.[13] Those who are familiar with the work of the Swiss theologian will know that his whole work is a constant circling around the person of Christ, and an exploration

13. Our differences with him will not only be theological, perhaps, since we must also wrestle with the failures of his personal life. See Tietz, *Karl Barth*. It is also worth noting that Barth also had experience in pastoral ministry and would perhaps have understood the very questions we wrestle with here.

of the implications of Christ (as the revelation of God) for various theological *loci*. As shall be observed, this Christological focus is no different when it comes to his reflection on human temporality.

In his discussion of creation and the reality of time, there is an intriguingly titled section, "The Unique Opportunity."[14] As the title suggests, Barth sees human life in creation and time, with all the constraints these imply, as promise and hope. Of course, human beings (perhaps especially modern, western humans) do not always think about our finite, bounded lives in this way. We often think of our lifespan (whether we have 40 or 60 or 00 years) as a mere restriction—more as a limitation to be suffered than a gift to be celebrated. Why? Because there is more of the world to be seen. There is more to learn, discover and experience. There is a longing for more time with loved ones. There is more work to be done. There is more beauty to encounter. For these reasons, we chafe at the mere decades we have. How can a few years or decades make sense on a planet that is four and a half billion years old, in a universe approaching 14 billion years? How can such an astonishingly short life be seen as a unique opportunity?

For Barth, the time constraint of each human life is an essential feature of God's good creation. God has loved the human into being as *this* limited creature. Which is also to say that we cannot have our lives outside of this form. The theologian insists: "Rather than tolerating our limitation with a sigh, we have every reason to take it seriously, to affirm it, to accept it, and to praise God for the fact that in it we are what we are and not something else."[15] To repeat: To be a limited human is to be precisely the creature that God has loved and blessed into being. According to Barth, to refuse or grumble about temporal limitation is a failure of gratitude and worship toward the Creator. So, each is invited to acknowledge the gracious and loving authority of God in relation to us as limited creatures. Barth, in fact, uses language that goes against the grain of contemporary spirituality by describing God as a "commander."[16] This commander has the right to require obedience of those he has created. But it also turns out that this obedience is equal to a joyful celebration of the gift of life in space and time.[17]

14. Barth, *Doctrine of Creation*, 569–98. The paragraph within which this section is located is entitled "Freedom in Limitation", which is also helpful and telling.

15. Barth, *Doctrine of Creation*, 571. He goes further and adds: "Those who resist it necessarily resist themselves, for they themselves are none other than those who are limited in this way." Barth, *Doctrine of Creation*, 573.

16. Barth, *Doctrine of Creation*, 571.

17. We would rightly hesitate over the deployment of the idea of God as a commander, given the idea's embeddedness in an inadequate deontological, moral framework. The concept of end and fulfillment within a teleological framework would better

As he writes about limited, human lives, Barth comes back, as always, to Christ. He reminds us that the incarnation, God's embrace of human life in Jesus, means God has entered into time-bound life—or that being time-bound is a part of the divine life on account of Christ. The Son of God embraced the same offer of temporal existence that we are invited to embrace.[18] Jesus was given a span of years between birth and death, in the same way each human is. In these years, he lived and loved and related and served. In this one, a person's existence as a singular and temporally finite being has been adopted and affirmed by God. This life of Jesus on earth and in time was not a "pitiful portion," says Barth, but a "rich dowry full of meaning and promise."[19] Yes, there is a kind of "humiliation" in the incarnation, since the Word has relinquished the divine glory. But in another sense, *this is no kind of humiliation*, since this limited human life is a good and beautiful thing. Jesus lived this unique opportunity in loving obedience to the one who called him to this path, and, even more remarkably, and also mysteriously, this means that each person can live their time/years fully through union with Christ. Human time, which is invariably lost time, becomes renewed. As Griswold puts it: "The gracious and free intersection of God's time with lost time in the time of revelation is an act of grace and healing."[20] Through union with Christ, we are able to live out the unique opportunity of our lives as he did, in faith and love and obedience—with meaning and purpose.

These are complicated theological questions, but it is not necessary to sort out all of the answers.[21] Rather, it is important simply to acknowledge the fundamental meaning in what has been argued. Namely, that God is good, that life is truly a gift, and that the good and precious gift of our lives can only be lived in limitation. And: "The time in which we live is our place. It may be a modest place, but it is ours."[22] This applies to everyone, of course, and not only to pastors. Retracing the steps that have been traced, and returning to the autobiographical beginning, I can say that the unfinished nature of my relationship with my grandfather has been put in perspective. Yes, I experience a sense of loss at what could have been, but I

capture the specific nature of the material universe and the path of our fulfillment within time.

18. As Barth puts it, plainly: "This is the very same offer which He Himself accepted when He became man in Jesus Christ." Barth, *Doctrine of Creation*, 575.

19. Barth, *Doctrine of Creation*, 574.

20. Griswold, *Triune Eternality*, 167.

21. For a helpful exploration of many of these questions, see my colleague's work: Langdon, *God the Eternal*.

22. Barth, *Doctrine of Creation*, 582.

am also invited to live this incompleteness as the good and beautiful form of life into which I have been graciously birthed by God. The same applies to pastoral ministry. Living with the unfinished in pastoral ministry is a matter of living the beautiful incompleteness of human life in God's good creation. In one sense, this will feel like a contradiction, and it will invariably be experienced as a contradiction. But it is also possible to live this contradiction faithfully. This is also so in relation to the persistent decline of the church and of congregations in the western context, where pastoral ministry is pursued against a backdrop of deep uncertainty and frequent future.

To live faithfully within limitation, and to be set free within limitation and contradiction, means turning ones focus toward gifts given, rather than results achieved. By the Spirit, each has gifts for the service of Christ's people and for the blessing of our neighbor. Gifts that may be celebrated as they are shared in daily life. The gifts particular to pastoral ministry are various, but they include teaching, pastoral insight, hospitality, leadership, evangelism, and compassionate service. It can be said, in fact, that there is *never* anything incomplete in the faithful sharing of our gifts. There is never anything unfinished about service extended through the Spirit is gifting. There is nothing unfinished about a word of compassion offered to someone in pain. There is nothing unfinished about a prayer offered for the flourishing of a marriage. There is nothing unfinished about a sermon on "blessed are the peacemakers." There is nothing unfinished about a campaign for affordable housing in the neighborhood. This is nothing unfinished about sharing the forgiveness of Jesus with someone weighed down by shame.

The pastor may not know the outcome of the gift having been offered; they cannot know the long-term result of what they have done. What they may know is that these are relational moments in which the grace, love, and mercy of Christ are extended and embodied—when his healing of time is realized. These are moments in which the pastor is fully alive, and fully alive in the ministry to which they have been called. To have a vocation to pastoral ministry is to have a vocation to precisely such moments.

All of this insists on being expressed personally and not only abstractly and objectively. When I struggle today with the unfinished nature of my own pastoral ministry—when I wonder about the results of my time and efforts—it is helpful to think of moments of meaningful encounter in the congregations I have served. I recall the moment when I was able to share faith with a young woman who was inquiring about Jesus. I recall a powerful and loving prayer offered, for me, by an elderly woman who had the gift of prayer. I think of a time when a passage of scripture brought light and joy to someone's eyes. I reflect on the experience of a man who found a moment of grace in the midst of a difficult separation and divorce. As I reflect back in this way, the loss of the unfinished and the uncertain fades, and gratitude and grace come to the fore of heart and mind. In this moment, I also recognize that in these past experiences, God by the Spirit, has given the gift of abundant life. Within the temporal boundedness of my life and being, grace emerged. How else could we describe it?

Pastors live with this tension, then: On the one hand, profound joy and gratitude for moments of abundance in ministry, and on the other hand, a backdrop of uncertainty about the difference we will finally make. Living with this tension need not translate into a denial of the uncertainty and loss that is part of human and pastoral experience. In fact, denial will only allow frustrations and uncertainty to make their way back into the pastor's life, by the back door. It will do so in the form of self-judgment at pastoral inadequacy or a deeper dejection at what is unknown and unfinished.

In the face of the unfinished, then, the response can only be one of prayer—prayer in the name of the one whose kingdom is coming. This is not to say that prayer is merely a form of therapy to help us cope with the reality of a bounded life. Rather, prayer draws us into conversation and encounter with the God who, in Christ, is bringing his purposes to fulfillment in the world. The God who gives us abundant life in present moments is the same God who has revealed himself to be lovingly preoccupied with our world and its future. What can we do, in the face of the unfinished, except reach out to the God who has shown himself to be grace and love? There is no "solution" to the unfinished here, and no solution is needed. There is only an invitation to joyful gratitude in abundance, and finally to prayer.

A PASTOR'S MORNING PRAYER

O living God, I find myself alive in the world, drawing breath, awakening to a new day. In the hours ahead of me, the mystery of my being will confront me; the wonder that I am here as a creature in the world you have given; the deeper wonder that it is through Christ that the world is made and that I am made. I praise you for this mystery; this gift and this grace.

I rush into each day, frequently forgetful—forgetful of your grace and inattentive to your Spirit. In this day open my eyes to the moments of abundant life you give. Let me celebrate love given and received. Let me see strength expended in service. Let me hear beauty in conversation and in the sounds of your wide world. Let me receive graciously and give generously.

Help me, O loving God, to trust you; to trust you in a world where your kingdom is more unseen than seen. I confess my deep wish to see more of what you are doing. I long for a birds-eye view of my life, and the lives of neighbours and friends. I want to see that long line of cause-and-effect laid out with clarity; to see where it all goes. To be more than the creature I am. To see that to which I have finally contributed.

O God who shows love in Jesus, who gives gifts by the Spirit—let these be enough for me in this day. Let it be enough that I have received love, and that I have offered love. Let it be enough that gifts have been exchanged compassionately and with joy. In this day, let it be enough that I will see something that opens a curtain on the world you will finally bring.

Through Christ, and by the Spirit. Amen.

BIBLIOGRAPHY

Baak, Gerrit. "As I Think Back." Translated by Annie Saddler. Unpublished manuscript.

Barth, Karl. *The Doctrine of Creation*. Vol. 1, pt. 4, Church Dogmatics. Translated by A.T. McKnight et al. Edited by G.W. Bromiley and Thomas F. Torrance. Edinburgh: T&T Clark, 1961.

Griswold, Daniel M. *Triune Eternality: God's Relationship to Time in the Theology of Karl Barth*. Minneapolis: Fortress, 2015.

Langdon, Adrian. *God the Eternal Contemporary: Trinity, Eternity, and Time in Karl Barth*. Eugene, OR: Wipf & Stock, 2012.

Larsen, Matthew D. C. *Gospels Before the Book*. Oxford: Oxford University Press, 2018.

Powell, J. Enoch. *The Evolution of the Gospel: A New Translation of the First Gospel with Commentary and Introductory Essay*. New Haven: Yale University Press, 1994.

Tietz, Christine. *Karl Barth: A Life in Conflict*. Oxford: Oxford University Press, 2021.

4

Maintaining a Godly Society

Offences and Forgiveness in the St. Andrews Burgh Court in the Later Sixteenth Century

Elizabeth Ewan

In his important study, *The Witches of Fife: Witch-hunting in a Scottish Shire 1560–1710*, Stuart Macdonald demonstrated the value of examining the early modern Scottish witch-hunt in its local and regional context. He began his chapter on cases prosecuted in the Presbytery of St. Andrews with a discussion of the accusation of an unnamed woman in 1572.[1] According to the diarist Mr. James Melville, recalling his youth in St. Andrews, the woman was placed on the pillar of repentance in the parish kirk of Holy Trinity, preached at by none other than John Knox, before her execution on 28 April.[2] Knox's secretary, Richard Bannatyne, who was present at the time, reported that she was accused of many horrible things. It was, however, the discovery of a strange and suspicious object concealed on her body, a white cloth "like a collore craig," that seems to have been the conclusive proof leading to her conviction, especially as she lamented its loss with its

1. Macdonald, *Witches of Fife*, 55–57.
2. Pitcairn, *Autobiography*, 58.

protective powers.[3] Unfortunately for historians, there are no extant court records to provide more details about the case.[4]

Further research on the witch-hunt by Macdonald and others has revealed the myriad of factors leading to witchcraft accusations in the local community.[5] Those suspected often had a long-standing reputation as quarrelsome troublemakers, causing disruption to their neighbors.[6] What is striking in the 1572 case is Bannatyne's description of one of the suspected witches' misdeeds. She had refused to forgive a man who, she alleged, had "done her some offence." When a bystander warned her that if she did not forgive the offender, God would not forgive her and she would be damned, she retorted that she did not care whether she went to heaven or hell and also uttered many other "execrable words."[7] Whether intentional blasphemy or a reply hurled in the heat of the moment, her words, in connection with the suspicious object, proved damning. As Macdonald says of her conviction, "her heretical views, her unneighbourliness, and the presence of the 'collores crag' seem to have been enough" evidence to secure her conviction.[8]

Witch accusations did not arise out of a vacuum; they reflected already-existing tensions within the community. Sometimes these exploded into accusations of witchcraft, but more commonly, the local authorities, both ecclesiastical and secular, attempted to dampen them down before they reached such a critical state. In doing so, they sought to create and

3. Bannatyne, *Transactions in Scotland*, 339. The nature of this object is unclear; it is discussed by Macdonald, *Witches of Fife*, 57. Most Scots-language records have been given here in English, except where the original Scots words are important to the argument. Dates are given in modern form.

4. This episode was turned into a play in St. Andrews in 1994, described at the beginning of Macdonald, *Witches of Fife*, 1. When I first met Stuart many decades ago, I immediately noticed his St. Andrews University scarf. Further conversation reveal that we had both spent time at St. Andrews as students, and moreover, in the arcane world of St. Andrews academic families, we were academic aunt and nephew. Since our first meeting, I have benefited greatly from his valued role as both friend and colleague in investigating the society of early modern Scotland, and also as ordained minister, including his presiding at my marriage. I hope this study from our joint student haunt will honour our friendship.

5. The literature on the Scottish witch-hunt is now vast and growing rapidly. For discussions of the historiography see Macdonald, "Godly Society" and "Counting Witches."

6. Martin, "Witch"; Cordey, "Reputation."

7. Bannatyne, *Transactions in Scotland*, 339.

8. Macdonald, *Witches of Fife*, 57. For the power of words in witchcraft accusations, see Dye, "Disorderly." Dissension and hatred between two women featured in another witchcraft case in 1581, although in this instance the witchcraft charge proceeded no further, Macdonald, *Witches of Fife*, 58.

maintain in newly-Reformed Protestant Scotland a "godly society." This chapter examines some of the ways in which the municipal authorities in St. Andrews strove to do this, focusing particularly on the role of rituals of forgiveness.

St. Andrews has featured in several studies examining how the early Reformed Kirk worked to impose the new model of a reformed society on parishioners after the Protestant Reformation. Medieval St. Andrews, with its shrine of St. Andrew, archbishop, university and religious houses, had been the leading center of the Scottish church.[9] From 1559, the city took pride in being one of the first communities to adopt the Protestant Reformation, established in Scotland 1559–60, and to establish a kirk session, a local church court consisting of the minister and lay elders and deacons, chosen from among the leading men of the parish. Among its responsibilities was ensuring the repression of vice and the nourishing of virtue through the imposition on the congregation of discipline, the third mark of the Scottish Reformed Kirk.[10] With admirable self-confidence, the local kirk session described its church as "the perfyt [perfect] reformit kirk" by 1564.[11]

Michael Graham, Margo Todd, and John McCallum, among others, have used evidence from the St. Andrews kirk session and presbytery, as well as church courts elsewhere, to examine the working of kirk discipline more broadly in Scotland as the kirk worked to establish a "godly society."[12] They have also drawn attention to the cooperation between the local ecclesiastical and secular authorities, pointing out, for example, the overlap of personnel on kirk sessions and town councils, and the practice of the kirk session occasionally asking the civil magistrates to impose certain penalties such as banishment on convicted offenders. At St. Andrews, this close cooperation can be seen from the very beginning in 1559 when its first elders and deacons were chosen by the kirk, the town and the university.[13] In his 1996 study, Michael Graham discussed the role of the town council in maintaining the peace briefly, but there has been little work done on the burgh court since then; this chapter builds on his discussion.[14]

While cooperation was important, the kirk session and the town administration did function independently. McCallum has drawn attention

9. For the medieval town, its university and its church, see Brown and Stevenson, *Medieval St. Andrews.*

10. Graham, "Theory and Practice," 422.

11. Dawson, "Face of Perfyt Kyrk," 413.

12. Graham, *Uses of Reform*; Todd, *Culture of Protestantism*; McCallum, *Reforming the Parish.* Dawson, "Face of Perfyt Kyrk," focuses on St. Andrews specifically.

13. McCallum, *Reforming the Parish*, 43–44.

14. Graham, *Uses of Reform*, 216–17 and notes 53–55.

to the distinctiveness of the two bodies.[15] This chapter examines how the burgh government of St. Andrews trod its own path in creating and maintaining a godly community. It worked in concert with the kirk session and presbytery on occasion, but it also had its own methods by which it aimed to organize and maintain a godly society.

As in other Scottish towns, the burgh court met in the tollbooth (the town hall), the seat of municipal government, and was presided over by the burgh magistrates, the provost and bailies.[16] In some cases, an assize of men was appointed to hear cases which involved disturbances of the peace or other controversial causes. The court's personnel were drawn from "the good men" of the town, primarily those who enjoyed the status of burgess and were substantial property-holders in the town, and many of whom also served as elders or deacons in the kirk session. A town clerk noted the court proceedings in the burgh court record.

Unfortunately, most of the sixteenth-century burgh court records for St. Andrews are no longer extant, leaving historians with only a snapshot from the one remaining volume, which covers the period from February 1589 to 14 November 1592.[17] However, the records are detailed enough to illustrate how the town dealt in these years with threats to the harmony of the community. As in 1572, unreconciled disputes between individuals were of concern to those trying to maintain peace and order. This chapter will focus on how the authorities dealt with two threats to that peace, physical assaults and the verbal offences of slander and defamation, both of which were sometimes described as "offences and injuries." Such injuries could range from insults and accusations of malfeasance to striking opponents and even seriously wounding them with deadly intent. Central to the court's efforts to deal with such disturbances to the peace of the community was the reconciliation of offender and victim through the asking of forgiveness.

FRACTURING THE GODLY SOCIETY

On 20 May 1589, Jonet Scott, widow of David Williamson, appeared before the court and complained against Bessie Kenzow and Jonet Kenlowy, her

15. McCallum, *Reforming the Parish*, 176–80, 188.

16. For example, Aberdeen, Falconer, *Crime and Community*, 13–17.

17. St. Andrews University Library [St. AUL], B65/8/1, St. Andrews Burgh Court Book. The manuscript is irregularly foliated, so references to cases are cited by date. Some extracts from earlier burgh court proceedings show the court in operation earlier in the sixteenth century, e.g., St. AUL, B65/22, Calendar of St. Andrews Charters, no. 322, 331.

daughter, as well as their husbands "for their interest", that they had called her "harlot, whore and glengorie [syphilitic] thief."[18] Mother and daughter, in turn, countered that Scott had called them "common thieves." After due deliberation, the assize found that mother and daughter had wronged in the "shameful slandering and defaming of the said Jonet Scott," calling her the specified words as well as "many other injurious and slanderous words." Scott was found innocent, as the charge was not proven. She asked that a record be made of the court's decision. The court ordered Kenzow and Kenlowy to pass to Scott's gate where the offence had occurred; there they were to "sit down upon their knees" and ask her forgiveness for their words. They were to pay a fine of 20s immediately to the collector of the poor's alms. Furthermore, it was decreed that if they ever "offended, troubled, molested, defamed or injured" Scott again in word or deed, or if Scott ever offended them in like manner (implying that the court was not wholly convinced of her innocence), the offender was to pay £10 to the common works of the town each time she did so.

This was not the end of the dispute, however. Just over four months later, Kenzow's husband, Robert Kenlowy, was placed in a ward (temporary imprisonment) until he could persuade his wife to carry out the sentence imposed on her in May, that is, going to Jonet Scott's gate and ask forgiveness.[19] Not only had she refused to do this, but on 18 September, she had insulted Scott again in the presence of the bailie. Scott had tried to get the bailie to enforce the decreet of 20 May. Kenzow's response was pointed: Scott "could wipe her arse" with it. For her defiance and new insult, Kenzow was fined £10, and her long-suffering husband was held liable for the sum. No more is heard of the case, so probably Kenzow eventually obeyed the decree. Suggesting that the apple did not fall far from the tree, however, her daughter Jonet Kenlowy was found guilty by the kirk session of quarrelling with her neighbors in 1599, so she may not have absorbed her lesson entirely either.[20]

The case, the only one with more than a single entry in the surviving burgh court record, illustrates several aspects about the burgh authorities' attempts at peace-keeping and the challenges they faced. It shows the types of insults that were thrown between townspeople. It demonstrates the town

18. St. AUL, B65/8/1, 20 May 1589. Husbands were often cited in cases against their wives "for their interest" in order to ensure that they could be held legally liable for any fines or other punishments incurred.

19. St. AUL, B65/8/1, 19 Sept 1589. Placing someone in ward was used by the court to enforce its decisions, although people could be released by providing another individual as surety that they would obey.

20. Fleming, *Register of the Ministers*, 890.

trying to reconcile parties through public demonstrations of contrition and forgiveness. There was also the stick of threatened sanctions for those who did not obey or, more commonly, for any repetition of the defense. It also shows that sometimes these official efforts were resisted by individuals who were not perhaps as deeply committed to the model of a godly society as were the authorities. Kenzow not only reoffended, thus incurring the financial penalty for doing so, but she did so in a way that demonstrated contempt for a burgh official.

This case was one of 65 verbal and physical assaults heard by the court in these four years. Both men and women featured as perpetrators and victims, and received similar punishments, except the cuckstool (discussed below). There were usually about 15–16 cases yearly, although the existence of clusters of cases in particular periods (for example, September and October 1589) mean that they were not evenly spread out over the year. There is no clear reason for these clusters, unlike those in kirk sessions, which, in some towns at least, appeared before the time of communion when the kirk, and indeed some of the parishioners themselves, worked especially hard to reconcile their differences.[21] This number compares with only four assault cases, all of them verbal, heard by the St. Andrews kirk session in the same period.[22] The court treated both verbal and physical assaults as offences and injuries, not only to the individual victim but to the town as well. In dealing with them, the authorities not only punished the perpetrator but, even more importantly, attempted to repair the rift which had been caused within the community as a whole. In St. Andrews, in the majority of cases, this meant ensuring the perpetrator sought the forgiveness of the victim, and usually in a way that would be witnessed by at least some of the neighbors of the town. Not only was justice done, but perhaps just as importantly, the authorities themselves were being seen to do justice, not just by the community but also by God.

PUNISHING THE PERSON AND THE PURSE

Historians of early modern Europe have argued that the punishment of the body was a major tool for enforcing acceptable behavior for governments of the period, but the magistrates of St. Andrews, at least from 1589 to 1592, were reluctant to make much use of such methods.[23] Although certain

21. Graham, "Church Discipline," 436–37.

22. *St. A KS*, ii, 636–785. Graham, *Uses of Reform*, 214–15, provides annual figures for types of offences heard by the St. Andrews Kirk Session in the years 1582–1600.

23. For the use and effect of such punishments in early modern Scotland, see

punishments, such as the cuckstool, jougs (an iron collar), and stocks, were threatened if the convicted person reoffended, they were rarely used in practice. However, the existence of these instruments of punishment acted as an effective reminder of the power of the authorities to correct wrongdoing.[24]

The cuckstool was used only once by the burgh court in 1589–92, although its use was threatened for repeat offenders in seven cases.[25] Jonet Husband and Kait Moffat, who had "offended and injured each other," were warned that if either repeated their offence, the guilty party would be sentenced to sit three hours in the cuckstool as often as they did so.[26] Beatrix Bell, convicted for striking and insulting Christian Ferr, was threatened with four hours in the cuckstool if she offended Ferr or anyone else in the future.[27] The only offender who spent time in the cuckstool was the servant Margaret Wood, who called Bessie Black, wife of an important citizen, "an old stinking rotten witch carling [old woman]."[28] Reflecting the seriousness of her offence, she was threatened with banishment if she repeated her action.

The jougs, an iron collar, used by both kirk sessions and burgh courts, was imposed as a penalty twice by the St. Andrews court in late 1589, once on Robert Tailor who had struck an officer on the head, drawing blood, and once on Marjorie Clink who had called Patrick Broun a false common thief along with several other words which the clerk reported were "unworthy to be put in writ."[29] The clerk noted that Clink was a frequent offender who had been threatened with banishment previously. The town's use of the jougs may have increased after 1592, as in December 1593, the kirk session and the magistrates agreed to enforce a 1567 act of parliament ordering the jougs to be used against fornicators, but whether this had an impact on the punishment of verbal and physical assault is unclear.[30]

Groundwater, "Powerful Objects."

24. Groundwater, "Powerful Objects," 184, 197–98, 205.

25. In most towns, the cuckstool was primarily used on women, although in some towns such as Dundee, men might be placed in it as well; Maxwell, *Old Dundee*, 354. The cuckstool was also used by kirk sessions for a variety of offences, generally with the assistance of the civic authorities (Todd, *Culture of Protestantism*, 176, 203).

26. St. AUL, B65/8/1, 4 March 1590.

27. St. AUL, B65/8/1, 21 November 1589.

28. St. AUL, B65/8/1, 13 January 1590.

29. St. AUL, B65/8/1, 16 December 1589 (Tailor); 19 December 1589 (Clink). For use of the jougs by both kirk sessions and burgh courts see Groundwater, "Powerful Objects," 197.

30. *St. A KS*, ii, 767. The kirk session used this punishment for sexual offences, e.g., *St. A KS*, ii, 767, 794, 819.

When assaults were so severe as to be life-threatening, stronger punishments, sometimes combined with the ones above, might be decreed. These sometimes involved both civic and church punishments if they broke both secular and ecclesiastical laws. Walter Adesoun, a tailor who assaulted the aged and frail kirk reader Thomas Wood to the peril of his life in 1592, was sentenced to the jougs and the stocks, along with several other penalties carried out both in the kirk and in the town before being banished.[31] A miller who wounded a tailor in several places in his back, leaving him for dead, was banished; the court warned him that if he remained or returned, his right hand would be struck off as an example to deter all others from such actions.[32] Offences against one's parents, breaking the Fifth Commandment, were also severely punished and threatened with harsh measures if repeated. William Liston, a baxter, was found guilty of "unnatural and wild behaviour" in violently assaulting his father in 1590; as well as doing repentance in the kirk, he was threatened that if he repeated his offence, he would be whipped through the streets and banished forever, as a warning to others against such deeds.[33]

Far more common than physical punishments were financial penalties. In many towns, such fines were described as "amerciaments of court" or "bailies unlaws. "They were usually imposed immediately and paid to the court for unspecified purposes, but in St. Andrews, the scribe usually recorded the use to which they were to be put. Their use underlined the authorities' attempts to repair rents torn in the social fabric of the godly community. Bessie Kenzow and Jonet Kenlowy, who insulted Jonet Scott, were ordered to immediately pay a 20s fine to the collector of the poor's alms, and were threatened with a much larger fine of £10 to the town's common works if they repeated their offence.[34] In two cases, money was paid to the victims; in one a payment was also made to the doctor who treated the victim who was wounded by a sword, while in two other cases of physical injury, the total fine went to the medical man.[35]

31. This burgh court record is recorded in the presbytery record rather than the burgh court record where there is only a marginal note for it beside a blank section of the page, suggesting close cooperation between the civic and church authorities in an attack on a member of the kirk. It is printed in *St. A KS*, ii, 710, note 1.

32. St. AUL, B65/8/1, 14 April 1590.

33. St. AUL, B65/8/1, 6 February 1590. The repentance in the kirk suggests close cooperation between kirk and court in this case.

34. St. AUL, B65/8/1, 20 May 1589, 19 September 1589. Other cases with fines to the poor include 23 September 1589, 26 September 1589.

35. Fines to victim, St. AUL, B65/8/1, 10 Oct 1589. Fines to doctor, 23 May 1589, 28 October 1589. Fines to both victim and doctor, 10 October 1589.

Most fines were due only if an offence was repeated. The amounts threatened were relatively large, which probably helped their function in discouraging repeat offenders. They were generally directed towards "the common works," projects that benefited the community as a whole. Sometimes they reflected particular projects in progress at that time. In 1589, for example, when the west port of the town was being repaired and improved, a number of these fines were directed to that work.[36] From late 1591 to 1592, many potential fines were directed towards the harbor works.[37] In this way, the magistrates attempted to ensure that future ruptures to the peace would result in financial aid to the well-being of the community as a whole.

FORGIVENESS IN THE GODLY SOCIETY

In just over 80% of the sentences imposed by the St. Andrews burgh court for verbal and physical assaults, the offender was ordered to ask forgiveness of the victim. Although further research is needed, it appears that St. Andrews was unusual among Scottish urban communities in the prominent role it gave to the ritual of forgiveness. These acts were important beyond the individuals involved. As Nikki Macdonald has pointed out, "the public performance of repentance was a demonstration to a watching God of the community's awareness of, and response to, the consciousness of sin in their midst."[38] Were the St. Andrews magistrates particularly aware of their role as the civil counterpart to the "perfect Reformed kirk," and eager to demonstrate this by showing their eagerness to respond to sin?

The early modern ritual of forgiveness had earlier roots in Scottish towns, drawing from the medieval church's sacrament of confession, which involved confession, contrition and penitence. Sentences imposed by pre-Reformation town authorities involved the repentant offender bringing a wax candle to the parish kirk to donate to the high altar or another specified altar, and kneeling and asking forgiveness of the person offended (and often also of God, the burgh magistrates and the congregation). In the fifteenth and early sixteenth centuries, such ritual performances might also take

36. St. AUL, B65/8/1, 27 May 1589, 2 September 1589.

37. For example, St. AUL, B65/8/1, 18 September 1591, 23 October 1591 (three cases), 10 March 1592, 2 May 1592.

38. Macdonald, "Reconciling Performance," 3. Graham, "Church Discipline," 436, also stresses the "performative nature of public repentance" in the kirk.

place in more secular sites, such as the place where an offence had occurred. Some involved a specific verbal formula to be voiced by the offender.[39]

The Reformed Kirk, dispensing with the sacrament of confession, nevertheless kept some of its penitential aspects and developed its own forms of public repentance. In some cases, it allowed relatively private repentance before the kirk session, although more commonly it ordered public repentance in the parish kirk, involving sitting or standing on a stool of repentance and confessing one's offence for a specified number of Sundays during the service before the congregation. Occasionally, offenders had to ask for forgiveness at the site of the offence.[40] The St. Andrews burgh authorities drew on both civic and ecclesiastical practices when they made use of their own forms of the performance of forgiveness. Sentences involving public repentance or the asking of forgiveness were certainly not regarded as a "soft option."[41] Indeed, it has been argued that "The humiliation incurred through the public performance of repentance by individuals provided one element of sacrifice in a culture that was honor-based and thus acutely aware of the importance of reputation and status." Bessie Kenzow's reluctance to apologize to Jonet Scott and Scott's pursuit of her for this refusal suggest the importance of the ritual to both offender and victim.

Towns differed on where they required offenders to ask forgiveness of their victims. St. Andrews magistrates varied between ordering somewhat more private forgiveness in the burgh court itself, more openly-visible forgiveness in the place where the offence had occurred, and most public of all at the market cross. The town appears to have been unusual in how much use it made of the market cross as a site, although more research needs to be done on the use of forgiveness rituals in other towns at this period.[42] Unfortunately, the court entries are not detailed enough about the specifics of a case to indicate why one place might be chosen in preference to others, although in some cases this can be surmised.

In about a fifth of the cases involving forgiveness, the site was not specified, although since the offender might be ordered to ask the victim's pardon immediately and the authorities would want to see that the order had been obeyed, the act probably took place either in or just outside the court. In 1590, John Mutto, who had struck Isobel Kay, was ordered to ask

39. Ewan, "'Tongue You Lied,'" 115–36; Macdonald, "Reconciling Performance," 20–30, 56–67.

40. Todd, *Culture of Protestantism*, 127–82, provides a detailed description of the ritual of public repentance in the kirk.

41. McCallum, *Reforming the Parish*, 218, 223–4.

42. I am grateful to Rob Falconer and Kevin Hall for discussion of the evidence from Aberdeen and Edinburgh in this period.

her forgiveness, while Jonet Husband and Kate Moffat, who had "offended and injured" each other, were each to ask the other forgiveness.[43] Two cases on one day in October 1591 involved women uttering a curse-like insult against a man, wishing that neither sea nor salt water should bear him above.[44] Perhaps the authorities preferred such words to be kept relatively private in order to avoid associations with witchcraft accusations. These two cases, coming around the time of the North Berwick witch trials in 1590, where some of the accused were suspected of raising storms which threatened to drown James VI and his new bride, Anna of Denmark, may have had more resonance than usual.[45]

Asking forgiveness in the court itself, described usually as "asking forgiveness at the bar," was prescribed in about a third of the cases, and probably took place as part of the court proceeding itself. The bar divided the judges in the court from the pleaders, marking off the space of judgment; being "at the bar" meant that one was physically present and pleading one's case in the court. Here, the offender acknowledged wrongdoing before the magistrates and elite men of the town present in the court, and in the seat of local administrative power, the tollbooth. This ensured that the act of reconciliation was witnessed by the leading members of the community, and those who had the power to enforce sanctions in the case of a repeated offence. For those further down the social hierarchy, especially, performing such an act before one's social superiors served as a powerful reminder of the control of the local authorities. The act was also imbued with the solemnity of the proceedings of the court.

On the other hand, this ritual took place within an enclosed space, away from the public gaze of the entire community. Perhaps, like the kirk, session repentances in front of the session, asking forgiveness at this site was regarded as less severe than the public ritual.[46] A hint that this might also be the case with the burgh court comes in September 1591 when William Hewtoun, a baker, who had "most heinously offended, slandered and injured" the minister Mr. Robert Buchanan with many injurious words, was reported by the scribe to have realized the enormity of his offence and, "moved by conscience freely of his own will unforced," sat down at the bar and craved God and the minister forgiveness.[47] This unforced act of contri-

43. St. AUL, B65/8/1, 22 May 1590, 4 March 1590.

44. St. AUL, B65/8/1, 23 October 1591. Similar insults could be found elsewhere in Fife in this period, McCallum, *Reforming the Parish*, 195.

45. The other Fife cases involving these insults were treated as slander rather than witchcraft accusations, McCallum, *Reforming the Parish*, 195, 203.

46. Todd, *Culture of Protestantism*, 140.

47. St. AUL, B65/8/1, 18 September 1591. This case may have been heard before

tion not only worked to convince the authorities of his genuine remorse but also spared him from the more public rituals of repentance that might have been imposed by civil and religious authorities on those who attacked the representatives of the church.

Sometimes, offenders were ordered to ask forgiveness at the place where the offence had taken place.[48] In 1589, James Fyfe younger who called his opponent a common thief and then struck him on the face was ordered to go to the street where he had done this and kneel and ask his forgiveness, while in 1592 Catherine Brown who had called Genie Flicter a common whore and thief was ordered to pass to the place where the offence was committed and ask forgiveness of both Genie and her husband.[49] In the Bessie Kenzow case, mother and daughter were ordered to go to the Jonet Scott's gate, the entrance to her property, where the offence had occurred. Such a site had the additional significance of highlighting Scott's status as a respectable married woman. These acts of forgiveness took place within full sight of the neighbors who had perhaps witnessed the original offence. As Todd has pointed out for kirk-ordered forgiveness rituals at these sites, they also emphasized the fact that in breaking the peace of the community, the offenders injured the neighbors as well as the individual victim.[50] Neighbors also acted in place of the court and assise who had heard the case. They had the power to enforce the reconciliation, bringing any repeated disreputable actions by the offender before the court.

The importance of the forgiveness ritual to the St. Andrews magistrates is suggested by the fact that the most common place ordered for the ritual was the market cross, being decreed in about 40% of the cases.[51] The cross represented the heart of the community, as well as the peace of the town, been broken by the offender's actions. Other crimes were also punished there.[52] The market cross was not just a place of publicity, however. It also carried other important symbolism. As seen above, it was the site of corporal punishment, by the cuckstool, jougs and stocks, a reminder of the power

---

the burgh court because the minister was from another parish outside St. Andrews.

48. This practice was followed in other towns as well, see Falconer, "Believing na evill," 71.

49. St. AUL, B65/8/1, 27 May 1589; 16 May 1592. Other examples include 21 November 1589, 2 May 1592, 9 June 1592.

50. Todd, *Culture of Protestantism*, 249–51.

51. Other towns also used the market cross occasionally, although it appears that St. Andrews may have used it more frequently. Further research is needed on other towns. Falconer, "Believing na evill," 70–71. I am grateful to Dr. Falconer for sharing his records of punishments in early modern Aberdeen.

52. Falconer, "Believing na evill," 70–71; Todd, *Culture of Protestantism*, 249–51.

of the authorities to punish the body as well as the mind. It was a symbol of the king's peace, the peace which had been broken by the offenders' verbal or physical actions. The cross was also the site of public proclamations, which governed the well-being of the community. Moreover, it was the site at which banishments were proclaimed, a reminder of the ultimate sanction of removal from the community which one had offended.

Asking forgiveness at the market cross was in some sense the equivalent of the public repentance in the parish kirk ordered so frequently by kirk sessions, although it did not occur as often. As public repentance in the kirk was witnessed by the "godly society," gathered as a congregation to hear the word of God, acts at the market cross were carried out in full view of the community gathered to buy and sell in the marketplace. Indeed, the potential audience extended beyond the town to those who had come from outside the community to trade, including foreigners from overseas. It thus acted as a reminder to those outside the community that this was indeed a godly town, devoted to enforcing proper behavior upon its inhabitants.

St. Andrews had one further refinement which so far has not been identified in other towns. It had different levels of the market cross on which offenders were to stand. Possibly this concept was borrowed from the reformed public repentance as several kirk sessions refer to different levels of penitent stools.[53] In 1575, a St. Andrews man convicted of drunkenness by the kirk session was warned that if he reoffended, he would be required to sit "upon the uppermost penitent stool."[54] In four cases before the burgh court in 1589–92, offenders were ordered to stand on the "upper tangs" of the market cross. In 1589, when a tailor slandered Patrick Boncle, the common clerk, accusing him of corruption in wrongly noting the votes in the recent election, he was found to have done "manifest wrong" and was to pass to the utmost tange of the market cross to confess his offence and crave Boncle's forgiveness.[55] Thomas Welwye, who was found guilty of several offences against his master, including refusing to do him service when his master required it of him, was to stand bareheaded on the highest degree of the cross for three hours, before asking his master's forgiveness.[56] In 1592, two women who had insulted two other women were each ordered to ask forgiveness of their victim, and then stand on the highest degree for two hours.[57]

53. Graham, "Church Discipline," 438.

54. *St. A KS*, i, 409–10.

55. 10 October 1589.

56. 31 December 1591.

57. 2 June 1592. Both cases were heard the same day. Unfortunately, the brief entries

The act of asking forgiveness, like the public repentance enforced by the Kirk, was usually tightly scripted in gesture and word. Central to most sentences was the requirement that the offender sit down on his or her knees, that is, kneel, before the person whose forgiveness was being sought. Kneeling before another carried highly significant connotations, symbolizing one's inferiority to the standing person. In cases where the social status of the offender was greater than that of the victim, this must have been particularly humiliating. Enforcing this part of the act was important in reversing the offender's attempt through his or her actions to make the victim inferior to the offender.[58] Moreover, it attempted to redress the balance between offender and victim by restoring power to the wronged person through the positive act of granting forgiveness to the offender. The ritual, of course, also depended on the victim's willingness to participate. It was the outright refusal of the accused witch of 1572 to forgive those who had offended her that had counted so heavily against her.

In some cases, specific words were also dictated. Most crucial in the eyes of the community and of the victims themselves was the necessity to restore a reputation which had been lost either through insults or through physical vulnerability. In some instances, the offender was ordered to say that they knew nothing of the person but good and honesty, or a version of these words.[59] When John Yuill, who was involved in a court case with John Gray, "most grievously offended" Gray by saying he should prove him mansworn in the presence of the bailies, he was ordered to confess his offence immediately to the bailies and say he knew nothing of Gray but honesty.[60] Such formulae reinforced the victim's good long-standing in the community, emphasizing the falsity of accusations and restoring the victim's injured reputation.

On occasion, another ritual was used when insults were involved, which emphasized the untruth of the offender's words. This was the formula "false tongue you lied" which was also used occasionally by the kirk session.[61] It did not originate with the kirk session, however, as town courts had imposed the formula occasionally on offenders from at least the early

do not provide any reason for them being subjected to this particular punishment.

58. Todd, *Culture of Protestantism*, 150; Macdonald, "Performing Repentance," 62.

59. St. AUL, B65/8/1, 3 June 1589, 23 September 1589 (2 cases), 26 September 1589,17 April 1590. For its use by kirk sessions, see Graham, "Theory of Discipline," 429.

60. St. AUL, B85/8/1, 30 January 1590.

61. *St. A KS*, i, 441 (1579) This case is discussed by Graham, "Women and the Church Courts," 157, 271.

sixteenth century.[62] In the two cases in the St. Andrews burgh court, the social status of the victims may have been important, as in both cases, they were magistrates. David Robertson, a flesher who had called Mr. David Russell the dean of guild a thief and a loun (low fellow, rascal), was ordered, as part of asking forgiveness at the market cross, to take himself by the tongue and say false tongue you lied and that he knew nothing of Mr. David but good and honesty. He was threatened with further sanctions if he reoffended against Russell or any magistrate.[63] William Lowson, a slater, who hit the same dean of gild in the face and injured the bailie, who was David Russell's son, was ordered in 1591 to kneel at the market cross and "to take himself by the tongue saying these words false tongue you lied."[64] He was then to pay 20 merks to the shore work and be banished forever.

For those who used additional weapons as well as their tongues, the court might order that such items be put in a place where the offender could no longer use them for harm. As part of the sentence on David Robertson, who insulted the dean of gild in 1589, as well as asking forgiveness, Robertson was ordered to deliver his "whinger" (a short sword or knife) by its heft to his victim.[65] In handing over his knife to the man he had attacked, the offender in such rituals symbolically made himself vulnerable and dependent on the mercy of his opponent, lowering his own status in relationship to that of his former victim.[66]

When William Turnbull insulted both John Paterson and his spouse and threatened to strike Paterson with his whinger, the court decreed that Turnbull ask forgiveness of them at the market cross, but also that his whinger be stuck on the north gable of the tollbooth (town hall), there to remain as a perpetual reminder of his misbehavior.[67] The kirk also used such methods—as part of a sentence on a man who attacked his father in 1594, the session ordered him to do public repentance in the kirk, and the hammer and stone used in the assault were to be shown.[68] Other towns, such as Perth, might also involve weapons in their rituals of forgiveness.[69]

62. Ewan, "Tongue You Lied," 128–29; Macdonald, "Reconciling Performance," 65–66.

63. St. AUL, B65/8/1, 3 June 1589.

64. St. AUL, B65/8/1, 8 June 1591.

65. St. AUL, B65/8/1, 3 June 1589.

66. Macdonald, "Reconciling Performance," 63.

67. St. AUL, B65/8/1, 10 March 1592.

68. *St. A KS*, ii, 785–6. This case is discussed in Graham, "Church Discipline," 434–35.

69. Macdonald, "Reconciling Performance," 63–64.

MAINTAINING THE GODLY SOCIETY?

How successful were the St. Andrews magistrates in maintaining their ideal of the "godly society"? As pointed out by several scholars of Scottish Reformed Kirk discipline, the goal of a perfect godly community on earth was ultimately unachievable.[70] However, what could be created was a society that tried its best to follow God's laws, even if it fell short. For those in charge of governing, both ecclesiastical and secular, it was important to strive to uphold the accepted moral standards and discipline. In the case of the St. Andrews burgh court, acting to reconcile disputing individuals, and moreover doing so with the publicity associated with rituals of asking forgiveness, demonstrated to the community, and most importantly to God, that it was doing its best to maintain such standards. By means of individual acts of reconciliation, the authorities hoped that they would avoid bringing down God's wrath on the entire community.

Michael Graham has argued that for kirk discipline to be effective, the elders had to be "relatively well-behaved themselves to as not to be vulnerable to charges of hypocrisy."[71] Ironically, the St. Andrews magistrates themselves failed this test in the years following the end of the surviving volume of records. A disputed election in October 1593 led to the ousting of the faction led by James Learmonth of Dairsie that had long dominated the town government, and resulted in violent resistance to the new order, including attacks on individuals and properties, a threat to attack the town, appeals to the Privy Council, and general disruption and disorder. Moreover, municipal politics were tied up with a long simmering feud between two prominent St. Andrews families going back to 1586, which flared up again around the same time.[72] Both disputes were eventually settled in the later 1590s through the joint efforts of the Privy Council, the kirk session and the Presbytery, but the ordinary inhabitants of St. Andrews might have been forgiven for wondering to what extent their social superiors were themselves model representatives of the "godly society."

BIBLIOGRAPHY

Bannatyne, Richard. *Journal of the Transactions in Scotland During the Contest Between the Adherents of Queen Mary and Those of her Son, 1570, 1571, 1572, 1573*. A. Constable, 1806.

70. For example, McCallum, *Reforming the Parish*, 38–39, 220–28, 230; Graham, "Church Discipline," 437.

71. Graham, "Theory of Discipline," 423.

72. John W. Cairns, "Academic Feud"; Graham, *Uses of Reform*, 296–8.

Brown, Michael, and Katie Stevenson, eds. *Medieval St. Andrews: Church, Cult, City.* St. Andrews Studies in Scottish History. Boydell, 2017.

Cairns, John W. "Academic Feud, Bloodfeud and William Welwood: Legal Education in St Andrews, 1560–1611—Part II." *Edinburgh Law Review* 2.3 (1998) 255–87.

Cordey, Anna. "Reputation and Witch-hunting in Dalkeith." In *Scottish Witches and Witch-Hunters. Palgrave Historical Studies in Witchcraft and Magic,* edited by Julian Goodare, 103–20. London: Palgrave Macmillan, 2013.

Dawson, Jane E. A. "'The Face of Ane Perfyt Reformit Kyrk': St. Andrews and the Early Scottish Reformation." In *Humanism and Reform: The Church in Europe, England, and Scotland, 1400–1643.* Vol. 8, Studies in Church History Subsidia, edited by James Kirk, 413–35. Ecclesiastical History Society, 1991.

Dye, Sierra. "Disorderly, Deviant, Dangerous: Defining Words as Witchcraft in Early Modern Communities." In *Deviance and Marginality in Early Modern Scotland,* edited by Allan Kennedy, 45–60. Boydell, 2025.

Ewan, E. "'Tongue You Lied': The Role of the Tongue in Rituals of Public Penance in Late Medieval Scotland." In *The Hands of the Tongue: Essays on Deviant Speech,* edited by Edwin D. Craun, 115–36. Medieval Institute, 2007.

Falconer, J. R. D. "'Believing na evill nor injury': Space, Place, and Crime in Sixteenth-Century Scottish Burghs." In *Deviance and Marginality in Early Modern Scotland,* edited by Allan Kennedy. Boydell, 2025.

———. *Crime and Community in Reformation Scotland: Negotiating Power in a Burgh Society.* Pickering & Chatto, 2013.

Fleming, D. H., ed. *Register of the Ministers, Elders and Deacons of St. Andrews 1559–1600,* 2 vols. Scottish History Society, 1889–90.

Graham, Michael. "The Theory and Practice of Church Discipline." In *A Companion to the Reformation in Scotland, ca. 1525–1638. Frameworks of Change and Development,* edited by William Ian P. Hazlitt, 420–50. Leiden: Brill, 2022.

———. *The Uses of Reform: "Godly Discipline" and Popular Behavior in Scotland and Beyond, 1560–1610. Studies in Medieval and Reformation Thought.* Leiden: Brill, 1996.

———. "Women and the Church Courts in Reformation-Era Scotland." In *Women in Scotland c.1100–c.1750,* edited by Elizabeth Ewan and Maureen M. Meikle, 420–42. Tuckwell, 1999.

Groundwater, Anna. "Powerful Objects: Coercion, Restraint, Torture and Punishment in the Scottish National Collections." In *The Scottish State and the Experience of Authority,* edited by Martha McGill and Alasdair Raffe. Edinburgh: Edinburgh University Press, 2025.

Macdonald, Nikki. "Reconciling Performance: The Drama of Discipline in Early Modern Scotland." PhD diss., University of Edinburgh, 2013.

Macdonald, Stuart. "Counting Witches: Illuminating and Distorting the Shape of Witchcraft Accusations in Scotland." *Journal of Scottish Historical Studies* 37.1 (2017) 1–18.

———. "Creating a Godly Society: Witch-hunts, Discipline and Reformation in Scotland." *Historical Papers* 10. Canadian Society of Church History (2010) 5–20.

———. *The Witches of Fife. Witch-hunting in a Scottish Shire, 1560–1710.* Tuckwell, 2002.

Martin, Laura. "The Witch, the Household and the Community: Isobel Youngs in East Barns, 1580–1629." In *Scottish Witches and Witch-Hunters, Palgrave Historical*

Studies in Witchcraft and Magic, edited by Julian Goodare, 67–84. London: Palgrave Macmillan, 2013.

Maxwell, Alexander. *Old Dundee, Ecclesiastical, Burghal, and Social Prior to the Reformation.* David Douglas, 1891.

McCallum, John. *Reforming the Scottish Parish: The Reformation in Fife, 1560–1640.* Ashgate, 2010.

Pitcairn, Robert, ed. *The Autobiography and Diary of Mr. James Melvil with a Continuation of the Diary.* Wodrow Society, 1842.

St. Andrews University Library (St. AUL). *St Andrews Burgh Court Book.* B65/8/1.

St. Andrews University Library (St. AUL). *Calendar of St Andrews Charters.* B65/22.

Todd, Margo. *The Culture of Protestantism in Early Modern Scotland.* New Haven: Yale University Press, 2002.

5

What to Make of History in the Study of Mission?

Charles Fensham

In her landmark study *"Begotten not Made": Conceiving Manhood in Late Antiquity*, Virginia Burrus points out that the study of history is always inextricably linked to the present. To put it in her own words,

> I am implicitly placing Wiles's question about doctrinal continuity into the context of contemporary concerns about gender, sexuality, and the body. The answer to the question will not, however, be a simple affirmation of discontinuity—not least because the very act of addressing the very difference of the past always implicates the present in the past (and vice versa).[1]

As we will see below, the study of mission involves a description of the past—mission history—and reflection upon it as the normative dimension of Missiology. It is therefore worth considering not just how we normatively or constructively reflect on history, but also how the writing of history is implicated by the present. In this essay, I hope to offer an opinion, as someone who is not a historian, on the relationship between constructing mission history and theological reflection upon it. The experience of a different culture and the impact of that experience will impact our writing and

1. Burrus, "Begotten not Made," 3–4.

understanding of history and our theological and ethical reflection upon it. I offer these thoughts in honor of the Rev. Dr. Stuart Macdonald and his profound contribution to historical research, both in his work on the distant past as he examined 16th century Scottish witch hunts, his groundbreaking work on Christianity in contemporary Canadian culture, and his study of the history of the Presbyterian Church in Canada since 1945.

In 1982, I was working as a youth worker with L'Église Protestante Māòhi (EPM). This denomination traces its roots back to the first London Missionary Society missionaries who established it in 1797. It is the largest Protestant Church in French Polynesia and is a denomination in the Reformed Tradition. As I spent my time learning the Māòhi language while using French to communicate, a slow but sure relationship of trust started to build with one local pastor. At that time, though young and inexperienced, I was an ordained Presbyterian minister, and the pastor recognized the things we held in common. After about four months working with youth, at the end of a Sunday service, the pastor took me aside and pointed out one of the very active members of the church. Then he explained that he felt comfortable talking to me about this person. He started by saying he did not think the guest missionaries from the Église Réformée in France would approve, but he felt he needed to confide in me because I might understand. Then he explained that this church member was highly valued in the community for wisdom, providing advice, and helping with child-care, and that this person was called *Māhū*. At that time, there was little awareness in my world about the Pacific and Indigenous traditions that recognized two-spirited people—people who are considered a third gender with both male and female roles in society. The reticence that this pastor felt in speaking honestly about this person and their role in the community was born from the homophobic Christian tradition brought to Tahiti by the missionaries and further supported, at that time, by the "mother denomination," the Église Réformée of France. I suspect that the United Protestant Church of France would have a different attitude today. The pastor was probably worried that this person might be hurt if I treated them in a judgmental fashion. By that time, he knew that I was trained both in Theology and Cultural Anthropology, so he thought I might understand with some compassion. Over the years, as I came to terms with my own sexuality, I have often thought of this experience and the implications for mission history, theology, and ethics.

As alluded to above, the classic way the methodology of Missiology was defined during the 20th century was coined by David Bosch, who claimed that Missiology is a discipline born from a descriptive tradition—mission history—and a normative tradition—reflection on Scripture and history.[2] He was also the theologian who framed a comprehensive definition of mission: "Mission has to do with the crossing of frontiers. It describes the total task which God has set the Church for the salvation of the world."[3]

The history of mission is therefore studied with a particular theological purpose, to describe and understand how the church crossed frontiers of culture, language, and geography as it brings the gospel to people who have not heard or understood it well before. It also requires deep theological and ethical reflection on what we can learn from that history and how to measure it against our evolving understanding of the gospel, Scripture, ethics, and theological traditions. All this sounds rather fine, but the collection of data and the writing of history of any kind is an exceedingly complex enterprise fraught with challenges. For example, to return to the Māòhi people of the South Pacific, the account of the missionary exploits of John Williams, who was the first missionary to reach those shores, is shrouded in stories that have been questioned. Williams kept a diary, which is published and is full of data, but how reliable is the data? How much of the stories told, though likely very true to his own experience, is colored by his own judgments and cultural perspective? The story of the Christianization of the Māòhi people includes a description of a mass conversion after a tribal leader, Pomare II, cooked and ate a sea turtle. Such turtles were considered to be the beings with the strongest and sometimes dangerous *mana* power according to Polynesian tradition, and the fact that Pomare survived was taken as a sign of the superiority of the Christian faith over the powers that be. At least, that is how the story is told. As time unfolded and historians started to dig into some of these stories, how they were recorded and transmitted, and so on, doubts developed that things transpired in the exact way the stories are remembered. Kealani Cook records the story with much greater nuance.[4] History is complicated, and having a mission agenda in telling it can potentially skew the picture.

There is no doubt that the Protestant Christian faith is strong amongst the Māòhi people of French Polynesia. It is a vibrant faith that integrated Māòhi cultural, language, the love of music and singing performances, the love of their food culture, and their exceptional island hospitality into their faith. This even includes the tacit protection of the pre-Christian tradition of the two-spirited *Māhū* despite the disapproval of some colonial church leaders.

2. Bosch, "Sendingwetenskap," 247.

3. Bosch, "Witness to the World," 17.

4. Cook, "Burning the Gods."

The problem of theological or missiological bias in the writing of church history or mission history was not something I learned a lot about as a theological student doing the obligatory church history courses. In fact, as I review some of the texts I was exposed to during the early 1980's, I am quite surprised by what I now perceive as a sense of myopia. However, the introductory text did introduce me to the concept "historiography" and the idea that the collection and writing of history should also be part of an academic commitment in church history, and there is mention of a certain "critical unrest" in historical academia.[5] Thus, I became aware of the problem of those who seek to discern the human and the Divine in church history, and those who critique this approach. Integrated with this is the problem of the role of theological conceptions in the writing of church history. The question, "What is the church?" is a theological matter, but different theological perspectives will lead to different ways of writing its history. The same is true for mission history. In addition, the framework used by the creator of any history will also inevitably shape and perhaps bias that history. One example that my instructor, J. A. Stoop, described in his introduction to church history was the idea that church history tells the story of the unfolding of God's church over time, which was shaped and in some ways completed in the early apostolic era. It could be argued that this idea is still influential in much of Roman Catholic and Orthodox thought on church history, perhaps best represented in the approach of Pope Benedict XVI.

Another favorite trope is the idea of the ideal early church and its subsequent decline which takes many forms over time. In the twentieth century, it became popular to advance the idea that the church took a turn for the worse due to its acceptance within the Roman Empire and how it accommodated itself within that empire. In the medieval period, the idea of the corruption of the church and a historical vision of different eras of divine decree gained influence through Joachim of Fiore and his followers. This in turn, was picked up by the Cathar and Waldensian movements and also became the major theme of Protestantism in its drive towards the reformation of the church. A parallel concept of church decline is identified with the idea of the Hellenization of the church, an idea particularly developed by Adolf von Harnack.

There is also the role of the conception of the relationship between the Scriptures and church history to consider. Early Christianity wrestled with the idea of the story of the church and the fulfilment of Scripture and tried to account for the tensions between the Jewish religion and emerging

5. Stoop, "Kerkgeskiedenis," 107.

Christianity. More recently, Gerhard Ebeling would argue that church history is the history of the exposition of the Scriptures.[6]

Another idea that arose more clearly in the late 19th century was the idea of "salvation history" (*heilsgeschichte*). This idea of salvation history has a very long presence in the understanding of the church and the people of God. Connected to this is a theme that reoccurs through the history of ideas of the church, the people of God, as the chosen or elected ones. Eusebius of Caesarea is sometimes described as the "father of church history," and he highlighted the theme of the church as "the people of God spread throughout the world wherever the sun is shining." Thus, he presents the church as a group of special people.[7] He also had a profoundly universal and inclusive understanding of this election, which for him started at Creation and included all people through history who received God's light. To support this, he argued that there was the "scattering of seeds of the true religion" throughout history, thus aligning himself with the early Christian apologetic doctrine of the *logos spermatikos.*[8] This theme of the "elect," or "the chosen people," would play a major role in the telling of church history and also, perhaps in the shaping of history both for good and for ill. One of the implications of this idea for the construction of church and mission history is that it imagines the church as both a historical entity and something that is beyond history. In turn, this dual way in which the church is conceived complicates what counts as history and what counts as theological insight. Assuming that theological reflection upon history is considered a valid activity of the academy and faith, as I do, this dual nature of how we understand church in relation to history keeps presenting an ongoing challenge. The idea of salvation history is of necessity something supra-historical and therefore theological, and thus identifying it directly with "history" is potentially problematic.

During the twentieth century, the concept of the people of God participating in God's salvation history became a major theme of ecumenical, theological and missiological reflection. When Christians of many different stripes unite to confess the church as one, holy, catholic, and apostolic, the universal character of this idea of church colors all of world history and perhaps also how academic church and mission history is conceived. In addition, during that century, the impact of the rise of the disciplines of social science, particularly sociology, cultural anthropology, and economics, also started to have an impact on how church and mission history is conceived.

6. Stoop, "Kerkgeskiedenis," 112.

7. Stoop, "Kerkgeskiedenis," 114.

8. Ferguson, "Problem of Eusebius," 9.

These lenses offered a new set of data to be considered when constructing church and mission history. For example, two questions raised are what impact did economics and its related political machinations have on the Reformation period, or how did mass refugee movements impact the way Reformation history is conceived?[9]

Given the vastness of the task of recording the history of a concept like church that is hard to define, combined with a two-thousand-year time span, also presents the problem of how to organize any historical account. One option is to devise chronological periods. Very early on, in the Epistle of Barnabas as well as in the work of Irenaeus of Lyon, the idea of dividing church history in seven eras arose. Behind this idea lay the seven periods in the astrological theory of history in the cultural world of that time, but, within Christian thought, the seven days of creation served as inspiration for conceiving seven periods of history.

Although already present in the thought of Tertullian, the sixteenth-century thinkers moved from seven to three eras, creating theological categories for every era, as "the era of nature," "the era of the law," and finally "the era of grace."[10] This threefold division was also conceived by others as the eras of "the Father, the Son, and the Holy Spirit." Other divisions identified patristic, medieval, Reformation, early modern and modern periods with various explanations of when and what determines the transitions among periods. To finish my less-than-expert description above, it must be noted that other ways of doing the task of church and mission history also include particular divisions based on content, such as the history of dogmatics, of patristic theology, of church law, of church archaeology, of church art, and of mission. There are, of course, other divisions and rationales, but the point here is that these kinds of chronological, typological, and content divisions often have theological origins, which again highlights the tension between academic critical history and theological reflection. The one inescapable reality that no church or mission historian can escape is the dramatic turn towards the role of critical science in the practice of these disciplines.

This turn to theology as critical science is generally attributed to Friedrich Schleiermacher and the debates around the place of theology in the University of Berlin in the early 19th century. To fit into the understanding of the modern university as a place where all disciplines are practiced based on an understanding of critical science, Schleiermacher argued for the place of theology as a "positive science" in the University, one that is focused

9. For a brilliant use of the refugee lens on Reformation history see Terpstra, "Religious Refugees."

10. Stoop, "Kerkgeskiedenis," 117.

on the church and its practices, examined through a rational and critical lens.[11] In this light, Schleiermacher argued for theology to be considered as one of the three "higher departments" within the University that also include law and medicine as disciplines focused on praxis.[12] This logic then leads to an understanding of theology and its various sub-disciplines as a "historical and empirical theory of religion."[13] This conception of theology elevates historical science as a practice at the core of the work of theology in a university. Schleiermacher described this as "historical theology," and thereby meant that the role that church history plays in this way of doing theology is at the heart of the discipline. For Schleiermacher, this meant that the practice of theology in the University should be interacting with all the different sciences while engaging responsibly and rationally with the history of the existence of the phenomenon of Christianity.

In his excellent article on Schleiermacher that I cite here, Wilhelm Gräb argues that, despite suspicion from the other parts of the University that theologians are incapable of maintaining critical distance, it is manifestly not the case.[14] However, if we consider the many layers of nuance in the production of academic church history outlined above, I would argue that the assumption of the ability to maintain critical distance is not that easily affirmed. The problem does not only potentially lie with being a person of faith who might have some kind of bias, but also with the presence of bias in all critical sciences in the University. If the roles were to be reversed and theologians were to look at the practice of Sociology and History in the University, are there not also biases present that might impact the writing of history? Even the very culture of critical science potentially creates bias. Simply said, there is no completely unbiased science unless one is focused on a very small empirical experiment and its results. Whether it is medical science that publishes results of studies conducted only on men and then takes the results as also applying to women, or whether it is the writing of history that ignores the cultural bias of the author, bias always plays a role. Both church and mission history cannot escape this.

I am not a church historian, but as a missiologist following David Bosch's definition of Missiology as the discipline that relies on the descriptive—mission history—and the normative—theological reflection on Scripture and history, I am bound to engage with the history of the church and mission as part of my work. I do so with much trepidation because of my

11. Gräb, "Schleiermacher's Conception," 335–36.

12. Gräb, "Schleiermacher's Conception," 339.

13. Gräb, "Schleiermacher's Conception," 340.

14. Gräb, "Schleiermacher's Conception," 337.

lack of expertise. In the middle of my career, when seeking to make missiological and theological sense of my experience as a gay person, I engaged in a major project to examine the history of the treatment of people with diverse sexualities in the history of the church and its mission. I wondered what the suppressed history of the maligning of the two-spirited *Māhū* by colonial missionaries and the quiet resistance by the indigenous church community signifies in mission studies. How were people who had diverse sexualities and perhaps gender identities treated in church and mission history? As I researched the topic and engaged with some global theologians in Africa on this topic, I discovered that there was very little examination of this matter in standard church history texts. When I made a presentation to a group of African theologians on the need to talk about this topic and to examine it critically, one theologian from Kenia responded by telling us how, in traditional Kenyan culture within his own tribal world, the love between men is known as "shepherd boy love." He claimed that the current animosity and vocal homophobia in many African churches was a colonial import due to the influence of the legal structures that the British Empire imposed on colonies and the support rendered for this by British colonial churches.

As I continued my research, I was surprised to discover a wealth of research on sexual diversity and the way Christianity interacted with it within the *secular* version of academic history, going back to early Christianity. However, bona fide church historians, except for a few, remained silent on this topic. The two most prominent church historians I encountered who did not remain silent on sexual diversity in church history both self-identified as gay. John Boswell's groundbreaking work, *Christianity, Social Tolerance, and Homosexuality,* is perhaps the best-known text.[15] Suffice to say that it did not receive a resounding acceptance in church history circles. Of course, some of the critiques of Boswell's work and his conclusions are valid, but the vehemence of the opposition indicates bias.

The other notable author, Mark Jordon, focused on the history of doctrine. His landmark work, "*The Invention of Sodomy in Christian Theology,*" is a most excellent piece of work.[16] When I asked a Reformed Church Historian with expertise on early Christianity to review my research, he commented on the quality of Jordon's work, which I was citing at length. However, he hastened to say that anything I, or another person "known to be gay," might write on the topic is by definition biased and therefore invalid. He then proceeded to assure me that being gay is unacceptable within Christianity. The lack of awareness of his own "straight" bias is, in my

15. Boswell, "Social Tolerance."

16. Jordon, "Invention of Sodomy."

opinion, quite revealing. His logic, if taken seriously, would of course mean that no woman could write about the history of the treatment of women within the history of the church, nor could he write anything unbiased that examines cisgender straight men. Bias is inescapable, no matter what our identity, so what do we do with it when we engage with church and mission history?

As I read through the historical documentation of secular historians on how the Christian church treated sexual diversity, I literally became depressed. The documented stories were so consistently present, extremely violent, the rationale often so cruel, and the scapegoating so apparent and self-serving that it surprised me that good people who researched and wrote church history would simply ignore these stories. I asked myself, is there not something to be learned from the cruelty, misconstrued as Christian faithfulness? I asked myself, why the myopia specifically among church historians? Stuart Macdonald, whom we honor in this volume, is an example of a church historian who fearlessly examined something similar in his work on witch hunts in Scottish church history. Why then did other church historians, aware of the cruelty and scapegoating of sexual and gender diverse people in the historical contexts not describe and examine these events?

The impact of this lacuna in church history became apparent as I engaged in debates in the Presbyterian Church in Canada about the treatment of sexual and gender diverse people. Literally no one knew of this cruel dimension of church history. People were concerned about what they called "the issue" and how people would leave the church if sexually and gender diverse people were welcomed as full members of the church, but there was no awareness of a dark history of abuse based on homophobic and transphobic doctrinal assumptions. In turn, because of the ignorance about the historical record, there was very little ethical reflection on the implications of such homophobia and transphobia. The operating model of moral conviction and ethical discernment was based on the very theology that tortured people, burned them alive, or held them under water until they drowned.[17] I would argue that it is reasonable to critically examine the unexamined dimensions of history and the theological biases that create such lacunas. This is why rational and critical historical reflection is essential for the doing of Missiology and, of course, also theology in general. Core to such a commitment is identifying bias, including one's own bias, and allowing ethical reflection and self-examination to clarify conclusions.

17. For a detailed examination of some of these stories and their theological origins see Fensham, "Misguided Love," specifically chapters 5–10.

Earlier, I asked, "So what do we do with it (bias) when we engage with church and mission history?" Because some form of bias is always present, the only thing we can do if we want to engage in critical academic work with integrity is to put our bias on the table. We must examine our bias and make the readers of our work aware of our bias so that they can carefully and critically weigh our arguments. If a missiologist is to practice the discipline by attending to the history of mission as one fundamental data set within the methodology that is descriptive as well as normative, then working hard at making that information as true as possible to what we understand as reality is required. Even as missiologists and historians strive to do so, we always need to examine and expose our own biases. The descriptive dimension of Missiology does not simply include the telling of the story of mission but also examining the story of the use of the Christian Scriptures in the telling of that story. As we do so, we need to recognize the role of our biases in what we record and what we omit and even how bias appears in how we frame things.

David Bosch tried to do this in his landmark work, "Transforming Mission," by ordering the telling of the story of mission history according to what he identified as paradigms operating in different periods of church history.[18] Another example of such missiological taxonomy is that of J. H. Bavinck, who used a periodic taxonomy combined with thematic questions.[19] In addition, there is Bevans and Schroeder's landmark Missiology "Constants in Context," which employs theological themes to order the discussion of mission history.[20] For Bosch, his selected taxonomy of paradigms was linked to the way certain Scripture texts operated in the mind of those who engaged in Christian mission. There is no doubt that Bosch's own bias played a role in his decisions about what part of the story to tell and what Scripture texts to identify. As a New Testament scholar who was practicing Missiology, his commitment to the historical critical method within Biblical Studies, and the development of his own hermeneutical framework also played a key role. This is inevitable. At the point where Scripture and history are linked in doing Missiology, the line between the descriptive and the normative becomes blurred because, even as one identifies what one considers dominant stories in history, one is also starting to make normative discernments and even judgments. Nevertheless, with biases on the table and openness to critical examination of assumptions, the missiological task is necessary and worth it.

18. Bosch, "Transforming Mission."

19. Bavinck, "Inleiding," 284–302.

20. Bevans and Schroeder, "Constants."

BIBLIOGRAPHY

Bavinck, Johan H. *Inleiding in de Zendingweteschap*. Kampen: Koj, 1954.

Bevans, Stephen B. and Roger Schroeder. *Constants in Context: A Theology of Mission for Today*. Maryknoll, NY: Orbis, 2004.

Bosch, David J. "Sendingwetenskap." In *Inleiding in the Teologie: Tweede Uitgawe*, edited by I.H. Eybers et al. Pretoria: Kerkboekhandel, 1978.

———. *Transforming Mission: Paradigm Shifts in Theology of Mission*. Maryknoll, NY: Orbis, 2011.

———. *Witness to the World: The Christian Mission in Theological Perspective*. Atlanta: John Knox.

Boswell, John. *Christianity, Social Tolerance, and Homosexuality*. Chicago: University of Chicago Press, 1980.

Burrus, Viginia. *"Begotten not Made" Conceiving Manhood in Late Antiquity*. Stanford: Stanford University Press, 2000.

Cook, Kealani. "Burning the Gods: Mana, Iconoclasm, and Christianity in Oceania." In *Violence and Indigenous Communities: Confronting the Past and Engaging the Present*, edited by Susan Sleeper-Smith et al., 93–113. Evanston, IL: Northwestern University Press, 2021.

Ferguson, Everett. "The Problem of Eusebius." *Christian History* 20.4 (2001) 8–12.

Gräb, Wilhelm. "Schleiermacher's Conception of Theology and Account of Religion as a Constitutive Element of Human Culture." In *Schleiermacher, the Study of Religion, and the Future of Theology: A Transatlantic Dialogue*, edited by Brent W. Sockness and Wilhelm Gräb, 335–49. Berlin: de Gruyter, 2010.

Jordon, Mark. *The Invention of Sodomy in Christian Theology*. Chicago: University of Chicago Press, 1997.

Stoop, J.A. "Kerkgeskiedenis." In *Inleiding in the Teologie: Tweede Uitgawe*, edited by I.H. Eybers et al. Pretoria: Kerkboekhandel, 1978.

Terpstra, Nicholas. *Religious Refugees in the Early Modern World: An Alternative History of the Reformation*. New York: Cambridge University Press, 2015.

6

The Formation of Pastoral Leaders in the Twelfth Century

The Genesis Commentary of Stephen Langton (ca. 1150–1228) in Context

James R. Ginther

INTRODUCTION

The catalyst for this essay has been manifold. In the first instance, an historical investigation of pastoral formation intersects so well with the academic career of Stuart MacDonald, which is why I so readily agreed to offer this piece in his honour. I have only known Stuart since 2015, when I came to Toronto as the new Dean of the Faculty of Theology at the University of St Michael's College (USMC). As one of the founders of the Toronto School of Theology (TST), USMC had a seat on its executive council, and at that point in time, Stuart was the representative for Knox College. It was clear to me from the very beginning that he was an able administrator because he first and foremost engaged in administration to support the work of pastoral formation at TST. As equally important to me, however, was the fact that Stuart was a historian, and we soon discovered we had a common commitment to the role that historical research and teaching can play in the formation of ministers of the Gospel. That common commitment led to a desire to team-teach *History of Christianity II, 848–1648,* for the basic degree programs at TST. For the last five years, Stuart, as a Protestant social historian of the Reformation and I, as a Catholic intellectual historian of the later Middle Ages, collaborated in one of the most enjoyable experiences in my thirty-plus years of university teaching. As we challenged our students to appreciate the complexities of church history, we wanted them in particular to think about different ways in which ministers and pastors have approached their vocation. This essay examines one way in which Christian leaders undertook pastoral formation.

The second catalyst is a recently completed research project that entailed editing and translating a commentary on Genesis by Stephen Langton (ca. 1150–228).[1] Langton is best known as the Archbishop of Canterbury from 1207 to 1228. His time as archbishop was turbulent, to say the least, but most students of English history know of him because of the role he played in the issuing of the *Magna Carta* in 1215 and its subsequent defense during the rest of his archiepiscopate. Prior to being elected to this position, however, Langton was a master of the sacred page in Paris during a period in which the cathedral school there was transformed into one of the first universities in medieval Europe. He lectured on Scripture, disputed theological questions, and preached to the university community and at other venues for over twenty-five years. He commented on nearly every book of the Bible (and perhaps several times) during his magisterial career, including the book of Genesis.

Langton is considered a very traditional exegete who engaged in a multivalent reading of Scripture: the literal, allegorical, tropological, and, at times, the anagogical. While Tristan Sharp and I, as editors of Langton's commentary, would argue that his hermeneutic was more sophisticated than many scholars have suggested, we still found some of his readings to be jarring. Perhaps the most curious for us was Langton's regular insistence that a text from Genesis could be understood to be about Christian leaders. His terminology rarely included the word "pastor," but instead he favored the term "prelate" (*prelatus*). This essay explores the rationale for why Langton returned to this exegetical theme throughout the commentary, and

1. *Stephani Langton super Genesim,* 1–11, edited and translated by Tristan Sharp and James R, Ginther. This volume has been submitted to a publisher and will likely be published in the next two years. Given the current state of this text, I will cite the edition based on the paragraph divisions we established for each biblical chapter (e.g., Gen. 1, n.20), but I will also provide the foliation for the base manuscript of the edition: Cambridge, Peterhouse College MS 112 (hereafter cited as *P).* The commentary has four prologues, which I will cite as P1 to P4, and the relevant paragraph number. All the translations used here are from our forthcoming publication.

indeed, I will argue that his interpretative strategy in Genesis was part of his larger approach to theological education at the nascent University of Paris.

There is also a third catalyst for this essay. Almost two decades ago, the eminent medieval historian, John Baldwin, published an article in which he argued that the political theory that undergirded the *Magna Carta* could be traced back to Stephen Langton's days at the University of Paris.[2] Baldwin's essay was part of an ongoing debate among historians about what role (if any) Langton, as archbishop of Canterbury, had in the crafting of the *Magna Carta*.[3] While that is a fascinating question to examine, the real import of Baldwin's study for me was to raise a parallel question: if Langton's political theories were embryonic in his theological writings prior to entering the political fray of England as archbishop of Canterbury, would it be possible to trace out any of his ecclesiology that governed his archiepiscopacy in those same writings? One entry point for answering this question is to reflect on what Langton said about prelates.

To assess the rationale of Langton's treatment of prelates in his Genesis commentary, it is important to understand the various contexts for his teaching. I will begin by establishing the institutional contexts, of which there are two: the ecclesial and the educational. Then, I will outline Langton's exegetical strategy, and this will require some reorientation on what historians have asserted about the task of spiritual exegesis at the medieval university. Finally, I will bring to the reader's attention the liturgical context, namely how Christians (and especially students at the University of Paris) encountered Scripture and why this would have some import on Langton's exegetical strategy. With these contexts established, I will then analyze the central themes of his theology of prelacy.

2. Baldwin, "Master Stephen Langton." This article was translated into French to be included in a collection of essays on Langton: Baldwin, "Maître Etienne Langton."

3. The scholarship has oscillated from the notion that Langton played a central role in the formation of the Charter, to having a negligible role. There seems to be a more recent consensus that while Langton may not have been party to drafting the *Magna Carta*, he was certainly responsible for the inclusion of the section on the liberty of the church and would later in 1225 issued a sentence of excommunication for anyone who rejected or opposed the document. This resulted in the English bishops basically becoming the de facto guardians of the *Magna Carta*. See Ambler, "Thirteenth Century," 41–45; Carpenter, "Archbishop Langton"; Vincent, "Archbishop of Canterbury"; and Baumann, *Erzbischof von Canterbury*, 149–89.

THE INSTITUTIONAL CONTEXTS

First, however, I must clarify the terminology at play. In English, the term "prelate" has become synonymous with a bishop or a higher position in an ecclesiastical hierarchy. This was certainly the case by 1500 in England as well as for its cognates in other European languages. However, for the Middle Ages the term was far more elastic. It had originated as a term applied to nobles and governmental authorities in the Late Antique period, and by the tenth century, it was applied almost exclusively to church leaders.[4] It often was used synonymously for a bishop and this is how Langton uses this term in his writings. While it can certainly be a catch-all term for various ecclesial ministers who would have the responsibility of pastoral care for Christians (*cura pastoralis, cura animarum*), Langton consistently distinguishes between prelate and priest (*sacerdos*), and this is most evident in a sermon he preached while teaching in Paris. The sermon was delivered to a group of bishops and Langton spends most of this very long sermon focusing on the ideal life and practice of a prelate or bishop. There are moments, however, in which he focuses on priests under a prelate's care, but the two categories are clearly distinct in his mind, even though they share a common commitment to pastoral care.[5]

Pastoral care had gained a legal definition by the end of the twelfth century in that it combined two distinct notions of ecclesial power: the power of order (*potestas ordinis*), that is the power to "bind and loose" in terms of the sacrament of penance and the concomitant responsibility to discipline those under a pastor's care; and the power of jurisdiction (*potestas jurisdictionis*), that is the power over, or more importantly the responsibility for, a specific group of Christians in terms of sacramental ministry and ecclesial discipline. Both concepts of ecclesial power had been implicit in Christian ministry for centuries, but it was not until the twelfth century that we see an explicit articulation of those two spheres and how they relate to one another.[6] One might argue that this assertion of the two powers was an attempt to reconfigure the concept of prelacy.

4. Heale, *Prelate in England*, 2–5.

5. *Sermo ad episcopos* (Sermo 300), fols. 123vb–126vb. I have consulted the digital facsimile: https://uurl.kbr.be/1578829. Given how Langton begins the sermon by noting he is not a bishop, this sermon was delivered while he was teaching in Paris. See Franco Morenzoni, "Pastorale et ecclésiologie dans la prédication d'Etienne Langton," in *Étienne Langton, prédicateur, bibliste, théologien*, 449–66 at 454–57.

6. Benson, *Bishop-Elect*, 45–55. I readily admit that my account here is a bit simplistic considering the complex arguments presented by medieval canonists and theologians who followed the work of Gratian in the early twelfth century. The terminology that emerged could be highly complex and often used inconsistently, but the

For nearly a thousand years, bishops had configured their responsibilities primarily in terms of their jurisdictional power. In Western medieval societies, the bishop was as much a political leader as he was a spiritual one.[7] The execution of the ministry required economic resources to build and maintain churches, employ individuals to manage those resources, provide remuneration for those in major holy orders (sub-deacon, deacons, and priests), purchase and maintain the fabrics for all liturgical activities, and provide care for the poor. Collectively, those resources were called the bishop's "temporalities," and in an agrarian society, that meant a bishop was often a major landowner and so had jurisdiction not only over ecclesiastical entities, but also over the men and women who worked the fields and produced goods for food and commerce. What added a further political and economic dimension to a bishop's temporal responsibilities was his familial connections. It had become common for a bishop to be chosen from a leading noble family in a diocese, and so there were not only the financial pressures to ensure a diocese had the means to support liturgical and pastoral tasks, but also how to manage those resources in terms of their impact on the economic interests of the bishop's family, and even the larger scope of the diocese's nobility. Even when cities began to exert greater social and economic influence beginning in the middle of the eleventh century, bishops still had to manage, and often govern, the political and economic forces of merchants who were not so intimately tied to the land.

The explicit articulation of pastoral care as a combination of the powers of order and jurisdiction, therefore, had the intention of bringing the actual pastoral responsibilities of prelates to the forefront of their positions: the temporalities were meant to be at the service of their spiritual responsibilities and should not work in opposition to them. This was no easy task, as the political pressures on a bishop were often severe and ever-present. It was one thing to assert the ecclesial power of order should be of greater importance; it was another thing to instill that mentality in a candidate for the episcopate.

The change in how bishops were selected went some way to implementing this shift in mentality. The redefinition of who could be an elector of a bishop, which had emerged as one of the outcomes of the so-called "reforms" of the eleventh century, was an attempt to draw a hard distinction between two other spheres of power: secular (*regnum*) and sacerdotal (*sacerdotium*) power. No longer was the king or the local lord the final selector

two concepts of power reflect the general distinction in those discussions.

7. The most relevant studies of the medieval episcopate are: Swanson, "Apostolic Successors," esp. 29–36; Crosby, *Bishop and Chapter*; Ott, *Bishops, Authority and Community*; Trumbore and Ott, *Bishop Reformed*.

of a bishop, but rather, following the model of how a pope was to be elected by the college of cardinals, a bishop was to be elected by the canons of the diocese's cathedral. The clergy would, in theory, be less interested in the political interests of an episcopal candidate and instead select a man who would understand his pastoral responsibilities emanating from his power of order.[8]

In theory, this was a significant change in ecclesial governance, but, in practice, it could make little difference. Cathedral canons were populated by members from noble (and, later, merchant) families, who had often been sent into the ecclesiastical system as a means of protecting and advancing familial interests.[9] And, it was not uncommon for the canons to be strongly reminded of the priorities of a king or lord prior to an election.[10] Where this change to episcopal election did make a difference was that often the successful candidate had administrative experience in an ecclesiastical context, which could easily be applied to the episcopal office.[11] This did mean that bishops of the twelfth century were more conscious of the fact that their temporal responsibilities were for the sake of ministry. However, it was not the full solution to bringing balance to prelacy.

As it has often been the case in the history of Christianity, the more effective solution was education. The only way to ensure that a newly elected bishop would adopt this balance in his responsibilities was to provide a way to form him with a good theological education. The problem was that there was no school for future bishops, per se. Indeed, the focus of theological education for most of the twelfth century was mainly on the formation of

8. Peltzer, *Canon Law*, esp. 20–72. See also Pennington, "Golden Age," 154–62.

9. Barrow, *Clergy in the Medieval World*, 269–309.

10. Langton himself would experience royal interference firsthand. In 1206, he travelled to Rome where he was soon after elevated to Cardinal priest of St. Chrysogonus, but more significantly he ended up in the middle of a contested election for the next archbishop of Canterbury after the death of Hubert Walter in 1205. Three delegations had travelled to Rome to gain the support of Pope Innocent III: one for the monks of Canterbury represented by Reginald, their prior, whom the monks have provisionally elected as archbishop; a second representing the bishops of England, who had demanded a role in the election of a new archbishop; and, a third representing the interests of king John, who wanted his own candidate, John de Grey, to be confirmed by the papacy. By December of 1206, Innocent III rejected both candidates, ruled the bishops' claim out of order, and insisted that the Canterbury monks present in Rome hold another election. The result was that the pope's former master, Stephen Langton, was elected the next archbishop. While the monks had capitulated, the king did not. His resistance led to an interdict on the English church from 1207 to 1214, at which point king John relented. It was only in that year that Langton was able to travel to Canterbury. See Baumann, *Erzbischof von Canterbury*, 77–98.

11. Ott, *Bishops, Authority and Community*, 29–33.

priests. Cathedral schools had arisen almost organically in this period; that is, they sought to respond to two demands: to create a general education in the liberal arts that would form men (with women clearly excluded) for future work in business and government; and to form men for priestly ministry through a thorough education grounded in the exposition of Scripture.[12] Schools housed in cities like Chartres, for example, sought to meet the first demand; schools in cities like Laon and Paris were more interested in the second, but with an understanding that a good theological education was built upon a solid formation in the liberal arts. The emergence of a formal theological education was one of the major reasons for the eventual emergence of the medieval university from those schools.[13]

Both the cathedral school and the university, as its successor, were committed to educational formation that sought to create "habits of mind." While the modern notion of pastoral education is configured to create specific skill sets along with mental habits in students, the medieval master of theology was only interested in those mental habits. There were no classes on homiletics or anything remotely resembling the practicalities of pastoral theology; instead, they taught their students to read Scripture and come to understand its multivalent meanings. They challenged students to explore theological ideas through debate or disputation. They taught their students to preach by modelling it themselves as they preached before the academic community, the bishop's court, and, where possible, the court of a lord or even the king.[14] How long such a formation lasted in the late twelfth century is anyone's guess. In Langton's time at Paris, we do not know if any formal degree was granted to a student, nor do we know how long a student remained under the tutelage of a master. Degree regulations for the University of Paris were first published in 1215, and there is no evidence to indicate whether those regulations formalized existing practices or created new ones. All we can say is that students attended classes for an unknown period of time. Even if that period were only one year, it was a significant improvement over previous centuries when most future priests had prepared for ministry by apprenticing to the local priest to learn their pastoral craft.[15]

Who taught a future bishop? In one sense, it is a pointless question since there was no way of knowing which student in a cathedral school

12. Smith, "Use of Scripture in Teaching," 229–43.

13. See Southern, *Scholastic Humanism*. See also Ferruolo, *Origins of the University*.

14. See Muessig, *Preacher, Sermon and Audience*.

15. It was also expected that a future priest would have progressed through holy orders or at least had been ordained as a sub-deacon or a deacon and thereby had taken a vow of celibacy. This would have meant that a man preparing for sacerdotal ministry would have at least known the practice of liturgy of the mass intimately.

or university would eventually rise to the rank of a prelate. And, since the episcopate was differentiated from the priesthood not by being a separate order but rather by the difference in jurisdiction, one might conclude that whatever a student could adapt to his sacerdotal vocation could also be of use to the pastoral dimension of his prelacy. That is an eminently historical observation, but it then raises two questions: why were their resources available in the twelfth century that were aimed at forming prelates? And second, if Langton understood that the priesthood and the episcopate were of the same holy order, why does he consistently make comments about the nature of prelacy in his biblical commentaries, and in his Genesis commentary in particular?[16]

An Ancient Resource: The *Regula pastoralis* of Gregory the Great

Let's address the resources first. One of the literary traditions that originated in the Carolingian period has come to be known as the "mirror of princes" (*speculum principum*). These texts were composed to provide both a moral compass for rulers and practical advice on how a prince ought to rule his kingdom. It would appear that these *specula* were a response to the recognition that Western Europe was a de facto Christian society and that had to include rulers who were aligned with Christian virtue—at least in principle! One of the interesting features of these texts was that many of them drew from an early medieval text, the *Regula pastoralis* written by Pope Gregory I (d. 604). A number of Carolingian authors found Gregory's account of a virtuous leader to be applicable not only to bishops, but to princes as well.[17]

While this literary genre eventually disappeared by the beginning of the tenth century, Gregory's *Regula pastoralis* continued to be copied.[18] Between the seventh and sixteenth centuries, around 500 copies have survived, and not only was the text preserved but read and integrated into other texts. In the twelfth century, there were at least seventy-six copies executed.[19] The text, while originally penned as a guide for a sixth-century Italian bishop, was considered applicable to various contexts. Gregory began by describing

16. Quinto, "Parabola del Levitico," 187–267; Bain, "Commentateur des Proverbes," 303–4. Berardi, "*Vita, scientia, doctrina*," 130–85, argues that Langton's concept of an ideal master is based on his view of prelacy. I would suggest the inverse is the case.

17. Ubl, "Carolingian Mirrors for Princes," 80.

18. There was a resurgence of this literature after 1150, but it was far more variable than the Carolingian antecedents. See Briggs and Nederman, "Western Medieval Specula," 160–96.

19. Clement, "Handlist of Manuscripts." My count also includes manuscripts that may be dated as 11th–12th century and 12th–13th century.

what he considered to be the qualities of a true pastor (book 1) and then what kind of life a good bishop should embrace (book 2). The third book gave advice on how to minister to various kinds of people who inhabited the bishop's diocese: Gregory lays out thirty-eight contrasting types of people, beginning with how pastoral care differs when ministering to men versus women, and so on. In the final book, Gregory focuses on how a bishop ought to care for himself in order to be an effective pastor.[20]

One can see immediately why the *Regula pastoralis* remained such a prime resource for forming bishops into good pastors. However, even stellar texts like this were never read in a vacuum. As influential as Gregory's masterpiece was, it was digested along with other texts. One excellent example of this is the manuscript, *Paris, Bibliothèque nationale de France, MS lat. 12262.*[21] This is a composite manuscript of four booklets that were sewn together in the last quarter of the twelfth century, so co-terminus with Langton's magisterial period at Paris. It would seem that the manuscript was put together at the Benedictine abbey of Saint-Eloi in Noyon, France, which would have made it a possible resource for the archdiocese of Reims, if not all of Northern France.[22] The copy of the *Regula pastoralis* is from the tenth century and is written in a clear Caroline script. The other three booklets demonstrate that Gregory's text did not address all the elements of the pastoral office of bishop. Jerome's commentary on Ecclesiastes, copied out in the eleventh century, follows the *Regula,* but it is an incomplete copy of Jerome. The third booklet, written in a late-twelfth century protogothic hand, continues Jerome's commentary where the previous booklet had ended in mid-sentence.[23] That same booklet also contains two small texts by Yves of Chartres, along with copies of five of his letters, which are followed by a copy of Gregory the Great's commentary on the Song of Songs.[24] The fourth booklet, also in a tenth-century hand but a different

20. The Latin critical edition is found in Gregory I, *Règle pastorale*; the English translation is found in Gregory I, *The Book of Pastoral Rule.*

21. I have examined a digital facsimile of this codex which can be accessed at https://portail.biblissima.fr/en/ark:/43093/mdata12f24232529399751110 38c973c0351ccc9f2864. This manuscript deserves closer study than I can provide here.

22. The abbey was founded in 640 but was subsequently destroyed by Viking invaders in 860. However, it was restored in 945, and so the booklets from the tenth and eleventh centuries may have been originally written in this monastery's scriptorium. See Barubé, *L'Abbaye du Mont-Saint-Eloi.*

23. *Jerome, Commentarius in Ecclesiasten.* The English translation is *St. Jerome: Commentary on Ecclesiastes.*

24. Not all of Yves's letters have been edited but see Yves de Chartres, *Correspondance.* Gregory's commentary on the Song of Songs has been published: Gregory I, *Expositio in Canticum canticorum*, 3–46.

scribe from that of the first booklet, contains two pieces by Leidrad (ca. 745–821), archbishop of Lyon: a treatise on the sacrament of baptism and a companion piece on the implications of renouncing Satan and all his works (*De abrenuciatione diaboli*).[25]

This stitched-together manuscript points to some important facets of what a bishop should know and do. It may seem odd that Jerome's exposition of Ecclesiastes would find its way into this "handbook," but a careful read of Jerome's exposition suggests two important lessons for a bishop. First, Jerome orients his reading of the Preacher in this biblical book as a type of Christ and how he teaches his church. Additionally—and this had some relevance to the late twelfth century—Jerome clearly advances the thesis that human beings cannot be successful in answering the questions posed by the Preacher. Ultimately, the answers to the questions are beyond the capability of the human mind and querying such topics can easily lead to misery and not to union with God. It is therefore instructive that the twelfth-century booklet of this manuscript includes a copy of Gregory's commentary on the Song of Songs, which offers another more accessible route for union with God, one that is more affective and dependent upon receiving God's love rather than exploring the world discursively. This exegetical counterbalance in fact reflects a continual challenge to bishops as teachers, along with theologians, namely to see the greater value in Christian life of *caritas* over *curiositas* (see below).

The inclusion of some small works and letters of Yves of Chartres (ca. 1040–1115) is not accidental. Yves had played a pivotal role in assessing the implications (and applications) of the reform movement that had originated with Pope Gregory VII. He was well versed in canon law and theology, and as a former abbot who then became bishop of Chartres in 1090, Yves was well experienced in being a prelate. He was also gifted in stating things clearly and succinctly, as his short account of sacred orders found in this manuscript well demonstrates. He was also committed to pastoral care as bishop. His second piece, copied here, a sermon to ordained clergy, ends with this observation:

> Offer the sacrifice, namely the bread and the wine, for the living and the dead. That which has been sacrificed transforms by the Holy Spirit into the true body and blood of Christ. When water is mixed with the wine in the chalice, the people are united with Christ. For if anyone only offers the wine, it is [Christ's] blood without us; if is it water alone, it is the people without Christ. When both are mixed together the heavenly sacrament

25. Mabillon, *Veterum analectorum*, 3:1–45.

> is perfected, by whose reception the body and soul of all faithful Christians is vivified. Bishop, priest, Levite, these are names of offices not of merits, nor therefore are we holy unless we would possess the virtue associated with our <official> names. Let each hear, believe, and protect true fraternity which has been poured out from the true office.[26]

A Contemporary Resource: The *De moribus et officio episcoporum* of Bernard of Clairvaux

A second literary resource was composed within the twelfth century, but because of its origins, it did not result in a wide readership. This treatise was penned by Bernard of Clairvaux (1090–1153) early in his time as abbot, probably around 1127.[27] The treatise originated as a letter to Henry Sanglier, who was bishop of the French diocese of Sens from 1122 until his death in 1142. Bernard begins his letter with the claim that his account of the conduct and office of bishops (*De moribus et officio episcoporum*) was in response to Henry's request for counsel. Bernard's goal in writing to Henry was to make a theological and ecclesiastical connection between the conduct and office of a bishop and the monastic life.[28] Even though Bernard clearly acknowledged that a bishop has greater authority than a monk or even an abbot, Henry ought to listen carefully to Bernard's advice and correction. Indeed, at the heart of the moral character of a bishop lay the monastic virtues of chastity, charity, and humility. Of those three, the most important was humility, and Bernard spends almost half of his treatise describing what this virtue is and how a bishop ought to practice it.[29] In

26. Paris, Bibliothèque nationale de France, MS lat. 12262, fol. 117v: "Pro uiuis et defunctis offerte [*corr. ex* offerre] sacrificium, panem scilicet et uinum, que sacrificata per spiritum sanctum, in uerum Christi corpus et sanguinem transeunt. Quando autem in calice aqua uino miscetur, Christo populus adunatur. Nam si uinum quis offerat tantum, sanguinis est sine nobis; si uero aqua sit sola plebs est sine Christo. Quando autem utrumque miscetur sacramentum celeste perficatur, cuius perceptione corpus et anima fidelium uiuificatur. Episcopus, sacerdos, leuita nomina sit officiorum, non meritorum, nec ideo sancti sunt [quia hec sunt, *interlin.*], nisi uirtutem habuerint nominum suorum. Audiat, credat, conseruet fraternitas uera que de officio uero prelibata svnt."

27. Bernard of Clairvaux, *De moribus* is printed in *Sancti Benardi Opera* volume 7, 100–31. See also the English translation with a critical introduction in Newman and Stiegman, *Bernard of Clairvaux*, 37–82.

28. Newman and Stiegman, *Bernard of Clairvaux*, 24–25.

29. Bernard of Clairvaux, *De moribus*, c.3.8 (7.107), translation in Newman and Stiegman, *Bernard of Clairvaux*, 47; cc. 5.17–8.32 (7.113–27), translation in Newman and Stiegman, *Bernard of Clairvaux*, 56–77.

the last chapter, Bernard turns his attention to the pride and arrogance of monastic communities that were seeking exemption from episcopal jurisdiction. This is an odd way to end the treatise, given the fact that the Cistercian order lobbied the papacy continually for such exemptions, and by the thirteenth century, the order's monasteries could not be visited by a local bishop.[30] One scholar has argued that the whole point of Bernard's letter to bishop Henry was to remind him that if he did claim any jurisdiction over a Cistercian monastery, he must have the correct disposition as a good bishop, and that this disposition would prevent him from doing any harm to a monastic community.[31]

The particularity of *De moribus* may explain why it had limited dissemination. It was certainly included in nearly every collection of Bernard's letters, but there are very few copies of it circulating as a separate work.[32] Some of these witnesses treat the text as a resource for moral theology, and only one is explicit in recognizing that this text could educate a future bishop. That witness, *Munich, Clm 14834*, is a manuscript composed of three booklets from the late twelfth-century. The third booklet, based on the scribal hand and its contents, originated in northern France and may have been bound later with the other two booklets (both of which were copied in Germany during the same period) in the fourteenth century.[33] This third booklet begins with Bernard's complete treatise, which is followed by a set of *sententie*, or short theological statements, that concern the nature of the church and its leaders.[34] For example, the first statement reads:

> It was said to Peter three times: *Feed my sheep*. Every pastor ought to feed <his sheep> in three ways: namely, by the example of a good life and of a holy manner of life; exhortations, which are to be accomplished in teaching and in instructing in a moral

30. Pfurtscheller and Schreiber, *Die Privilegierung des Zisterzienserordens*.

31. Boquet, "Le gouvernement de soi et des autres," 279–96.

32. I have found only ten manuscript copies of *De moribus* as a treatise from the twelfth century, and two of them are only partial copies: Paris, Bibliothèque nationale de France (=BNf), MS lat. 576, fols. 106r-118r; Paris, BNf MS lat. 2939, fols. 91v–111v; Paris, BNf MS lat. 2943(1), fols. 82v–84v; Munich. Bayerische Staatsbibliothek, Clm 14834, fols. 71r–84v; Paris, BNf MS lat. 3702, fols. 109r-v (excerpt, cc. 2–3); Paris, BNf MS lat. 2571, fols. 92v–101r (excerpt, cc. 6–9); Troyes, Mediatheque de Troyes MS 343, fols. 1r–16v; Admont, Stiftsbibliothek, MS 380, fols. 79r–91r; Melk, Stiftsbibliothek, MS 248, fols. 84v–94b; Neustift/Novacella, Augustiner-Chorherrenstift, Cod. 282, fols. 15r–25v.

33. See the catalogue description by Anja Freckmann on handscriftenportal.de: https://resolver.staatsbibliothek-berlin.de/HSP0006DCD00000000.

34. Munich. Bayerische Staatsbibliothek, Clm 14834, fols. 71r–84v (*De moribus*); 85r–90r (*sententie*), which may be attributed to Bernard.

> manner; by prayer that he <the pastor> may be worthy to be heard on behalf of the laity.[35]

The third item on this last booklet is a copy of the *Formulae for spiritual understanding* (*Formulae spiritalis intelligentiae*) by Eucherius of Lyon (ca. 380–ca. 449), which is a patristic primer for spiritual exegesis. There follows a series of theological *sententie* from the school of Anselm of Laon on the Trinity and the creation of humanity, a homily by Anselm of Canterbury, an anonymous sermon on Matthew 11.12 (which concerns those who would violently plunder the kingdom of God, and could easily be applied to how a bishop treats his temporalities), a letter of Jerome about the interpreting the parable of the prodigal son, an anonymous treatise on baptism and additional theological *sententie* from the school of Anselm of Laon. All in all, this is similar to our manuscript example of Gregory's *Regula pastoralis*: Bernard's text is joined with other resources that would contribute to the formation of a good prelate.

SPIRITUAL EXEGESIS AND SCRIPTURE IN THE LITURGY

Given that it was acceptable to add relevant texts to these two major resources for forming prelates, one might expect that if Langton were interested in this topic, he could have composed a companion text. He was not averse to writing treatises that were beyond his teaching responsibilities, and so it would have been a natural response to the formation of prelates to compose a text with a title such as *De prelato*.[36] However, no such text has emerged and instead we find Langton continually returning to what a good prelate ought to be and to do in his lectures on Scripture. To determine why he approached this topic in his biblical lectures, we must outline two additional contexts: the nature of biblical exegesis in the late twelfth century and the liturgical context.

35. Munich. Bayerische Staatsbibliothek, Clm 14834, fol. 85r: "Ter dictum est: *Pasce oves meas.* Omnis pastor tribus modis debet pascere : exemplo scilicet bone uite et conuerascionis sancti ; exhortationes que fit docendo et moraliter instruendo ; oratione ut dignus sit exaudiri pro subditis." The term *subditus* literally means "subject" and could refer to anyone under the jurisdiction of a prelate, clergy and laity alike. However, in most uses the author has the laity in mind—and Langton, as we shall see, certainly uses the word with that intention.

36. See Quinto, *Stefano Langton*, 41–57, 77–90.

Medieval Spiritual Exegesis and Classical Rhetoric

In the narrative of twelfth-century theology, Stephen Langton has been assigned to the "biblical-moral school." This category was an invention of the German historian Martin Grabmann as he traced out the development of scholastic theology to the time of Thomas Aquinas.[37] The category's content and contours, however, were really provided by Beryl Smalley in her lifelong research on the study of the Bible in the Middle Ages.[38] While Smalley intended to establish the importance of biblical scholarship primarily in the twelfth and thirteenth centuries, the unintended consequence was that the "biblical-moral school" became shorthand for unsophisticated and often facile exegesis. There was apparently an obsession with spiritual interpretation among exegetes like Langton, which was free-ranging, arbitrary, and more focused on moral teaching without possessing necessarily any theological and philosophical rigor. There was certainly a theoretical nod towards the importance of literal exegesis (which was purportedly a sign of more sophisticated theological work), but the actual hermeneutical activity of this school often demonstrated little commitment to the dictum, "spiritual expositions come from the literal sense itself."[39] Added to this account was another negative assessment: Langton and his contemporaries apparently were deeply suspicious of speculative theology, especially when the point of departure was not the exposition of the sacred page.[40]

I would argue that we need to reconfigure this account in order to establish a more historically accurate intellectual context of Langton's exegetical work. This reconfiguration requires two important modes of explanation: first, we need to conceptualize Langton's practice of expounding the Bible in the larger theoretical framework that had been provided by Augustine of Hippo. Second, we need to account for the practical resources that classical rhetoric provided for a theologian like Langton, because therein lay an important pedagogical strategy.

37. Grabmann, *Geschichte der scholastischen Methode*, 2:476–509.

38. Smalley, *Bible in the Middle Ages*, 196–263.

39. Langton himself states this relationship between literal and spiritual exegesis more than one occasion. In his second prologue to his lectures on Genesis, he plays on the signification of the four horns emanating from the ark of the covenant: *In Exodo legitur*, *Super Genesim*, P2.6 (P fol. 2rb): "Per iiii cornua quibus aduersarios uentilare debemus, iiiior modi expositionis in scriptura: historice, allegorie, tropologice, anagogice. Historice Ierusalem ciuitas illa terrena, allegorice ecclesia militans, tropologice anima, anagogice ecclesia triumphans. Et ita cornua procedunt ex ipso, quia ex ipsa littera proueniunt expositiones."

40. Baldwin, "Master Stephen Langton," 811–12. See n.58, below.

Augustine's *De doctrina christiana* had an inordinate impact on medieval thought as it was one text from his corpus that was consistently copied and read throughout the Middle Ages. Among the many methodologies and concepts that Augustine advanced, two in particular played an important role in biblical exegesis as almost aphorisms for medieval theologians in the twelfth and thirteenth centuries. The first was that Christians were to "meditate on what we read <in Scripture> till an interpretation be found that tends to establish the reign of charity."[41] This provided a great deal of flexibility and creativity in presenting how one could understand a particular passage, and that flexibility emerged in the three forms of spiritual interpretation. Augustine, however, did advocate for the importance of the literal reading of the sacred page, and so the second aphorism was that "nothing is entirely drawn from allegorical obscurities which is not stated plainly elsewhere."[42] The argument, put forward by Smalley and others, is that as biblical exposition developed in faculties of theology in the medieval university, the expositors made a tighter connection between the literal sense of a given passage and any allegorical or tropological reading of that same passage. The connection became so tight that it ultimately collapsed for some theologians as they drew upon a developing theory of authorial intent: this collapse allowed some to argue that what was previously read as allegory could now be understood as the literal sense of Scripture because it was the meaning that God as author had intended.[43]

For theologians like Langton, however, the relationship between literal and spiritual exegesis was more in keeping with the two Augustinian aphorisms: as long as the spiritual reading furthered charity and its content was found to have been stated more plainly elsewhere in Scripture, then the exposition was both valid and coherent. While the allegorical and tropological exposition might appear to be arbitrary to the modern reader in relation to how Langton read the passage before him literally, the former was based on a broader vision of the teaching of Scripture as a whole and so based on the assumption that Scripture interprets Scripture.[44]

41. Augustine, *De doctrina christiana*, 3.15.23 (91).

42. Augustine, *De doctrina christiana*, 2.6.7–8 (35–6).

43. Minnis, *Medieval Theory of Authorship*. On the collapse between literal and spiritual readings, see Smalley, "William of Auvergne," 121–82 and Ocker, *Biblical Poetics*. See also Ginther, *Master of the Sacred Page*, 64–72.

44. The commitment to this Augustinian framework demanded that the literal sense receive scholarly attention. Langton is inconsistent to how much attention he gives to the literal sense in the Genesis commentary (sometimes providing detailed expositions of the grammatical, historical and philosophical elements of the sacred text, while at other times simply stating: *littera patet*—"the literal meaning is clear"). However, Langton was the first to provide a detailed set of lectures on Peter Comestor's

What often goes unmentioned is the fundamental role that classical rhetoric played as a pedagogical resource in medieval exegesis, in addition to providing some of the basic analytical tools for reading Scripture. I want to point to the importance of memory in biblical exegesis in particular, but the important point is not necessarily about calling to mind the relevant biblical and patristic sources to expound (although this was a key element in Langton's intellectual culture). Instead, it is important to consider the role Scripture itself could function as a mnemonic tool. Classical rhetoric, according to the *Rhetorica ad Herennium*, taught that connecting well-known physical objects and space to abstract concepts trained the mind to recall those concepts quickly and accurately. This is often called a "memory palace" that one could traverse in one's mind.[45] While classical rhetoric assumed that this art of memory would draw upon familiar objects in the real world, medieval thinkers often used biblically based images to accomplish the same type of mnemonics. Perhaps the clearest example is Hugh of St-Victor's *De arca Noe*, which used the description of the ark to create a virtual space upon which to hang various theological concepts.[46]

Using Scripture as mnemonic device was a strategy Langton appears to have embraced right from the beginning of his teaching. His inaugural sermon, from which he launched his magisterial career, is a prime example of his exegetical strategy in terms of his hermeneutical commitments, but it also reveals an important pedagogical strategy.[47] The sermon draws upon the Exodus narrative and is presented in three parts: first, he uses the ten plagues to spell out the ten dispositions that can be obstacles to good theological study, where each plague signifies a sinful act or attitude that must be countered by the appropriate virtue. Then, he uses the fact that the Israelites took grain from the Egyptians as an opportunity to talk about the importance of the liberal arts as a propaedeutic to studying theology.[48] In the final section, he uses the story of the reception and nature of manna as an opportunity to discuss the role Scripture plays in the discipline. The Exodus

Scholastic Histories (*Historia scholastica*), a resource for literal exegesis that was a complete historical account of all of Scripture. See Clark, *Making of the* Historia scholastica.

45. *Rhetorica ad Herennium*, 3.16–24 (204–24).

46. Lewis, "History and everlastingness," 203–22; Sicard, *Hugues de Saint-Victor*.

47. The sermon was edited by Roberts, *Studies in the Sermons*, 224–37 (hereafter cited as Langton, "Inaugural Sermon").

48. This is reminiscent of Augustine's imagery of the Israelites plundering the Egyptians of their gold and silver prior to their exit. Augustine had used this narrative moment to justify the value of using "secular" learning for the sake of Christian teaching: Augustine, *De doctrina Christiana*, 2.40.60. Langton has a similar strategy but uses the image of the Israelites taking grain from the Egyptians because it first had to be beaten (separating the wheat from the chaff) into a useful resource and then consumed.

narrative becomes a structure to which Langton can attach key theological ideas with the intent that when the auditor of his sermon hears that Scriptural text read again, he could call to mind the concepts of Langton's sermon.[49]

Was this calling to mind simply a hopeful thought on Langton's part? Possibly, but it was grounded in the fact that Langton and his students repeatedly encountered nearly the whole of Scripture on an annual basis. Scripture was embedded into the liturgy of the Eucharist, although by the twelfth century, continuous reading of Scripture (such as reading the entire Pentateuch during Lent) was replaced by excerpts or pericopes. It did mean that Langton and his students would have heard much of the book of Genesis as part of the Eucharistic liturgy during Lent as well as part of the readings of the divine office. As equally important was the fact that students of theology were required to read Scripture continuously. While they could not take the leisurely pace of monastic meditation in their reading, students were nonetheless challenged to read the sacred page repetitively as a form of discipline and practice.[50] This continual reading certainly contributed to a memory drenched in biblical imagery and terminology. At the same time, we ought to keep in mind that lectures like that of Langton could be called to mind as they encountered again and again a part of Scripture at a Sunday Eucharist, the celebration of a feast day that was replete with Scriptural readings, parts of the divine office, or in their own private readings.[51]

LANGTON'S ACCOUNT OF PRELACY

In this manner, Langton subtly contributed to the formation of prelates by connecting his accounts of prelacy to his biblical exposition, first for his students in the classroom and then for later readers of his commentaries. Each commentary was almost a silently added text to either Gregory's *Regula pastoralis* or Bernard's *De moribus*. In order to understand the scope

49. See also *Super Genesim*, 3, n.23 (P 9ra): "Hoc est quod filii Ysrael pasti sunt farina conspersa quam tulerant de Egypto, et postea manna in deserto, demum in terra promissionis fructibus terre illius. Ecce modus progrediendi: prius enim recordatio peccatorum, demum iusticia in presenti, tertio iocunditas in patria. Ysaias [Is. 30:21]: *erunt occuli tui uidentes preceptum Domini, et aures tue audientes post tergum monentis.* Peccatores enim habent Deum a tergo qui monet eos ad penitentiam. In Euangelium [Mt. 18:11]: *uenit Filius Hominis saluare quod perierat.*"

50. Hugh of St-Victor, *Didascalicon*, 3.6–7; 6.1 (PL 176.769–770, 799); *Didascalicon of Hugh of St-Victor*, 90–91, 135.

51. Reilly, "Bible as Bellwether," 10–11.

and content of Langton's account of prelacy, it would be helpful to return momentarily to his inaugural lecture.

Langton's exposition of the ten plagues produces a rather odd account of what things can be obstacles to theological study. Some are commonplace: corruption of the world that drowns out good works (water into blood); vain talk (frogs); harmful speech of a biting tongue (stinging insects); anxiety (flies); brutish behavior (cattle death); and pride (boils).[52] But the signification of the four remaining plagues is perhaps unexpected: secular power that oppresses the powerless or the poor (hail); soothing flattery (locusts); approbation of another person's sin (darkness); and the loss of temporal prosperity (firstborn death).[53] These four are more social challenges than just moral failings, and one might push this further by noting that these are challenges that are connected to leadership. Taken together, these last four plagues signify actions of a leader whose integrity is undermined when he fails to confront these problems: If they do not speak up on behalf of the poor and powerless, if they act contrary to the Gospel because of someone's flattery, if they approve of another person's sin, and if they are obsessed by any loss of temporal goods because of their leadership position—all this diminishes their capability to be good leaders. The role of a master of the sacred page converges with a prelate because both are charged with teaching the faithful, and ultimately, the students of the master would one day become teachers themselves, as future masters, priests, archdeacons, or bishops.[54] Reading the plagues as signifying these obstacles to good leader-

52. Langton, "Inaugural Sermon," 226–28.

53. Langton, "Inaugural Sermon," 228–30.

54. *Super Genesim*, P1.7 (P 2ra): "Predicator autem ad modum prelati [*corr. ex.* philosophi] debet respondere, scilicet *ducentorum denariorum panes non sufficient eis* [Io. 6:7]. Centenarius perfectionem notat; ducenti ergo duplicem perfectionem notat in prelatis: unam uite, aliam doctrine. Et prelatus debet intelligere quod hec duo non sufficiunt ad pascendum si ne gratia. Sed dicit Andreas: *est puer unus hic*, etc. [Io. 6:9] Similiter et predicator, si sit Andreas id est uirilis in opere, et frater Simon id est obediens Christo, dicit: *est puer unus hic*, etc. Puer quasi paruam et minus sufficientem habens doctrinam. Si uelit loqui de aliqua auctoritate v librorum Moysi, dicat: *est puer unus hic habens v panes ordeaceos*. Si de Psalmis et prophetis, dicat: *est puer unus hic habens duos pisces*. Et si ita faciet, Dominus in tantum multiplicabit predicationem suam quod sufficiet illis quibus predicat, et etiam in tantum de residuo habebit quod poterit predicare etiam immundissimam uitam habentibus. Et hoc est replere xii cophinos de fragmentis. Per cophinos enim qui sunt uasa in quibus stercora deportantur, inmunditia uite designatur; per fragmenta subtilitas predicationis diuine intelligitur. Bene autem dicitur, *est puer unus hic*. Predicator enim mundam et angelicam debet habere uitam et 85 innocentem, sicut puer innocens est. Unde in Apocalpysi legitur quod Iohannis accepit librum de manu angeli [vid. Apc. 10:8–10]; uitam enim debet habere angelicam a quo suscipiunt subditi exemplum et disciplinam."

ship points to a central component of Langton's account of prelacy: power as it is understood in relation to leaders and their followers.

Leadership and the Creation of Humanity

In the Genesis commentary, Langton's understanding of pastoral leadership has its context in the creation of humanity in general. He notes in his literal exposition that the *Ordinary Gloss* (a highly authoritative source for Langton and his students[55]) describes that there are three facets to human dignity in its creation: "in the deliberateness of creation because humanity was created with deliberateness; in the dignity of leadership because humanity was made to be 'lord of all things;' <and> in the excellence of formation because humanity was made IN THE IMAGE AND LIKENESS OF GOD."[56] Langton distinguishes image as referring to humanity's nature and likeness to grace conferred at creation, and humanity lost the latter through sin.[57] This lays the groundwork for his allegorical reading: Genesis 1:26 can be read about the church: humanity in this verse signifies the prelate as a judge related to the dignity of leadership. His calling is not to harass good Christians, but rather to coerce evil people. To have dominion over all living things then is to have dominion over those who are overly inquisitive (signified by the fish),[58] those who are proud (fowl), and those who lack

55. Smith, *Glossa ordinaria.*

56. *Super Genesim*, 1, n.172 (P 6ra): ". . . in deliberatione creationis quia creatus est cum deliberatione, in dignitate prelationis quia factus est 'dominus omnium,' in excellentia formationis quia factus est *ad imaginem et similtudinem Dei.*"

57. *Super Genesim*, 1, nn.174–175 (P 6ra): "Loquitur Pater ad Filium et ad Spiritum Sanctum dicens, FACIAMUS HOMO AD IMAGINEM, etc. in naturalibus, ad SIMILITUDINEM in gratuitis. Gratuita amisit homo per peccatum sed non naturalia, licet uulneratus sit in eis. Unde uerumtamen in imagine pertransit. Unde homo qui *incidit in latrones* uulneratus est in naturalibus et spoliatus in gratuitis [vid. Lc. 10:30–4]. Diabolus enim rapit que potest et destruit que rapere non potest, sicut aduersarius facit. Item dicitur: 'sicut disposuit facere hominem, ita fecit.' Sed disposuit facere ad imaginem et similitudinem suam, ergo ita fecit eum, ergo homo factus est ad similitudinem Dei. Sed similitudo refertur ad gratuita, ergo homo factus est in gratuitis, ergo homo habuit gratuita in creatione sua. Responsio: non solum dicitur homo similis Deo per gratiam iustificantem sed per innocentiam. Ideo Adam erat similis Deo quia creatus est in innocentia. Unde interlinearis dicit super: 'ad similitudinem innocentie et iustitie.'"

58. The vice or sin of being "overly inquisitive" (curiosis) is a much-misunderstood complaint from the twelfth century (and to some degree into the thirteenth). Critiques of theological curiosity are cast as those who were deeply suspicious of speculative reasoning and the detailed investigation of theological topics. As noted above, the historian John Baldwin attempts to demonstrate that Langton was an "old school" theologian by citing a passage from his commentary on Amos: see above, n.41. However, if Baldwin had just read a few sentences further than what he quoted, he would

self-control (beasts). Langton reinforces this role of a prelate by citing two passages from Paul's letters and then reminds his readers that every prelate will have to account for the fact that he stands between God and the laity and will have to account for their actions.[59]

The loss of grace at humanity's fall did not abolish the natural dignity of leadership, but it clearly impaired it. Langton asserts that with both the image and likeness of God, humanity could have dominion over all living things, but with the loss of the likeness or grace, humanity was de facto inferior to all living things. And yet, this promise of God concerning humanity's dominion was not voided. To explain how this is the case, Langton invokes a rather clumsy analogy. Humanity's relationship to its Creator means that in one way God belongs to all, and having possessed him in this way, humanity possesses all things. If this is the case, then why do people go hungry? Langton responds with the analogy that humanity is like the lord and God is his steward, and one who knows best how to distribute such goods. But this wise steward is hampered by the fact that his lord is stupid and decides to

have created a more balanced portrait of Langton as a theologian: Paris, Bibliothèque nationale de France, MS lat. 505, fol. 46ra: "SUPER TRIBUS SCELERIBUS MOAB [Amos 2.1]. *Moab interpretur ex patre et significat hic theologos qui cum sint ex patre supremo quadem curiositate venerantur verba similiter cadencia et irreverenter secreta dei investigant tota die disputando de trinitate et notionibus et quibus aliis in quibus parva aut nulla est edificatio* animarum. Nec attendunt quod a quo dummodo dicto, stultas et sine disciplina questiones de uita. Theologos ergo talibus [dicens *om.*] dominat dicens: SUPER TRIBUS SCELERIBUS MOAB ET SUPER QUATUOR NON CONVERTAM EUM, id est, Moab, scilicet curiosum theologum, EO QUOD INCENDERIT OSSA REGIS IDUMAEAE USQUE AD CINEREM, id est, eo quod irreuerenter et impudento inuestigant secreta diuinitatis. Nam hoc est succendere usque ad cinerem ossa regis Ydumee, id est, secreta Dei qui est rex Ydumee, id est, terre sicut et celi. Rodere quidem eius ossa possimus sicut canes, sed non succendere uel comminuere" [the bold text is what Baldwin had transcribed]. Langton's complaint here is not inquisitiveness per se, but that in the "curious theologians" it lacks any pastoral goal, and that the inquiry is so obsessive those theologians end up incinerating the theological "bones.". Theologians "can indeed gnaw on those bones like dogs" ("rodere quidem eius ossa possimus sicut canes!"), but not to set them on fire or incinerate them.

59. *Super Genesim*, 1, n. 190 (P 6rb): "Uel de ecclesia. FACIAMUS HOMINEM AD IMAGINEM SUAM Per hominem prelatum intelligere iudicem, qui debet esse iudex non ut uexet bonos, sed ut coerceat malos. UT PRESIT PISCIBUS curiosis; UOLATILIBUS superbis; BESTIIS ferocibus. Unde Apostolus [1 Cor. 2:15]: *spiritualis omnia iudicat et a nemine iudicatur*. "Ubi non deliquimus, ibi pares sumus." Idem [Rm. 13:3–4]: *uis non timere potestatem? Bene fac. Si autem male feceris, time*. Ad Timotheum [1 Tim. 1:9]: *Lex iusto non est posita*. Iudex ergo attendere debet ut habeat Deum super se et homines infra se. Unde Iob [Iob 31:21]: *Si leuaui super pupillum manum meam*, etc. *Timor enim Domini super me* [cf. Ps. 54:6]. Iste enim erat memor quod erat in statu medio apud Deum. *Quod iustum est seruis prestate, scientes quod et Dominum habetis in celum* [Col. 4:1]. Item: *obedite prepositis uestris. Ipsi enim peruigilant quasi reddituri rationem* [Hbr. 13:17] Domino pro ominibus uestris."

distribute his goods in the worst way.[60] Good leadership, then, must avoid the stupidity, and for prelates that means being attuned to God's grace. He points to the sequence of actions in the next few verses: God first blesses, then he commands humanity to grow, and then he gives humanity dominion over all things:

> . . . because first it is necessary that there be God's grace and blessing, and then humanity grows in virtues, and in the multiplication of good works, and then humanity may have dominion over the fish, that is evil people, to direct and rule them; and then it may secure the labor <and> fruit of temporal things. Whence the Apostle [1 Cor. 9:11]: *If we have planted in you*, etc. Again [1 Cor. 9:13]: God thus has ordained that *he who serves at the altar, lives from the altar*. Again, in Galatians [Gal. 6:6]: *Let him who was instructed share with him who instructed him.* In Ecclesiasticus [Ecli. 14:15–16]: *In the division of lots give and receive.* This is the fate of the church, that certain people receive spiritual things while giving temporal or carnal things, SO THAT THEY MAY BE YOURS FOR EATING AND FOR ALL THE LIVING CREATURES OF THE EARTH, because prelates ought to receive so that they may share with the other faithful people those <temporal goods> because they were not only created for the use of human beings, but for animals and birds as it was said to Peter: *Feed, feed my lambs* [Io. 20:15–16], because those who do not have the fleece of temporal things ought to be fed by prelates in two-fold way, bodily and spiritually. He says once *Feed my sheep* [Io. 21:17] because he who has temporal things ought only to be fed spiritually.[61]

60. *Super Genesim* 1, n.191 (P 6rb): "Nota quod si prelatus habeat imaginem et similitudinem Dei, preest omnibus animalibus. Si uero amittit similitudinem, inferior est omnibus animalibus. ET PRESIT Apostolus [cf. Col. 1:16]: *omnia nostra in celo sunt et in terra*. Non mirum quod ipse Deus factus est noster, et in eo possesso possidemus omnia. Unde Ieronimus: "iusto totus mundus diuitie sunt." Et Apostolus [Rm. 8:32]: *filium suum tradidit pro nobis quomodo donauit cum illo*. Si querit quis fex quo ergo nobis omnia dedit qualiter facta sunt omnia nostra, id est iustorum, ergo ex quo disponit ita quod quandoque patimur inediam? Responsio: Ipse quasi procurator noster est, et optime disponit, et stultus est dominus qui uult aliter rem suam disponi quam disponat optimus procurator, qui melius scit disponere quam ipse dominus."

61. *Super Genesim*, 1, n.193 (P 6rb): "MASCULINUM ET FEMINAM CREAUIT EOS DEUS Per masculinum prelatum, per feminam plebem subiectam intellige. REPLETE TERRAM Sancte ecclesie, et subicite eam. Debet enim ecclesia subiecta esse per humilitatem. Et nota ordinem: prius BENEDIXIT DEUS et post dicit CRESCITE, etc, et post DOMINAMINI PISCIBUS MARIS, et post subiunxit ECCE DEDI UOBIS, etc.; quia primo oportet ut sit gratia Dei et benedictio, et post homo crescat in uirtutibus, et multiplicatione bonorum operum, et post dominetur piscibus, id est malis, ut eos dirigat et

The attention that a prelate must give to those who lack temporal goods is Langton's reminder to future prelates that their control of land and wealth was to serve those in greater need and not to serve those who are already rich and powerful. In his moral exposition of Genesis 2:1, Langton reminds his reader that Christ's crucifixion was for everyone, the insignificant and the great people equally, but especially for those who are powerless.[62]

This form of social justice should not obscure the fact that Langton was still a creature of his age. He never questioned that a properly ordered Christian society required a hierarchical understanding of power and responsibility. To begin with, the difference between prelacy and laity was defined in moral terms. In his spiritual exposition of Genesis 1:6, Langton asserts that the waters which the firmament separated signified prelates (*aquas superiores*) and the laity (*aquas inferiores*) "because the life of prelates ought to be separated by far from the life of the laity, <and> because prelates ought to have a higher standard of life by far."[63] The expectations of a prelate's exemplary life are one of only two topics about prelates on which Langton led a disputation. The question he raises is "whether a prelate is bound <to do> works of mercy more than anyone else." This had a secondary question: "whether a prelate is bound to have perfect love," which Langton later defines as being prepared to lose his life for the faith or on

regat, et post laborem fructum percipiat temporalium. Unde Apostolus [1 Cor. 9:11]: *si seminauimus uobis*, etc. Item ita ordinauit Deus ut *qui altario seruit, de altario uiuat* [1 Cor. 9:13]. Item ad Galatas [Gal. 6:6]: *communicet ille qui catechizatur illi qui catechizat eum*. In Ecclesiastico [Ecli.14:15–6]: *in diuisione sortis da et accipe*. Hec est sors ecclesie, ut quidam accipiant spiritualia dando temporalia uel carnalia, UT SINT UOBIS IN ESCAM ET CUNCTIS ANIMANTIBUS TERRE, quia prelati debent accipere ut aliis fidelibus communicent, quia non solum creata sunt ista in usum hominum, sed animalium et auium, ut dictum est Petro: *pasce, pasce agnos meos* [Io. 21:15–6], quia illi qui non habet uellus rerum temporalium dupliciter debent pasci a prelatis, corporaliter et spiritualiter. Semel dicit *pasce oues meas* [Io. 21:17] quia qui habet temporalia spiritualiter debent pasci tantum."

62. *Super Genesim*, 2, n.19 (P 6va–vb): "Et nota quod bene dixit PERFECTI SUNT, etc. Aliter enim uidetur quod crucifixus esset pro maioribus et non pro minoribus, sed pusillum et magnum ipse fecit equaliter, et illi cura est de omnibus reuera crucifixus est pro minoribus et pauperibus, etiam qui sunt pauperes expressius. Item *opera manuum eius* [Ps. 18:2]. Pendens enim in cruce non habuit ubi corpus reclinaret. Unde Apostolus [Rm. 14:15]: *noli cibo perdere illum pro quo Christus mortuus est*; pro peccatoribus enim passus est. Hoc probat latro quem unicum momordit in cruce." We have translated *pauper* as "powerless" rather than "poor" because the former captures both the economic and social implications of this category of humanity.

63. *Super Genesim*, 1, n.69 (P 4va): "Uel allegorice ecclesia est firmamentum quasi in bono confirmata, que habet aquas superiores, id est prelatos, et inferiores, id est subditos. *Et diuidit aquas ab aquis* quia uita prelatorum debet esse longe a uita subditorum diuisa, quia longe excellentiorem debuerunt habere uitam prelati."

behalf of his laity. He clearly answers in the affirmative, and the last part of his solution addresses how a prelate ought to faithfully manage his temporalities for the sake of others.[64]

That moral separation, moreover, was governed by a hierarchical one. As he expounds the second creation narrative of humanity and especially the creation of the first woman (Gen 2:18–25), Langton takes the opportunity to outline the relationship between prelate and laity. When Adam is unable to find a helper among the animal population, this signifies that a prelate ought not to allow a layperson to be equal to him, even though this often happens. The prelate is the leader, and the layperson is his helper, and the relationship is defined by submission of the former to the latter.[65] That submissive relationship had an inviolable rule: if a prelate who was called to a higher standard of morality betrayed that calling, a lay person could not publicly accuse him of immoral behavior. This is Langton's reading of Genesis 9, where Ham discovers his father, Noah, drunk and asleep in the nude. Ham is the evil layperson who "reveals the sin of a prelate to others," whereas his brothers are good laypeople who "conceal the crime of this same prelate and thus to hide it is to do good." The two good sons cover Noah with a blanket while averting their eyes, and therefore, "the faces of the laity ought to be turned away from the evil works of the prelate as it is displeasing to them."[66] This account of "hiding" the crimes of a church leader is certainly offensive to our modern ears, considering the events of the last two decades in the global Roman Catholic Church. However, Langton's position

64. Cambridge, St John's College MS C.7, fol.196ra–vb: The disputed questions begins: "Queritur utrum prelatus pre ceteris ad opera misericordie teneatur. Et ita plusquam alii subuenire [subuenire, *bis*] subditus corporaliter. Hanc questionem precedit alia qua queritur utrum prelatus teneatur habere perfectam caritatem. Quod si est constat quod plusquam ceteri ad opera misericordie tenetur. Quod autem perfectam teneatur habere caritatem."

65. *Super Genesim*, 2, n.132 (P 8va): "Repete hoc: NON EST BONUM ESSE HOMINEM SOLUM QUASI FACIAMUS EI ADIUTORIUM, et est intelligendum de prelato cui cedit in adiutorium plebs subdita, et ex hoc ita faciendum erat ei adiutorium."

66. *Super Genesim*, 9, n.23 (P 12va): "Bibere ergo uinum est delectari in fructu subditorum, sed quando lapsum contrahit ex regimine, sic inebriatur, et sic NUDATUS IN TABERNACULO SUO id est inter subditos, QUIA CUM UIDERIT CAM, PATER CANAAN, id est aliquis malus subditus, nunciat et manifestat aliquis potest relati. Unde autem Cham dicitur pater Canaan. Cham enim interpretatur 'calliditas', Canaan 'commotio', et calliditas, id est sapientia secularis que inimica est Deo, generat commotionem, de qua dicitur: *commouebuntur a fundamentis* [Sap. 4:19]. AT UERO SEM, actiui scilicet, ET IAFETH, boni scilicet subditi, ocultant crimen ipsius prelati, et sic occultare est bene operari. Unde dicit quod pallium imposuerunt humeris suis. Per humerum enim opus designatur. FACIESQUE EORUM ERANT ADUERSE Quod displicet tibi non libenter intueris. Ita ergo facies subditorum debent esse diuerse ab operibus malis prelati ut eis displiceant."

is in keeping with the medieval theological and canonical consensus on the sin of scandal. To expose publicly the sin of a priest or bishop (and often it was a case of sexual sin) undermined the credibility and authority of any church leader, so theologians and canonists argued, and thus threatened the efficacy of sacerdotal ministry.[67]

The separation between prelate and laity was not unbreachable. While prelates may be above the laity, they cannot stay there. In the same way that Eve was intimately connected to Adam by the mode of her creation, so too a prelate must always come down (*condescendat*) to the level of the laity.[68] This "condescension" was not meant as a way of further marking a prelate's superiority, but rather drawing upon a more recent analogy, the prelate ought to be a "shepherd with the smell of the sheep."[69] Langton clarifies that his intention here is positive and ministerially focused by pushing his allegorical reading further: since the "rib" that a prelate gives to the Church is the cardinal virtue of fortitude, and it is joined with the flesh, he is to be a bone for the strong and the flesh for the feeble. This means that a prelate's condescension is accomplished through compassion.[70] The two most common ways to overcome the separation between prelates and laity were preaching and the sacrament of penance. In his spiritual exposition of the

67. Bryan, "Threefold Truth," 29–47.

68. *Super Genesim*, 2, n.135 (P 8vb): "Assumpsit costam Per costam fortitudinem, per carnem intellige infirmitatem, et ad hoc quod ecclesia sit similis prelato, oportet quod prelatus condescendat subditis. Unde Apostolus [1 Cor. 4:16]: *imitatores mei estote*, etc."

69. Pope Francis, quoted in Gomes, "Pope to Priests," https://www.vaticannews.va/en/pope/news/2021-06/pope-francis-priests-students-church-louis-french.html.

70. *Super Genesim*, 2, n.135 (P 8vb): "Hoc nunc Per ossa fortes, per carnem fragiles intellige. Prelatus enim debet esse os fortibus et caro debilibus, et tunc poterit dicere hoc nunc, etc. Apostolus os erat cum dixit [1 Cor. 2:6]: *sapienciam loquimur inter perfectos*; caro fuit cum dixit [1 Cor. 2:2]: *nihil iudicaui me scire nisi Iesum*, etc. Nota: prelatus condescendit subditis per compassionem." This connection between a prelate's "condescension" and compassion is echoed in a sermon Langton preached before a group of bishops: *Sermo ad episcopos* (Sermo 300, Brussels, Bibliothèque royale MS II 953, fols. 123vb–124ra): "In pretaxatis itaque uerbis [=Ps. 106:23–24], septem notare potest lectoris diligentia omnibus qui gubernandis ecclesiis preficiuntur admodum necessaria, quorum tria notari possit in uerbo *descendendi*. Omnis enim qui descendit ab altiori ad imum tandem in eo notatur altitudo. Quia uero qui uilis uiolentia impellere non proprie descendere [*recte*, doscendere *ms*], immo potius cardere uel ruere dicitur. In eo intelligitur spontanea humiliatio. Et quoniam ad eos quibus compatimur sine corpore, tamen mente descendimus. In eodem innuitur compassionis affectio. Quia uero omnis homo timet in mari, nomine maris datur intelligi sollicitus timor sine timida sollicitudo. In eo autem quid subiungitur *facientes operationem*, suo nomine designatur operatio. In eo quod subidicitur *in aquis multis,* operis continuatio quia non debet prelatus tantum laborare circa diuites et potentes, sed circa pauperes et ignobiles et generaliter cura totam in latitudinem sibi commissam."

sin of Adam and Eve in Genesis 3:10, Langton draws an intimate connection between preaching and confession: if people avoid hearing a preacher because they say it is better to be ignorant than to know of their sins, ". . . they speak foolishly because so many times the obstinate are called upon through grace at the occasion of preaching." Those who avoid the words of the preacher are like Adam and Eve, who hid when they heard the voice of God after they had eaten the fruit of the tree of knowledge of good and evil.[71]

Bishops had been charged with preaching since the very beginning of Christianity, and it is one of the responsibilities highlighted in Gregory's *Regula pastoralis*. Langton's magisterial career took place in a period of major changes to how Christians were taught, and that included expanding the category of who was able to preach. Itinerant preachers had become a phenomenon by the mid-twelfth century, and bishops, along with the papacy, were concerned that uneducated or misinformed people were preaching ideas and practices that were contrary to the Christian faith. This led to the introduction of new canon law to regulate (and really, restrict) itinerant preachers. Such preachers would have to be licensed by the bishop before they could speak publicly. As parish priests gained a theological education at a local cathedral school or a university, they too were granted permission to give regular Sunday homilies.[72] Sometimes lost in this narrative of change is the constant of episcopal preaching. For Langton, a prelate had a responsibility to preach and, furthermore, to preach with his words and with his actions, both of which had been touched by God's grace: "the prelate must understand that these two things [perfection of life and doctrine] are not sufficient for feeding <Christians> if there is no grace."[73]

71. *Super Genesim*, 3, n.27 (P 9ra–rb): "Adam audiuit uocem Domini et timuit, et nichilominus se abscondit. Eodem modo contingit in ecclesia: multi enim sunt qui audita predicatione siue uerbo Dei timent, et tamen abscondunt peccatum latebris consciencie, nec uolunt illud confiteri. Sed tamen deberent occurrere omino cum Adam per confessionem, et non dicere cum | seruo pigno: *Domine, timui te, quia homo austerus es* [Lc. 19:21], *et ideo abscondi talentum tuum* [Mt. 25:25]. Et sicut Adam fugit a facie Domini, ita multi fugiunt ab instantia predicationis ne eam audiant, dicentes: 'nolimus audire predicationem; melius est ignorare quam scire, quia *seruus sciens ualpulabit*,' [cf. Lc. 12:47] etc. Sed stulte dicunt, quia multitociens uisitantur per gratiam etiam obstinati occasione predicationis."

72. The literature on medieval preaching is vast, but see the summative account in Muessig, "Sermon, Preacher and Society"; as well as Bériou, *Pouvoirs de l'éloquence*.

73. Super Genesim, P1, n.7 (P 2ra): "Predicator autem ad modum prelati debet respondere, scilicet d*ucentorum denariorum panes non sufficient eis* [Io.6:7]. Centenarius perfectionem notat; ducenti ergo duplicem perfectionem notat in prelatis: unam uite, aliam doctrine. Et prelatus debet intelligere quod hec duo non sufficiunt ad pascendum si ne gratia."

The history of penance from the twelfth century onwards rarely gives attention to the prelate. This is understandable as this century saw the formal establishment of the parish priest hearing confession and imposing satisfaction. But what became the standard practice of the sacrament of penance did not reach its full articulation until the thirteenth century. The Third Lateran Council (1179) began to regularize the role and function of a parish priest, but it was not fully completed until the Fourth Lateran Council (1215).[74] This "inter-conciliar period" was a period of change in practice and doctrinal development, and this was the theological and ecclesial context that Langton inhabited. His assertion that prelates had a role in penance is in part an echo of Gregory's *Regula pastoralis*, but also because he saw that episcopal involvement was, like preaching, a required constant in a period of immense upheaval and change.

It was clearly impractical for a bishop to be solely responsible for the sacrament of penance, given the size of most dioceses in the medieval Latin church. That did not void the fact that canon law asserted that the bishop was the "proper priest" of everyone in his diocese.[75] There were specific cases that had to be reserved for the bishop to hear the confession and impose satisfaction, but these were the most egregiously sinful acts.[76] By the time Langton left Paris for Canterbury, most bishops were delegating their personal role in penance to an official in their household, and later Langton, as an archbishop, would recognize that even diocesan clergy were hesitant to confess to their ordinary.[77] And yet, Langton, as a master of theology, insisted that a prelate ought to be involved in hearing confession and imposing satisfaction, a point he makes while expounding the account of Adam naming all the animals brought to him by God (Gen 3:19–20).[78]

74. Cusato, "Radical Renewal," 307–18.

75. Goering, "Internal Forum," 184.

76. Goering, "Internal Forum," 182, 196–97.

77. Goering, "Internal Forum," 185, quoting Langton at the Council of Oxford (1222).

78. Super Genesim, 2, n. 123 (P 8va): "ADDUXIT Nota: Deus format animalia et adducit ad Adam. Ita Deus innouat hominem per gratiam, et cum conteritur, confugit ad prelatum et confitetur. Hoc est quod dicit in Euangelio [Lc. 5:14; Mt. 8:4]: *mundare ualde, et ostende te sacerdoti.* UT UIDERET QUID UOCARET Nota: prelatus non statim debet dare absolutionem et remissionem, etc., sed prius debet uidere utrum contristatus sit nec ne, et postea cum discrestione absoluere. OMNE ENIM QUOD, etc., hoc est dixit: *Quodcumque solueris super terram* [Mt. 3845 16:19], etc. APPELLAUIT NOMINIBUS SUIS. Nota: prelatus dat alicui quandoque nomen suum, quandoque alienum. Dat nomen suum, id est sibi congruum, quando iudicat de eo secundum quod est. Dat nomen alienum quando palpat uitium subditi de quibus dicit: *ue uobis qui iustificatis impium pro muneribus* [cf. Is. 6:22–23]. Item Osee [Os. 4:8]: *peccata populi mei commedunt.* Item Ysaias [Is. 5:20]: *ue hiis qui dicunt bonum malum*, etc."

CONCLUSIONS

Langton's discussion of prelates and penance perhaps points to the fact that he was more idealistic than practical, and this may simply be because his vantage point was from the magisterial chair and not the cathedral chair. Nevertheless, his account of prelacy demonstrates that he shared a common concern with many of his fellow theologians and ecclesiastical reformers about the state of the episcopacy. The life and actions of a bishop could not be overwhelmed by the political and economic pressures of being a bishop in the later Middle Ages. Current and future bishops must be made aware that all the power they possess and all the responsibility laid upon them must be driven by a commitment to pastoral care. That could only be accomplished through shaping habits of mind. At the heart of that formation was reading Scripture as both as a resource for thinking theologically about the prelate's role and as a mnemonic tool to recall what that theology was.

It is difficult to assess how successful Langton was in educating Christian leaders in the late twelfth century. On the one hand, the decades that followed Langton's magisterial career saw an increased focus on pastoral care, and much of that was due to the leadership of bishops across medieval Europe.[79] However, we cannot say with much confidence that Langton's teaching at Paris was a major catalyst. He was part of a circle of masters who shared a common commitment to theological education.[80] And, it is not coincidental that a certain Lothar of Segni studied at Paris in the 1180s (leaving to go to Bologna around 1187), who would go on to become Pope Innocent III in 1199 and later spearhead the Fourth Lateran Council. Whether this future pope ever sat at the feet of Langton, we cannot say. Indeed, it has been difficult to determine who exactly were members of Langton's school at Paris, as the documentary evidence rarely provides insight into the names of students at a medieval university. Perhaps the only hope of assessing the impact of Langton's account of prelacy while a Parisian master is to take a more careful look at his approach to pastoral care and prelacy while archbishop of Canterbury. That, however, is a project that is outside the scope of this essay and awaits future analysis.

79. See in particular the changes that occurred in England and the role that many bishops played in Gibbs and Lang, *Bishops and Reform*; Boyle, "Robert Grosseteste." For a more recent account of the changes in pastoral care generally, see the essays in Stansbury, *Companion to Pastoral Care*.

80. See the classic study of Baldwin, *Masters, Princes, and Merchants*.

BIBLIOGRAPHY

Ambler, Sophie T. "The Church and Magna Carta in the Thirteenth Century." In *Magna Carta: History, Context and Influence. Papers Delivered at Peking University on the 800th Anniversary of Magna Carta*, edited by Lawrence Goldma, 41–50. London: University of London Press, 2018.

Augustine. *De doctrina christiana*. Edited by J. Martin. Corpus Christianorum Series Latina 32. Turnhout: Brepols, 1982.

Bain, Emmanuel. "Etienne Langton, Commentateur des Proverbes." In *Etienne Langton, Prédicateur, Bibliste, Théologien: Etudes Réunies*, 285–326. Bibliothèque d'histoire Culturelle du Moyen Age 9.Turnhout: Brepols, 2010.

Baldwin, John W. "Maître Etienne Langton, Futur Archevêque de Canterbury: Les Écoles de Paris et La Magna Carta," in *Etienne Langton, Prédicateur, Bibliste, Théologien: Etudes Réunies*. Bibliothèque d'histoire Culturelle Du Moyen Age 9. Turnhout: Brepols, 2010.

———. *Masters, Princes, and Merchants: The Social Views of Peter the Chanter & His Circle*. Princeton: Princeton University Press, 1970.

______. "Master Stephen Langton, Future Archbishop of Canterbury: The Paris Schools and Magna Carta." *English Historical Review* 123.503 (2008) 811–46.

Barrow, Julia. *The Clergy in the Medieval World: Secular Clerics, Their Families and Careers in North-Western Europe, c.800–c.1200*. Cambridge: Cambridge University Press, 2015.

Barubé, Odile. *L'Abbaye du Mont-Saint-Eloi des origines au XIVe siècle*. Poitiers: Imprimerie l'Union, 1977.

Baumann, Daniel. *Stephen Langton: Erzbischof von Canterbury Im England der Magna Carta (1207–1228)*. Studies in Medieval and Reformation Traditions 144. Leiden: Brill, 2009.

Benson, Robert L. *The Bishop-Elect; a Study in Medieval Ecclesiastical Office*. Princeton: Princeton University Press, 1968.

Berardi, Alessia M. "*Vita, scientia, doctrina*: Stephen Langton and the Biblical Model of the 'Good Master' in the Twelfth-century Schools." PhD diss., University of Toronto, 2023.

Bériou, Nicole. *Les pouvoirs de l'éloquence: prédication et pastorale dans la chrétienté latine, XIIe-XIIIe siècles*. Geneva: Droz, 2024.

Bernard of Clairvaux. *De moribus et officio episcoporum*. In *Sancti Benardi Opera*, edited by J. Leclercq and H. Rochais, 8 vols, 7:100–31. Rome: Editiones Cisterciensis, 1957–74.

Boquet, Damien. "Le gouvernement de soi et des autres selon Bernard de Clairvaux Lecture de la lettre 42, De moribus et officio episcoporum." In *Le pouvoir au Moyen Âge Idéologies, pratiques, representations*, edited by C. Carozzi and H. Taviani-Carozzi, 279–96. Aix-en-Provence: Publications de l'Université de Provence, 2007.

Boyle, Leonard E. "Robert Grosseteste and the Pastoral Care." In *Medieval and Renaissance Studies: Proceedings of the Southeastern Institute of Medieval and Renaissance Studies, Summer 1976*, edited by Dale B. J. Randall, 3–51. Medieval and Renaissance Series 8. Durham: Duke University Press, 1979.

Briggs, Charles F., and Cary J. Nederman. "Western Medieval Specula, c.1150–c.1450." In *A Critical Companion to the "Mirrors for Princes" Literature*, edited by Noelle-

Laetitia Perret and Stéphane Péquignot, 160–96. Reading Medieval Sources 7. Leiden: Brill, 2023.

Bryan, Lindsay. "Peter the Chanter's Threefold Truth and the Sin of Scandal." In *From Learning to Love: Schools, Law, and Pastoral Care in the Middle Ages. Essays in Honour of Joseph W. Goering*, edited by Giulio Silano et al., 29–47. Toronto: Pontifical Institute of Mediaeval Studies, 2017.

Caplan, Harry, ed. and trans. *Rhetorica ad Herennium*. Loeb Classical Library. Cambridge: Harvard University Press, 1954.

Carpenter, David A. "Archbishop Langton and Magna Carta: His Contribution, His Doubts and His Hypocrisy." *English Historical Review* 126.522 (2011) 1041–56.

Clark, Mark J. *The Making of the* Historia scholastica, *1150–200*. Studies and Texts 198. Toronto: Pontifical Institute of Mediaeval Studies, 2015.

Clement, Richard W. "A Handlist of Manuscripts Containing Gregory's Regula pastoralis." *Manuscripta* 28 (1984) 23–44.

Crosby, Everett U. *Bishop and Chapter in Twelfth-century England: A Study of the Mensa Episcopalis*. Cambridge: Cambridge University Press, 1993.

Cusato, Michael. "The Radical Renewal of Pastoral Care in the Italian Communes, 1150–250: Prelates, Secular Clergy, and the Mendicant Orders." In *A Companion to Priesthood and Holy Orders in the Middle Ages*, edited by C. Colt Anderson and Greg Peters, 306–45. Brill's Companion to the Christian Tradition 62. Leiden: Brill, 2015.

Ferruolo, Stephen C. *The Origins of the University: The Schools of Paris and Their Critics, 1100–215*. Stanford: Stanford University Press, 1985.

Gibbs, Marion E., and Jane Lang. *Bishops and Reform, 1215–1272: With Special Reference to the Lateran Council of 1215*. London: Oxford University Press, 1934.

Ginther, James R. *Master of the Sacred Page: The Theology of Robert Grosseteste, ca. 1229/30–1235*. Aldershot, UK: Ashgate, 2004.

Goering, Joseph W. "The Internal Forum and the Literature of Penance and Confession." *Traditio* 59 (2004) 175–227.

Gomes, Robin. "Pope to Priests: Be 'Shepherds with "the Smell of the Sheep."'" *Vatican News*, June 7, 2013. https://www.vaticannews.va/en/pope/news/2021-6/pope-francis-priests-students-church-louis-french.html.

Grabmann, Martin. *Die Geschichte der scholastischen Methode*. 2 vols. Darmstadt: Wissenschaftliche Buchgesellschaft, 1909–11.

Gregory I. *The Book of Pastoral Rule*. Translated by George E. Demacopoulos. Crestwood, NY: St Vladimir's Seminary, 2007.

———. *Expositio in Canticum canticorum*. Edited by Pierre-Patrick Verbraken. Corpus Christianorum, Series Latina 144, 3–46. Turnhout: Brepols, 1963.

______. *Règle pastorale*. Edited by Floribet Rommel. Sources chrètiennes, 381–82. Paris: Cerf, 1992.

Heale, Martin. *Prelate in England and Europe, 1300–1560*. York: York Medieval, 2014.

Hugh of St-Victor. *Didascalicon*. PL 176.741–838.

———. *L'Oeuvre de Hugues de Saint-Victor, 3: De archa Noe. Libellus de formatione arche*. Edited by Patrice Sicard. Sous la Règle de saint Augustin 17. Turnhout: Brepols, 2024.

Jerome. Commentarius in Ecclesiasten in *S. Hieronymi opera I: opera exegetica*, Corpus Christianorum Series Latina 72, 147–361. Turnhout: Brepols, 1958.

Lewis, John A. H. "History and Everlastingness in Hugh of St Victor's figures of Noah's Ark." In *Time and Eternity: The Medieval Discourse*, edited by Gerhard Jaritz and Gerson Moreno-Riaño. International Medieval Research 9, 203–22. Turnhout: Brepols, 2003.

Mabillon, Jean. *Veterum analectorum: complectens varia fragmenta et epistolia scriptorum ecclesiasticorum, tam prosâ, quàm metro, hactenus inedita.* 3 vols. Paris: Billaine, 1675–82.

Minnis, A.J. *Medieval Theory of Authorship: Scholastic Literary Attitudes in the Later Middle Ages.* 2nd ed. Philadelphia: University of Pennsylvania Press, 1988.

Muessig, Carolyn. "Sermon, Preacher and Society in the Middle Ages." *Journal of Medieval History* 28.1 (2002) 73–91.

———, ed. *Preacher, Sermon and Audience in the Middle Ages.* New History of the Sermon 3. Leiden: Brill, 2002.

Newman, Martha G. and Emero Stiegman. *Bernard of Clairvaux: On Baptism and the Office of Bishops. On the Conduct and Office of Bishops, on Baptism and Other Questions; Two Letter-Treatises.* Kalamazoo MI: Cistercian Publications, 2004.

Ocker, Christopher. *Biblical Poetics before Humanism and Reformation.* Cambridge: Cambridge University Press, 2002.

Ott, John S. *Bishops, Authority and Community in Northwestern Europe, c.1050–1150.* Cambridge Studies in Medieval Life and Thought, 4th ser., 102. Cambridge: Cambridge University Press, 2015.

Peltzer, Jörg H. *Canon Law, Careers and Conquest: Episcopal Elections in Normandy and Greater Anjou, c.1140–c.1230.* Cambridge Studies in Medieval Life and Thought, 4th ser., 71. Cambridge: Cambridge University Press, 2008.

Pennington, Kenneth. "The Golden Age of Episcopal Elections (1100–300)." In *Episcopal Elections in the Churches: Laws, Practices, Doctrines*, edited by Alberto Melloni and Federico Ruozzi, 154–62. Bologna Studies in Religious History 2. Leiden: Brill, 2025.

Pfurtscheller, Friedrich and Georg Schreiber. *Die Privilegierung des Zisterzienserordens im Rahmen der allgemeinen Schutz- und Exemtionsgeschichte vom Anfang bis zur Bulle Parvus Fons [1265]. Ein Überblick unter besonderer Berücksichtigung von Schreibers Kurie und Kloster im 12. Jahrhundert.* Bern: Lang, 197.

Quinto, Riccardo. "La Parabola del Levitico." In *La Bibbia del XIII secolo: storia del testo, storia dell'esegesi: Convegno della Società Internazionale per lo Studio del Medioevo Latino (SISMEL), Firenze, 1–2 giugno 2001*, 187–267. Florence: SISMEL—Edizioni del Galluzzo, 2004.

———. *Stefano Langton (1228) e La Tradizione Delle Sue Opere: "Doctor Nominatissimus."* Beiträge zur Geschichte der Philosophie und Theologie des Mittelalters, n.F. 39. Münster: Aschendorff, 1994.

Reilly, Diane J. "The Bible as Bellwether: Manuscript Bibles in the Context of Spiritual, Liturgical and Educational Reform, 1000–1200." In *Form and Function in the Late Medieval Bible*, edited by Eyal Poleg and Laura Light, 9–29. Library of the Written Word 27. Boston: Brill, 2013.

Roberts, Phyllis B. *Studies in the Sermons of Stephen Langton Stephanus de Lingua-Tonante.* Studies and Texts 16. Pontifical Institute of Mediaeval Studies, 1968.

Smalley, Beryl. *The Study of the Bible in the Middle Ages.* University of Notre Dame Press, 1970.

———. "William of Auvergne, John of La Rochelle and St. Thomas Aquinas on the Old Law." In *Studies in Medieval Thought and Learning from Abelard to Wyclif*, 121–82. London: Hambledon, 1981.

Smith, Leslie. *The* Glossa ordinaria*: The Making of a Medieval Bible Commentary.* Commentaria 3. Leiden: Brill, 2000.

———. "The Use of Scripture in Teaching at the Medieval University." In *Learning Institutionalized: Teaching in the Medieval University*, edited by J. van Engen, 229–43. Notre Dame: University of Notre Dame Press, 2000.

Southern, R. W. *Scholastic Humanism and the Unification of Europe, Volume I: Foundations.* Oxford: Blackwell, 1995.

St. Jerome: Commentary on Ecclesiastes. Translated by Richard J. Goodrich and David Miller. Ancient Christian Writers 66. New York: Newman, 2012.

Stansbury, Ronald J., ed. *A Companion to Pastoral Care in the Late Middle Ages (1200–1500).* Brill's Companions to the Christian Tradition 22. Leiden: Brill, 2010.

Swanson, Robert N. "Apostolic Successors: Priests and Priesthood, Bishops, and Episcopacy in Medieval Western Europe." In *A Companion to Priesthood and Holy Orders in the Middle Ages*, edited by C. Colt Anderson and Greg Peters, 4–42. Brill Companions to the Christian Tradition 62. Leiden: Brill, 2015.

Tayler, Jerome, trans. *The* Didascalicon *of Hugh of St-Victor.* New York: Columbia University Press, 1961.

Trumbore, Anna and John S. Ott, eds. *The Bishop Reformed: Studies of Episcopal Power and Culture in the Central Middle Ages.* Church, Faith and Culture in the Medieval West. London: Routledge, 2016.

Ubl, Karl. "Carolingian Mirrors for Princes: Texts, Contents, Impact." In *A Critical Companion to the "Mirrors for Princes" Literature*, edited by Noelle-Laetitia Perret and Stéphane Péquignot, 74–107. Reading Medieval Sources 7. Leiden: Brill, 2023.

Vincent, Nicholas. "Stephen Langton, Archbishop of Canterbury." In *Etienne Langton, Prédicateur, Bibliste, Théologien: Etudes Réunies*, 51–123. Bibliothèque d'histoire Culturelle du Moyen Age 9. Turnhout: Brepols, 2010.

Yves de Chartres. *Correspondance.* Edited by J. Leclercq. Paris: Belles Lettres, 1949.

Manuscripts

Admont, Stiftsbibliothek, MS 380
Brussels, Bibliothèque royale, MS II 953
Cambridge, Peterhouse College, MS 112
Cambridge, St John's College, MS C.7
Melk, Stiftsbibliothek, MS 248
Munich. Bayerische Staatsbibliothek, Clm 14834
Neustift/Novacella, Augustiner-Chorherrenstift, Cod. 282
Paris, Bibliothèque nationale de France, MS lat. 576
MS lat. 2571
MS lat. 2939
MS lat. 2943(1)
MS lat. 3702
MS lat. 12262
Troyes, Mediatheque de Troyes, MS 343

7

Reading Reginald Scot in Scotland

Michael F. Graham

While researching and writing books about early modern witchcraft beliefs has been a growth industry in both scholarly and popular publishing in recent decades, this was not always the case. Serious academic study of the European witch-hunt (as distinct from the work of earlier antiquarians and folklorists) was really only born in the late 1960s and early 1970s.[1] This nascent area of inquiry reached Scotland as the 1970s turned into the 1980s and has continued to attract many participants.[2] The popularity of the field makes it hard to see, from today's vantage point, how pioneering Stuart Macdonald's 2002 monograph, the first regional study of the Scottish witch-hunt based on local church court records, actually was. One of Stuart's working hypotheses was that the idea of the demonic pact, which cast Satan as an integral part of what made witchcraft a threat to Christian society, was slow to take hold in Scotland, not really becoming widely accepted until around 1610.[3] One controversial work circulating in English-language print early in the seventeenth century, which challenged the idea that Satan could possibly operate in the way most of those concerned about

1. See, for example, Macfarlane, *Witchcraft*; Thomas, *Decline of Magic*; Midelfort, *Witch Hunting*.

2. For Scotland, the pioneering work was Larner, *Enemies of God*. Many works have been published since then, but see in particular Goodare, *Scottish Witch-hunt*.

3. Macdonald, *Witches of Fife*, 9–10.

witchcraft thought he did, was the Englishman Reginald Scot's *Discoverie of Witchcraft*.[4]

Scot's work was radically skeptical; he was arguably the most skeptical of all sixteenth-century demonologists. In a nutshell, he argued that witchcraft was an impossible crime, that spirits (including the Devil) could not take physical form, and that those who blamed their misfortunes on witches were refusing to recognize that God might allow bad things to happen for God's own unknowable reasons. In other words, Scot argued, they refused to accept the idea of divine providence unless it seemed to be working in their favor. He also held that those who ascribed so much power to the Devil and witches were essentially dethroning God from God's place as lord of all creation. Writing in England in the 1580s, when Catholicism was seen as both heretical and a political threat, Scot likened witchcraft beliefs to Catholic "superstition".

While family tradition holds that Scot's family was originally Scottish, he called Kent home and is known as "England's First Demonologist" (to quote the title of a study by Philip Almond).[5] *The Discoverie of Witchcraft* makes only one brief reference to Scottish witchcraft, a reference which suggests that Scot had very little knowledge of the beliefs and practices of those north of the Tweed. Nevertheless, Scot's book, in its various early modern printings, was read in Scotland and by prominent figures, such as James VI and Sir Walter Scott. It certainly influenced the discussion of witchcraft in Scotland. In this essay, I'd like to discuss how Scottish readers and writers read Scot, based both on writings by Scottish authors which mentioned him, and readers' marks in copies known to have had Scottish owners.

But before looking at Scot's Scottish readers, let's pause briefly to look at Scot's reading of practices surrounding Scottish witchcraft. Outside of one passing reference to St. Andrew's association with Scotland (in a passage likening Catholic saints to "heathen idols,") he mentioned Scotland only once, in a tome of over 550 pages. Early in book two of the work, in a section highlighting what Scot saw as the very loose standards under which legal procedures against suspected witches could be launched, he referred matter-of-factly to a putative Scottish custom according to which each kirk had a wooden box with a slot "into the which any bodie may freelie cast a little scroll of paper, wherein may be conteined the name of the witch, the time, place and fact, &c." Scot wrote that this box would have three locks, the

4. Scot, *Discoverie of Witchcraft* (1584), STC 21864. There were further printings of this work, with little variation in text, in 1651 (Wing S943, Wing S943A) and 1654 (Wing S944), and a slightly expanded edition, including material not by Scot, in 1665 (Wing S945, Wing S945A).

5. Almond, *England's First Demonologist*.

keys to which were held by three different "inquisitors or officers appointed for that purpose," who would open the box every fifteen days, thus allowing someone to accuse a neighbor anonymously without being "shamed with the reproch of slander or malice to his poore neighbour."[6] The personal pronoun implies that Scot assumed that only men would place accusations in the box, despite the prominence of women as accusers and witnesses in Scottish witchcraft cases.[7] In the text, Scot cited the French jurist and demonologist Jean Bodin as the source of this information, although unlike so many of his other (usually disparaging) references to Bodin, Scot did not note where in Bodin's *De la Démonomanie des Sorciers* this nugget could be found. In fact, it comes early in Bodin's book four, where he referred to a "praiseworthy custom of Scotland [also] practiced at Milan" which allowed for such anonymous accusations.[8] Scot and/or his publisher William Brome, doubtless aware that his English-language book would find the vast majority of its readers in Britain and Ireland, were careful to mark it with a printed marginal note: "The Scottish Custo[m]e of accusing a witch." In this context, it is noteworthy that Scot, so critical of Bodin's assertions throughout the work, accepted this claim uncritically, suggesting the Scots had a reputation in England for loose evidentiary standards. While the accusation box with the three "inquisitors" (a term which allowed Scot to associate Scotland with continental, Roman law-based procedures) may have grown out of some sketchy knowledge of the disciplinary procedures of the Scottish Reformed Kirk, it certainly does not reflect any known practice there.

Scot's attitude toward Scottish legal practices may have landed well with his English readers, many of whom would have regarded Scotland as primitive and backward. Other material on Scottish witchcraft printed in England, most notably *Newes from Scotland*, about the North Berwick witch-hunt of 1590–91, while presenting King James VI as a strong and godly ruler eager to rid his kingdom of Satan's servants, also described the torture used against suspects (something not generally done in English witchcraft cases) in grisly detail, perhaps intending to reassure English readers that they lived in a more civilized country.[9] This attitude creeps in despite the fact that the probable author of the pamphlet was a Scot, albeit one who had spent

6. Scot, *Discoverie of Witchcraft*, STC 21864, II.2, 20. The reference to St. Andrew is in the appended "Discourse on Devils and Spirits," 526–27.

7. For women as both accusers and witnesses, see, *inter alia*, Martin, "Devil and the Domestic."

8. Bodin, *Demon-Mania of Witches*, 176.

9. Carmichael, *Newes from Scotland*.

several years during the 1580s in London: James Carmichael, minister of Haddington.[10]

However ill-informed Reginald Scot may have been about Scotland, some Scottish readers felt well-informed about him. The most famous of those, of course, was the royal demonologist King James VI. The king, writing sometime between 1591 and 1597, (and probably with Carmichael as his editor) went right after Scot in the preface to his *Daemonologie*, stating that he felt compelled to write against the damnable opinions of two principally in our age, whereof the one, called Scot, an Englishman, is not ashamed in public print to deny that there can be such a thing as witchcraft; and so maintains the old error of the Sadducees in denying of spirits. The other, called Wierus, a German physician, sets out a public apology for all these craftsfolk, whereby, procuring for their impunity, he plainly betrays himself to have been one of that profession.[11]

Thus, he impugned Johann Weyer as a diabolical fellow traveler, and Scot as a radical skeptic. The king was probably more correct in the second charge than the first, and yet his own work was moderately skeptical, and he drew on Scot to buttress its arguments. Just before calling out Scot and Weyer, James wrote that his work aimed to "resolve the doubting hearts of many, both that such assaults of Satan are most certainly practised, and that the instruments thereof merit most severely to be punished." Either he was overstating the need for his tract, or else suggesting that Scot and Weyer had indeed tapped into wider doubts about the reality of witchcraft.[12]

Daemonologie is presented as a dialogue between two speakers, Philomathes and Epistemon. The former is very skeptical, reflecting many of the views of Reginald Scot (as well, to a lesser extent, of Weyer). Epistemon is made to win the argument, but even he expresses skepticism about some extreme demonological beliefs before concluding at the end that witchcraft is a clear and present danger. In their preface to one version of the work, Lawrence Normand and Gareth Roberts noted that "all the authorities mentioned in the preface to *Demonology* are [also] cited in Scot."[13] They also detected James' borrowing of Scot's interpretation of the Witch of Endor (1 Sam 28) and placing parts of it in the mouths of both of his speakers.

The biblical passage tells of a visit by the Hebrew king Saul to a conjuring woman, despite having previously banished all sorcerers and magicians

10. Normand and Roberts, *Witchcraft in Early Modern Scotland*, 292–3; Goodare, "Witch-hunting," 138.

11. James VI, *Daemonologie*, STC 14364, preface "To the Reader." For Carmichael's role, see Normand and Roberts, 328; Goodare, "Scottish Witchcraft Panic," 65.

12. Ibid.

13. Normand and Roberts, 330.

from his kingdom. Seeking advice in a very difficult period in his war against the Philistines, the king asks her to raise the spirit of the recently deceased prophet Samuel. Saul gets his wish, but the news is not good; he is told that he will suffer defeat and he and his three sons will be slain. This passage was interpreted by most early modern authors on witchcraft as biblical proof that both witchcraft and conjuring were possible, but also to be condemned, given Saul's hypocrisy and the bad end to which he came. In James' *Daemonologie*, the skeptic Philomathes says the witch did not really raise a spirit, and merely tricked Saul into thinking she had, while even the more credulous Epistemon suggests that Saul was not in the room where the alleged spirit was raised, a suggestion which was apparently unique to Reginald Scot.[14]

While that last possibility raised by Scot found its way into Epistemon's side of the dialogue, it would appear that Scot was the source for much of the Philomathean viewpoint in *Daemonologie*. Philomathes, when asked what part of witchcraft belief *he* doubts, says "even of all, for ought I can yet perceive: and namely, that there is such a thing as witchcraft or witches"—a viewpoint much more clearly in line with Scot's than Weyer's.[15] Of course that statement comes early in the first book of the dialogue, and Epistemon will eventually win the argument, despite casting doubt on some maleficient powers. For example, Epistemon denies that spirits can carry human sperm in order to impregnate women, thereby undermining the claims about *incubi* and *succubi* that were central to so many demonological beliefs.[16] Likewise, Epistemon argues, as did Scot, that witches cannot transform themselves into small animals in order to pass through keyholes.[17] Thus James the royal demonologist, while keen to denounce Reginald Scot's foundational views about spirits, nevertheless absorbed significant elements in his critique of demonological theory. James' discussion of demonic hierarchies and the demons associated with the four compass points are even reminiscent of Scot, although Scot likely got these from the *Pseudomonarchia Daemonum* or "Lesser Key of Solomon" in later editions of Weyer.[18] And, contrary to an historical rumor given legs through repetition ever since it appeared in the article on Scot in the original *Dictionary of National Biography* in 1897, James did not order all copies of Scot's book burned when he succeeded to

14. Normand and Roberts, 336–37. Scot's discussion of the Witch of Endor is in Scot, *Discoverie of Witchcraft*, 139–52.

15. *Daemonologie*, 2.

16. *Daemonologie*, 67–868.

17. Clark, "King James's *Daemonologie*, 169. For such transformations see Scot, *Discoverie of Witchcraft*, V.i, 91.

18. Normand and Roberts, 330.

the English throne in 1603.[19] It should be noted here that Stuart MacDonald has questioned the extent to which some of the key demonological concepts that King James argued for, such as the witches' sabbath, or meetings of witches in churches, had much influence in Fife witchcraft cases.[20] Much of his evidence was drawn from kirk session and presbytery registers, where those testifying were neighbors who were probably more concerned about evil done to them by witches than the grander Satanic conspiracy feared by elites such as judges, ministers, theologians and kings.

There are numerous copies of the early printings of the *Discovery of Witchcraft* in Scottish collections, and some of them have early modern readers' notes in them, offering the tantalizing possibility of understanding how less prominent readers read Scot's work. Unfortunately, when one tries to narrow that down to Scottish readers, one faces the problem that many of those books passed through English (or Irish) hands before landing in Scotland. Thus few marginal notes can be explicitly connected to Scottish readings of Scot. (Of course, it should also be noted that many of the copies in libraries outside of Scotland may have been marked by Scottish readers; in some cases, all one has is an owner's name. While certain names may be distinctly Scottish, English or Welsh, some are less obviously so. And it is not always clear that particular notes can be connected with an owner who inscribed their name in a copy.) It is also difficult to gauge how easy it would have been to locate Scot's work in Scottish bookshops, since the necessary sources for that kind of information are scanty. The Edinburgh bookseller/binder Robert Gourlaw did not list it among the 116 London-printed titles in his inventory in September 1585, but then again, it had not been out that long; only thirteen of his titles were from 1584–5.[21] One might wonder how King James and Carmichael acquired the copy or copies that they read. Possibly, Carmichael got one during his exile in England, which ended late in 1587.

One copy of the 1584 printing of Scot's *Discoverie* which appears to have been marked by a Scottish reader in the early seventeenth century, is held in the National Library of Scotland.[22] It was purchased in 1604 by a Mr. Robert Gordon, and, conveniently, is currently bound with the same owner's undated copy of the 1597 printing of King James' *Daemonologie*. The binding containing the two books probably dates to the nineteenth century, so it is not clear that these two books always travelled together,

19. Almond, "King James I," 209–13.
20. MacDonald, *Witches of Fife*, 167, n. 53.
21. Ferguson, "Edinburgh Printers and Stationers."
22. Scot, *Discoverie of Witchcraft*.

but they shared the same owner. The designation "Mr" before a Christian name would probably indicate ministerial credentials, or at least a university degree. It is likely, although not certain, that this was Robert Gordon of Straloch, who would have attained that place-name with his 1608 purchase of the lands of Straloch, ten miles north of Aberdeen. He was a 1597 graduate of Marischal College in Aberdeen who then spent a few years in Paris with the minister Robert Bruce, among others, returning to Scotland by 1601. He became known as a cartographer, and one of his seventeen children was the more famous mapmaker James Gordon of Rothiemay.[23] While Gordon left his copy of *Daemonologie* essentially unmarked, save for his name on the frontispiece, he made a few notes in his copy of the *Discoverie*, suggesting a careful reading of at least the first parts of the book.

On its frontispiece, he inscribed "In otio negotium" [literally: in leisure, labor]. In humanist culture, "negotium" could also mean "the active life," with learning applied in service to country.[24] Perhaps Gordon, who would certainly devote a lot of service to charting and mapping his country, saw in the Kentish gentleman Scot (who had served in the English parliament, written about hop cultivation, had done some of the surveying for the construction of the sea walls at Romney and had chronicled the reconstruction of Dover Harbor) a kindred spirit. If so, he became somewhat skeptical of the English witchcraft skeptic once he started reading.

In the third chapter of the second book of Scot's *Discoverie*, in which he discussed what he thought were the weak evidentiary standards of witch trials, as well as Jean Bodin's credulousness, Scot argued that "if any come in, or depart out of the chamber or house, the doores being shut, it is an apparent and sufficient evidence to a witch's condemnation, without further triall: which thing Bodin never sawe. If he can shew me that feat, I will subscribe to his follie." Gordon, whose time in Paris may have given him some respect for Bodin's writings, underlined the phrase "if he can shew me that feat", and then wrote in the right margin "he wald sei[m] verie curiou[s] to conceif th[e] thing maiste [e]videntlie kn[a]win be all m[as]taris off this art."[25] The tone of the note is suspicious of Scot's true intentions, and echoes King James' doubts about Weyer's motives: "he plainly betrays himself to have been one of that profession." Later on, in book nine, chapter six, where Scot discussed the prophecies contained in the Hebrew Scriptures, particularly Daniel and Joseph's interpretations of royal dreams, Gordon caught him in an error and corrected it, using superscript numbers. Scot's text made

23. Vance, "Gordon, Robert of Straloch."

24. Watson, "Ennobling Reform," 86.

25. Scot, *Discoverie of Witchcraft*, 23.

Pharaoh into a Persian and Nebuchadnezzar into an Egyptian.[26] While that mistake probably originated with the compositors working to print Scot's very typographically complex book, and not with its author, perhaps Gordon of Straloch, with his knowledge of scripture, became disillusioned and gave up reading here; he seems to have left no further marks after this point. If he kept his copy of Scot alongside his copy of James' *Daemonologie*, he seems to have agreed more with the latter, even if he didn't mark it up.

The *Discoverie of Witchcraft* continued to attract Scottish readers throughout the early modern period, but it is a challenge to find anyone who agreed substantially with its arguments. The philosophy professor and mathematician George Sinclair denounced Scot's skepticism in his apparently very popular *Satan's Invisible World Discovered* of 1685. Sinclair, like the conservative English author Joseph Glanvill, from whom he borrowed material (while also bragging that Glanvill had made use of his own earlier printed account of the "Devil of Glenluce") associated the late-seventeenth century growth of witchcraft skepticism with a decline in religious faith, in part because it also questioned the reality of spirits. On the surface the Anglican Glanvill and the committed Presbyterian Sinclair seem like unlikely allies, but they shared a view that religious belief was in decline and that authors such as Reginald Scot and his (mostly) English disciples bore some responsibility for that. Aiming his preface at Scot and some more recent English witchcraft skeptics, Sinclair wrote:

> The other reason why Folk disbelieve Witches and Spirits is atheism. For if a man take good notice, he will find there is of it lurking at the root of the *Saducean Principle*. 'Tis probable that the *Saducees* in Christ's time, were as great Patrons and Advocates of Witches as either *Scot* the *Inglishman*, the *Father of the Witch Patrons, whom King James mentions in his Demonology*, or [John] *Webster*, [John] *Wagstaff*, or the *Author of the Namle Pamphlet*, Printed *Anno* 1659.[27]

Sinclair perhaps read Scot, but rejected his views, a century after their publication. He also praised James VI's *Daemonologie*, calling it "a piece as far beyond all other men's writings on that subject, as [James] himself was beyond all Princes in his time."[28]

But Sinclair's work was a product of a very different age than Scot's own, with witchcraft skepticism put in the general category of "atheism"

26. Scot, *Discoverie of Witchcraft*, 174.

27. Sinclair, *Satan's Invisible World*, A.2.v. I base my assessment of this work's popularity on its frequent reprintings even into the nineteenth century.

28. Sinclair, *Satan's Invisible World*, A.4.v.

(such as that of Thomas Hobbes or Benedict Spinoza, with whose views Scot and King James had not needed to contend).[29] And while a late seventeenth-century Scottish (and anti-presbyterian) jurist like Sir George Mackenzie of Rosehaugh might criticize lax evidentiary standards in witchcraft trials, he never suggested, as Scot did, that the crime itself was an impossible one; the presbyterian Sinclair was careful to remind his readers of this.[30]

It seems surprising that Mackenzie of Rosehaugh, in his compendious *Laws and Customs of Scotland in Matters Criminal* (1678), while specifically citing various demonologists in his discussion of legal issues surrounding witchcraft, never mentioned Reginald Scot. He made several negative references to Weyer, calling him "that great Patron of witch-craft" and used material from Jean Bodin and Martin Delrio (both Catholic authors) to support his view that witches, if properly convicted, should be condemned by the law.[31] But while Scot's name may be absent from Mackenzie's discussion, his ideas are not. Near the beginning of the section treating witchcraft, Mackenzie wrote:

> That there are Witches, Divines cannot doubt, since the Word of God hath ordain'd that no Witch shall live; nor Lawyers in Scotland, seing our Law ordains it to be punished with death. And though many Lawyers in Holland, and elsewhere, do think, that albeit there were Witches under the Law, yet there are none under the Gospel; the Devils power having ceased, as to these, as well as in his giving Responses by Oracles.[32]

Where might those lawyers in Holland have gotten such an idea, which doubtless contributed to the witch-hunt ending much earlier in the Netherlands than elsewhere? Perhaps from reading one of the Dutch translations (and abridgements) of Reginald Scot's work printed in the early seventeenth century, the only versions of Scot's work to appear in a language other than English.[33] A few pages later, Mackenzie bewailed the distortions in testimony created when authorities were too quick to torture suspects, noting that "Many of them confess things which all Divines conclude impossible, as transmutation of their bodies into beasts, and money into stones, and their going through walls and closs doors, and a thousand other ridiculous things, which have no truth nor existence but in their fancy." In fact, not

29. Sharpe, "Witch Historiography," 195–96.

30. Sinclair, *Satan's Invisible World*, A.4.v; Levack, "End of Scottish Witch Hunting," 168.

31. Mackenzie, *Laws and Customs*, 81–84, 90–91, 94, 98.

32. Mackenzie, *Laws and Customs*, 81.

33. *Ondecking van Tovery* (1609); *Ondecking van Tovery* (1637).

all Scottish divines considered such things impossible, but Reginald Scot certainly did.[34]

Ian Bostridge has found that the growing divergence between Scottish and at least some English witchcraft beliefs forced a delay in the publication of Francis Hutchinson's *An Historical Essay Concerning Witchcraft* as Thomas Tenison, Archbishop of Canterbury, was concerned it would anger Scottish opinion during sensitive negotiations over the Act of Union.[35] This skeptical book, which echoed Scot in many ways, did not appear in print until 1718. On the other hand, we know that William Annand, Dean of Edinburgh, had acquired a copy of the 1651 printing of Scot's book; it was listed in the contents of his library up for auction after his death in 1690. Annand's esoteric interest apparently also led him to purchase works by the sometime magician Cornelius Agrippa.[36] It may be worth noting that Annand's Episcopalianism views could have given him a very different religio-political worldview than Sinclair or many of the Scottish negotiators of the Union. Indeed, he had spent the years of the covenants in England, where he attended Oxford University, only returning at the Restoration.[37]

Annand's book collecting points us to the changing role of owning and reading Scot in Scottish (or for that matter, British) intellectual culture as the hunting of witches stopped being a regular occurrence. In 1665 the London stationer Andrew Clark came out with a new, expanded version of the *Discovery of Witchcraft*.[38] This was a book fit for a gentleman of curiosity, and indeed, one of its purchasers was Samuel Pepys, who bought his copy in August 1667. Unlike the printings of 1584, 1651 and 1654, which were compact quartos, this was a fine folio. It also featured additional material which was not by Scot, and which in fact took a much more credulous viewpoint than Scot. Among those apocryphal insertions was a "second" book added to the "Discourse on Devils and Spirits" which Scot had appended to the original *Discoverie of Witchcraft*. This was presented by the publisher in 1665 as "succedaneous to the former [i.e., the original discourse] and conducing to the completing of the whole work, but in fact it was at war with the fundamental concepts of the original.

It was this version of Scot's book that came into the hands of a Scottish gentleman of curiosity (but not leisure), long after the witch-hunt had

34. Mackenzie, *Laws and Customs*, 87.

35. Bostridge, *Transformations*, 34–35.

36. *Catalogue of Excellent and Rare Books* (1690) 8, 13.

37. Mullan, "Annand, William."

38. Scot, *Discovery of Witchcraft* (1665), wing S945 and S945a (slight variations on frontispiece).

ended. Sir Walter Scott apparently purchased it for one pound and one shilling.[39] His copy still had a seventeenth-century binding and had suffered some water damage. The only note he left in the book itself indicated that he found it "very curious." But in other writings, Walter Scott showed evidence of having read Reginald Scot, and he clearly read this particular version of the *Discovery of Witchcraft*, if not this particular copy. Walter Scott appreciated Reginald Scot for his anti-Catholicism as well as for his uses as a source of folkloric belief and a how-to guide to the performance of magic, writing in his own *Letters on Demonology and Witchcraft* that Scot:

> seems to have been a zealous Protestant, and much of his book. . .is designed to throw upon the Papists in particular those tricks in which, by confederacy and imposture, the popular ideas concerning witchcraft, possession and other supernatural fancies were maintained and kept in exercise; but he also writes on the general question with some force and talent, considering that his subject is incapable of being reduced into a regular form, and is of a nature particularly seductive to an excursive talent. He appears to have studied legerdemain for the purpose of showing how much that is apparently unaccountable can nevertheless be performed without the intervention of supernatural assistance, even when it is impossible to persuade the vulgar that the Devil has not been consulted on the occasion.[40]

Walter Scott was obviously reading Reginald Scot as a curious repository of esoteric ideas, not as a controversialist in current debates. With confidence in progress, Walter Scott declared that Reginald Scot's catalogue of witchcraft-related beliefs "serves to show what progress the English have made in two centuries in forgetting the very names of objects which had been the sources of terror to their ancestors of the Elizabethan age."[41]

At the time of his death in 1832, Scott was in the early stages of writing a novel about which both his publisher Robert Cadell and his son-in-law J.G. Lockhart had serious doubts. Bordering at times on self-parody, Scot intended to write it as a report from a correspondent describing the impressive collection of books and other historical artifacts amassed by "Jonathan Oldbuck of Monksbarns," with Oldbuck as a thinly-veiled stand-in for Scott himself and Monksbarns representing his estate of Abbotsford in the Scottish Borders. As it happens, this fragmentary work did not find its way into

39. *Discovery of Witchcraft* (1665). MS note on half-title, across from frontispiece.

40. Scott, *Letters on Demonology*, 115.

41. Scott, *Letters on Demonology*, 111.

print until 2004.[42] As of the summer of 2025, the volumes it mentions as being part of Scott/Oldbuck's library were still in place at Abbotsford as described in this whimsical catalogue. After some discussion of Shakespearean editions and some other works of sixteenth- and seventeenth-century literature, Scott went on to describe the section he categorized as "demonology," devoting several pages to it.[43] Here he listed the 1665 edition of Scot's *Discovery of Witchcraft* as well as books by the Dutch clergyman Balthasar Bekker, a witchcraft skeptic influenced by Scot, and several Anglophone puritan authors, such as Richard Baxter and Cotton Mather, who believed that witchcraft was a real threat to Christian society. The work on which he spent the most words was Sinclair's *Satan's Invisible World Discovered*. Among other things, he described it as "a very curious book"–strikingly similar to the assessment he inscribed in Scot's *Discovery of Witchcraft*, despite the obvious contrast between Sinclair's credulity and Scot's skepticism.[44] He called the former "this father of fables," and *Satan's Invisible World Discovered* a "masterpiece of the terrible."[45] Scott was certainly a voracious reader and a broadminded collector, proud of the library he had amassed. Describing Scot's *Discovery of Witchcraft* near the end of this "demonology" section (its appearance delayed because, as an oversized folio, it was kept on a lower shelf) he called it "a rare book in excellent order which may also be said of a great part of its companions."[46]

But despite his obvious appreciation of England's first demonologist, Walter Scott must not have read his 1665 *Discovery of Witchcraft* too closely. (In his defense, he wrote his *Letters on Demonology and Witchcraft* while recovering from a stroke in 1830). For example, he appears not to have noticed the clear difference in tone between the material that was original to Reginald Scot and that which had been inserted by the "apocryphal Scot" of 1665. Thus, Walter Scott quoted a story from the second book of the "Discourse on Devils and Spirits" about a man who met someone who, it became apparent after a while, was the spirit of someone dead for a century–one of the Learmonths of Dairsie in Fife, perhaps, who were associated with Thomas the Rhymer, according to Walter Scott's note.[47] In the course

42. Scott, *Reliquiae.*

43. Scott, *Reliquiae*, 55–64, 67.

44. Scott, *Reliquiae*, 55.

45. Scott, *Reliquiae*, 58.

46. Scott, *Reliquiae*, 67.

47. Thomas the Rhymer was the subject of manuscript poetry dating to the fifteenth century as well as a ballad collected in the late nineteenth century by Francis Child, which told of Thomas being seduced by the Queen of Elfland at the Eildon tree in the Eildon Hills (not far from Walter Scott's Abbotsford estate) and taken on a

of the story, apparently told of a journey in England, the narrator supposedly is taken, at least in imagination, to Fife. The story was allegedly told to "apocryphal Scot" by the person to whom it happened, who ended up selling a horse to the spirit in question, paid for by a beautiful woman in a cave. Walter Scott took this as evidence that Reginald Scot "seems to have given some weight to the belief of those who thought that the spirits of famous men do, after death, take up some particular habitations near cities, towns and countries, and act as tutelary and guardian spirits to the places which they loved while in the flesh."[48] In fact, Reginald Scot would have believed nothing of the sort.

It is perhaps cruelly ironic that when Reginald Scot finally found (in the person of Sir Walter Scott) a prominent Scottish admirer, that admirer misapprehended some of his views. Based on the handful of examples I have been able to find, Scottish readers didn't really get Scot. Granted, few English readers embraced him either, but this was changing by the late seventeenth century, when his reception north of the Tweed was still very frosty. While Stuart MacDonald argued that beliefs about the Devil's association with witchcraft were slow to take hold in Scotland, those beliefs had a firm grip on Scottish attitudes by the second decade of the seventeenth century, if not earlier, and Scottish readers seemed little interested in Reginald Scot's efforts to shake them, or any other aspects of his attack on demonological theory for that matter. In fact, Sinclair's rejection of Scot in 1685 was implicitly reinforced in several subsequent Scottish witchcraft pamphlets.[49] As it turned out, from the Elizabethan/Jacobean age until that of romantic nationalism and its interest in folklore, readers frequently mined Scot's book for what they wanted, not what he wanted them to get. The second copy of the 1584 *Discoverie of Witchcraft* held by the National Library of Scotland, whose reader(s) were probably English, and which evidently faced rather hard use, was marked by one reader who was apparently attempting to (or at least thinking about) conjuring spirits.[50] This certainly highlights the fact

mystical journey to Elfland, where he is held captive for seven years. When he returns to the everyday world, he has been given the gift of prophecy and can never tell a lie. See Henderson and Cowan, *Scottish Fairy Belief*, 36, 142–51.

48. Henderson and Cowan, *Scottish Fairy Belief*, 86–87. The story is told in the second book of the "Discourse" in the 1665 *Discovery of Witchcraft*, chapter 3, sec 19–20, 48.

49. For example, *Witch-craft Proven* Wing B1800A (Glasgow 1697) and *The Tryal of Witchcraft* (Glasgow, 1700) Wing B1800aA. Both of these have been attributed to John Bell, minister of Gladsmuir (d. 1707), but Christina Larner has convincingly argued that he probably only wrote the second, and she suggests a different John Bell as the author of the first. See Larner, "Late Scottish Witchcraft Tracts."

50. Scot, *Discoverie of Witchcraft* (1584), 377–400, 419–20.

that once a book passes from author to printer to reader, the last will use it however they want, regardless of the author's intentions.

BIBLIOGRAPHY

Almond, Philip C. *England's First Demonologist: Reginald Scot and "The Discoverie of Witchcraft."* London: Tauris, 2011.

———. "King James I and the Burning of Reginald Scot's The Discoverie of Witchcraft: the Invention of a Tradition." *Notes and Queries* 56.2 (2009) 209–13.

Annand, William. *Library catalogue (posthumous auction listing).* Edinburgh, 1690.

Bekker, Balthasar. *The World Bewitch'd; or, An Examination of the Common Opinions Concerning Spirits.* Amsterdam, 1691–1693.

Bodin, Jean. *De la démonomanie des sorciers.* Paris: du Puys, 1580.

———. *On the Demon-Mania of Witches.* Translated by Randy A. Scott. Toronto: Center for Reformation and Renaissance Studies, 2001.

Bostridge, Ian. *Witchcraft and Its Transformations, c.1650–c.1750.* Oxford: Clarendon, 1997.

Carmichael, James. *Newes from Scotland.* London: William Wright, [1591?]. STC 10841a.

A Catalogue of Excellent and Rare Books, to Be Sold by Auction the 25th Day of February. Which Was the Library of Mr. William Annand Late Dean of Edinburgh Deceased. Edinburgh: Society of Stationers, 1690.

Clark, Andrew. *The Discovery of Witchcraft.* Expanded folio edition. London, 1665.

Clark, Stuart. "King James's Daemonologie: Witchcraft and Kingship." In *The Damned Art: Essays in the Literature of Witchcraft*, edited by Sidney Anglo, 156–81. London: Routledge, 1977.

Delrio, Martin. *Disquisitionum magicarum libri sex.* Louvain, 1599–1600.

Ferguson, F. S. "Relations Between London and Edinburgh Printers and Stationers (-1640)." *The Library*, 4th Series, 8 (1927) 145–98.

Glanvill, Joseph. *Saducismus Triumphatus.* London, 1681.

Goodare, Julian. "The Scottish Witchcraft Panic of 1597." In *Scottish Witch-hunt in Context*, edited by Julian Goodare, 51–72. Manchester: Manchester University Press, 2002.

———, ed. *Scottish Witch-hunt in Context.* Manchester: Manchester University Press, 2002.

———. "Witch-hunting and the Scottish State." In *Scottish Witch-hunt in Context*, edited by Julian Goodare, 122–45. Manchester: Manchester University Press, 2002.

Gordon, Robert of Straloch. Marginalia in *The Discoverie of Witchcraft.* London, 1584. National Library of Scotland.

Gourlaw, Robert. *Inventory of Books and Bindings.* Edinburgh, 1585.

Graham, Michael F. *The Uses of Reform: "Godly Discipline" and Popular Behavior in Scotland and Beyond, 1560–1610.* Leiden: Brill, 1996.

Henderson, Lizanne, and Edward J. Cowan. *Scottish Fairy Belief: A History.* East Linton: Tuckwell, 2001.

Hutchinson, Francis. *An Historical Essay Concerning Witchcraft.* London, 1718.

James VI. *Daemonologie.* Edinburgh, 1597.

Larner, Christina. *Enemies of God: The Witch-hunt in Scotland.* London: Chatto & Windus, 1981.

———. "Two Late Scottish Witchcraft Tracts: *Witch-craft Proven* and *The Tryal of Witchcraft.*" In *The Damned Art: Essays in the Literature of Witchcraft*, edited by Sidney Anglo, 227–45. London: Routledge, 1977.

Levack, Brian. "The Decline and End of Scottish Witch Hunting." In *Scottish Witch-Hunt in Context*, edited by Julian Goodare, 166–81. Manchester University Press, 2002.

Macdonald, Stuart. *The Witches of Fife: Witch-Hunting in a Scottish Shire, 1560–1710.* East Linton: Tuckwell, 2002.

Macfarlane, Alan. *Witchcraft in Tudor and Stuart England.* London: Routledge, 1970.

Mackenzie, George. *Laws and Customs of Scotland in Matters Criminal.* Edinburgh: Glen, 1678.

Martin, Laura. "The Devil and the Domestic: Witchcraft, Quarrels and Women's Work in Scotland." In *Scottish Witch-Hunt in Context*, edited by Julian Goodare, 73–89. Manchester University Press, 2002.

Midelfort, H. C. Erik. *Witch Hunting in Southwestern Germany, 1562–1684.* Stanford: Stanford University Press, 1972.

Mullan, David George. "Annand, William." *Oxford Dictionary of National Biography*, 2:176. Oxford: Oxford University Press, 2004.

Normand, Lawrence, and Gareth Roberts, eds. *Witchcraft in Early Modern Scotland: James VI's "Daemonologie" and the North Berwick Witches.* Exeter: University of Exeter Press, 2000.

Ondecking van Tovery (Leiden: Basson, 1609), USTC 1011512.

Ondecking van Tovery (Leiden: Willem Chrisiaensz vander Boxe, 1637), USTC 1028328.

Pepys, Samuel. *The Diary of Samuel Pepys.* Edited by Robert Latham and William Matthews. London: Bell & Hyman, 1970–1983.

Scot, Reginald. *The Discoverie of Witchcraft.* London: Brome, 1584. STC 21864. NLS Shelfmark H.2.d.29(1).

———. *The Discoverie of Witchcraft.* London, 1651.

———. *The Discoverie of Witchcraft.* London, 1654.

———. *The Discovery of Witchcraft.* Abbotsford Collection/Advocates Library, Shelfmark: Abbotsford. London, 1665.

Scott, Sir Walter. *Letters on Demonology and Witchcraft.* London: Murray, 1830.

———. *Reliquiae Trotcosienses, or The Gabions of the Late Jonathan Oldbuck esq of Monkbarns.* Edited by Gerard Carruthers and Alison Lumsden. Edinburgh: Edinburgh University Press, 2004.

Sharpe, James. "Witch-hunting and Witch Historiography: Some Anglo-Scottish Comparisons." In *Scottish Witch-Hunt in Context*, edited by Julian Goodare, 182–97. Manchester University Press, 2002.

Sinclair, George. *Satan's Invisible World Discovered.* Edinburgh: Reid, 1685.

Tenison, Thomas. Correspondence concerning the publication of Hutchinson's *Historical Essay*. Lambeth Palace Library.

Thomas, Keith. *Religion and the Decline of Magic.* London: Weidenfeld & Nicolson, 1971.

Vance, Shona MacLean. "Gordon, Robert of Straloch." *Oxford Dictionary of National Biography*. Oxford: Oxford University Press, 2004.

Watson, Samantha. “Ennobling Reform in Tudor Ireland.” *Sixteenth Century Journal* 46 (2015) 83–104.
Weyer, Johann. *De praestigiis daemonum.* Basel, 1563.

8

Leaving Christianity Revisited

An Anglican Update

Alan L. Hayes

Stuart Macdonald deserves this Festschrift! He has modelled excellence in research and teaching in the history of Christianity. He has explored and connected a variety of themes, embraced interdisciplinary research methods, rethought conventional assumptions, excavated relevant primary sources thoroughly, organized data patiently, constructed fresh interpretations sensitive to social and cultural contexts, and presented his results in a clear and persuasive style of scholarly reporting. In the following pages, I will focus on a splendid example of his craft: the book which he and our mutual friend Brian Clarke published in 2017, *Leaving Christianity: Changing Allegiances in Canada since 1945*.

That Canadians had been "leaving Christianity" for several decades came as no surprise to anyone who has spent time in Canadian churchland over that period. But this was a historical phenomenon that, Macdonald and Clarke realized, required a more nuanced interpretation than it had usually received. For their research, they gathered and plumbed a multitude of data, notably the decennial census, annual denominational statistical returns, the General Social Surveys administered by Statistics Canada, the Project Canada surveys conducted by the sociologist Reginald Bibby, and a series of Canadian Gallup Polls, which take a particular interest in religion.

The authors recognized that statistics were not the only possible index of Christian commitment, but they offered plausible arguments as to why they can be particularly useful and, treated carefully, reliable. Their findings illuminated similarities and differences among the denominations, regions, and decades in ways that problematized some familiar metanarratives. They brought balanced judgments and fresh perspectives to their topic, and they concluded with hints as to how churches might respond.

The reviews were positive and appreciative. My favorite came from a professor of religious studies, a field which was established in the 1960s as a secular, outsider corrective to the blinkered and biased efforts of theological studies. Still, in 2018, the interdisciplinary rivalry seemed fresh to her. She was thrilled that these "theologian authors" had somehow managed to steer clear of "fantasies" and had succeeded in producing "detailed and realistic" scholarship. But for herself, she said, she preferred churches as "great concert venues."[1]

What I propose to do here is to explore some of the more recent data for "leaving Christianity." The last main sources of data in their book come from 2011. Since then we have had the Canadian census of 2021 and some fresh denominational and survey data. Now, none of these new sources challenges the narrative of decline in *Leaving Christianity;* on the contrary, they confirm it. But the task I have set for myself here is a bit different from Macdonald and Clarke's. In this short space I can't match the broad, ecumenical perspective which was among Macdonald and Clarke's most ambitious and brilliant achievements. Instead, I will be looking at a single denomination—my own, the Anglican Church of Canada. By taking a more granular look at the Anglican case, I can supplement the broader explanations in *Leaving Christianity* with some more humdrum but possibly suggestive reasons why so many Canadian Christians have left their churches, and haven't been replaced by a similar (or greater!) number of seekers.

STATISTICS OF CHURCH DECLINE IN CANADA

In the two tables in this section, I have updated the Anglican statistics of *Leaving Christianity* by adding the census data for 2021, and denominational

1. Beaman, review of *Leaving Christianity*, *Canadian Historical Review*, 664–66. Other reviews include Turcotte, review of *Leaving Christianity*, *Études d'histoire religieuse*, 80–83; Rady-Shaw, review of *Leaving Christianity*, *Ontario History*, 235–37; Reimer, review of *Leaving Christianity*, *Journal of Contemporary Religion*, 600–601; Bramadat, review of *Leaving Christianity*, *Church History*, 963–64; Badertscher, review of *Leaving Christianity*, *Touchstone*, 69–70.

data for 2022 and 2023. I have also added some other statistical categories not included in *Leaving Christianity.*[2]

Macdonald and Clarke treated the data of the Anglican Church of Canada (ACC) in connection with the data from two other large "mainline" Protestant denominations, the United Church of Canada (UCC) and the Presbyterian Church in Canada (PCC). These three denominations followed similar patterns of increase and decline after World War II. In fact, in the way they organize their book, Macdonald and Clarke effectively present these three denominations as the baseline against which the other churches can be compared. The significant statistics they considered included affiliates (i.e., those self-identifying with the denomination for census purposes), members, Sunday attenders, Sunday school children, persons baptized, and persons confirmed (or professing their faith). The general pattern of these three denominations was this: their significant numbers generally peaked in the early 1960s, declined modestly in the 1970s, fell more precipitously in the 1980s, showed some incipient signs of correction in the 1990s, and then continued their collapse in the first decade of the 2000s.

These various numbers didn't decline synchronously. The decline in baptisms was a leading indicator for a later decline in Sunday school registration, which in turn signaled a later decline in confirmations (or professions of faith). In other words, fewer parents were having their babies baptized, and those who were baptized either weren't brought up in the Christian faith or began dropping out. Even if their parents kept them in church, when they reached early adolescence (the age of confirmation) they were usually free to decide to exit. These declines had a snowballing effect. The children who weren't in church in the 1970s became parents whose children also didn't go to church.

As a result, towards 2000, a disproportionately large number of those who remained active in the church were those born before 1950—the leading edge of the "Boomer" generation and their elders. Younger "Boomers" who no longer attended church often still identified as Christians on their census returns, because they had a residual sense of Christian identity. But

2. Scans of the original publications of parish statistics from 1959 to 2001 are available on the Anglican Church of Canada website, https://www.anglican.ca/ask/faq/number-of-anglicans/statistical-archive/. The most recent ACC statistics for most categories can be found in Neil Elliot, "Statistics Report to General Synod 2025," https://gs2025.anglican.ca/wp-content/uploads/Report-006-Appendix-A-Statistics-Report.pdf. However, for the number of clergy, parishes, and congregations, the most recent data is for 2022, in Neil Elliot, "Anglican Church of Canada: the State of the Church," *NumbersMatter*, March 6, 2025, https://numbersmatters.ca/2024/03/05/anglican-church-of-canada-the-state-of-the-church/. References below to parish statistics in any given year will be found in the appropriate year's document as cited here.

increasing numbers of young Canadians had no experience of church at all and looked on churchland as *terra incognita*. These told the census-takers that they had "no religion."[3]

For the decade ending in 2011, Macdonald and Clarke found, Anglican numbers were missing.[4] Readers might have wondered about this gap. The problem was that in 2002, the ACC's national Department of Financial Management and Administration lost patience with the frustrating process of persuading dioceses to collect, organize and report the data, which they in turn were trying to persuade their parishes to collect, organize and report. No ACC statistics were published after that until a denominational Statistics and Research Officer, the Rev. Neil Elliot, was appointed in 2016. The statistics resumed, a little irregularly, in 2017.

Macdonald and Clarke rightly observe that denominational statistics are generally viewed with skepticism by researchers. They particularly note that numbers of members and attendees may be inflated: for instance, inactive members may be left on the rolls for a while, or leaders may want their congregations to look popular.[5] But the situation is more complicated than that, as we'll consider next. At the diocesan level, data categories aren't consistently defined from year to year; at the parish level, data are collected by different individuals with varying degrees of scrupulosity. For some categories of the ACC data, it is probably wise to assume a margin of error of at least 10%, and probably much more.

Total Number on Parish Rolls

The most significant single category for numbers of Anglicans involved in their church is the category that the ACC states as "total number on parish rolls" (sometimes "souls" or "members").

In fact, the ACC has no formal document called a "parish roll," and there's no agreement among dioceses as to whom to include in the category. The word "members," when used in the ACC, is misleading, since there's no defined system by which a person becomes a member of the ACC, as there is for the UCC and PCC (adult profession of faith or transfer of membership).

3. The Angus Reid Institute has done polling for the Canadian think tank Cardus suggesting a refinement distinguishing "Non-Religion," "Privately Faithful," and "Spiritually Uncertain." *Cardus*, "The Shifting Landscape of Religion in Canada," November 23, 2022, https://www.cardus.ca/research/faith-communities/reports/the-shifting-landscape-of-faith-in-canada/.

4. Clarke and Macdonald, *Leaving Christianity*, Tables 1.6 and 1.7, 56, 58.

5. Clarke and Macdonald, *Leaving Christianity*, 42.

This looseness is presumably an echo of church establishment in England, where, by default, everyone living within the geographical bounds of a parish was entitled to the services of the parish church.

In practice, each diocese has its own way of telling parishes how to calculate "number on parish rolls." Here is the current situation, as of 2025, in several of our ACC dioceses:

- The diocese of Niagara asks for the number of "all to whom ministry is offered." (But probably many clergy aim to offer ministry to anyone in need.)
- The diocese of Rupert's Land, a little more restrictively, includes "everyone of any age for whom the parish assumes pastoral care."
- The diocese of Islands and Inlets (formerly called the diocese of British Columbia) tells the parish returning officers to exclude persons under the age of 16.
- The diocese of Toronto wants only the number of *baptized* persons, thus excluding seekers, catechumens, and those who (like William Powell's character in the 1947 movie *Life with Father*) may be Anglican stalwarts but unbaptized. This criterion would tend to underestimate the number of people involved in congregations. On the other hand, the diocese gives parishes the option—the *option*—to include online attenders.
- The diocese of Huron is also interested only in baptized persons, but it adds its own peculiarity: "People should only be removed from this figure through death, a move, or a request for removal from the parish list."
- The diocese of Kootenay asks the parish returning officer for the number of persons on the parish "snail mail" list, and also (in a separate box) the number of persons on its email list. Presumably, the diocese sums the two numbers to arrive at the "total number on parish rolls," though it is not clear how it avoids double-counting people who appear on both lists.
- The diocese of Fredericton instructs to include whoever "claims to be Anglican."[6]

6. These documents, usually forms, are hard to find through a Google search, and will not likely remain on diocesan websites long. Some may continue to exist archived on the "Wayback Machine," https://web.archive.org. Diocese of Niagara, "Parish Treasurer's Manual," 58, https://niagaraanglican.ca/uploads/documents/2018/01/treasurers-manual-2022.pdf; Diocese of Rupert's Land, "2024 Annual Parish Demographic Statistics," https://dq5pwpg1q8ruo.cloudfront.

Whatever the diocesan instructions, in practice there can be no guarantee that every parish returning officer will fastidiously follow them—or, indeed, even read them. In short, the published "number on parish rolls" in any given year, though not exactly fictional, doesn't have anything like an agreed meaning.

Identifiable Regular Givers

This category was added in 1967. Its numbers are likely quite reliable, usually being the number of envelope subscribers. It tells us little, however, about the number of people in the parish church who are actively involved. For one thing, there will probably be only one envelope subscriber per family. For another thing, some regular (and sometimes quite generous) givers may not come to church at all, while some highly involved parishioners may not take out offering envelopes.

Easter Communicants or Attenders

Easter and Christmas are the only days of the church year when the ACC can reasonably expect that the greatest number of people with a sense of Anglican identity will attend worship. That, presumably, is the rationale for requiring these statistics. Until 1986 parish returning officers were asked to report the number of communicants in the octave of Easter (i.e., from Easter Sunday to the following Sunday, inclusive). Adding the numbers of communicants at all services would certainly count many individuals more than once, yielding an inflated number of actual Anglican numbers. In another respect, however, the reported number would underrepresent attendance,

---

net/2025/02/01/01/49/55/89cf2e64-5999-41a0-ba09-425b2f40f0b2/4.%20Parish%20 Demographic%20Statistics%202024.pdf; Diocese of Inlands and Inlets, "2025 Parish Information Return," item 17, https://forms.office.com/Pages/ResponsePage.aspx?-id=Dwfg1yZtcoSstdgiSVSMLhhcEzgCCgRCuwT0LXTbSYNUMTlISVdRMElaRF UyTjAyM1c4NzQxU1I3QS4u. Diocese of Toronto, "Incumbent's Annual Statistical Return Handbook," 4, https://www.toronto.anglican.ca/parish-administration/finance/annual-returns/?lang=en; Diocese of Kootenay, "Form F: Parish Statistics for the year ending December 31, 2024," https://docs.google.com/spreadsheets/d/1ByuvHyzyBK36 HcSf3lexjKa4LyIfGGIz4x9QKGmCreY/edit?usp=drive_link; Diocese of Huron, "2024 Parish Statistic Form," https://forms.office.com/pages/responsepage.aspx?id=Sk-bN-87w60yh3iuh8wvYDPXLPPLUIn5Kgi-WwU1RL8VURDAyTllVRjNWRE81QjhM-NFlXMV05UklYSS4u; Diocese of Fredericton, "Parish Statistics Return for 2024," https://forms.office.com/pages/responsepage.aspx?id=ivnPw2EbmEie2mqkTSZvwg-xmXmCpaBFBruCASKW5zbxUM09DVjJPM1NWOVZLOTY0WFVDSTZKSUtNUy-QlQCN0PWcu.

since until 1969 members of other churches who might attend weren't supposed to receive communion in the ACC, and until 1981 children (that is, unconfirmed persons) were ineligible to receive communion. In 1987 this category was dropped. In 2017 it reappeared as "Easter attendance."

Average Sunday Attendance

All Anglican services are supposed to be recorded in parish registers, and for each service, the number in attendance and the number of communicants are supposed to be entered as well. In 1988, parishes began to be asked to calculate the *average* Sunday attendance throughout the year. Persons who attended more than one Sunday service must have usually been double-counted, since the numbers in the parish register are total numbers for each service, unless the parish returning officer, when completing the statistical form in the following year, tried to estimate how many attended more than once a Sunday.

Typically the sidesmen (ushers) are responsible for counting numbers, and, at least in larger churches, relaying the number to the priest during the offertory, to ensure that the right minimum number of communion wafers are consecrated. In my own experience, not all sidesmen are equally observant, especially at services without communion. I have seen numerous cases where someone (perhaps the team that counts the offering after the service) enters an estimate in the register. In the fuzzy theory, the statistic for *average* Sunday attendance is calculated by totaling the numbers at every service, and dividing by the number of services. In practice, I expect that this number often reflects a plausible estimate.

Is It Important

Macdonald and Clarke suggest that even if specific numbers are often wrong, "we can reliably discern trends and the change they represent." I accept this point; as a premise in statistics, a large sample size reduces the margin of error. And even if the ACC's 1961 numbers and its 2021 numbers are off by 10% or 20%, we can see from the tables in *Leaving Christianity* that the overall declines are much more dramatic than that. It is not wrong, however, for readers to be skeptical of the finer calculations.

	1961	1971	1981	1991	2001	2021, 2023	%
Census affiliates	2,409,068	2,543,180	2,436,375	2,188,115	2,035,500	1,134,310	−52.9%
On parish rolls	1,358,459	1,109,221	921,545	801,963	685,845	294,382	−78.3%
Members - census	56.39%	43.62%	37.82%	36.65%	33.69%	25.95%	
Easter	476,535	399,221	406,164			127,011	−73.3%
Avg Sunday attendance				184,673	162,138	58,871	−68.1%
Attendance - members				23.0%	23.6%	20.0%	
Identifiable givers			250,647	248,260	212,577	106,402	−57.5%

Table 8.1: Anglican numbers on parish rolls, affiliation, and attendance 1961–2023 (Including membership as a percentage of census affiliation, and attendance as a percentage of numbers on parish rolls)

A Few Comments

In this table, the most recent figures for affiliated (census) Anglicans are taken from the 2021 census. The numbers on parish rolls and the numbers for average Sunday attendance are taken from a denominational report referenced earlier for the year 2023, the most recent year available.

The considerably greater proportional decline of Anglican census affiliates compared to numbers on parish rolls, between 1961 and 2023, suggests that Anglican memory was more robust than Anglican involvement, and increasingly so in later decades. This may possibly qualify the suggestion of *Leaving Christianity* that Anglican identification waned with the aging of the population (as younger Canadians with little or no experience or memory of churchgoing grew older).

Leaving Christianity discusses the importance of the decline of Sunday school registrations from 1961 to 2011. It is noteworthy, therefore, that when Anglican statistics resumed in 2017, Sunday school involvement wasn't reported. My own observation is that relatively few Sunday schools remain across the ACC.

The ratio of average attendance to numbers on parish rolls has remained relatively stable. One reason could be that the numbers on parish rolls are generally constructed by parish officers on the basis of mailing lists, which are in turn constructed on the basis of whom they see in church.

Other Statistical Data

The ACC annual statistical documents discussed above help us delve further into changes and trends in church governance, structure, and activities. No numbers are published for the ordinations of priests in recent years.

	1961	**1971**	**1981**	**1991**	**2001**	**2022–2023**	%
Baptisms	45132	28722	23384	21003	13354	3651	−91.9%
Confirmations	35253	21965	15021	8267	5506	1549	−95.6%
Marriages	11982	16197	12343	9552	6009	1145	−90.4%
Funerals	20499	21108	19043	18316	15635	7645	−62.7%
Clergy	2004	1859	2058	2112	2193	1895	−5.4%
Priested	87	47	97	83	65		
Parishes	1768	1727	1656	1781	1792	1498	−15.3%
Congregations	3644	3417	3255	3006	2884	1978	−45.7%

Table 8.2. Occasional services, and number of clergy, parishes, and congregations, 1961–2023

Reliability

The numbers of baptisms, confirmations, marriages, and funerals can be considered highly reliable, for reasons given by Macdonald and Clarke.[7] For the same reasons, the number of parishes and congregations can be considered reliable.

My summary of numbers of clergy has required some judgment on my part, since the categories under which clergy were reported over the years changed several times. My aim has been to include all active clergy (bishops, priests, deacons), paid or unpaid, regardless of their sphere of ministry. This number excludes clergy on leave of absence, clergy in secular positions, and clergy "retired" or "pensioned" (even though many retired Anglican clergy continue in ministry).

Baptisms and Confirmations

As I have noted, *Leaving Christianity* describes a pattern of a decrease in baptisms leading to a decrease in confirmations (or professions of faith) some years later and an increase in "no religion" some further years after that: in other words, the decline in Christianity in Canada is in large measure a cohort-related legacy of defections in the late 1960s and 1970s. Macdonald and Clarke use the UCC as an example.[8] If one runs the ACC numbers in the way that Macdonald and Clarke do for the UCC, the decline in confirmations will look catastrophic, but in fact, the ACC statistics of confirmation are an irrelevant indicator after about 1980. In 1981, baptism began to be considered full Christian initiation in the ACC, and confirmation was no longer required for admission to communion (though many parishes, or parents, continued older practices for a while). Confirmation became "a rite in search of a purpose;" young people had little incentive to pursue it. That said, there is no doubt that the number of young people did decline considerably after 1980.

Closings of Parishes and Congregations

The statistics distinguish parishes (both self-supporting parishes and mission parishes) from congregations. Many Canadian Anglican parishes, especially in small towns and rural areas, are multi-point: that is, congregations

7. Clarke and Macdonald, *Leaving Christianity*, 42.

8. Clarke and Macdonald, *Leaving Christianity*, 52–53, figure 1.8.

meet in different, geographically distributed church buildings for worship, but share a priest and parish governance. Although the closure of 46% of congregations between 1971 and 2022 is dramatic, it appears almost moderate in contrast to the 78% collapse of Anglican membership between 1961 and 2023, discussed earlier. Thus, the average size of an Anglican congregation has dropped considerably during this period. The much smaller decline of 15% in the number of parishes reflects the consolidation of multi-point parishes by the closure and merger of congregations. We'll return to these points later.

Marriages and Funerals

The decline in the number of parish-related funerals can be largely explained by the greater decline in Anglican membership. The collapse in the number of marriages can be explained in part by the decrease in the number of young churchgoing Anglicans. (In "the old days," many marriages developed from relationships formed in the Anglican Young People's Association.) Another explanation, of course, is the increase in common-law marriages.

Number of Clergy

The only significant Anglican statistic that has hardly decreased at all since 1961 is the number of clergy. But the reality is a little more complex than the figures reflect. The greatest single change in ordained ministry in the ACC in the last four decades has been the explosion of "vocational," "perpetual," or "permanent" deacons—three alternative terms all referring to deacons who are not intending to proceed to ordination as priests, as "transitional" deacons do. The ACC statistics for 1981 break out the number of vocational deacons, and the number is zero. In the ACC statistics for 2022, by contrast, 325 vocational deacons were identified, 45 of them paid and 285 unpaid.

This statistic hints at broad changes in the structure, style, and ministry of Anglican congregations, as I will discuss later.

Ordinations

In the late 1960s and early 1970s, fewer priests were ordained annually than before or since. From my own conversations with people who contemplated or sought ordination in that era, I gather that many young people who might otherwise have sensed a call to ordained ministry were discouraged by the traditional structures, expectations, and styles of the church and not hopeful about the future of institutional Christianity. This is one of the clearest indications of the thesis that the decade of the 1960s represents a turning point in ACC history.

WHY IS THE ANGLICAN CHURCH OF CANADA DECLINING?

Interpretations of Decline

Leaving Christianity is particularly helpful for its even-handed and instructive survey of academic studies of the decline of religion in modern Canada, the United States, and Britain. The authors whom they consider, all sociologists, social historians, or religious historians, include Reginald Bibby of the University of Lethbridge, Hugh McLeod of the University of Birmingham, Callum Brown of the University of Glasgow, Rodney Stark of the University of Washington, Jeffrey Cox of the University of Iowa, Grace Davie of the University of Exeter, Robert Putnam of Harvard, Joel Thiessen of Ambrose University (Calgary), Bryan Wilson of Oxford, Michael Gauvreau of McMaster University, and Nancy Christie of the University of Western Ontario. (This is an aging group: Bibby, McLeod, Davie, Gauvreau, and Putnam are retired; Cox, Stark, and Wilson are deceased. Maybe younger scholars are no longer curious about Christian decline!)

Macdonald and Clarke draw from the insights of all these writers, but they (rightly) eschew identifying a master explanation for church decline. They believe, though, that many of the chief causes are to be found in the 1960s, since, otherwise, how is it that the booming, robust Canadian Christianity of the 1950s began its decline so abruptly in the 1960s?

They are rightly skeptical of "the secularization thesis" (which, as they point out, is a bit inchoate, since it takes several different forms).[9] If the secularization thesis says that people give up on a belief in God because they think that science has disproven it, the religious surveys suggest otherwise: they "consistently show that the vast majority of Canadians" believe in God or an afterlife, Macdonald and Clarke say. Only a minuscule number of Canadians, about 1.1% in 2011, identify as atheists or agnostics.[10] By comparison, the theme of Owen Chadwick's magisterial *The Victorian Church* is that the national life of late nineteenth-century England was characterized by both religious doubt and thriving churches. In other words, doubts

9. Clarke and Macdonald, *Leaving Christianity*, 229.

10. Clarke and Macdonald, *Leaving Christianity*, 164, 231.

about faith do not automatically lead people *out of* the church: they may lead people *into* it.

Macdonald and Clarke, therefore, look for other cultural and social changes that shook the 1960s, changes that transformed values and priorities and loyalties. They take a particular interest in what's sometimes called a drain in "social capital," that is, the "social networks and the norms of reciprocity and trustworthiness that arise from them."[11] Partly because of rising affluence, the decade turned towards individualism, consumerism, and an orientation towards "self-fulfilment," and away from civic engagement, a trust in institutions, social conformity, and volunteerism. Another impetus to cultural change was the introduction of oral contraceptives, which simplified family planning, and which together with the changed economic environment opened up unprecedented social and economic opportunities for women—including those millions of women who until then had had time on their hands to run church women's missionary societies, raise funds for the churches, teach Sunday schools, meet in sewing circles, sing in choirs, cook and clean up after parish suppers, decorate church buildings, and look after the altar linen.

In short, the cultural changes of the 1960s weren't specifically anti-religious, but they destabilized "Christendom," which was a Christianity that had been inculturated into the values of the waning era. The churches might have envisioned and constructed a post-Christendom Christianity. In the end, they didn't.

Now, my personal experience of the 1960s leads me to agree with Macdonald and Clarke that that decade was a crucial turning point in North American social history. It also leads me to agree that the churches had to wrestle with changing social values. That said, however, my personal story is that in the 1960s, I felt a hope that I hadn't experienced before for the churches. They seemed to be positioning themselves to give the moral and spiritual leadership that the new age required. I was inspired by the Christian justice movements of the period, and by the many church leaders who so passionately and effectively critiqued the moral legitimacy of the old order and set out to help build a better one. Their example led me *into* Christianity, not out of it. No doubt I was in a minority, but I do not think I was unique. Although *Leaving Christianity* makes a plausible case that statistics of church decline reflect the church's failure to meet the new era, it is noteworthy that its statistics of ACC affiliates show an *increase* between 1961 and 1971.[12]

11. Clarke and Macdonald, quoting Robert Putnam, *Leaving Christianity*, 240.

12. Clarke and Macdonald, *Leaving Christianity*, Tables 6.1 and 6.2.

The Case of the ACC

The advantage of the broad-brush picture in *Leaving Christianity* is that it gives an account of Christianity in general—indeed, religion in general—across Canada. This is exactly what a reader wants from a study as ecumenical and inclusive as *Leaving Christianity.* But in shifting our attention to the particular case of the ACC, I'm proposing that there lies an advantage also in turning from the "macro" to the "micro," so that some finer-grain details come into focus. True, these details won't all apply to all other denominations. But some may be suggestive.

My own experience as a parish priest was that I could usually understand why some people left, but I didn't know how to attract new people in. From that perspective, church decline has two dynamics: what moves people to leave, and what fails to move people to enter, where the former is usually unspectacularly mundane, and the latter a bit of a mystery. In addition, we need to note that, especially among some Indigenous Anglicans and immigrant Anglicans, there's another story to be found besides decline.

Mundane Reasons for Leaving Churches

My first example of the mundane character of the decline of the ACC is that, when we look closely at the statistics, it was slow and incremental. Now, indeed, the decline of 78% in ACC membership from 1961 to 2023 looks catastrophic. But tracked on an exponential curve it is only about 2% per year, compounded. Thus, arguably, church decline in the twentieth century is the inverse of church growth in the first three centuries of the common era. The sociologist Rodney Stark, in disagreeing with the nineteenth-century historian Adolf Harnack that the growth of the early church displayed "inconceivable rapidity" and "astonishing growth," turned to the leverage intrinsic to the exponential curve. Working from numerous scholarly estimates of the population of the church in its first three centuries, he calculated that church growth was a modest 3.6% per year, compounded annually. Raising Christian children and inviting friends to meet Jesus could easily account for such growth.[13]

Equally ordinary things can explain the gradual decline in Christian numbers. One category of causes is demographic. People die. People become sick or disabled housebound. People move away. Couples get divorces that, in effect, require one of them to bow out of their church.

13. Stark, *Rise of Christianity*, esp. 17–42.

Another influence is competition for Sunday time. In the 1980s, Lord's Day legislation was repealed or judicially overturned, and people found Sunday a convenient time to shop, or to schedule ice time for kids' hockey teams, or to go to movies or entertainment parks, or to relax at home and watch television—maybe even religious television.

Another reason why some people pull back from church is that, frankly, congregations can be really annoying places. People who work very hard, often invisibly, can feel unappreciated. Their feelings can get hurt. They can feel abandoned, or disappointed, or let down, or angered, when they aren't visited enough, or are asked for money too often, or are harangued from the pulpit, or experience bullying or even abuse, or aren't consulted in decision-making, or have unresolved arguments, or feel out of the loop. And such everyday issues can generate something of a spiritual crisis because they seem so anomalous in an organization that makes such high claims for itself as the community of saints, the body of Christ, the fellowship of love. People sense hypocrisy.

Then, note the statistics above on the closures of congregations. Each congregation's closure results in several people lost to the church forever. Technically, the closure is probably presented as the merger of the closed church into a surviving church, where members of the old church are supposed to start attending the surviving church. But if the surviving church is too distant, or too different in liturgical or musical or preaching style, or too unfriendly, not all members of the closed church will care to adapt. Some may refuse to continue due to resentment of the church authorities who imposed the changes. A 2020 article in the *Anglican Journal,* the monthly ACC newspaper, explored congregational mergers. It looked at the example of a merger of four ACC congregations in Nova Scotia. The article reports, "The number of parishioners has diminished by about 30% since the churches merged, [the church wardens] say, a number consistent with what the diocese told them to expect."[14]

LTBTQ+ Issues

Let's name a reason for leaving that *can* be quantified, at least in small part: disputes about the place of LGBTQ+ folks in the life of the church. The specific presenting questions of these disputes are whether people living in same-sex relationships should be married in church, and whether they should be eligible for ordination. These issues have roiled the ACC since

14. Joelle Kidd, "The Changing Face of the Church," *Anglican Journal,* 7 January 2020, https://anglicanjournal.com/the-changing-face-of-church/.

the 1970s, and they still aren't formally resolved. Modern Canadian Anglicans have a live-and-let-live attitude when it comes to the Trinity, the empty tomb, Christ's real presence in the Eucharist, predestination, penal substitutionary atonement, and other issues that used to get people ejected or jailed or immolated, but they have been unable to resolve these apparently lesser matters of sexuality. In this respect, the turn away from the ACC reflects its *involvement* in the larger culture, not the disengagement that Macdonald and Clarke suspect. But to be fair, underneath these presenting questions of the role of LGBTQ+ people in the church lie deeper questions about tradition and the interpretation of Scripture, values and tolerance and justice.[15] (The other consuming Anglican arguments of the period since the 1960s, the ordination of women and liturgical change, have largely died down.)

Those who take a progressive position on these matters often claim that the church has lost members because of its stuck-in-the-mud traditionalism, while those who take a conservative position often claim that the church has lost members because it abandoned orthodoxy.[16] Both may well be true, though I see no persuasive way to decide which is *more* true. And possibly an even greater number of ACC members have exited not because they had strong feelings about these issues, but because the fighting has gone on for decades, and it can be very tiring. In any event, while some have no doubt left the ACC over these issues, *Leaving Christianity* helpfully provides considerable support that neither a liberal orientation nor a conservative one is in itself the key to church survival, let alone church growth. To me, a particularly telling statistic in the book is that the conservative branch of Canadian Lutheranism and the progressive branch have comparable statistical trends.[17]

Nevertheless, there is one kind of statistical evidence for the numbers leaving the ACC because of their conservative views on LGBTQ+ issues. Dozens of ACC congregations and thousands of ACC members have seceded from the ACC in protest against the ACC's liberal drift on LGBTQ+ issues. The most notorious such case was St. John's Anglican Church, Shaughnessy, in Vancouver, which in 2008 was reportedly the largest congregation in the ACC, with a weekly attendance of about 800. In 2008, it disaffiliated, after the bishop, breaking an agreement with his brother and

15. Anglican Church of Canada, Committee on Faith, Worship, Ministry, "Same Sex Blessings/Homosexuality," https://www.anglican.ca/faith/focus/hs/ssbh/.

16. An example of the latter by an author who proves what he assumes is David Goodhew, "The Collapse of the Anglican Church of Canada," *Covenant: TLC's Online Journal*, 5 August 2024, https://livingchurch.org/covenant/the-collapse-of-the-anglican-church-of-canada/.

17. Clarke and Macdonald, *Leaving Christianity*, 61.

sister bishops, pushed forward liberal LGBTQ+ policies, and brooked no dissent. After a court battle, the church building returned to the ACC. The new St. John's, Shaughnessy, now has a Sunday attendance of 85.[18]

The story of these many congregational secessions, with their shifting alliances, reorganizations, litigations, defections, and counter-schisms, is complex. But as of 2025, most of the surviving seceding churches are members of the diocese of Canada of an alternative Anglican denomination, not in communion with the archbishop of Canterbury, called the Anglican Church of North America. Globally, the Anglican movement of disaffiliation from Canterbury has involved millions of people, but according to its 2024 statistics, the ACNA diocese of Canada has only 5,159 members. Interestingly, this figure represents a 20% decline from 2023.[19]

Why Are So Few New People Coming to the ACC?

The mundane things we've been considering help explain why individuals leave the ACC. But why aren't the departures matched, or more than matched, by additions? Macdonald and Clarke suggest several reasons that apply to most or all Canadian Protestant denominations: birth rates are generally low; parents do not encourage their children to go to church; Protestant immigration is thin; "social capital" has been chipped away.[20] But, again, there are some particular issues to identify for the ACC.

First, most ACC parishes are small, in what's often called a "pastoral" range of 50 to 150 members. This development is reflected in the tables above, where it will be seen that the "total number on church rolls" divided by the number of parishes has fallen by over 70% since 1961 (from about 770 to 200, of whom only a fraction are active). Typically, in pastoral-sized churches, some studies suggest, the clergy leader is the hub and is expected to have a personal relationship with everyone; programming is thin; pastoral assistants and skilled lay volunteers are few; and the congregation functions as an interplay of three or four social networks of family and friends. Such

18. For a general survey of this history, see "St. John's Shaughnessy" on *Wikipedia*, https://en.wikipedia.org/wiki/St._John%27s_Shaughnessy. For the recent attendance, see Terry Shields Dirbas, "Third Sunday of Lent," *St. John's Shaughnessy*, 1 March 2024, https://www.stjohnsshaughnessy.org/2024/03/01/third-sunday-of-lent/.

19. A long list of Anglican groupings not in communion with Canterbury can be found at Anglicans Online, "Not in the Communion," 31 August 2025, https://anglicansonline.org/communion/nic.html. A spreadsheet of ACNA statistics for 2024 is available by link from the ACNA Provincial Council Documents Center, https://drive.google.com/drive/folders/1FVBHbqpMQmgecAr-EgtZadD5T_bDRwHf.

20. Clarke and Macdonald, *Leaving Christianity*, 36, 70, 240–42.

a style limits growth—indeed, it can limit even the desire for growth, since congregants may fear that adding too many more people would disrupt the comfortable, familiar character of their Sunday experience. Moreover, those seeking a church, not least those with young children, will very likely prefer a larger church with a variety of programs, a number of skilled lay leaders, diverse opportunities for involvement, and a wider choice of social groups to which to attach themselves.[21]

Second, it is significant that the number of Anglican clergy has remained roughly the same since 1961, while membership has declined by almost 80%. A higher ratio of clergy to laity is necessary partly because ACC's small congregations use clergy time less efficiently than larger congregations do. Also, since congregations are smaller, fewer full-time clergy are needed, requiring the deployment of more clergy in part-time positions.

As a result, since fewer people are likely to produce less income to support roughly the same number of clergy, it is likely that clergy salaries are becoming less competitive in the wider Canadian economy.[22] Those contemplating a clergy career need to face the prospect of low salaries (almost never starting above $40,000 plus housing[23]) that will leave them with long-term student debt after a four-year B.A. and a three-year M.Div., and some challenges in trying to support a family. In response, many dioceses will now ordain priests on the basis of a shorter, academically reduced alternative training, and appoint them to a part-time or even non-stipendiary position so that they can seek additional salary income elsewhere.[24] Prospective students discouraged for these reasons who have transferable leadership skills may well seek meaningful work in more affluent organizations.

Has the quality of ACC leadership declined as a result? I can't envision a statistical project that could measure changes in the quality of leadership, so this must remain a question.[25] The matter is important because many

21. See, for example, Rothauge, *Sizing Up a Congregation*.

22. While most deacons and most Indigenous priests are non-stipendiary, their leadership does involve smaller costs for their dioceses.

23. I have consulted clergy remuneration data at several diocesan websites: for example, Diocese of Nova Scotia and Prince Edward Island, "Financial Information," https://www.nspeidiocese.ca/pages/financial-information.

24. André Forget, "Conference Explores Alternatives to Seminary Education," *Anglican Journal*, February 27, 2017, https://anglicanjournal.com/conference-explores-alternatives-to-seminary-education/, where the clergy base salary is below $37,000 plus rectory.

25. Concerns about falling standards for clergy aren't new. In 1954, the Fund for Theological Education was established in the USA because "a national group of top seminary educators, clergy and civic leaders had become increasingly concerned that the quality of those entering the ministry had declined and that many of the most talented

visitors to a church will likely consider the quality of the clergy leadership when they think about returning, and church members may make a decision about remaining partly on the same basis.

Third, another reason religious seekers might be skeptical about the ACC may be its reputation and "optics." Its unsavory history with Indian residential schools has shocked many consciences, later apologies notwithstanding. News stories about the convictions of clergy leaders, choirmasters, and others for sexual predation take a toll. A CBC story reporting the ACC primate's self-protective response to the release of the names of victims of sexual misconduct must have reinforced some viewers' negative views of ecclesiastical institutionalism.[26]

Fourth, more recently, the closures of churches during the COVID pandemic from March 2020 to (roughly) March 2022 may have permanently changed some patterns of church involvement and attendance. So far, Statistics Canada reports "no visible effect of the pandemic on religious affiliation trends,"[27] but it is too early to be confident.

Finally, I think there's something to Macdonald and Clarke's suggestion that Canadian churches have suffered because they have failed to engage "the new cultural and religious context" of post-Christendom.[28] But I suggest a revision to their generalization with respect to the ACC, and probably some other denominations as well.[29] From the late 1960s to the mid-1980s, the ACC navigated a surprisingly quick and broad *aggiornamento* (or updating) in response to the cultural upheavals of the 1960s, despite a fair measure of internal dissent. Hugh McCullum has described the mood of General Synod, ACC's national governance, when in 1971 it met to choose a new primate to head the denomination. That process was

---

students were choosing professional careers outside the ministry." This statement was on the FTE website until the organization recently changed its name and mission, but an archived screenshot is available at https://web.archive.org/web/20090310134631/https:/thefund.org/about/about_history.phtml.

26. Paige Parsons, "Anglican Church of Canada put interests of alleged abusers ahead of victims," *CBC News*, May 11, 2022, https://www.cbc.ca/news/investigates/anglican-church-newspaper-breach-1.6448578.

27. Two differing views: Statistics Canada, "The Impact of the COVID-19 Pandemic on the Religiosity of Canadians," July 18, 2022, https://www150.statcan.gc.ca/n1/pub/45-28-0001/2022001/article/00005-eng.htm; Religious Media Centre, "COVID accelerated 'trend towards secularisation' says report," https://religionmediacentre.org.uk/news/covid-accelerated-trend-towards-secularisation-says-report/.

28. Clarke and Macdonald, *Leaving Christianity*, 239, and elsewhere.

29. Macdonald and Clarke are suggesting, not proposing a thesis, which would require some considerable unpacking and qualification, given the diversity of Canadian churches and Canadian cultures.

steered by "the progressives in a moribund church," he writes, "the people who wanted openness, inclusivity, change."[30] The election went to Archbishop Ted Scott, whose personal humility, dialogical style, "radical compassion," and devotion to justice dominated the ACC's agenda and style during his primacy (1971–1986). Along with several likeminded bishops, a remarkable senior management team in the national office, and mixed but sometimes enthusiastic support from the pews, he led the ACC into dismantling hierarchical structures, introducing greater transparency to its operations, bringing Indigenous leadership into Church House, ordaining women to the priesthood, replacing the sixteenth-century *Book of Common Prayer*, and embracing a sizable social justice agenda.[31]

This period was particularly distinguished by the work of several ecumenical social justice coalitions, including the Roman Catholic Church—an unprecedented phenomenon in Canadian Christianity. For the ACC wasn't the only reinvigorated denomination during these years; the Roman Catholic Church in Canada was buoyed after Vatican II and the UCC in the same years was being led by such edgy moderators as Robert McClure, Bruce McLeod, Lois Wilson, and Bob Smith (although these denominations, too, were internally divided). These coalitions tackled issues of Indigenous justice, apartheid in South Africa, corporate social responsibility, the equitable treatment of poorer nations in international trade, and the treatment of third-world workers by Canadian resource companies, among other things. The most conspicuous coalition—apart from the Toronto School of Theology!—was likely Project North, which opposed the construction of an oil pipeline in the Mackenzie River Valley through the territory of the Dene Nation.[32]

But the coalitions, perhaps especially Project North, stirred considerable blowback, especially from among the wealthy and influential. Sandra Beardsall has traced how the UCC in the 1980s retreated from solidarity with Indigenous peoples into an "everyone-has-a-valid-point" orientation, and developments in the ACC were no doubt similar.[33] Since Ted Scott's retirement, although ACC leaders have often "talked the talk," their infrequent statements about public policy are seldom visionary, and their budget priorities and energies and policy tendencies have looked inward.

30. McCullum, *Radical Compassion*, 143.

31. A similar development has been studied in Anglicanism in the USA. Tobin, *Privilege and Prophecy*, argues that the image of the Episcopal Church changed from a "bastion of WASP wealth and respectability" to an institution committed to progressive causes, a change that triggered divisions and resentments.

32. See for example Hutchinson, *Prophets, Pastors*, and Pratt, *In Good Faith*.

33. Beardsall, "Into the South," 94.

ACC STORIES THAT AREN'T ABOUT DECLINE

While the narrative of decline works reasonably well with most largely white settler parishes (even if many of them have West Indian, Asian, and African members), it doesn't work so well for Indigenous Anglicans or some new immigrants.

As for Indigenous Anglicans, Statistics Canada has published local profiles for many First Nations census tracts based on the 2021 census. Several show robust Anglican affiliation, signs that an Indigenous nation has adopted Anglicanism not as a western, settler colonial phenomenon, but as a resource for, and expression of, their own culture.

Let me start with the Gwich'in. Mark Macdonald, the former National Indigenous Anglican Archbishop, sometimes said, as much seriously as facetiously, that the Gwich'in were the most Anglican nation on the planet.[34] The 2021 census profile for Fort McPherson, Northwest Territories, reports a total population of 645, of whom 530 reported Gwich'in nationality, and of whom 535 people self-identified as Anglican. The statistical table doesn't cross-tabulate Gwich'in and Anglican, but even if all 115 non-Gwich'in residents of this census area were Anglican, that would still mean that 78% of the Gwich'in were Anglican. Most likely the percentage is much closer to 100.[35]

Historically, the Gwich'in became Anglican through the ministry of the missionary Robert McDonald (1829–1913), a man of triracial heritage (Scots, Ojibwe, Jamaican mulatto), who spent almost four decades among these people (then called the Tukudh or the Loucheux). He became fluent in the language, and translated the Scriptures; he married a Gwich'in woman, Julia Kutug, and raised a family of nine children; so far from trying to "Improve" the people, he embraced a Gwich'in identity; rather than seeking to distinguish Gwich'in teaching and spirituality from Christian, he affirmed the commonalities; rather than making church decisions on his own, he promoted a healthy lay leadership so that the Gwich'in could take responsibility for their own faith.[36]

34. Among other places, he made this comment in a course on Canadian Indigenous Christianity that we taught together at Wycliffe College in the late 2010s.

35. Government of Canada, "Fort McPherson, Hamlet [Census subdivision], Northwest Territories," Indigenous Population Profile, 2021 Census of Population, https://www12.statcan.gc.ca/census-recensement/2021/dp-pd/ipp-ppa/details/page.cfm?Lang=E&SearchText=Fort%20McPherson&DGUID=2021A00056101015&GENDER=1&AGE=1&HP=0&HH=0.

36. Peake, "Robert McDonald"; Gaver, "Solitudes in Shared Spaces."

For the Nisga'a, in the census area called Nisga'a land, the 2021 Statscan profile reported a total population of 1,875, of whom 1,530 identified primarily as Nisga'a (all others were also First Nations). The top religious group was Anglican (810 persons, 45.1%), followed by "other Christians" (235, 13.1%).[37] Nicholas May, in a PhD thesis of 2013, found that the complex process by which the Nisga'a became Christian (1860–1920) was based in the cultural stance of the Nisga'a themselves that valued and integrated new knowledge. They did not surrender their identity and accept a colonial Christianity; rather, they made Christianity a Nisga'a religion.[38]

Chisasibi, in Nunavik (northern Quebec), is a Cree nation which was moved to its present location to spare it from the consequences of the James Bay hydroelectric dam construction of the 1980s. Formerly, it was located on Fort George Island, which had a Hudson's Bay trading post (1803), an Anglican mission (1852), and an Anglican school (1907) which became an Indian residential school (1933). The census profile reports a population of 4,985, of whom 3,245 (65%) self-identified as Anglican.[39] This remote place has retained its cultural identity, which suggests to me that it has made Anglicanism its own. Its clergy leaders are a Cree couple. A Facebook posting for the parish in 2023 listed 57 children who were candidates for confirmation; I would be surprised if any settler Anglican parish in Canada ever achieves such numbers these days.[40]

The Inuit of what is sometimes called "the Anglican Arctic" have, to a significant degree, retained an Anglican identity. The 2021 census reports 26,380 self-identified Anglicans out of a total population of 70,540 (37.4%).[41] The anthropologists Frédéric Laugrand and Jarich Oosten have rejected the familiar narrative that a traditional Inuit past was replaced or subverted by a Christian present. Rather, they found, traditional Shamanism always borrowed "outside" elements, and Inuit Christianity, particularly Anglicanism, embraced some Shamanistic cosmology.[42] A writer

37. Government of Canada, Nisga'a, "Nisga'a land," Focus on Geography Series, 2021 Census of Population, https://www12.statcan.gc.ca/census-recensement/2021/as-sa/fogs-spg/page.cfm?topic=10&dguid=2021A00055949035&lang=E.

38. May, "Feasting on the AAM."

39. Governement of Canada, "Chisasibi, Terres réservées aux Cris (TC) Quebec," Census Profile, 2021 Census of Population, https://www12.statcan.gc.ca/census-recensement/2021/dp-pd/prof/details/page.cfm?Lang=E&SearchText=chisasibi&DGUIDlist=2021A00052499814&GENDERlist=1,2,3&STATISTIClist=1,4&HEADERlist=0.

40. St-Philip's Anglican Church Chisasibi, Facebook group, https://www.facebook.com/groups/493246808476874/.

41. Government of Canada, "Religion by Indigenous Identity: Canada, Provinces and Territories," https://www150.statcan.gc.ca/t1/tbl1/en/tv.action?pid=9810028801.

42. Laugrand and Oosten, *Inuit Shamanism*.

identifying as Inuk wrote on an Internet post in 2025: "Anglicanism stuck in Nunavut because the missionaries really connected with the Inuit learning their language, translating the Bible, and respecting their traditions . . . In a place as isolated as Nunavut, the church became more than religion; it is also a hub for support and connection."[43]

Unfortunately, the way Statistics Canada frames its census questions about religion obscures the religious character of Indigenous peoples, by forcing respondents to choose just one religion. In real life, many Indigenous peoples embrace both Christianity and Indigenous spirituality, without paradox or tension. (Other Indigenous peoples do indeed reject that mixture.)

As for new immigrant Anglicans, I have space for only one example. In my own diocese of Niagara, the ACC is being buoyed by an influx of Mandarin-speaking Chinese members, served by Chinese Anglican clergy and lay leaders under the general mentorship of the Rev. Canon Garfield Wu Adams, who was converted to Christianity in a Chinese prison, of all places. Their worship and fellowship functions bilingually, though mainly in Chinese. Among this group, it is not Christianity that has an unfortunate reputation to live down, but atheism. Many new Chinese Canadians have been initially attracted to Garfield Adams' meetings where English is practiced, then stay for the fellowship, and then are moved by the preaching and music and prayers to embrace Christianity.[44]

CONCLUSION

Leaving Christianity is a highly successful synthetic treatment of the fortunes of the Christian Church in Canada from after World War II to the time of the book's publication, as illuminated by a range of statistical data. Although the reliability of any individual data point is inevitably subject to some margin of error, the sweep of the book's timeline and denominational coverage, the number and variety of the statistical sources, and the absence of any apparent unidirectional bias in the data collection, give the reader considerable confidence in the book's conclusions.

The title *Leaving Christianity* reflects the fact that, as a whole, the population of Canada is less churchgoing than it once was. When I look at

43. "Why are there so many Anglicans in Nunavut?," Reddit thread, https://www.reddit.com/r/nunavut/comments/1hyqhgz/why_are_there_so_many_anglicans_in_nunavut/.

44. Anglican Diocese of Niagara, "Mission in Acts," https://niagaraanglican.ca/ministry/chinese-anglican-ministry.

the data of the ACC in particular, it becomes clear to me that the number of individuals who have left Christianity over the past seventy years isn't surprising: it is a slow leak of roughly 2% per year, compounded annually, easily explained by demographic events, frustrations with congregational life or the denomination, and competition for Sunday leisure time. What needs to be explained is that numbers haven't been replaced. For that failure, *Leaving Christianity* provides several explanations that seem right to me, relating to birth rates, immigration patterns, and child-rearing decisions. More sweepingly, the book suggests that the Canadian churches have failed to engage with post-Christendom culture. This is a trickier explanation to demonstrate, but I think it has merit, with one caveat. I think = that the ACC and some other denominations actually did experience quite an exciting period of *aggiornamento* from the late 1960s to the mid-1980s, when it was routed by a conservative reaction. Ironically, the ACC's retreat into a self-protective stance may well have resulted in part from its anxiety about declining numbers.

Nevertheless, Canadian Anglicanism retains strengths in some Indigenous communities where it has been inculturated and has found new strength in at least one local immigrant community. And worldwide, we shouldn't forget that the number of Anglican Christians has roughly doubled since 1970. Indeed, Anglicanism's distinctive weakness in first-world affluent colonial and predominantly white societies lends considerable support to Macdonald and Clarke's suspicion that "leaving Christianity" has a great deal to do with the church's relation to its cultural context.

BIBLIOGRAPHY

Badertscher, John. Review of *Leaving Christianity: Changing Allegiances in Canada since 1945* by Brian Clarke and Stuart Macdonald. *Touchstone* 38.1 (2020) 69–70.

Beaman, Lori G. Review of *Leaving Christianity: Changing Allegiances in Canada since 1945* by Brian Clarke and Stuart Macdonald. *Canadian Historical Review* 99.4 (2018) 664–66.

Beardsall, Sandra. "'Getting their Story into the South': Project North and the United Church of Canada, 1975–1987." *Historical Papers: Canadian Society of Church History* (2018) 89–96.

Bibby, Reginald W. *Fragmented Gods: The Poverty and Potential of Religion in Canada.* Toronto: Irwin, 1987.

Bramadat, Paul. Review of *Leaving Christianity: Changing Allegiances in Canada since 1945* by Brian Clarke and Stuart Macdonald. *Church History* 87.3 (2018) 963–64.

Brown, Callum G. *The Death of Christian Britain: Understanding Secularisation 1800–2000.* London: Routledge, 2001.

Chadwick, Owen. *The Victorian Church.* 2 vols. London: Adam & Charles Black, 1966–1970.

Christie, Nancy. *Households of Faith: Family, Gender, and Community in Canada, 1760–1969*. Montreal and Kingston: McGill-Queen's University Press, 2002.

Clarke, Brian, and Stuart Macdonald. *Leaving Christianity: Changing Allegiances in Canada since 1945*. Montreal and Kingston: McGill-Queen's University Press, 2017.

Cox, Jeffrey. *The English Churches in a Secular Society: Lambeth, 1870–1930*. Oxford: Oxford University Press, 1982.

Davie, Grace. *Religion in Britain since 1945: Believing without Belonging*. Oxford: Blackwell, 1994.

Gauvreau, Michael. *The Catholic Origins of Quebec's Quiet Revolution, 1931–1970*. Montreal and Kingston: McGill-Queen's University Press, 2005.

Gaver, Cheryl. "Solitudes in Shared Spaces: Aboriginal and EuroCanadian Anglicans in the Yukon and the Northwest Territories in the Post-Residential School Era," PhD diss., University of Ottawa, 2011.

Hutchinson, Roger. *Prophets, Pastors and Public Choices: Canadian Churches and the Mackenzie Valley Pipeline Debate*. Waterloo, ON: Wilfrid Laurier, 1992.

Laugrand, Frédéric B., and Jarich G. Oosten. *Inuit Shamanism and Christianity: Transitions and Transformations in the Twentieth Century*. Montreal and Kingston: McGill-Queen's University Press, 2010.

Macdonald, Mark. Various public addresses and interviews as National Indigenous Anglican Archbishop.

May, Nicholas. "Feasting on the AAM of Heaven: The Christianization of the Nisga'a, 1860–1920," PhD diss., University of Toronto, 2013.

McCullum, Hugh. *Radical Compassion: The Life and Times of Archbishop Ted Scott*. Toronto: Anglican Book Centre, 2004.

Peake, Frank. "Robert McDonald (1829–1913), the Great Unknown Missionary of the Northwest," *Journal of the Canadian Church Historical Society* 17.3 (1975) 54–72.

Pratt, Renate. *In Good Faith: Canadian Churches against Apartheid*. Waterloo, ON: Wilfrid Laurier, 1997.

Putnam, Robert D. *Bowling Alone: The Collapse and Revival of American Community*. New York: Simon & Schuster, 2000.

Rady-Shaw, Julia. Review of *Leaving Christianity: Changing Allegiances in Canada since 1945* by Brian Clarke and Stuart Macdonald. *Ontario History* 110.2 (2018) 235–37.

Reimer, Sam. Review of *Leaving Christianity: Changing Allegiances in Canada since 1945* by Brian Clarke and Stuart Macdonald. *Journal of Contemporary Religion* 33.3 (2018) 600–601.

Rothauge, Arlin. *Sizing Up a Congregation for New Ministry*. New York: Seabury, 1983.

Stark, Rodney. *The Rise of Christianity: A Sociologist Reconsiders History*. Princeton: Princeton University Press, 1996.

Statistics Canada. *Census of Population, 2021*. Ottawa: Government of Canada, 2022.

Statistics Canada. *General Social Survey*. Various years. Ottawa: Government of Canada.

Tobin, Robert Benjamin. *Privilege and Prophecy: Social Activism in the Post-war Episcopal Church*. New York: Oxford University Press, 2022.

Turcotte, Paul-André. Review of *Leaving Christianity: Changing Allegiances in Canada since 1945* by Brian Clarke and Stuart Macdonald. *Études d'histoire religieuse / Historical Studies*, Canadian Catholic Historical Association, 86.1–2 (2020) 80–83.

Wilson, Bryan. *Religion in Secular Society*. London: Watts, 1966.

9

"Between Evil and Less Evil"[1]

Canadian Churches and Area Bombing in World War Two

Gordon L. Heath

By late 1942, Germany was basically bombed "around the clock."[2] By 1945, the situation in Japan was similar. The Allied bombing efforts over Germany and Japan were punishing campaigns developed not only to destroy military personnel and infrastructure but also to break the will of citizens by subjecting them to dislocation, desolation, and death. The raw numbers provide a striking summary of the cost of the campaigns. The Allies lost roughly 81,000 airmen,[3] whereas by the end of the war, the cities of Germany and Japan were wastelands marked by piles of massive rubble, including two eradiated cities. The immediate civilian deaths in cities were approximately 410,000 Germans and 340,000 Japanese.[4] Those figures do not account for injury and dislocation.

1. "Protest Indiscriminate Bombing," *Presbyterian Record*, May 1944.

2. De Bruhl, *Firestorm*, 76.

3. Bashow, *None but the Brave*, 121–22.

4. Numbers vary. See Bashow, *None but the Brave*, 121–22; Wilson et al., *Bombing Japan*, ch. 6; Hoyt, *Inferno*.

Randall Hansen notes that the most often asked questions about the bombing campaigns revolve around two issues: "was bombing justified and did it work?"[5] This research is not concerned with the latter question, but is related to the former; more specifically, can the bombing be considered morally justified? Note, the moral issue being addressed here was not strategic bombing of specific military targets; the moral issue in focus was the shift from precision bombing to area or carpet bombing[6] of civilian populations. The memory and memorialization of the desolation caused by such bombing has a long and complicated history.[7] The morality of shifting from precision bombing to area bombing was debated at the time and has, at various times, come under further criticism. In the last generation or so in Canada, the morality of area bombings became a heated issue due to various revisionist histories.[8] As Tim Cook notes, the CBC-TV miniseries *The Valor and the Horror* (1992), in particular one episode entitled *Death by Moonlight: Bomber Command*,[9] played a key role in stoking debate.

The focus of this chapter is not to provide a history of the bombing campaigns, for that has been ably carried out by others.[10] Nor is it an attempt to solve the ethical issue by making a statement on the morality of the bombing campaigns. What this research focuses on is the public response of Canadian Protestant churches to the urban conflagrations. Significant research has been carried out on the churches and their reactions to the war effort against German and Japanese fascism,[11] but, at this point in time, no one has specifically examined the Canadian churches' reactions to the bombing campaigns.

While the churches were officially supportive of the overall war effort against the Axis powers, there was little enthusiasm expressed for the conventional area-bombing campaigns, nor for the atomic bombing of

5. Hansen, *Fire and Fury*, 269.

6. There are a variety of terms that are virtually synonymous: area bombing, carpet bombing, saturation bombing, fire-bombing, and obliteration bombing. What those terms share in common is (1) they are not precision bombing, and (2) they are indiscriminate (thus civilians are targeted). Precision bombing, on the other hand, intends to target military personal and infrastructure.

7. Arnold, "Beyond Usable Pasts," 26–28; Bowe, "Framing Memory."

8. Hall, "Black, White and Grey," 7–8.

9. Cook, *Fight for History*, ch. 13. See also Nelson and Waters, "Allied Bombing," 113–15.

10. For instance, see Ross, *Strategic Bombing*; Addison and Crang, *Firestorm*; Webster and Frankland, *Strategic Air Offensive*; Messenger, *"Bomber" Harris*; Biddle, "Bombing by the Square Yard"; Shaffer, *Wings of Judgment*.

11. Rudy, "Cause of Righteousness." For further sources on the churches and the war, see Rudy, "Protagonist of Justice"; Sinclair–Faulkner, "For Christian Civilization."

Hiroshima and Nagasaki. The churches seemed reticent to openly criticize the efforts of the area bombing campaigns, as well as reticent to endorse the bombing (although they appreciated the victory it wrought). However, they did at times raise pressing ethical questions on the subject, revealing a striking and poignant distaste for such seemingly morally suspect conduct by a side that was supposed to be fighting against evil, not copying it. Such critical commentary on the war effort provides nuance and complexity to what is sometimes seen to be wartime churches unconditionally supporting the nation's war effort. The best the churches could publicly say in support was that there seemed to be no other option if victory was to be attained. At worst, the actions of the allies on that particular matter were a profound moral failure requiring remorse and repentance. The reason for the tepid support or even open criticism of the bombing of civilians *en masse* was that such a practice went contrary to the just war tradition of non-combatant immunity. It also made the allies complicit in actions they once criticized as barbaric. Nevertheless, the underlying reason—or compromise—for tolerating the bombing was that evil needed to be done to defeat an even greater evil, in common parlance it was "the better of two evils," or as one churchman at the time wrote a position "between evil and less evil."[12] What follows is the range of commentary on area bombing, demonstrating how the churches were torn between patriotism or prophetic witness, loyalty or ethical convictions, and national leadership or Christian identity.

THE CHURCHES

The Canadian Protestant churches comprised close to 60% of the population of Canada, with the other 40% being Roman Catholic. The focus here is on the Protestant churches, with hopes that in the future attention can be directed to the Catholic and Eastern Orthodox churches. Unless noted otherwise, when churches are referenced, it means those Protestant churches. It should also be noted that while the churches shared much in common, they were far from monochrome.

The Protestant churches can be categorized into two groups. The first, made up of the United Church of Canada (UCC), Anglicans, Presbyterians, and Baptists, were roughly 50% of the Canadian population, and of primarily—though not exclusively—British background. Those churches saw themselves as nation-builders, with a mission to shape Canada into a Christian (hopefully Protestant) nation. And that mission included speaking to the political events of the day, especially in wartime. The second, comprising

12. "Protest Indiscriminate Bombing," *Presbyterian Record*, May 1944.

about 10% of the Canadian population, was a mix of smaller denominations on the margins due to ethnicity (German Lutherans, German Mennonites) and/or theology (Mennonite pacifists, Pentecostals, Salvation Army).

SOURCES

The sources of this research are, with a few exceptions, denominational periodicals, usually published bi-weekly or monthly. The periodicals were read widely in the respective denominations, with some having a circulation close to secular daily papers. The religious press of the various denominations provided a broad range of local, national, and international denominational news, articles and editorials on international affairs, letters to the editor, as well as poetry, hymns, prayers, and stories. The advantage of such sources is that one gains a sense of the official and public position of the denomination, as well as opinions that the editor deemed worthy to publish. The limitations of using such sources are obvious. What did the people in the pews or pulpits think about what they read in the papers? And what role did the editor play in the shaping of views through the use of a heavy editorial hand? Nevertheless, the advantages of the papers are obvious as well, for they do provide a sense of the official positions or at least views popular enough to print in order to resonate with readers.

The Protestant periodicals accessed for this research include the *Observer* (UCC), *Canadian Churchman* (Anglican), *Montreal Churchman* (Anglican), *Presbyterian Record* (Presbyterian), *Acts and Proceedings* (Presbyterian), *Canadian Baptist*, *Maritime Baptist*, *Gospel Witness* (Baptist), *War Cry* (Salvation Army), *Canada Lutheran*, *Pentecostal Testimony*, and *Canadian Churches and the War* (a joint publication issued by the Wartime Information Board, Ottawa).[13] The *Gospel Herald* (Mennonite) was published in the US but distributed to the Mennonite community in Canada. One source providing a unique perspective is a newsletter entitled *Bulletin* published by R. Edis Fairbairn, a dissenting pacifist UCC minister who was critical of the United Church's support for the war.[14]

13. There are indications in the Roman Catholic press (e.g., *L'Action Catholique*; *L'Autorite*; *Catholic Register*; *Catholic Record*; *Casket*; *Northwest Review*) that attitudes may be similar to Protestants, but that primary source material has not been examined in any detail for this chapter. Thanks to Mark McGowan for leads on those Catholic papers.

14. Fairbairn (1880–1953) was active in arousing social awareness in the United Church, contributor to *Towards the Christian Revolution*, author of *Apostate Christendom* and *The Appeal to Reality*, pastor, founder and editor of a pacifist newsletter that circulated in the church, as well as one of the main leaders behind the pacifist movement

AREA BOMBING

After the fall of France in the summer of 1940, the British needed a way to strike back at Germany. Landing troops on the continent was not an option for the foreseeable future, but not to act could lead to further German successes (not to mention erode allied morale). The only way to strike back directly at Germany was through heavy bombers, and Britain eventually commenced a bomber offensive against the German homeland. Despite the misgivings of some clergy in the Anglican Church in Britain, some in the public, a few airmen, and even Prime Minister Winston Churchill (at times), the bombing was directed to cities and civilian populations. Any notion of non-combatant immunity was eventually abandoned for military necessity, and the firebombing of cities became commonplace.[15]

Area bombing grew to become a cathartic and morale-building strike at the hated Germans, a chance to placate the Russians who wanted a second front, an occasion to destroy infrastructure, and, hopefully, an opportunity to undermine German morale. Led by "Bomber Harris," there were those in Britain who believed that strategic bombing could win the war, especially with such power as demonstrated by the 1,000-bomber attack on Cologne in May 1942. By 1944, the Americans had begun the practice as well. And when US bombers gained airfields close enough to Japan, they started the same process over Japanese cities with devastating results.

As for in the war in Asia, the dilemma facing President Harry Truman in the summer of 1945 was multifaceted and vexing.[16] An invasion of Japan was projected to lead to over a million deaths and incalculable casualties. So what to do? Invade and see massive suffering or bomb two cities and kill 200,000 or so. It was a lose-lose option, for either option had horrifying ramifications. However, the Allies had already "crossed the Rubicon" with the firebombing of German and Japanese cities, and Truman chose the atomic bomb.

It should be noted that while the most denominational periodicals covered a significant amount of war-related matters, there was limited commentary on area bombing of civilians. However, by 1944 statements started appearing, and what was printed revealed conflicted churches—support for the war effort but not necessarily the way it was being fought in the air over Germany and Japan. What follows provides a summary and brief analysis of that coverage.

---

in the United Church. The *Bulletin* is located at the United Church Archives, Toronto.

15. Hansen, *Fire and Fury*; Hall, "Black, White and Grey."

16. Walker, *Prompt and Utter Destruction*; Allen and Polmar, *Code-Name Downfall*.

THE CHURCHES AND AREA BOMBING

The churches' view of war was shaped by the just war tradition, a tradition that can be traced to the earliest centuries of the church.[17] It was the view that the state was given authority by God to use violence for the purpose of justice; stated simply, both the cause must be just (*jus ad bellum*), and the means used to wage the war must be just (*jus in bello*). Anything else, the tradition held, was to be condemned and not supported. In the war against Germany and Japan, it was believed that the pressing issue of cause was clear and beyond debate—fascism was deemed to be an aggressive existential threat. What was vexing among those in the churches was the means—could the bombing of civilians be deemed to be just?

The initial answer to that question was negative; the churches made it clear in the opening months of the conflict that the bombing of innocents was barbaric and against the rules of war.[18] However, when the tide of war started to shift in the Allies favor in mid/late 1942, the churches faced a dilemma. What they used to condemn had, so it seemed, increasingly become standard Allied practice.

SIGNS OF SUPPORT

It should be noted that initially, there seemed to be a high degree of trust in the planning and motives of the Allied command. It was realized that citizens could not make a well-informed decision due to a lack of facts about the strategic necessities, and that a basic degree of trust was required when hearing what naysayers had to say about the actions of allied bombers. For instance, in 1942, one contributor to the Anglican *Canadian Churchman* declared that despite the statements to the contrary, the churches could trust the Allied leaders to carry out bombing raids within a humane framework:

> Last week Americans rejoiced to hear that American bombers had actually raided Japanese cities. We may well rejoice at this evidence of the power of American arms, and we may safely

17. Heath, *Christians.*

18. "It is aerial bombardment which is the most frightful side of this war, and the deliberate attempt to breakdown the morale of the nation by killing civilians. It is this which makes it so hard to keep from bitterness of spirit. When you think of German airmen turning their machine guns upon little children playing on the village green, deliberately dropping their bombs over residential districts where there are no military objectives whatever, and they know it,—it is then one feels that every spark of decency is outraged by such devilry." "John Bull Churchill," *Canadian Baptist*, 15 November 1940. See also John Pitts, "Is Hitler Anti-Christ?" *Presbyterian Record*, September 1940.

> ignore propagandist statements by Japanese authorities as to the bombing of nonmilitary objectives. We think that our leaders may be trusted to carry on military operations honourably and as humanely as possible, and the indiscriminate bombing of helpless citizens, of any race or nation, is neither honourable nor humane.[19]

However, as will be seen below, as the war progressed, and the rules of war as commonly understood (d)evolved, the churches began to realize that something was amiss.

That said, there were a few comments that indicate early support for the bombing of German cities, such as the 1942 comments in the *Presbyterian Record* that noted with approval the targeting of urban centers.[20] A few years later, in the face of criticism, with even more information on the bombing campaign in the skies over Germany, the same paper provided a more detailed defense of the bombing campaign.[21] It was critical of English clerics who raised moral qualms about the bombing campaign, claimed that it was not carried out by a vengeful spirit but with a concern for strategic value only, noted that the cities were not defenseless, and that, besides, the argument went, the Germans did it first. It went on to argue that in a total war, the definition of who was a noncombatant had changed. No longer were civilians free from being targeted, for "wars can only be won by destroying either the forces in the field or those in the factory towns supplying them, or both." It was accepted that the task was dehumanizing, but it was considered that the allied motives were pure, their cause was just, and those in bombers could die with a good conscience:

> In an unnatural interlude in civilian existence, in which men must either slay or be slain, they do, without hatred in their hearts, what they believe will prevent the complete victory of evil and the de-spiritualizing and de-moralizing of life. What higher course is possible? . . . They will go over enemy territory again tonight no doubt, and thousands of them will say their prayers, with no sense of hypocrisy, before going; And if they meet God in the air tonight there sure he will understand.

The article ended with Prime Minister Churchill's not-so-sympathetic advice to German citizens in cities; they needed to "get away to the hills and watch the home fires burning."

19. "Love Your Enemies," *Canadian Churchman*, 30 April 1942.
20. "Sinse Annyway," *Presbyterian Record*, November 1942.
21. "Protest Indiscriminate Bombing," *Presbyterian Record*, May 1944.

That mention of the Germans starting it first was used elsewhere,[22] not necessarily to deny that there were ethical issues at stake, but to at least place the allied response in a larger context of the course of the war. After all, there is an innate sense of moral virtue if you are not the one who started it. For instance, in the context of the devastation of war in general and German cities in particular, the *Maritime Baptist* published an article entitled "Chickens Come Home to Roost,"[23] a colloquial expression that no doubt resonated with those happy to see Germans getting their comeuppance. However, even those who noted that they did not start the policy of indiscriminate area bombing were aware of the moral quandary: "Today terrible things are happening for which someone is responsible. It is quite unlikely that any people or nation is entirely blameless. All have sinned and come short of the glory of God. All have in greater or lesser measure divorced politics from morals and made expediency the first law of their relations with others."[24]

RETICENCE, REGRET, AND REPENTANCE

Much of the commentary was marked by a combination of reticence, regret, and repentance. Canadian Anglicans took their lead from William Temple, the Archbishop of Canterbury. Earlier in the war the Church of England had raised pointed questions with the British government over the shift to area bombing and had settled on trusting the government and thus supporting the campaign.[25] Despite the brutality of modern area bombing, those in the churches were urged to wage war in such campaigns without malice or hate.

Reflecting the Augustinian concern for the right use of violence to be motivated by love and not hate or self-interest was a sermon preached by C. H. Adams, Canadian Chaplain overseas, on the anniversary of the Battle of Britain. Adams exhorted his listeners to forgive those who were their enemies, as professed in the Lord's Prayer. That expectation for forgiveness was rooted in the humbling recognition that allied hands were not spotless when it came to injustice: "We have the right to demand that our enemies should experience the same justice as we ourselves submit to. Certainly, we

22. "Bombing Policy," *Canadian Baptist*, 16 August 1943; H.H. Bingham, *Canadian Baptist*, 1 July 1944.

23. "Chickens Come Home to Roost," *Maritime Baptist*, 19 December 1943.

24. "Chickens Come Home to Roost," *Maritime Baptist*, 19 December 1943. See also "Bombing Policy," *Canadian Baptist*, 16 August 1943.

25. Lammers, "William Temple."; Chandler, "Obliteration Bombing."; Snape, *Church Militant*, ch. 3.

must not be vindictive in our treatment of them. We must first strive for a full understanding of their case, remembering that our own nation had its part in the policies which have borne such bitter fruit. On that understanding, we must build true and dispassionate justice."[26] A similar exhortation in the *Canadian Churchman* stated that

> We must strike, and strike hard. We must take the offensive and carry the war to the enemy's territory. We must outthink him, outmaneuver him, and outfight him, on land, at sea, and in the air. Above all we must keep our hands our heads clear—and we cannot do that if they are clouded by hate. Any reputable psychiatrist will testify to that. Not hate, but the consciousness of a righteous and imperative causes the mental attitude that will lead to final victory—to the only kind of victory that is worth winning.[27]

The church's clergy and chaplains were to work hard to ensure that the hearts of soldiers and citizenry reflected those high ideals. And, in the minds of some, they seemed to be successful, for it was stated numerous times that the Allied bombing campaign was being carried out in a spirit of humble necessity. In the words of a defender of the bombers, they were "modest, self-forgetting, gentle, generous, walking humbly with God; and with charity in their hearts towards all" and "knights of the air."[28] At a convocation address at McMaster University, the bombers were portrayed similarly: "Nobody flies a bomber over Germany for personal gain or advantage. Our sailors do not man corvettes in the hazards and storms of the North Atlantic for the sake of personal profi . . . . The fact is we have failed to realize that men are willing to live and to die if need be for supra-personal ends."[29] Those idealized impressions of airmen provided a moral imprimatur of sorts, their uprightness seemingly undermining any criticisms of the bombing campaign.[30]

Despite positive portrayals of those involved in the bombing of German cities, the most common narrative was increasingly a paradoxical mix

26. "Love Your Enemies," *Canadian Churchman*, 30 December 1943. See also "The Temptation to Hatred," *Maritime Baptist*, 7 April 1943.

27. "Love Your Enemies," *Canadian Churchman*, 30 April 1942. See also Walter R. Bowie, "Hate is a Moral Poison," *Canadian Churchman*, 23 September 1943.

28. "Protest Indiscriminate Bombing," *Presbyterian Record*, May 1944. For another example of evoking crusading idealism for allied soldiering, see "Christianity and War," *Canadian Churchman*, 19 August 1943.

29. James S. Thomson, "Preface to Reconstruction," *Canadian Baptist*, 1 June 1943.

30. For more detailed explanation of the expression moral imprimatur see Heath, "Queen Victoria and General Gordon."

of a need to win a just war, a need to do what was once considered to be barbaric and unethical, and a need to repent for one's actions. In some cases, concerns for the targeting of civilians led to condemnation of the bombing campaign. What follows are a few of the most poignant examples.

It was recognized that the pragmatism associated with military necessity was potentially a slippery slope to losing key convictions and giving up the moral high ground. One commentator lamented the dehumanizing and demonizing of the war in general. He wrote: "The spirit of war, a demonic possession, has obsessed the world . . . that devilish spirit has already lowered men to the animal level . . . and it threatens to annihilate all human values."[31] And the longer the war went on, the more likely both sides would descend into an abyss:

> When men and nations become desperately cynical, vengeful, and bitter, human life loses its value, justice and freedom become trivialities, spiritual worth becomes a dangerous luxury. The world is already rampant with the philosophy of an eye for an eye, and a life for a life. And as we become increasingly more thirsty for the blood of our enemies we are gradually forgetting that they are, like ourselves, made in the image of God; that they too possess, as their inalienable right, the justice and freedom of an individual personality; and that they are to be valued as spiritual entities beyond worth.

As the following comments indicate, such concerns for the sanctity of all human life—enemies included—led to both subtle and quite pointed criticisms of the targeting of citizens in cities. In fact, criticisms would evolve to such pointed statements made by one Presbyterian that captured well the sense of vexing moral compromise and uncertainty, "the choice between evil and less evil":

> The basic truth is at war itself is wrong, disgusting, stupid, an unchristian—the whole thing! You cannot argue that to destroy one class of men is Christian and to destroy another class is not Christian. The killing of fellow men is all unchristian! We have been forced by aggression into an unchristian atmosphere and our choice is not between good and evil, Christian and unchristian, but between evil and less evil.[32]

31. "Human Values," *Maritime Baptist*, 10 February 1943.
32. "Protest Indiscriminate Bombing," *Presbyterian Record*, May 1944.

And that vexing dilemma was reiterated in other statements, such as one made by the UCC as well as in a joint statement of the mainline British background churches in March–April 1945.

The UCC faced a dilemma, for in the opening months of the war, there had been serious dissent in the clergy ranks over the UCC's support for the war.[33] It was a public scandal for a church that was trying to take a leading role as the unofficial state church and the conscience of the nation, which Phyllis Airhart coined a church with the "soul of a nation."[34] The embarrassment was eventually dealt with in part by shutting down debate in the pages of the denominational periodical, the *Observer*. However, one of the key dissenting clergy was the indefatigable R. Edis Fairbairn. On his own initiative, he published a *Bulletin* that continued his criticism of the UCC's support for the war effort.[35] And in that criticism, there was commentary that reveals what one clergyman felt about the bombing campaign. In Old Testament prophet-like fashion Fairbairn made his case clear: the UCC had descended into "the moral hell of callousness."[36] He went on to state that callousness of their hearts had made the allies do terrible things, so much so he was convinced that "the price of vistory [*sic*] is that we have become what we went to war to eliminate."[37] Echoing the concern expressed by like-minded pacifists, the bombing of German cities was foremost in Fairbairn's mind when he stated "that by embarking upon this campaign of ruthless destruction of life, civilian and military, we have reduced ourselves to the moral level of German and Japanese militarists."[38] Even if the reported executions and cremations that were beginning to trickle out of Germany near the end of the war were correct, Fairbairn asked, "are they any more diabolical thsn [*sic*] our cremation alive with phosphorus bombs of the civilians of Hamburg?"[39] He went on to argue that the difference between German atrocities and the Allied atrocities (bombing) was a "matter of temperament

33. Rothwell, "United Church Pacifism."; Heath, "Rise and Fall."; Airhart, *Soul of a Nation*, 130; Manson, "United Church and the Second World War."; Orser, "World War Two."

34. Airhart, *Soul of a Nation*.

35. Bulletins were dated and given a number. There were no page numbers since the newsletter was just on a single sheet of paper, usually on both sides. There are some gaps in the collection. Fairbairn was the sole author of the *Bulletin*, but he did solicit comments and often responded to them. The *Bulletin* can be found at the United Church Archives, Toronto. See Heath, "Irreconcilable Differences."

36. *Bulletin #12*, 24 February 1944.

37. *Bulletin #27*, [n.d.].

38. *Bulletin #27*, [n.d.].

39. *Bulletin #27*, [n.d.].

and training. Our way seems more refined. Does it make the atrocity any less atrocious?"[40] Fairbairn placed the blame for this "degradation of civilization below the level of beasts" at the foot of the church, for the church "did have insight once into the nature of war, but forsook it quickly when called to heel by the State."[41] There is no way of knowing how widespread Fairbairn's critical views were held, but it certainly was a view that ran counter to much of the public narrative of the UCC as well as the other churches.

While Fairbairn may have had those who agreed with him, what most commentary in the denominational press revealed was a troubling and paradoxical tension in that doing evil was needed to stop those who were committing an even greater evil. Imbedded within such commentary was pointed critique, but it was in the context of support for the war effort in general, and the regretful need for area bombing in particular. There seemed to be no way to escape the war, so action was needed; in other words, bombing and repentance was the only way forward. The following examples provide a sense of that resolve and remorse. In a striking and bold prophetic statement in the closing weeks of the war in Europe the UCC posted an editorial that echoed some of Fairbairn's concerns with the morality of area bombing.

One of the most critical public comments in the denominational press was a statement in the *Observer*. The immediate context was the aftermath of the bombing of Dresden in February 1945. The reported devastation of that city seems to have tipped the scales of opinion among some key figures in the UCC. That shift is not surprising, for even Prime Minister Churchill was struck by the destruction and soon raised questions about such "terror" raids—a usage of a term that "rankled the RAF senior command."[42] In an editorial entitled "Terror Bombing" it was made clear that area bombing was both unBritish and unchristian. Its blunt criticism is worth quoting at length:

> Naturally, in bombing military objectives, it must be expected that many helpless people will be killed and injured. That is one thing, but certainly to drop bombs from the air designed not primarily to destroy military objectives but to kill men and women and little children whose only fault is that they happened to be born German and in all likelihood had no more to do with making this war than people in similar circumstances in other countries, is not British . . . To embark on a policy of terror bombing would in itself have been reprehensible enough but

40. *Bulletin #28*, 20 May 1945.

41. *Bulletin #27*, [n.d.].

42. Cook, *Fight to the Finish*, 374.

> to announce beforehand that the policy was to be inaugurated shows to what lengths a people may go once the dogs of war are unleashed. Gradually, we become case hardened, our feelings become seared and toughened until we can watch bombings, death and murder on the screen without a tremor. Had this announcement being made when the war first broke out there would have been such a public clamour that no government would have dared put it into effect. But now the announcement has all but passed unnoticed.[43]

The article concluded with the suggestion that it would be much "better to go on through to the end with a record of fair play and decency than to descend to the pagan practices of those against whom we struggle." That public indignation in the closing weeks of the war in Europe was immediately challenged by a reader who wrote a letter to the editor questioning his sudden squeamishness. After all, he wrote, they had known about such bombing for years, so why only criticize when the war was basically over?[44] After the use of atomic bombs, another letter to the editor decried the justification of such means of mass destruction as "justified under the guise of military necessity."[45]

Shortly thereafter followed a statement published in the bi-monthly *Canadian Churches and War.*[46] And the importance of the statement cannot be overstated, for not only was it was an agreed upon statement by the four mainline churches, it was also a nuanced position that supported the bombing campaign but acknowledged the moral ambiguity of such actions.

The formal statement of *Canadian Churches and War* began with an affirmation of the value of all human life, as well as an acknowledgment that the indiscriminate bombing of cities was a "test by which we may judge the depth and force of our ultimate beliefs." So how could the churches pass the test? What followed was a three-point response to questions raised about the bombing, no doubt with the hope of alleviating the consciences of those who were vexed or confused about the conduct of allied forces and/or the churches' lack of stated opinion of such matters.

First, it expressed a lack of sympathy for "those in this country and America who plead in the name of Christianity or humanity for restrictions on bombing" without providing another way forward for victory. It went on to say that those who refused to support the bombing effort needed to be

43. "Terror Bombing," *Observer*, 1 March 1945.
44. Harold A. Miller, "On 'Terror Bombing' Editorial," *Observer*, 15 April 1945.
45. "Ministers Protest Atomic Bomb," *Observer*, 1 November 1945.
46. "Obliteration Bombing," *Canadian Churches and War*, March–April 1945.

clear if they were willing to prolong the war, or even lose the war, in order to avoid the deaths of civilians.

Second, it acknowledged that the general rules of warfare mandated that civilians should not be targeted: "there is clear distinction between the use of violence necessary for the attainment of military objectives and wanton destruction." However, the decision as to what was appropriate or not was in the hands of the military, for civilians "seldom have the data required for a right judgement." Again, another example of the trust given to authorities. It did concede, however, that if there was a "flagrant use of violence in excess of military necessities" it would be incumbent upon citizens to protest.

Third, indiscriminate bombing revealed the "hideousness of modern war" that not only brought about an "immeasurable toll of human pain and misery" but also a corruption of "men's characters and souls." Reports coming from Europe gave credence to that concern, for repeatedly there was a marked degree of "apathy, callousness and complete indifference to the suffering of others" in such razed neighborhoods, what was coined a "vast scale of dehumanization" of the populace, something that was opposed to the "purpose of God." So what was to be done if such bombing led to such dehumanizing results? The answer provided was to carry on and end the war through bombing, if necessary, for there was yet a greater evil to destroy:

> If we are compelled to continue such actions in order to avert a still greater evil, this must not blind us to what we are doing, nor allow us to escape from its horror by taking refuge in the righteousness of our cause. We must not shrink from facing the anguish of our predicament that the only means that we can see of vindicating human rights is by participating in their violation and in a process of ruthless dehumanisation. The more vigorously we prosecute the war in the conviction that there is no road to better things except by going through it, the more every necessary act of war ought to become a prayer for forgiveness and for the reconversion of our hearts and minds to a love of mercy and justice, and of all the things that belong to humane society.

That answer was hardly a ringing endorsement of the bombing campaign, but it was nonetheless a common refrain coming from the churches as they struggled with the problem of facing off against greater and lesser evils. In one sense, the dropping of two atomic bombs on Hiroshima (6 August 1945) and Nagasaki (9 August 1945) did not change the fundamental question of the morality of targeting of civilians. After all, the conventional firebombing of cities such as Tokyo had led to more deaths than the usage of atomic bombs.[47] However, what did change was the scale of carnage using a single bomb.

In the immediate aftermath of the war in Europe the *Canadian Lutheran* printed a postwar address that praised the work of allies and expressed the view that the victory was a work of God. However, despite the justice of the cause the actions of the allies were still considered to be deeply troubling:

> As we rejoice over victory let us beware lest we gloat over the slaughter and devastation that we have attended the advance to victory . . . As we stand bared before God we dare not self-righteously assume that there were no sins of ours among those that weighted the scale to the depths of the bloodiest and most destructive war in all of history. We, too, need to seek forgiveness and the power to exercise mental balance in the midst of a surge of violent emotions.[48]

Lutherans in Canada had needed to be very careful how they expressed views on the war, for their German identity meant that any careless slip of the tongue could make them look like they were a dangerous enemy alien. Perhaps the end of the war emboldened the church to speak on issues—such as area bombing—they had been thinking about for a while but did not feel free to say. After all, the cities being flattened were, for many, the homes of German family and friends.

A more subtle criticism of the bombing of civilians can be seen in the *Gospel Herald*, a US-based but circulated-in-Canada Mennonite periodical. Mennonites were a part of the historic peace church tradition and publicly identified with pacifism. They were under significant criticism and restrictions in Canada for their lack of support for the war so it seems understandable if their public statements on war strategy were muted to a degree.[49] Their German origins only made them even more suspect. However, commenting on the bombing of Hiroshima and Nagasaki, it was stated that when "nations arm for total war, they no longer abide by any moral law. Any method, regardless of the amount of suffering which it may inflict upon innocent women and children, is urged as absolutely necessary if it

47. More people died in the conventional firebombing of Tokyo than the atomic bombing of Hiroshima or Nagasaki.

48. N. Willison, "A 'V-E' Day Address," *Canadian Lutheran*, June 1945.

49. While the movement was officially a pacifist movement, a significant number of Canadian Mennonites enlisted in the war. That said, those who refused to fight after conscripted faced ridicule and time in work camps. See Dirks, "War Without, Struggle Within"; Friesen, *When Canada Called*; Reddig, "Manitoba Mennonites."

aids in bring the enemy to the point of surrender."[50] Their commentary in the months following the atomic bombs was marked by a sober recognition that America had lost its moral compass and an exhortation for citizens to exercise their conscience and refrain from such horrors.[51]

Quickly after the dropping of two atomic bombs, Japan formally surrendered on 2 September 1945, thus ending the war against the Axis powers.[52] The churches rejoiced over the victory, but an ominous note remained due to the uncertainty surrounding the advent of the atomic age:

> The Presbyterians of Canada join with all loyal subjects of the British Empire and Commonwealth in rejoicing over the victorious conclusion of the Second World War, brought about the surrender of Japan . . . We thank God even for the *Atomic Bomb* which has hastened the collapse of the last of the Axis powers and greatly shortened the war. Shame to us if we do not lift grateful hearts to God for our deliverance . . . Let this Thanksgiving be also a consecration to the building of a better world wherein wars and rumours of wars shall be no more, and *justice and righteousness, liberty and brotherhood shall cover the earth as the waters cover the sea* . . . . The discovery of the *Atomic Bomb* has brought a new and dreadful force into the world. If that discovery is used for destructive purposes it may well lead to race annihilation. But long ago there was introduced into this world a new and vital force—which if used for constructive purposes—will produce a new social order wherein dwelleth happiness, righteousness and peace for ALL Nations and ALL Peoples. That force resides in the Gospel of Jesus Christ. That force alone can save the world.[53]

Commentary on the atomic bomb reflected uncertainty surrounding how such a weapon could, if ever, be used again. While some expressed the conviction that the use of atomic bombs had saved lives,[54] Canadian church leaders wrestled with the implications of the United States having such

50. H. Harold Hartzler, "Some Thoughts on the Atomic Bomb," *Gospel Herald*, 26 October 1945.

51. "C.P.S. Reaction to Atomic Bomb," *Gospel Herald*, 24 August 1945; "Items and Comments," *Gospel Herald*, 5 October 1945; "The Individual Conscience," *Gospel Herald*, 23 November 1945.

52. Germany had surrendered earlier on 8 May 1945.

53. J. M. Macgillivray, "Thanksgiving for Victory," *Presbyterian Record*, September 1945. Emphasis in original.

54. "On the Atomic Bomb," *Observer*, 1 November 1945.

awesome power at its disposal.[55] Some were repulsed by the Allied bombing of cities, whether conventional or nuclear.[56] Others saw the development of the bomb as "one of the Lord's instruments for the furthering of His plans."[57] Yet others shared the same hopes and fears—atomic power had the means to make life better or bring about the extinction of the human race.[58] In the stark words of the Salvation Army's *War Cry*, the hope was that atomic energy would "vitalize and not vaporize Man who discovered it."[59] Yet even others feared that the weapon could, someday, be used against the United States and its allies.[60] Finally, some believed that the second coming of Jesus was a comfort in the face of looming catastrophe.[61]

A more sophisticated and detailed response to atomic weapons developed in the postwar years.[62] Suffice it to say here that in the immediate aftermath of Hiroshima and Nagasaki, not to mention the destruction of a host of other cities by conventional bombing, it was thought the only way for the world to escape unfathomable destruction was for the churches to bring their influence to bear. As the *Observer* declared, "The responsibilities which are laid upon the church in these post war years are heavy indeed; to these is now added that of developing in men and nations, with all possible speed, strength of character, unselfishness and a spirit of universal brotherhood which alone will enable them to direct this new power to the happiness and a good life of all peoples throughout the world."[63] Or, in

55. "Christian Ethics and the Bomb," *Montreal Churchman*, September 1945; "A Moral Problem," *Observer*, 1 December 1945.

56. "As I See It," *Observer*, 1 October 1945; J. Lavell Smith, "Ministers Protest Atomic Bomb," *Observer*, 1 November 1945.

57. Chester A. Hofman, "On the Atomic Bomb," *Observer*, 1 November 1945.

58. "The Challenge of Peace and Victory," *Canadian Churches and the War*, September 1945.

59. "Atomic Energy," *War Cry*, 25 August 1945. See also "A New Factor," *Observer*, 1 September 1945; "Dr. Oldham Discusses Implications of Atomic Bomb," *Observer*, 15 September 1945; E. Gilmour Smith, "Atomic Power," *Observer*, 15 November 1945; "The Atomic Bomb," *Pentecostal Testimony*," 1 September 1945; "Atomic Bomb Invented," *Maritime Baptist*, 15 August 1945; T.T. Shields, "Will Atomic Energy Destroy or Save Mankind?" *Gospel Witness*, 16 August 1945; "The War That Never Ceases," *Gospel Witness*, 23 August 1945; "The Up-to-Date Word," *Gospel Herald*, 30 November 1945; "Romance of Uranium Find," *Canadian Baptist*, 1 October 1945.

60. "The Atomic Bomb," *Gospel Witness*, 9 August 1945; "The Frankenstein of the Air," *Maritime Baptist*, 15 August 1945.

61. "For the believer, there is a brighter prospect. The rapture of the church is his comforting hope." See "The Atomic Bomb," *Pentecostal Testimony*," 1 September 1945.

62. For instance, see Mojzes, *North American Churches*; Thrift, "Bible, Anti-communism"; Kirby, "Responses Within the Anglican Church."

63. "A New Factor," *Observer*, 1 September 1945. See also "The Old and the New,"

the words of the Mennonite *Gospel Herald*, "The only answer to the atomic bomb is the Sermon on the Mount."[64] Those exhortations for the church to save humanity from destroying itself provided motivation and a sense of urgency to churches engaging in the public square, thus bucking a trend to secularism and the concomitant marginalization of the churches. That sense that need was for the churches to be active in shaping the moral landscape was reinforced by none other than Canadian Prime Minister William Lyon Mackenzie King who stated that "only Christianity can save the world from doom in this era of the atomic bomb."[65]

CONCLUSION

In his moral evaluation of critical actions in World War Two, Michael Bess speaks of the allied area bombing as a "case of moral slippage."[66] What is important to note is that the wartime Canadian churches would seem to agree with his assessment. As this chapter indicates, despite their support for the war effort, and ardent nation-building impulses marked by active engagement in the public square, the churches recognized the corrosive nature of war that undermined once agreed upon ideals of what was—and what was not—acceptable in wartime. Such critical commentary on the war effort provides nuance and complexity to what is sometimes seen to be wartime churches unconditionally supporting the nation's war effort.

The best the Canadian churches could publicly say in support of area bombing was that there seemed to be no other option if victory was to be attained. At worst, the actions of the allies on the particular matter of area bombing were a profound moral failure requiring remorse and repentance. The reason for the tepid support or even criticism of the bombing of civilians *en masse* was that such a practice went contrary to the just war tradition of non-combatant immunity. It also made the allies complicit in actions they had once criticized as barbaric. Nevertheless, the underlying reason—or compromise—for tolerating the bombing was that evil needed to be done to defeat an even greater evil, in common parlance it was "the better of two

Observer, 1 January 1946; "On the Atomic Bomb," *Observer*, 1 November 1945; "A Moral Problem," *Observer*, 1 December 1945. For an earlier version of the same argument, see "Human Values," *Maritime Baptist*, 10 February 1943.

64. Howard H. Charles, "Peace Section," *Gospel Herald*, October 1945.

65. Rady-Shaw, "Ministering to an Unsettled World," 225.

66. Bess, *Choices Under Fire*, ch. 5.

evils," or, as one churchman at the time wrote, a position "between evil and less evil."[67]

BIBLIOGRAPHY

Acts and Proceedings of the Presbyterian Church in Canada. Toronto. Wartime volumes.

Addison, Paul, and Jeremy A. Crang. *Firestorm: The Bombing of Dresden, 1945*. Chicago: Ivan R. Dee, 2006.

Airhart, Phyllis D. *A Church with the Soul of a Nation: Making and Remaking the United Church of Canada*. Montreal and Kingston: McGill-Queen's University Press, 2014.

Allen, Thomas B., and Norman Polmar. *Code-Name Downfall: The Secret Plan to Invade Japan and Why Truman Dropped the Bomb*. New York: Simon & Schuster, 1995.

Arnold, Jörg. "Beyond Usable Pasts: Rethinking the Memorialization of the Strategic Air War in Germany, 1940 to 1965." In *Memorialization in Germany since 1945*, edited by Bill Niven and Chloe Paver, 129–49. New York: Palgrave Macmillan, 2010.

Bashow, David L. *None but the Brave: The Essential Contributions of RAF Bomber Command to Allied Victory during the Second World War*. Kingston: Canadian Defense, 2009.

Bess, Michael. *Choices Under Fire: Moral Dimensions of World War II*. New York: Knopf, 2006.

Biddle, Tami Davis. "Bombing by the Square Yard: Sir Arthur Harris at War, 1942–1945." *International Historical Review* 21.3 (1999) 626–64.

Bowe, Meghan Kathleen. "Framing Memory: The Bombings of Dresden, Germany in Narrative, Discourse and Commemoration after 1945." MA thesis, University of Victoria, 2011.

Canadian Baptist. Toronto. Various issues, 1940–1945.

Canadian Churches and the War. Ottawa: Wartime Information Board. Various issues, 1944–1945.

Canadian Churchman. Toronto. Various issues, 1940–1945.

Canadian Lutheran. Winnipeg. Various issues, 1945–1946.

Chandler, Andrew. "The Church of England and the Obliteration Bombing of Germany in the Second World War." *English Historical Review* 108.429 (1993) 920–46.

Cook, Tim. "Clio's Warriors: Canadian Historians and the Writing of the World Wars." Vancouver: UBC Press, 2006.

———. *The Fight for History: 75 Years of Forgetting, Remembering, and Remaking Canada's Second World War*. Toronto: Allen Lane, 2020.

———. *Fight to the Finish: Canadians in the Second World War, 1944–1945*, vol. 2. Toronto: Allen Group, 2015.

De Bruhl, Marshall. *Firestorm: Allied Airpower and the Destruction of Dresden*. New York: Random House, 2006.

Dirks, Nathan. "War Without, Struggle Within: Canadian Mennonite Enlistments during the Second World War." MA thesis, McMaster Divinity College, 2010.

67. "Protest Indiscriminate Bombing," *Presbyterian Record*, May 1944.

Fairbairn, R. Edis. *Bulletin*. Privately published newsletter, various issues, 1940–1945.

Friesen, Ronald. *When Canada Called: Manitoba Mennonites and World War II*. Steinbach: Ronald Friesen, 2006.

Gospel Herald. Scottdale, PA. Various issues circulated in Canada, 1945–1946.

Hall, David Ian. "'Black, White and Grey': Wartime Arguments for and against Strategic Bomber Offensive." *Canadian Military History* 7.1 (1998) 7–19.

Hansen, Randall. *Fire and Fury: The Allied Bombing of Germany, 1942–1945*. Toronto: Doubleday Canada, 2008.

Heath, Gordon L. *Christians, the State, and War: An Ancient Tradition for the Modern World*. Lanham, MD: Lexington Books/Fortress Academic, 2022.

———. "Irreconcilable Differences: Wartime Attitudes of George C. Pidgeon and R. Edis Fairbairn, 1939–1945." *Canadian Society of Church History Papers* (1999) 29–49.

———. "Queen Victoria and General Gordon: Heroes in the Age of Empires." In *Baptists and Gender*, edited by Melody Maxwell and T. Laine Scales, 68–101. Macon, GA: Mercer University Press, 2023.

———. "The Rise and Fall (and Resilience) of the Peace Movement among Presbyterians and the United Church in the Interwar Years, 1919–1939." *Canadian Society of Church History Papers* (2019) 51–77.

Hoyt, Edwin P. *Inferno: The Firebombing of Japan, March 9—August 15, 1945*. Oxford: Madison, 2000.

King, William Lyon Mackenzie. *The Mackenzie King Diaries*. Library and Archives Canada.

Kirby, Dianne. "Responses Within the Anglican Church to Nuclear Weapons: 1945–1961." *A Journal of Church and State* 37.3 (1995) 599–622.

Lammers, Stephen E. "William Temple and the Bombing of Germany: An Exploration in the Just War Tradition." *Journal of Religious Ethics* 19.1 (1991) 71–92.

Manson, Ian McKay. "The United Church and the Second World War." In *A History of the United Church of Canada*, edited by Don Schweitzer, 57–75. Waterloo, ON: Wilfrid Laurier University Press, 2012.

Maritime Baptist. Halifax. Various issues, 1942–1945.

Messenger, Charles. *"Bomber" Harris and the Strategic Bombing Offensive, 1939–1945*. London: Arms and Amour, 1984.

Mojzes, Paul, ed. *North American Churches and the Cold War*. Grand Rapids: Eerdmans, 2018.

Nelson, Robert, and Christopher Waters. "The Allied Bombing of German Cities from a Canadian Perspective." *Journal of the History of International Law* 14 (2012) 113–15.

Orser, W. Edward. "World War Two and the Pacifist Controversy in the Major Protestant Churches." In *Protestantism and Social Christianity*, edited by Martin E. Marty. New York: Saur, 1992.

Presbyterian Record. Toronto. Various issues, 1940–1946.

Rady-Shaw, Julia. "Ministering to an Unsettled World: The Protestant Churches, the Cold War, and Ontario 1945–1956," PhD diss., University of Toronto, 2017.

Reddig, Kenneth. "Manitoba Mennonites and the Winnipeg Mobilization Board in World War II." MA thesis, University of Manitoba, 1989.

Ross, Stewart. *Strategic Bombing by the United States in World War II: The Myths and the Facts*. Carolina: McFarland, 2003.

Rothwell, David R. "United Church Pacifism, October 1939." *Bulletin* XXII (1973–1975).

Rudy, Adam D. "The Cause of Righteousness and Freedom: Canadian Protestant Churches and The Second World War, 1939–1945." PhD diss., McMaster Divinity College, 2022.

———. "'The Protagonist of Justice Against the Forces of the AntiChrist': Christian Democracy and the Second World War in *The Silhouette* and *The Recorder.*" In *Christian Higher Education in Canada*, edited by Stanley E. Porter and Bruce G. Fawcett, 13–39. McMaster General Studies Series. Eugene, OR: Pickwick Publications, 2020.

Shaffer, Ronald. *Wings of Judgment: American Bombing in World War II.* Oxford: Oxford University Press, 1985.

Sinclair-Faulkner, Charles Thomas. "'For Christian Civilization:' Churches and Canada's War Effort, 1939–1942." PhD diss., University of Chicago, 1975.

Snape, Michael. *A Church Militant: Anglicans and the Armed Forces from Queen Victoria to the Vietnam War.* Oxford: Oxford University Press, 2022.

Temple, William. *Christianity and the Social Order.* London: Penguin, 1942.

Thrift, Gayle. "The Bible, Anti-communism, and the A-Bomb: Canadian Protestant Churches in the Cold War Era, 1945–1968." PhD diss., University of Calgary, 2005.

United Church of Canada. *The Observer.* Toronto. Various issues, 1939–1946.

———. Acts and Proceedings of the General Council. Toronto, wartime sessions.

Valor and the Horror. Directed by Brian McKenna and Terence McKenna. CBC Television miniseries, 1992.

Walker, J. Samuel. *Prompt and Utter Destruction: Truman and the Use of Atomic Bombs Against Japan.* Chapel Hill: University of North Carolina Press, 2004.

War Cry. Toronto: Salvation Army. Various issues, 1940–1946.

Webster, Charles, and Noble Frankland. *Strategic Air Offensive Against Germany, 1939–1945*, vols. 1–4. *Victory.* London: H. M. Stationary Off., 1961.

Wilson, Sandra, et al. *Bombing Japan, 1945: The U.S. and the War in the Pacific, 1941–45.* London: Routledge, 2022.

10

Two Calvinists' Understandings of the Scripture and Administration of the Biblical Ceremonies and Missional Implications

Joon Won Kim

INTRODUCTION[1]

In the sixteenth century, the wave of Reformation from continental Europe also washed over the British Isles. There is little doubt that one of the

1. I am honored to offer this contribution in celebration of the Rev. Dr. Stuart Macdonald, whose presence in my life has been nothing short of a gift. My academic journey—from the Th.M to the Ph.D—was shaped and sustained by his unfailing kindness, encouragement, and pastoral care. Dr. Macdonald has been, in the deepest sense, my mentor. He welcomed me with a warmth that put both mind and heart at ease, greeting me with a gentle expression and a tone that conveyed genuine interest in my work and academic life. His insights—always perceptive, always offered with joy—became steady lights on my path. During seasons when I met walls in my studies or in life, he was the first person I sought out. He listened patiently, asked questions that clarified my thoughts, and helped me find footing again. His scholarship, spanning the global history of Christianity, Scottish Reformation studies, and the complex relationship between church and society in Canada, reflects a rare combination of intellectual rigor and pastoral sensitivity. Yet for me—and for many students across the Toronto School of Theology—his greatest legacy lies in his commitment to mentoring with integrity, humility, and a sincere desire to form the next generation with wisdom

core issues of the Reformation in the sixteenth century, especially in continental Europe, was sacramental theology. This controversial issue took a different aspect in the British Isles, however, especially in England where the debate was not so much about theology as it was about liturgy or ceremony. After Thomas Cranmer's prominent liturgical work, the *Book of Common Prayer* (hereafter, the BCP), debates over the ceremony and *adiaphora* had lasted for several decades in England, and even among the Marian Exiles in Frankfurt-am-Mein and continental Europe. Several notable theologians and ministers were involved in these debates. John Knox, a Scottish reformer and the father of Scottish Presbyterianism, rejected the BCP because he thought that this book of worship was not reformed enough and that it still contained superstitious ceremonies. About forty-seven years after the 1552 publication of the BCP, Richard Hooker, defender of the Anglican Church and public worship, wrote an outstanding commentary in its defense entitled *Of the Lawes Ecclesiasticall Politie* (hereafter, the *Lawes*).

It is hard to find a point of contact between John Knox and Richard Hooker because they do not mention one another in their works. However, one cannot conclude that there is no correlation between them, because they both clearly reveal their opinions on the BCP and the English liturgy. Moreover, they also have something else in common, i.e., Calvinism. Many theologians and ministers in the late sixteenth and seventeenth centuries were influenced by Calvin, either directly or indirectly. Richard Hooker of England and John Knox of Scotland were two such ministers. It is hard to regard them as "Pure Calvinists," although in some ways both were strongly influenced by Calvin's theology and practice. Knox, who brought reformed theology into his country, was one of the successors to John Calvin. While there have been debates about whether Richard Hooker was a Calvinist or an anti-Calvinist, this defender of the Anglican Church and of Anglican theology takes an affectionate attitude towards Calvin and his theology.[2] For example, in the Preface to the *Lawes*, Hooker honors Calvin with the following phrases: "A founder [your discipline] had, whome, for mine owne part, I thinke incomparably the wisest man that ever the french Church did enjoy, since the houre it enjoyed him."[3] Thus, it is controversial, but still

---

and compassion. For these reasons, and with heartfelt gratitude, I dedicate this work to honour Dr. Macdonald's enduring influence and the countless ways he has shaped my academic journey.

2. Neelands, "Use and Abuse," 42. For a discussion that Hooker was not a Calvinist, see Joyce, *Anglican Moral Theology*, 56. Neelands' review on Joyce's argument is also helpful.

3. *Lawes*, Preface 2.1; *Folger Library Edition of the Works of Richard Hooker* (hereafter cited as FLE), 1:3.13–15. All references to the *Lawes* cite book, chapter, and section

reasonable to regard him as a Calvinist.[4] These two theologians nevertheless had quite different theologies and practices, particularly concerning the interpretation of Scripture and public worship.

In this essay, the different approaches to Scripture and the BCP of these two Calvinists will be discussed. The main argument of this paper is that neither Richard Hooker nor John Knox held the same understanding of biblical theology as Calvin; and these differences produced different approaches to public worship or the BCP. In order to support the argument, this paper is made up of the following sections: first, the historical background of Knox and Hooker, especially regarding the history of the BCP in the sixteenth century; second, the differences in their biblical interpretation and understanding of the authority of Scripture; and third, the liturgical application of scriptural ceremonies in Hooker and Knox, especially around the issue of the eucharistic posture—that is, kneeling at the altar. This essay then concludes that different hermeneutics and approaches to Scripture in Hooker and Knox led them to different liturgical theologies and applications.

However, this survey does not merely remain at the level of historical and theological analysis of the sixteenth-century Reformation era. Rather, this study seeks to reinterpret the differences between Hooker's and Knox's biblical hermeneutics and liturgical theology from the perspective of contemporary missional ecclesiology, and to derive implications applicable to the missional practice of the church today. The modern church faces the missional challenge of maintaining the essence of the gospel while simultaneously communicating appropriately with the times and culture amid rapid secularization and cultural pluralism. In this context, the two approaches to biblical interpretation demonstrated by Hooker and Knox—namely, Hooker's emphasis on the integration of scriptural authority with reason and tradition, and Knox's emphasis on the literal authority and omnicompetence of Scripture—provide crucial insights into how the contemporary church should navigate the tension between the essence of the gospel and cultural adaptation.

Particularly from the perspective of missional ecclesiology, the worship and rituals of the church become core elements that form the identity of a community participating in the *missio Dei* toward the world, transcending mere internal expressions of piety. The debate between Hooker and Knox was precisely about this point—namely, how the church should

followed by the standard FLE citation. References to FLE cite volume, page, and line numbers.

4. For full discussion, see Neelands, "Use and Abuse," 41–57.

remain faithful to scriptural authority while delivering the gospel within its cultural context. Therefore, this study explores what significance the theological heritage of the past can have for the missional identity and practice of today's church by applying the historical debates of the sixteenth century to the missional situation of the twenty-first century. This represents an attempt at hermeneutical expansion that is both practical-theological and missiological, moving beyond mere historical-theological research. Through this endeavor, this essay seeks to present the theological criteria necessary for the contemporary church to perform culturally appropriate missional practice while maintaining the essence of the gospel.

In order to support this research and argument, this essay is structured as follows. First, it examines the historical background of the BCP in the sixteenth century, along with the theological backgrounds of Hooker and Knox. Second, it compares how the two figures held different positions on biblical interpretation and the authority of Scripture. Third, it discusses Hooker's and Knox's application of scriptural ceremonies, particularly focusing on the issue of eucharistic posture (the issue of the kneeling at the Lord's Table). Fourth, it explores how these discussions can be connected to the perspective of missional hermeneutics and what implications they offer us. In conclusion, this essay seeks to demonstrate how the different biblical interpretations and approaches of Hooker and Knox resulted in differences in their liturgical theology and modes of application, and how these can be interpreted and applied missiologically.

CONTROVERSY OVER THE BOOK OF COMMON PRAYER

In 1547, King Edward VI ascended to the throne and there followed several liturgical changes in the Church of England. The Archbishop of Canterbury, Thomas Cranmer, led these liturgical reforms. He collected existing liturgical orders—including the Uses of Sarum (Salisbury), York, Bangor, and Lincoln—and issued an English vernacular communion preparation to be inserted in the Latin Mass. However, in 1549, through the Act of Uniformity, the BCP "replaced all Latin rites other than for ordination."[5] The BCP was revised again by Cranmer and his co-compilers in 1552. At this stage of the revisions, there was tension between the compilers and John Knox, a Scottish reformer. Knox did not want to accept certain postures and ceremonies he regarded as idolatrous or superstitious. In particular, he insisted that kneeling at the altar should be replaced with sitting at the table.

5. Spinks, *Remembrance of Me*, 313.

The debates over the ceremonies and postures were harsh. Both the supporters of the BCP and the revisionists hold fast to their positions. This controversy was even continued in Frankfort-am-Mein; where Knox, the leader of the revisionists, and Richard Cox, the co-compiler of the BCP, had heated debates over this issue. As a result, Knox was expelled by the city magistrates and moved to Geneva where Calvin was ministering. In 1559, after the death of Queen Mary I and Queen Elizabeth I's accession, the two groups of exiles were able to return to England and Scotland. On his way to Scotland, Knox acquired a couple of copies of a newly-compiled book of worship, *The Forme of Prayers,* which later became the authorized worship book for the Church of Scotland. For his part, Cox, as a bishop of Ely, played an important role in the early Elizabethan years in England. The controversy over the ceremonies and the BCP seemed to have ended in Scotland, but continued in England.

In England, there had been controversies between the Anglican Conformists and the Puritan nonconformists. John Whitgift and Richard Hooker defended the reformed English liturgy and the BCP, but Thomas Cartwright and Walter Travers denounced it because they regarded this form of worship as in some respects superstitious and abominable. Whitgift, the archbishop of Canterbury, and Cartwright, former Lady Margaret professor of theology at Cambridge, continued their dispute for six years from 1572 to 1577. The dispute was triggered by the anonymous publication of *An Admonition to Parliament*, or the so-called "the Puritan Manifesto." Whitgift responded with his *Answer to the Admonition* in 1572 and Cartwright with his *Reply to an Answer Made of Master Doctor Whitgift* in 1574. After these, three more tracts were published: one by Whitgift and two by Cartwright.

Sixteen years later, from 1577, Richard Hooker started to publish his *Lawes.* Books I–VI were published in 1593 and Book V in 1597. Although three other books—VI–VIII—were published in 1648 and 1660 after Hooker's death in 1600, the *Lawes* proved sufficient to refute the Puritans' arguments in government circles. Through this writing, Hooker defended the Anglican liturgy and public worship against attacks by the Puritans; in particular, in Book V he addressed the Puritans' criticisms of the BCP one by one. As Lee W. Gibbs evaluates, Book V of the *Lawes* "provides a constructive exposition of those practices by showing that in the Prayer Book '*True Religion*' could indeed be the '*roote of all true virtues and the stay of all well ordered common-wealthes*[.]'"[6] Although the dispute over the BCP

6. Gibbs, "Life of Hooker," 16; *Lawes* 5:1.1; FLE 2:16.1.

and public worship continued in the seventeenth century, Hooker and his *Lawes* provided adequate grounds for defending the Anglican liturgy.

TWO INTERPRETATIONS OF SCRIPTURE AND THE AUTHORITY OF SCRIPTURE

As many scholars have noted, the authority of Scripture and the illumination of the Holy Spirit are the two key elements of Calvin's biblical interpretation. In his Preface to the *Institutes of the Christian Religion*, Calvin calls Scripture "God's Sceptre": "Now, that king who in ruling over his realm does not serve God's glory exercises not kingly rule but brigandage. Furthermore, he is deceived who looks for enduring prosperity in his kingdom when it is not ruled by God's sceptre, his Holy Word."[7] He also emphasizes the role of the Holy Spirit as the teacher of Scripture: "Let this point therefore stand: that those whom the Holy Spirit has inwardly taught truly rest upon Scripture, and that Scripture indeed is self-authenticated; hence, it is not right to subject it to proof and reasoning."[8] Hooker and Knox both accept and develop Calvin's criteria or tools of biblical interpretation and the authority of Scripture. However, their ways of accepting and developing Calvin's hermeneutical principles are not the same.

Richard Hooker

There has been much debate over Hooker's identity as a reformer of the sixteenth century. Although he was labelled a father of Anglican theology, a theologian of the *via Media*, an Anglican conformist, or defender of the Elizabethan church, many scholars continue to agonize about giving him the description of "Calvinist." For example, O. T. Hargrave places Hooker in the "anti-Calvinist tradition," while Henry Hammond puts him "on the Calvinist side."[9] Actually, as with many second or third generation reformers, Hooker's theology was influenced not only by one or two senior reformers, but by contemporary reformers also. In other words, not only Calvin and Luther, but also many continental and English reformers had influence with Hooker. Categorizing Hooker in one tradition is difficult, especially as there have been several misapprehensions about a number of issues to do with his

7. Calvin, *Institutes of the Christian Religion*, Preface. Hereafter this reference will be cited as *Institutes*, followed by the appropriate book, chapter, and section.

8. *Institutes*, I, vii, 5.

9. Neelands, "Use and Abuse," 42, 50, 51.

theology. One of these is that he did not accept the so-called "continental reformed biblical theology," or Calvin's view on Scripture. This seems to be because Hooker did not hold the doctrine of Scripture's "omnicompetence" which the Puritans held fast to.[10] Nigel Atkinson introduces the notion that there are two misconceptions about this: first, "Hooker did not hold to a Reformed view of the Fall," and second, Calvin adopted "the doctrine of Scripture's omnicompetence."[11] Atkinson argues that those two statements are inaccurate because Hooker does not deny the doctrine of the Fall and Calvin does not assert Scripture's omnicompetence.

It is not easy to define Hooker's biblical theology and view on the authority of Scripture. However, it is reasonable to categorize his biblical hermeneutics as similar to those of Calvin. Much as Calvin's biblical hermeneutics focus on the authority of Scripture and the illumination by the Holy Spirit, Hooker too regards these as his tools of interpretation. As Neelands clearly shows, Hooker "acknowledges some important role for the Spirit with respect to assuring us of the truths found in Scripture: the truth of the Scriptures is supplied indeed 'by the testimony of the spirit, which assureth our harts therein' . . . [of] the foundation for the general authority of Scripture in the Church."[12]

Hooker goes a step further and links this doctrine to the authority of reason, although this development is already implicit in Calvin's theology. It is a misunderstanding that Calvin never endorsed human reason because of his belief in the total depravity of humankind. However, Calvin himself distinguishes reason between natural and supernatural and acknowledges human beings still possess the ability to discern natural laws: "[T]o perceive more clearly how far the mind can proceed in any matter according to the degree of its ability, we must here set forth a distinction. This, then, is the distinction: that there is one kind of understanding of earthly things; another of heavenly."[13] According to Atkinson, "Calvin held to Scripture where it spoke but was otherwise content to follow reason or tradition."[14] For Hooker, reason has a necessary and principal role in the authentication of Scripture;[15] he believed that reason is "necessary to elicit certain doctrines by consequence from Holy Scripture, and is also necessary for

10. Atkinson, *Richard Hooker*, 78. Atkinson defines the doctrine of Scripture's omnicompetence as "a view of Scripture that demanded a biblical warrant for every action."

11. Atkinson, *Richard Hooker*, 79.

12. Neelands, "Use and Abuse," 47–48; *Lawes*, III. 8. 15; FLE 1:232.33–233.9.

13. *Institutes*, II, ii, 13.

14. Atkinson, *Richard Hooker*, 79.

15. Voak, "Principle of *Sola Scriptura*," 135.

theological enquiry and debate."[16] This mutual interaction between the authority of Scripture and reason is the core argument in Hooker's theology.

Although his identification as a Calvinist is still disputed, his interpretation and acknowledgement of Scripture seems to be based on Calvin's approach. Above all, regarding his liturgical theology, Hooker's view on Scripture and reason is significant because his defense of the BCP and of ceremonies in public worship seem to be based on this premise. When he confronted Puritan complaints about the BCP, he used this theological and biblical premise logically and rhetorically.

John Knox

It has generally been assumed that Knox was a pure Calvinist or a sincere follower of Calvin. This is a reasonable evaluation because the relationship between those two reformers was solid. In a letter to Mrs. Locke, Knox praises Calvin's Geneva as "this place, whair I nether feir nor escahme to say is the maist perfyt schoole of Chryst that ever was in the erth since the dayis of the Apostillis."[17] Knox often wrote to Calvin to seek his advice and Calvin also kindly replied. However, recent scholars argue that although there are many similarities between the two reformers, it is hard to regard Knox as a pure Calvinist or a clone of Calvin. Jane Dawson, Richard Kyle, and Richard Greaves identify many differences between Calvin and Knox. In particular, this new perspective on the relationship between Calvin and Knox centers on their different views on biblical interpretation or on the authority of Scripture. For example, V. E. d'Assonville asserts that "the great difference between Knox and Calvin (and Luther as well) relates to Knox's view of Scriptures."[18] Greaves also argues that the doctrine of authority in Knox is slightly different from Calvin's.[19]

For Knox, the "Word of God" has the ultimate and supreme authority over all other authorities. Knox never made a concession about this and his resulting firm belief can be found throughout his works. The supreme authority of Scripture, as seen above, was not new in the sixteenth century. Knox took this concept, however, and reinterpreted it from his own perspective. In a letter to some Protestant women in Edinburgh, he argued strongly that "[i]n religioun thair is na middis: either it is the religioun of

16. Voak, "Principle of *Sola Scriptura*," 101.

17. Knox, *Works of John Knox*, 4:240. Hereafter this reference will be cited as *Works* followed by the appropriate volume and page number.

18. D'Assonville, *Institutes of Calvin*, 69.

19. Greaves, "Nature of Authority," 30–51.

God, and that in everie thing that is done it must have the assurance of his awn Word, and than is his Majestie trewlie honourit, or els it is the religioun of the Divill, whilk is, when men will erect and set up to God sic religioun as pleaseth thame[.]"[20] The role of the Holy Spirit in understanding Scripture was also important to both Calvin and Knox, but while this was vitally important to Calvin, it rarely appears in Knox's works. As Greaves indicates, "Knox himself gives more emphasis to the recorded words of Scripture than to an inner spiritual testimony of their validity and meaning."[21]

The supreme authority of Scripture, for Knox, means that "the Word of God" should be read literally, whereas Calvin tried to keep a balance between the substance and the letter of Scripture. Drawing on Deuteronomy 12:32, emphasizes the literal form over the substance of Scripture: "If I be well remembered, Moses, in the name of God, says to the people of Israel, 'All that the Lord thy God commandis thee to do, that do thow to the Lord thy God: add nothing to it; diminiyshe nothing from it.' Be this rewill, think I, that the Kirk of Christ will measur Goddis religioun, and notby that which seams good in thare awin eis."[22] From this premise, Knox tries to recover biblical worship, declaring that "inventit be the braine of man, without the express Word of God" is the service of devil.[23]

Calvin then expresses concern about Knox's strictly literal interpretation of Scripture in a letter from 1561: "[i]n regard to Ceremonies, I trust that your strictness, although it may displease many, will be regulated by discretion. . . . With this exception, you know well that certain things, though not positively approved, must be tolerated."[24]As Calvin's concern shows, Knox's literal interpretation of Scripture and its authority led him to fight against what he considered abominable and superstitious ceremonies without mercy or toleration. The BCP was no exception, and in particular, he felt kneeling at the altar was one of the main problems with the prayer book.

Both Richard Hooker and John Knox seem to accept and develop Calvin's biblical hermeneutics and the authority of Scripture; however, their points of application are quite different. Whereas Hooker accepts the authority of Scripture and the illumination of the Holy Spirit linked to the authority of reason, Knox emphasizes the literal form of Scripture and its omnicompetent application, rather than focusing on the role of the Holy

20. *Works*, 4:232.

21. Greaves, "Nature of Authority," 46.

22. *Works*, 1:197.

23. *Works*, 4:231.

24. *Works*, 6:124.

Spirit. These reformers' different understandings and applications seem to have influenced their liturgical theologies, especially their views on the BCP.

TWO VIEWS ON THE BOOK OF COMMON PRAYER AND THE KNEELING AT THE ALTAR

Although Calvin's general approach to Scripture was accepted or acknowledged by both Richard Hooker and John Knox, the latter two emphasize different points. While Hooker recognizes the first authority of Scripture and the role of the Holy Spirit, Knox puts his emphasis on the literal form of Scripture and its omnicompetence. These differing emphases also seem to influence their liturgical application to public worship, differences found in their attitudes to the BCP. In order to link their biblical approaches to their liturgical theologies, the issue of kneeling at the altar is reviewed in this section.

Richard Hooker

In Books IV and V of the *Lawes*, Richard Hooker defends some rites and administrations of the sacraments which the Puritans complained about. The Puritans criticized "baptism by women," "interrogatories proposed to infants and answered by godparents," "the use of the sign and ceremony of the cross in baptism," "confirmation by bishops," "the use of the singular *take thou* instead of Jesus' *ye*," "kneeling to receive communion," "the lack of required community self-examination before communion," "the admission of papists to communion," "communion for a part of the congregation only and not the whole congregation," and "private communion," which Hooker dealt with one by one, "after the general account of the sacrament or rite."[25]

One of the complaints raised by the Puritans was the posture at the Holy Communion or the Lord's Supper. As described in the previous section, this issue had a long history and several events. In Hooker's time, the debate was an ongoing issue. In Book IV, Hooker briefly introduces the controversy: "one Church esteemeth it not so good to receive the Eucharist sitting as standing, another Church not so good standing as sitting[.]"[26] In Book V, Chapter 68, Hooker introduces Thomas Cartwright's critique first: "Our second oversight is by gesture. For in knelinge there hath bene superstition; sittinge agreeth better to the action of a supper; and our Saviour

25. Neelands, "Christology and the Sacraments," 369.

26. *Lawes*, 4.13.8; FLE 1:333.15–17.

usinge that which was most fitt did him selfe not kneele."[27] Cartwright also claims that "Kneeling carieth a shew of worship, sitting agreeth better with the action of the Supper[;] Christ and his Apostles kneeled not."[28] In response Hooker argues:

> Our kneeling at communions is the gesture of pietie. If wee did there present our selves but to make some show or dumbe resemblance of a spirituall feast, it may bee that sitting were the fitter ceremonie, but comming as receivers of inestimable grace at the hands of God, what doth better beseeme our bodies at that hower then to bee sensible witnesses of minds unfainedly humbled? Our Lord himselfe did that which custome and long usage had made fit; we that which fitnesse and great decencie hath made usuall.[29]

Although he only writes a short passage about this controversy, Hooker's defense and counter-argument against Cartwright and the Puritans is clear and logical. For Hooker, "sacraments are a means of personal participation or communion, and through them God imparts grace."[30] According to Neelands, this passage can be read as follows: "Kneeling is appropriated for Communion because more than a feast is present: we receive inestimable grace at the hands of God."[31] Moreover, this passage seems to be based on his understanding of the authority of Scripture and reason. In order to understand this according to Hooker's intention, it is necessary to visit the previous section in Book V:

> [W]e herein doe otherwise then Christ did. Our imitation of him consisteth not in tyinge scrupulouslie our selves unto his syllables, but rather in speakinge by the geavenlie direction of that inspired divine wisdome which teacheth divers waies to one ende, and doth therein controle theire boldnes by whome any profitable way is cencured as reprovable only under coulor of some smale difference from greate examples going before."[32]

Hooker seems to deviate neither from the authority of Scripture nor from reformed biblical hermeneutics. Instead he seems to apply his premise of the relationship between the authority of Scripture and reason to this

27. *Lawes*, 5.68.1; FLE 2:344.9–12.
28. *Lawes*, 5.68.3; FLE 2:346.i. The full passage is found in FLE 6:771.
29. *Lawes*, 5:68.3; FLE 2:346.23–29.
30. Spinks, *Two Faces*, 132.
31. Neelands, "Richard Hooker."
32. *Lawes*, 5:68.1; FLE 2:345.17–24.

Eucharistic ceremony. He felt a reasonable application of ceremony or policy derived from Scripture and supported by the "voice of the Church" as not only allowable but also serviceable:[33]

> [W]hat scripture doth plainelie deliver, to that the first place both of creditt and obedience is due; the next whereunto is whatsoever anie man can necessarelie conclude by force of reason; after these the voice of the Church succeedeth. That which the Church by her ecclesiasticall authoritie shall probablie thinke and define to be true or good, must in congruitie of reason overrule all other inferior judgmentes whatsoever.[34]

While the authority of Scripture and reason might not be the only factors in Hooker's mind concerning liturgy and worship, it is nevertheless reasonable to suppose his approach to Scripture played a significant role in his liturgical theology. Although there are many aspects of Hooker's thought to be reviewed and compared, such as his concept of edification, it seems clear that Hooker developed and applied his own biblical perspective in defense of public worship and certain ceremonies.[35]

John Knox

Among his works on worship and liturgy, a sermon entitled "A Vindication of the Doctrine that the Sacrifice of the Mass is Idolatry," is one of the key texts for understanding Knox's liturgical theology and its relation to biblical theology. In this long sermon, Knox gives two syllogisms to identify false and idolatrous worship:

> [First,] All wirschipping, honoring, or service inventit by the braine of man in the religioun of God, without his own express commandment, is Idolatrie: The Masse is inventit be the braine of man, without any commandment of God: Thairfoir it is Idolatrie.[36]
>
> [Second,] All honoring or service of God, whairunto is addit a wickit opinioun, is abominatioun. Unto the Masse is addit a wickit opinioun. Thairfoir it is abominatioun.[37]

33. Gibbs, "Hooker's *via Media* Doctrine," 234.

34. *Lawes* 5:8.2.; FLE 2:39.8–14.

35. Bradford Littlehjohn argues that "the edification of the Church" is a key concept in understanding his theology on liturgy and ceremonies. For full discussion, see Littlejohn, "Edification of the Church."

36. *Works*, 3:34.

37. *Works*, 3:52.

Knox saw the purging of idolatrous worship and the restoration of true worship as the first and most urgent task. There were many new worship books, including the BCP and Calvin's *La Forme*, but he was not satisfied with them; he wanted a more reformed and Scripture-based worship book. As mentioned in the previous section, Knox once held a good opinion of the BCP. Although he had several debates with Cranmer and other English scholars over various issues, including kneeling at the altar, his attitude towards the BCP was not entirely negative. However, when he sent a letter to Calvin in March 1555, he levelled harsh criticism against the BCP: "[S]o because I do find in the English Book (which they so highly praise and advance above all other Orders) things superstitious, impure, unclean, and unperfect (the which I offered myself ready to prove, and to justify before any man,) therefore I could not agree that their Book should be of our Church received."[38] What had happened to Knox? The answer can be found in the debate between Cranmer and Knox over the appropriate posture to assume at the communion service.

One of Knox's main concerns was to restore the Lord's Supper in a biblical way. During his stay in England, he had challenged the revision of the BCP by Thomas Cranmer, Nicolas Ridley (1500–1555), and the other co-revisers. Knox's opinion on the BCP was delivered to his congregation in Berwick in 1552:

> To teach the point, kneeling at the Lord's Supper I have proved by doctrine to be no convenient gesture for a table, which has been given in that action to such a presence of Christ as no place of God's Scriptures teach unto us. And therefore kneeling in that action, appearing to be joined with certain dangers no less in maintaining superstition than in using Christ's holy institution with other gestures than either he used or commanded to be used, I thought good amongst you to avoid, and to use sitting at the Lord's Table, which you did not refuse, but with all reverence and thanksgiving unto God for his truth, knowing, as I suppose, you confirmed the doctrine with your gesture and confession.[39]

In another document addressed to the Privy Council,[40] Knox also presents his opinion on the correct posture to be maintained at the table: "Kneeling is the gesture most commonly of suppliants, of beggars, of such men as,

38. *Works*, 4:44.

39. Lorimer, *Knox and the Church of England*, 261.

40. Although it is not clear the author was John Knox, Iain R. Torrance asserts that it was "almost certainly Knox." For further discussion, see Torrance, "Reformed Piety."

greatly troubled by knowledge of misery or offense committed, seeks help or remission, doubting whether they shall obtain the same or not."[41]

Eventually Knox had an opportunity to preach for the first time before Edward VI and the assembled court at Windsor Castle. In this sermon, he claimed that sitting at the Lord's Table was the correct posture for communion. As a result, "the Privy Council instructed the printer to halt production of the book until 'certain faults' could be corrected[;] and the matter was urgent because the new Prayer book was due to be introduced across the land on 1 November."[42]

Neither Cranmer nor Knox wanted to concede their positions. After the short but harsh debates, the Council decided to add a rubric to the final version of the BCP on 22 October. This is the "black rubric," so called for the following reason: the "first printing of the new book had already come off the presses, so this disclaimer had to be printed separately and inserted into the existing books. Such liturgical instructions are called rubrics, and were typically printed in red ink, but regular ink was used in this case, so it came to be known as the Black Rubric."[43]

In 1556, after being banished from Frankfurt, Knox and his Marian exiled co-authors wrote *The Forme of Prayers*; and unsurprisingly inserted a rubric as follows: "The exhortation ended, the minister commeth doune from the pulpet, and sitteth at the Table, euery man and woman in likewise takinge their place as occasion best serueth, then he taketh bread and geueth thankes, either in these woordes followinge, or like in effect."[44] This is an interesting point, because the authors do not give any direction concerning the bringing of the bread and wine to the table, nor at what point in the service this is to be done; yet they do not forget to indicate sitting at the table. It is obvious from this that Knox did not agree with the BCP's practice of kneeling at the communion service, because he regarded it as a superstitious posture.

Although both Hooker and Knox agree about the supreme authority of Scripture and share Calvin's biblical hermeneutics, their perspectives are not the same. It seems that these different approaches to Scripture influence their liturgical applications. Their views on the issue of kneeling at the altar is a good example of their differences. Whereas Hooker interprets it with the authority of Scripture, reason, and even the "voice of Church," Knox

41. Lorimer, *Knox and the Church of England*, 271.

42. Dawson, *John Knox*, 73.

43. Jacobs, *Book of Common Prayer*, 54. See also MacCulloch, *Thomas Cranmer*, 527.

44. *Works*, 4:194.

emphasizes the literal form, origin, and omnicompetence of biblical ceremony and condemns the posture of kneeling. It is not easy to conclude that Hooker and Knox share no common opinions about worship, liturgy, or ceremony; however it is reasonable to suppose that their liturgical theologies are based, among other aspects, on their unique approaches to Scripture.

A MISSION REREADING OF THE SCRIPTURE AND WORSHIP IN HOOKER AND KNOX

The differences in biblical interpretation and liturgical application between Hooker and Knox examined thus far offer significant missional implications for church today. David Bosch articulates the missional perspective as transforming paradigms of mission, while Leslie Newbigin emphasizes missional practice understood through the interaction between gospel and culture.[45] Wright, through his concept of missional hermeneutics, underscores that the Scripture goes beyond merely providing grounds for mission—it is itself the narrative of God's mission.[46] From this perspective, Hooker's and Knox's biblical interpretation and liturgical application can be understood as missional endeavors undertaken within the specific cultural contexts of sixteenth-century England and Scotland.

Dean Flemming's theory of cultural contextualization enriches this understanding further. In his work, *Contextualization in the New Testament: Patterns for Theology and Mission*, Flemming analyzes Paul's cross-cultural communication strategies, presenting a method that flexibly adjusts cultural forms while maintaining the essence of the gospel. According to Flemming, Paul practiced gospel contextualization through cultural bridge-building, demonstrating a balance that remained sensitive to cultural contexts while preserving the transformative nature of the gospel.[47] From this perspective, Hooker's approach can be viewed as a good example of contextualization that considered the English cultural context. By acknowledging scriptural authority while emphasizing the roles of reason and tradition, Hooker sought harmony with the cultural and intellectual traditions of England at that time. Conversely, Knox's rigorous literalist approach can be understood within the context of Scotland's radical reform, aiming at the formation of a new identity based on the concept of the new Israel.

Richard Bauckham, on the other hand, presents a distinctive perspective on biblical interpretation. Bauckham's missional hermeneutics proposes

45. Bosch, *Transforming Mission;* Newbigin, *Gospel in a Pluralist Society*, 141–54.

46. Wright, *Mission of God*, 22–29, 48–51.

47. Flemming, *Contextualization*, 89–125.

a way of reading the entire Scripture with mission as the central concern.[48] According to Bauckham, biblical interpretation requires a balance between understanding the original context of the text and contemporary application.[49] He views Scripture's narrative as moving from particularity to universality—the concept that God reveals himself through specific individuals or nations and ultimately makes himself known to all. Bauckham also emphasizes the importance of connecting Scripture with critical issues in the contemporary world. From this viewpoint, Hooker can be seen as similar to Bauckham's balanced approach in that he acknowledged scriptural authority while seeking to interpret and apply its meaning through reason and tradition. Knox, conversely, gave absolute priority to the original context and authority of the Scripture, which may have been an effective strategy within the context of the radical reform that the Scottish church required at the time.

Such analyses provide important implications for contemporary ecclesial worship and missional practice. First, the form and content of worship can be contextualized with consideration for cultural context, and this need not undermine scriptural authority. Hooker's biblical interpretation and his liturgical approach grounded in reason and tradition demonstrate how traditional forms of worship can embody biblical truth. Second, cultural contextualization may sometimes require radical reform like that of Knox. Particularly when existing cultural forms distort or obscure the essence of the gospel, decisive separation may be necessary.

This finds application in the contextualization issues of worship faced by the global church today. For instance, the ancestor veneration question in Asian churches exemplifies the tension between Knox's rigorous approach and Hooker's cultural flexibility. In the Korean Christian context, this tension is clearly evident in the development of Christian alternatives to traditional memorial services and ancestral rites.[50] Similarly, the question of incorporating elements of traditional rituals into Christian worship in African churches serves as another example.[51] Many churches are striving to find balance between traditional worship forms and contemporary sensibilities. Hooker's approach offers a model that recognizes the value of tradition while pursuing cultural appropriateness, whereas Knox's approach reminds us that sometimes bold cultural innovation is necessary. Furthermore, this discussion helps acknowledge the diversity of missional practice.

48. Bauckham, *Bible and Mission*, 11–26.

49. Bauckham, *Hermeneutical Ventures*, 5–17.

50. Moon. "Han'gugin-ŭi Kajŏng."

51. Bediako, *Christianity in Africa*, 104–25.

As Fleming points out, cultural contextualization cannot be achieved in a single manner. The different approaches of Hooker and Knox each possessed their own validity and effectiveness within their respective contexts. It shows, in some cultural contexts, a gradual and inclusive approach like Hooker's may be more appropriate, while in others, a radical and separatist approach like Knox's may prove more suitable.

In conclusion, the cases of Hooker and Knox demonstrate how biblical interpretation and liturgical application can be realized differently within missional contexts. Their differences can be understood not merely as theological disputes, but as missional efforts to effectively communicate and embody the gospel within their respective cultural contexts.

CONCLUSION

While it might seem straightforward to label Richard Hooker and John Knox as Calvinist; when carefully parsed, it is not easy to identify them simply as Calvinists. For a more accurate identification, the following prefixes would apply: Hookerian Calvinism and Knoxian Calvinism. This essay began from the premise that Richard Hooker and John Knox had different approaches to the Scripture and these differences led them to different liturgical applications, especially concerning the BCP. In order to prove that argument, this essay identified and compared the differences between their biblical theology and liturgical theology. Whereas Knox emphasized the literalness and omnicompetence of Scripture and applied it to liturgical practices, Hooker linked the authority of Scripture to the authority of reason and made a rational application to ceremonies. In other words, their different applications of Calvin's biblical interpretation and view on the authority of Scripture gave Hooker and Knox different perspectives on public worship and ceremonies.

Knox, commonly called the father of the Presbyterian Church and a sincere disciple of John Calvin, seems to have held a slightly different biblical perspective from Calvin. Although Knox's starting point of a biblical approach seems to be based on Calvin's hermeneutics, he developed it from his own perspective and applied it very strictly. Throughout his works, Knox describes Scripture with many strict expressions such as: "The playn Word of God," "the express Word of God," "God's own express commandment," and "the strict Word of God."[52] D'Assonville comments that Knox understands Scripture literally, "in the strictest sense, precisely as it stands in the Bible."[53] As seen above, Knox's strictness is also applied to his liturgical

52. These expressions are recited in d'Assonville, *Institutes of Calvin*, 69.

53. D'Assonville, *Institutes of Calvin*, 69.

theology. Whether or not Knox's strict hermeneutics are similar to Calvin's could well require reconsideration.

It is common to call Hooker's theology a "theology of the *via media*" or a "theology of *adiaphora*," but his biblical approach must also be taken into account, because he applies scriptural criteria to defend church polity, including liturgical ceremonies. For Hooker, liturgical ceremonies in the BCP are reasonable applications of the biblical rites. As he states in *Lawes* Book V, some ceremonies, including the kneeling posture at Holy Communion, belong to the issue of piety. For Hooker, since Scripture remains silent about exact or detailed means of administration, ceremonies do not need to be just as they are in Scripture. As Neelands states, "Church polity, since it must account for its temporal, historically-bound reality, can and should, when reasonable, conform to what is 'convenient' for the greater purpose of the common good."[54] One of Hooker's theological contributions to the English Church, can be found here. As Haugaard notes, the English Church "blossomed" based on Hooker's scriptural interpretation; his biblical interpretation broadened the meaning and administration of biblical worship.[55]

Although Hooker and Knox did not actually meet, it is worthwhile comparing and studying their biblical and liturgical theologies because both men learned from and developed Calvin's biblical theology and applied it to their liturgical theologies. While it seems that their interpretations of Scripture and liturgy are not the same, both Hooker and Knox had significant impact on the way biblical worship would be conducted. Although only the scriptural approach and its liturgical administration are reviewed in this essay—and these aspects need more research—the effort might be considered worthwhile for greater understanding of the relationship between Anglican and Presbyterian liturgies.

This historical analysis, however, extends beyond mere historical interest to offer vital insights for contemporary missional practice. Viewed through a missional hermeneutic lens, the approaches of these two reformers each provide vital insights for the contemporary church. Hooker's approach highlights the importance of cultural engagement and contextualization, while Knox's approach emphasizes the necessity of maintaining scriptural fidelity. The modern church continues to face the challenge of balancing these two essential perspectives. Moreover, Bauckham's concept of movement from particularity to universality and Flemming's contextualization theory offer valuable frameworks not only for reinterpreting the Hooker-Knox debate but also for addressing contemporary missional

54. Neelands, foreword to *Hooker's Use of History*, vi.

55. Haugaard, "Scriptural Hermeneutics."

challenges, particularly in understanding how the universal message in the Scripture can be authentically embodied within diverse cultural contexts.

The significance of this study lies in its reinterpretation of historical theological controversies from a contemporary missional perspective, yielding fresh insights into the challenges facing church today. This historical-missional approach demonstrates that church history is not merely a record of past events but a vital resource for contemporary ministry. The theological tension between Hooker and Knox mirrors the tension experienced by the modern church as it seeks to maintain both cultural relevance and biblical integrity. Their debate reveals that contextualization is far more than simple cultural adaptation—it is a complex task requiring deep theological reflection and pastoral wisdom.

Future research should explore how these theoretical insights can be applied in specific cultural contexts, particularly in non-Western settings. The multi-religious and multi-cultural situations of Asia and other regions present challenges quite different from those of the West, requiring fresh applications and developments of Hooker's and Knox's insights. This is not merely an academic concern but a critical issue with direct implications for the missional practice of the contemporary church.

BIBLIOGRAPHY

Atkinson, Nigel. *Richard Hooker: The Authority of Scripture, Tradition, and Reason.* Carlisle, UK: Paternoster, 1997.

Bauckham, Richard. *Bible and Mission: Christian Witness in a Postmodern World.* Grand Rapids: Baker Academic, 2003.

———. *The Bible in the Contemporary World: Hermeneutical Ventures.* Grand Rapids: Eerdmans, 2015.

Bediako, Kwame. *Christianity in Africa: The Renewal of Non-Western Religion.* Edinburgh: Edinburgh University Press, 1995.

Bosch, David J. *Transforming Mission: Paradigm Shifts in Theology of Mission.* Maryknoll, NY: Orbis, 1991.

Calvin, John. *Calvin: Institutes of the Christian Religion.* The Library of Christian Classics. Volumes XX and XXI. Edited by John T. McNeill. Translated by Ford Lewis Battles. Philadelphia: Westminster, 1960.

D'Assonville, V. E. *John Knox and the Institutes of Calvin: A Few Points of Contact in Their Theology.* Durban, SA: Drakensberg, 1969.

Dawson, Jane E. A. *John Knox.* New Haven: Yale University Press, 2015.

Flemming, Dean. *Contextualization in the New Testament: Patterns for Theology and Mission.* Downers Grove, IL: InterVarsity, 2005.

Gibbs, Lee W. "Richard Hooker's *via Media* Doctrine of Scripture and Tradition." *Harvard Theological Review* 95.2 (2002) 227–35.

———. "Life of Hooker." In *A Companion to Richard Hooker*, edited by Torrance Kirby, 1–26. Leiden: Brill, 2003.

Grislis, Egil. "Reflections on Richard Hooker's Understanding of the Eucharist." In *Richard Hooker and the English Reformation*, edited by Torrance Kirby, 207–23. Dordrecht: Kluwer Academic, 2003.

Greaves, Richard L. "The Nature of Authority in the Writings of John Knox." *Fides et historia* 10.2 (1978) 30–51.

Haugaard, William P. "The Scriptural Hermeneutics of Richard Hooker." In *This Sacred History: Anglican Reflections for John Booty*, edited by Donald S. Armentrout, 161–74. Cambridge, MA: Cowley, 1990.

Hooker, Richard. *The Folger Library Edition of the Works of Richard Hooker* (FLE). Volumes I, II, and VI. Edited by W. Speed Hill. Cambridge, MA: Belknap, 1977.

Jacobs, Alan. *The Book of Common Prayer: A Biography*. Princeton: Princeton University Press, 2013.

Joyce, A. J. *Richard Hooker and Anglican Moral Theology*. Oxford: Oxford University Press, 2012.

Keble, John, ed. *The Works of . . . Mr. Richard Hooker: With an Account of His Life and Death by Izaac Walton*. 7th ed., revised, edited by R. W. Church and F. Paget. 3 vols. 1888; repr. Anglistica and Americana, vol. 181. Hildesheim: Olms, 1977; Ellicott City: *Via Media*, 1994.

Kindred-Barnes, Scott N. *Richard Hooker's use of History in his Defense of Public Worship: His Anglican Critique of Calvin, Barrow, and the Puritans*. New York: Mellen, 2011.

Knox, John. *The Works of John Knox*. Edited by David Laing. 6 Volumes. Edinburgh: Thomas and George Stevenson, 1854–64.

Littlejohn, W. Bradford. "'The Edification of the Church': Richard Hooker's Theology of Worship and the Protestant Inward / Outward Disjunction." *Perichoresis* 12, no. 1 (2014) 3–18.

Lorimer, Peter. *John Knox and the Church of England: His Work in Her Pulpit and His Influence Upon Her Liturgy, Articles, and Parties*. London: King, 1875.

MacCulloch, Dairmaid. *Thomas Cranmer: A Life*. New Haven: Yale University Press, 1996.

Moon, Okpyo. "Han'gugin-ŭi Kajŏng Ŭirye-e Mich'in Kidokkyo-ŭi Yŏnghyang: Cherye-rŭl Chungsim-ŭro" [The Influence of Christianity on Korean Family Rites: Focusing on Ancestral Rites]. Inmun Kwahak 79 (1998) 157–69.

Neelands, W. David. "Hooker on Scripture, Reason, and 'Tradition.'" In *Richard Hooker and the Construction of Christian Community*, edited by A. S. McGrade, 75–94. Tempe, AZ: Medieval & Renaissance Texts & Studies, 1997.

———. "Christology and the Sacraments." In *A Companion to Richard Hooker*, edited by Torrance Kirby, 369–401. Leiden: Brill, 2003.

———. Foreword to *Richard Hooker's Use of History in His Defence of Public Worship*, Scott Kindred-Barnes, i–vi. Lampeter: Mellen, 2011.

———. Review of *Richard Hooker and Anglican Moral Theology* by A. J. Joyce. *Journal of British Studies* 52.2 (2013) 509–10. https://doi.org/10.1017/jbr.2013.14.

———. "The Use of Abuse of John Calvin in Richard Hooker's Defence of the English Church." In *Between the Lectern and the Pulpit*, edited by Rob Clements and Dennis Ngien, 41–57. Vancouver: Regent College, 2014.

———. "Richard Hooker." Lecture presented at Trinity College, Toronto, ON, March 6, 2019.

Newbigin, Lesslie. *The Gospel in a Pluralist Society*. Grand Rapids: Eerdmans, 1989.

Spinks, Bryan D. *Two Faces of Elizabethan Anglican Theology: Sacraments and Salvation in the Thought of William Perkins and Richard Hooker*. Lanham, MD: Scarecrow, 1999.

———. *Do This in Remembrance of Me*. London: SCM, 2013.

Torrance, Iain R. "A Particular Reformed Piety: John Knox and the Posture at Communion." *Scottish Journal of Theology* 67.4 (2014) 400–13.

Voak, Nigel. "Richard Hooker and the Principle of *Sola Scriptura*." *Journal of Theological Studies* 59.1 (2008) 96–139.

Wright, Christopher J. H. *The Mission of God: Unlocking the Bible's Grand Narrative*. 2nd ed. Downers Grove, IL: IVP Academic, 2023.

11

Evangelism in a Quiet Voice

A Historical Reflection on the Emphasis on Active Evangelism in the FLAMES Initiative of the Presbyterian Church in Canada

Ross Lockhart

"We do not really *do* evangelism as Presbyterians, do we?" The question emerged in a dimly lit Presbyterian church basement during coffee hour, after I spent the morning preaching on the theme of Christian witness. My kind-hearted and well-meaning conversation partner went on to explain that they had been born into a Presbyterian family and attended the same congregation their whole life. Letting the question linger a while, the church member shifted their cup and saucer to the other hand and continued, "Ross, when I say we do not do evangelism as Presbyterians I understand that we need to share our faith, I'm just not sure *how* we do that. I like to *live* my faith but I'm not really comfortable talking about it, do you know what I mean?"

Encouraging Mainline Protestants to share and show the gospel through their words *and* actions remains an ongoing process, with deep roots within the Presbyterian Church in Canada (PCC). As recently as 1998, the 124th General Assembly of the PCC adopted the FLAMES initiative to articulate and demonstrate the priorities of the denomination as it entered a new century. From 1999–2005, this renewal campaign was encouraged throughout congregations, presbyteries, and synods with an annual focus on a different aspect of the church's mission as follows:

F ocus on Children, Teens and Young Adults
L aity Equipping
A ctive Evangelism
M ission, International, National and Justice
E ducation For Laity and Clergy
S pirituality

When introducing the year of Active Evangelism to the General Assembly, it was noted "*that evangelism is something Presbyterians talk about with a quiet voice.*"[1] This chapter explores the attempt to amplify that "quiet voice" and to discern ongoing lessons for the practice of evangelism in the PCC over twenty years after the FLAMES initiative.

In his recent work on the history of the PCC, Stuart Macdonald notes that evangelism played an important role in the life of the denomination in his study from 1945 to 1985. Macdonald notes the important work of the Board of Evangelism and Social Action over the decades raising the profile of evangelism, with Presbyterians encouraged in the 1950s to approach the evangelistic task as an obligation, "to speak conviction, with conviction flowing from a true understanding of the Bible and areal experience of the grace of God."[2] Through rapid cultural change in the 1960s, Macdonald notes the PCC faced the reality of declining church membership by turning to evangelism as a solution as a report to General Assembly in 1971 stated, "we have been dealing with an erosion of faith" that required a "relevant proclamation of the Gospel, supported by an authoritative teaching ministry," in order for the PCC to have a "distinctive witness only in so far as it becomes a community of believers able to articulate its faith and declare God's Word."[3]

Macdonald describes the ambitious goal approved by the General Assembly to "Double in the Eighties," seeking to turn around church decline. Alongside the Committee on Church Growth tasked with this doubling of the PCC membership in the 1980s, the work of the Board of Congregational Life also equipped and encouraged Presbyterians to articulate Christian faith in ways that connected with their neighbors. The Congregational Life report to the 1981 General Assembly makes clear the urgency for evangelism declaring, "We will need to explore and develop new ways and new language

1. PCC, *Acts and Proceedings of the General Assembly 2003*, 341.
2. Macdonald, *Tradition and Tension*, 130.
3. Macdonald, *Tradition and Tension*, 149.

if we are to reach these persons with the Good News of Jesus Christ. The making of disciples to engage in this ministry is a necessity in fulfilling our commission. This is not something that can be left to the 'professional'; it is the work of the whole Church."[4] Evangelism was stressed not only in General Assembly reports, denominational resources and congregational workshops in the 1980s, but also through the development of a new statement of faith. *Living Faith (Foi Vivant)* would not achieve subordinate standard status alongside the Westminster Confession and the Declaration of Faith Concerning Nation until the next decade, however, the appearance of the "little green book," in pews and homes throughout the 1980s demonstrated its popularity with church members. Section 9 of *Living Faith* is focused on evangelism and mission in a changing Canadian context. Drawing on the denomination's focus for both evangelism and social action, the new statement of faith declared:

> 9.1.2 Mission is evangelism,
> the offer of salvation to all people
> in the power of the Holy Spirit,
> to be received through faith in Christ.
> It asks people to repent of their sins,
> to trust Christ,
> to be baptized,
> and to enter a life honouring Jesus as Lord.
>
> 9.1.3 Mission is service,
> a call to help people in need and
> to permeate all of life with the compassion of God.

While missional theology would note that mission is both an attribute and action of the Triune God *before* it becomes mixed with human agency, *Living Faith* makes clear that evangelism was not just an optional practice, but both core and confessional in the life of Presbyterians. Indeed, while the PCC's goal of doubling the number of members in the 1980s failed to live up to its own high bar of accomplishment, the desire to continue to engage in evangelism and church growth remained.

Indeed, a decade later when the PCC launched the FLAMES initiative, it is noteworthy that "Active Evangelism" was given a whole year of focus, suggesting perhaps that passive sharing of the Christian faith was thought to be more of a default setting for Presbyterians. As we examine more closely this year of evangelism for the PCC, we might ask what were the aims of this initiative to motivate Presbyterians to speak, share and show their faith in Jesus Christ? How was "Active Evangelism" explained and understood at

4. Macdonald, *Tradition and Tension*, 160.

the time? What impact, if any, may be discerned from this year of emphasis on the speech act of faith sharing for Presbyterians across Canada? Indeed, when we look back on this specific evangelism initiative in a long line of commitments of the PCC to sharing the gospel, what might it say to leaders in the PCC today, as we study the goals, activities and impact of the church's understanding of evangelism in the FLAMES initiative in the fading light of Christendom in Canada.

WHAT DO WE MEAN BY EVANGELISM?

Before going further, it would be helpful to spend a moment on the question of evangelism itself. What is evangelism? Evangelism certainly is an ancient Christian practice, but today it can often feel like the "problem relative" within the wider family of practical theology. Preaching, pastoral care, ethics, catechesis and other areas of practical theology are thoroughly studied and taught at mainline Protestant seminaries today, however, evangelism often meets with silence or slight embarrassment. As a Presbyterian professor who regularly teaches courses on evangelism, I find myself often having to go back to define what we mean by this particular Christian practice. The biblical roots of evangelism come from the Triune God who chooses, in God's own sovereign way, to be revealed in creation, covenant, Christ and church. The word "evangelism" comes from a New Testament Greek word *euangelion.* This word is a compound word made up of "eu", meaning good and "angelion" meaning message or news.[5] So, the word "evangelism" comes from a Greek word that means Good News. It is translated into English with the word "Gospel". Walter Brueggemann reminds us that the Hebrew word *bissar* means "tell-the-news" and that this message *announced* is critical. Someone has to share the gospel and tell the saving story of Jesus, but that proclamation is in light of God's action and is announced in anticipation of God's ongoing redeeming and reconciling love at work in the world, including through the church. Brueggemann suggests interpreting evangelism in three scenes: 1) conflict between powerful forces; 2) the witness who gives testimony and tells the outcome (Peter in Acts at Pentecost would be an example); and 3) the listener then is invited to make an appropriate response.[6] I often interpret Brueggemann's threefold description is in terms of:

1. WHAT—What's the truth, the reality of this world we are living in and experiencing with our human lives

5. *Angelion* is the word we get angel from, a messenger of God.
6. Brueggemann, *Biblical Perspectives on Evangelism*, 15–18.

2. SAY WHAT—Someone has to make meaning of what we are experiencing in this world. Someone has to be a witness.
3. SO WHAT—the invitation is offered to those who hear the witness. Considering this witness, how will they respond?[/NL 1–3]

Noting this basic outline of evangelism, what did Presbyterians at the turn of the twenty-first century mean when they launched the FLAMES initiative focusing for a whole year on the theme of sharing the good news with a waiting, watching world?

"ACTIVATING" EVANGELISM IN THE PCC

In anticipation of the focus on evangelism, the Presbyterian theological colleges partnered with the History Committee of the PCC to host a two-day conference May 24–25, 2002, at Knox College entitled, "Active Evangelism: The Canadian Presbyterian Story." Participants were offered a program that reminded them of the PCC's evangelistic heritage and vision, and a challenge to live as heirs of that heritage by laying a biblical, historical, theological, and practical foundation for "Active Evangelism." This laid a groundwork for the General Assembly that met in Cornwall, Ontario the next month to officially mark the beginning of the theme of "Active Evangelism: Sharing Christian Hope and Hospitality."

The General Assembly noted that the goal of the year was to elevate the profile of evangelism and to be more intentional in reaching people for Christ's church. Synods were encouraged to use "Active Evangelism" as a theme for their meetings in the fall, in order to support local leaders in contextual evangelism initiatives. At the General Assembly, commissioners were divided into small groups to engage in faith sharing, followed by a time of singing (noted as "contemporary Christian music") led by Rev. Glen Soderholm. While no clear definition was given at the time what was meant by evangelism, the Committee on History in their report noted that their conference in advance of General Assembly defined evangelism in the following way:

> Christian evangelism is the intentional proclamation, through words, deeds of kindness, the faithful discharge of daily duties, and acts of worship, of the good news of the triune God's gracious invitation to all humanity to become God's people. God's invitation is seen most clearly in Jesus the Messiah. The prayerful goal of proclaiming the good news is that individuals and whole peoples hearing and seeing God's invitation will respond

to the working of the Holy Spirit, accept the invitation, and become members of the Kingdom of God.[7]

EVANGELISM ACTIVATED IN *THE PRESBYTERIAN RECORD*

One intriguing source for reflection upon the year of Active Evangelism is found in *The Presbyterian Record*. The PCC's national magazine published a monthly column featuring curated voices dedicated to the theme offering different perspectives on evangelism. Incoming Moderator Rev. Mark Lewis introduced the year of Active Evangelism to the wider church in the July 2002 issue of *The Presbyterian Record*. Lewis noted that many Presbyterians were familiar with negative aspects associated with evangelism, however, in its proper sense evangelism "is the true foundation of growth and vitality in the church. We all need to answer God's call to become evangelists. The word *evangelism* simply means 'sharing the good news'; The good news is that God is love and, in the person of Jesus Christ, died to pay the price for our sins and was raised again to give us life eternal. Our church will be revitalized and renewed when every member accepts his or her own calling to evangelism with joy and enthusiasm."[8] Lewis went on to note the Life and Mission Agency's definition of evangelism as, "Witnessing in word and action to the transforming love of God in Christ with integrity and compassion in personal, church and public realms." And while evangelism is, technically speaking a "speech act," Lewis acknowledged how hard it was for many Presbyterians to put their faith into words, and instead encouraged them into acts of mercy, compassion and peace.

Along with a monthly guest columnist exploring the topic of Active Evangelism, the denominational magazine also highlighted ways in which congregations could practically engage the theme through articles written by Rev. Jim Czegledi, associate secretary for evangelism, church growth and worship. Each month Czegledi suggested specific ways to put Active Evangelism into action including through bible studies and small group studies, offering the Alpha Program, practices to encourage faith sharing, hosting an Active Evangelism Special Sunday, visiting larger churches like Willow Creek, and engaging in diagnostic tools like the Natural Church Development program.

7. PCC, *Acts and Proceedings of the General Assembly 2002*, 264.

8. *The Presbyterian Record* (July 2002), 9.

In fact, Czegledi was also the next guest columnist for Active Evangelism in the September 2002, placing an emphasis on the sharing of faith in personal relationships. Czegledi's article had a different feel than Moderator Mark Lewis' introduction to the year of Active Evangelism in the previous issue. Lewis earlier stated, "I have heard countless faithful Presbyterians say: "I cannot be an evangelist. 1 am no good with words.' I assure all of those people that they do not need words to be an evangelist."[9] Instead, Czegledi wrote in September, "There is no getting around it. Evangelism does involve sharing our faith with others. While deeds can speak as loudly as words, the New Testament church grew, and churches continue to grow, through people who tell others about Jesus Christ, invite them to church and live lives of Christian discipleship."[10] Czegledi asked, "is there an official Presbyterian approach to evangelism?" And then answered by arguing that

> The model endorsed by the General Assembly of The Presbyterian Church in Canada is relational evangelism. Relational evangelism is One-on-one evangelism. It was the method used by Jesus and his disciples in the New Testament. The Gospels tell us Jesus' primary concern was not with programs to reach multitudes but, rather, with training disciples who would follow him and share the good news with others. The Presbyterian way of doing evangelism honours this biblical approach to evangelism. How can we share our faith? Relational evangelism happens when God's Spirit leads people to share their faith in words or action, inside or outside the church. It happens when people engage one another in faith-sharing conversations and when unchurched families, friends, business associates or neighbours are invited to come to church. The local church is the heart of evangelism efforts.[11]

Other guest columnists included Rick Horst in October who offered a reflection on Jesus sharing his identity as Messiah in Luke 7 as one who brings healing to those in need. Horst urged Presbyterians to turn outwards and find those for whom the Good News was indeed new news. He wrote, "God has given gifts and resources to each of us for addressing the hurts and hopes of those who are beyond the walls of our buildings or outside the reach of our traditional ministries. In a mission-post congregation, we share those gifts beyond ourselves. In doing so, we begin to see afresh the dynamic

9. *The Presbyterian Record* (June 2002), 9.
10. *The Presbyterian Record* (September 2002), 16.
11. *The Presbyterian Record* (September 2002), 14.

ministry of Jesus Christ in tangible, life-changing ways."[12] Horst warned that Presbyterians had deluded themselves into believing that "maintenance and survival is the mission of the church. Instead of conserving and protecting, we are called in this exciting time to expand and invest—to give ourselves away in the name of Jesus Christ."[13]

In November, Terry Ingram stressed the importance of leadership (a common theme throughout the year long column on evangelism) and wrote, "The role of leadership is critical. I am convinced that, while clergy cannot make congregations healthy and vibrant by themselves, they certainly have the power to pour cold water over those things with which they disagree. As this is true of clergy, so it is true of strong sessions." Ingram went on to argue that if "active evangelism is going to be lived out in our congregations, the leadership needs to be on board. And this means more than passing a motion of concurrence at a meeting or setting up some committee to investigate and report back on the matter."[14]

In December, Heather Vais wrote a reflection on evangelism and worship, noting the opportunity that congregations have to reach out in Advent and Christmas to neighbors and friends in the community. Vais stated, "I go into every congregation I serve with a mind for growth. After all, that is what we are called to do as a people of God. As well as the vital aspects of our Christian ministry of offering care to people in need and justice for those who are oppressed, we are called by Jesus Christ to a ministry of evangelism: to share the good news and make disciples of all the nations."[15]

In January 2003, Rev. Carey Nieuwhof challenged the ways and forms of Presbyterian worship as possible barriers to evangelism. Nieuwhof wrote, "We are free to adapt . . . the form with which we express the Christian faith. Did the Early Church express its worship with an organ and 17th-century hymns? Did the Early Church dress in suits and sip coffee and juice after worship services? Did they meet only once a week? Were their services characterized by moderation and mediocrity?"[16] Reflecting on his own congregational ministry in Oro, Ontario Nieuwhof observed, "At Trinity, we've become so convinced of the importance of both evangelism and discipleship to the mission of the church, we've decided to offer two distinct types of services each week. We've given our prime-time services (two identical weekend services) over to the purpose of evangelism. By

12. *The Presbyterian Record* (October 2002), 38.
13. *The Presbyterian Record* (October 2002), 38.
14. *The Presbyterian Record* (November 2002), 40.
15. *The Presbyterian Record* (December 2002), 38.
16. *The Presbyterian Record* (January 2003), 34.

using contemporary Christian songs, secular music that raises theological issues, prayer, drama, video clips and biblical preaching designed for people with no biblical knowledge, we're trying to create a service that anyone can access." Nieuwhof noted the challenge for Presbyterians to attend to the needs of their neighbors and move beyond worship that simply met the personal preferences of church members. He wrote, "There is some measure of blessing in this kind of service for Christians, but the real purpose is to help those who are not yet Christians come to a safe place where they can hear a dangerous message. We encourage our people to attend this service and bring their friends whenever possible. Think of it as doing Billy Graham every weekend."[17]

The monthly column on Active Evangelism rarely appeared in the following month's "Letters to the Editor," with Nieuwhof's article being the exception. Indeed, it appears not everyone shared the same enthusiasm for evangelism that brought a change in the way Presbyterians worshipped God. A letter to the editor from Niagara Falls challenged Nieuwhof's rosy picture of evangelistic renewal, asking whether attending to new believers came at the cost of long time members writing, "Perhaps the reason seniors find it harder to change is that the 'milk' suitable to new believers is insufficient and unsatisfying for more mature Christians who desire more 'meat' than is offered by some contemporary services."[18] The letter went on to challenge Nieuwhof's pastoral sensibilities to those who had left the congregation after a change to a more evangelistic form of worship asking (perhaps rhetorically),

> How many once-valued and longtime members have left your church because of the change in service? And how many others have remained while feeling unhappy and unfulfilled because of the changes; yet, they are determined to stay in the faint hope that things will change some day or because no one is going to chase them out of their church? Do you care about such people even if they are only a minority? Some people finally transfer their membership because they feel their church simply doesn't care about them anymore.[19]

Rev. Kirk Summers talked about church extension as evangelism in the February 2003 issue, that also included a profile on Western Han-Ca's emphasis upon evangelism and church extension. Summers reflected on his work over many years in Calgary-Macleod Presbytery with the Church Extension

17. *The Presbyterian Record* (January 2003), 35.
18. *The Presbyterian Record* (February 2003), 8.
19. *The Presbyterian Record* (February 2003), 8.

Committee that sought out the best practices and people to identify new church planting opportunities and support the work of founding new churches. Summers concluded with a charge for judicatories: "Presbyteries, pray for Christ's church to be extended and developed within your bounds. Learn from where you've been, assess where you're at and decide where you want to go. And, of course, if you do not have one already, strike a committee full of people eager to serve the Risen Christ and extend his Kingdom, In the light of his resurrection, the future for his church is blazing bright."[20]

Next, Rev. Chuck Congram wrote in the March about the struggle in the 1980s with attempting to double the membership of the denomination and how leadership is critical to successful evangelism. He noted the experience of critics who suggested "that God was far more interested in our faithfulness than in our success. In our current denominational culture, significantly more time is spent trying to define what evangelism is and the appropriate Presbyterian way of doing it than in the actual practice. The time has come for leadership to set aside the philosophical rhetoric in order to engage more fully in being personally involved in evangelism. In addition, individuals associated with our congregations must be challenged and trained to seek ways to introduce others to the life-transforming power and love of Jesus Christ. This mandate, which is enormous, is first and foremost a leadership issue."[21] He went on to encourage leaders to practice evangelism regularly as a way to model the importance of reaching out to others and building relationships with non-Christians in the community.

Tom Dickey continued this theme of leadership in the April 2003 issue, noting the result if congregations were not encouraged by their leaders to change, or unwilling to do so would be, "some congregations will continue to decline and some will die. Congregations must move away from an institutionally driven agenda toward a mission-driven one if they are to connect with the community."[22]

In May, Keith Knight explored the potential for evangelism through technology noting, "Internet technology has opened the floodgates of possibility for today's spiritual seeker. There is an incredibly wide range of information on religion, faith, spirituality and church on the Internet. The biggest challenge for any spiritual seeker is to separate the wheat from the chaff."[23] The Presbyterian Record wrapped up its focus on Active Evangelism by asking Don Posterski from World Vision to offer an "outsiders"

20. *The Presbyterian Record* (February 2003), 44.

21. *The Presbyterian Record* (March 2003), 44.

22. *The Presbyterian Record* (April 2003), 39.

23. *The Presbyterian Record* (May 2003), 40.

perspective. Posterski encouraged Presbyterians to move away from the dour stereotypes so often associated with the denomination to embrace a more joyful expression of the gospel. As Posterski wrote, "Presbyterians, unshackle yourselves! Surrender your demeaning self-images and rethink the assumption that others are not interested in spiritual matters. Get rid of the stereotypes that curtail you and take a fresh look at the people who surround you. Together, let's celebrate our life in Christ and enjoy engaging and responding to the people God brings within our reach."[24]

REFLECTIONS FROM THE MODERATOR

In researching this theme of Active Evangelism and the FLAMES[25] initiative, the Rev. Dr. Mark Lewis generously shared his time and thoughts with me looking back on the theme over two decades later. Having served as Moderator of the General Assembly during the "Year of Active Evangelism" in 2002–2003, Lewis' contributions provide a crucial "insider" perspective on the campaign. Lewis noted, during our discussion, the extensive background on the FLAMES initiative beginning in 1995 with the Long-Range Planning Committee, on which he served as Convenor, that examined previous denominational studies in its mandate to define and promote the priorities of the Presbyterian Church as it entered a new century.[26]

Lewis shared how the Committee felt that the church had fallen into a cycle of introspection and visioning that led to little action, like an athlete in an endless cycle of training, but never competing. As Lewis remarked, "sometimes 'visioning' is what we do when we do not want to do ministry."[27] Lewis noted that the committee in an effort to compile the results of numerous studies and encourage church members to take action, through the Assembly Council, hosted the "Think Tank" in 1996. Lewis described this gathering as a diverse group of Presbyterians from across the country that encouraged them to share their hopes and dreams for the denomination.

24. *The Presbyterian Record* (June 2023), 51.

25. Mark Lewis shared that he continues to type "FLAMES" in bold capitals in the Mistral font. The Mistral is a wind system that brings clear, fresh air to the Mediterranean, adding for interest that Mistral is now an AI start-up company.

26. Lewis noted in particular The LAMP Report (1969), The Administrative Council Re: Planning (1988), Changing Times, Changing Choices (1988), Catching the Vision (1988), From Vision to Reality (1989), The Administrative Council Re: Strategic Planning (1989), The Task Force on Restructuring (1990), The Special Committee on Restructuring (1991), Live the Vision (1993), The State of the Church Report (1993), and the Reports Re: Staffing and Structuring (1994).

27. Mark Lewis, Personal Correspondence, 24 September 2025.

The observations that emerged from the "Think Tank" were shared across the wider church with an invitation for responses. While views were diverse, six priorities emerged that later formed the FLAMES initiative: Education for Laity and Clergy, Mission: International, National and Justice, Empowering Laity, Teen and Young Adult Ministry, Evangelism, and Spirituality.

Lewis recalled that the goal of the program was to present and promote the priorities in a way that would encourage church members to action. To that end, Lewis recounted how the committee hosted several contests, including a songwriting contest and an essay writing contest entitled "Who Fanned Your Flames," to encourage nationwide participation. The motto "Fanning the Flames" was adopted, and the updated image of the classic Presbyterian symbol of the burning bush from Exodus 3 was created, "with the intention of revisiting our sense of being called to a great mission in the same way that Moses was called, with the seven red flames represent the seven years of the initiative."[28] Lewis recalled how the five green leaves represented the living church filled with grace and the two brown stems represented the Old and New Testaments. He described how the three blue swirls represented the Holy Spirit fanning our flames to new life before adding playfully, "The extent to which Presbyterians took such convoluted numerology to heart is questionable; however, they were quick to point out that the new symbol bore a strange resemblance to the Kellogg's Cornflakes rooster."[29]

When asked about the specific year 2002–2023 with a focus on "Active Evangelism," Lewis humorously recalled that "despite what cynics say, the adjective 'active' was not just added to 'evangelism' for fear that the "FLEME"

28. Mark Lewis, Personal Correspondence, 24 September 2025.

29. Mark Lewis, Personal Correspondence, 24 September, 2025.

initiative would only have induced a lot of throat clearing. It was added to emphasise that evangelism must be active."

Lewis traced the highlights for me of the year of Active Evangelism, beginning with the Committee on History's conference at Knox College before General Assembly highlighted earlier in the chapter. In his role as Moderator of the General Assembly in 2002–2003, Lewis recalled in detail the way in which different agencies of the church engaged the theme of evangelism. For example, the Life and Mission Agency defined evangelism as "Sharing Christian hope and hospitality" and provided resources to the wider church and invited people to share their stories of evangelistic witness. Lewis noted that International Ministries invited Canadian Presbyterians to renew their interest in international evangelism in the many nations served by the Presbyterian Church in Canada. Justice Ministries were remembered for drawing attention to the reality that upholding justice for the marginalized and poor is always a crucial part of evangelism. Lewis emphasized that, "It was deeply satisfying and encouraging to see all the agencies of the national church rededicate themselves to active evangelism under the banner of the initiative."[30]

More than two decades later, Lewis offered his thoughts on the legacy of the year of Active Evangelism, and the questions it raises for Christian witness today. Lewis wrote,

> If evangelism is inviting others to join God's people, then the most challenging question about evangelism in 2025 is, "What does it mean to be God's people?" Throughout the twentieth century, "God's people" were aligned with the dominant colonising forces of society. We evangelised from a position of strength and with the view that all people should conform to a European worldview and religious system. We must ask, "How must our sense of evangelism change in light of our understanding of the harm we rendered to those persons whom we were evangelising, including, but not limited to First Nations persons and 2SLGBTQI+ persons?" To be faithful to the Gospel call to evangelise, we must constantly ask, "What was Jesus doing in the world?" And, "What does Jesus want us to do today?"

30. Mark Lewis, Personal Correspondence, 24 September 2025.

LOOKING BACK ON THE YEAR OF ACTIVE EVANGELISM

In the Acts and Proceedings of the General Assembly that followed the "Year of Active Evangelism," congregational resources provided to enhance evangelistic work were noted, as well as a recommendation that relational evangelism be the priority for Presbyterians moving forward. The report stated that from time to time, "we are asked about the Presbyterian approach to evangelism. In 1994, the General Assembly endorsed face to face evangelism as a priority for The Presbyterian Church in Canada. Evangelism face to face means the kind of evangelism, which is conducted at a personal or relational level, individually and in small groups. It is relational evangelism."[31] But what did Presbyterians mean exactly by relational evangelism? It was defined as "outreach to people by people, one on one or face to face. It works hand in hand with Christian hospitality and was the method used by Jesus and his disciples in the New Testament."[32] In reflecting upon this approach to sharing and showing the gospel through a Christ-centered lens, Presbyterians reflected on the year of Active Evangelism by noting that "The gospels tell us about Jesus calling others to follow him. His primary concern was not with programs to reach multitudes, but rather with training disciples whom the multitudes would follow. It is the model or style of evangelism endorsed by the General Assembly of The Presbyterian Church in Canada.[33]

WHAT DOES THIS MEAN FOR EVANGELISM IN THE PCC TODAY?

As this book seeks to honour the life and work of our colleague Stuart Macdonald, including his scholarship and teaching on the history of Mainline Protestant Churches in Canada, we have explored the practice of evangelism during a particular historical moment in the life of the PCC. As a missiologist, with a love of history, I am left to ponder like Mark Lewis' reflections above, what we mean by evangelism today. Many of my treasured colleagues in practical theology across North America are wrestling with these same questions. Rick Osmer encourages us to move away from evangelism as conversionism, instead approaching evangelism as "the invitation to respond to the gospel, the good news of God's salvation of the world in Jesus Christ, which is offered to others as the witness of the church under the guidance

31. PCC, *Acts and Proceedings of the General Assembly 2003*, 343.
32. PCC, *Acts and Proceedings of the General Assembly 2003*, 343.
33. PCC, *Acts and Proceedings of the General Assembly 2003*, 343.

and persuasive power of the Holy Spirit."[34] Priscilla Pope-Levison wrestles with the biblical, theological, historical and practical aspects of various models of evangelism in Christian practice, and ultimately ends her study by asking what is "good" about evangelism. She advocates for evangelism today that includes five "key qualities of good evangelism," namely hospitality, relationship, integrity, message bearing, and church rootedness.[35] Andy Root revisits the Christian practice of evangelism in our current "age of despair," focusing on consolation in the real sorrow that many feel today. Root reimagines evangelism by attending to the sacramental shape of divine-human encounter, offering us a vision that feels far more pastoral than locked in the traditional mode of proclamation. Root writes, "evangelism, if we can see it through consolation as sacramental, invites others to receive a blessing. It is to invite other to be blessed by the ministry of the Christian, of the church, of the living God who is ontologically a minister. God enters all our sorrows for the sake of redemption and participation in God's infinite life."[36] From this contemporary scholarship on evangelism, we can see that the Presbyterians in this study from two decades ago are part of a longer and broader conversation on the nature of Christian witness that will continue into the future. In the end, Presbyterians may share their devotion to the Lord Jesus with neighbors in a quiet voice, but even a whisper can be a witness in a world longing for hope, beauty and truth.

BIBLIOGRAPHY

Brueggemann, Walter. *Biblical Perspectives on Evangelism: Living in a Three-Storied Universe*. Nashville: Abingdon, 1993.

Macdonald, Stuart. *Tradition and Tension: The Presbyterian Church in Canada, 1945–1985*. Montreal/Kingston: McGill-Queen's University Press, 2025.

Osmer, Richard. *The Invitation: A Theology of Evangelism*. Grand Rapids: Eerdmans, 2021.

Pope-Levison, Priscilla. *Models of Evangelism*. Grand Rapids: Baker, 2020.

Presbyterian Church in Canada (PCC). *Acts & Proceedings of the General Assembly 2002*.

Presbyterian Church in Canada (PCC). *Acts & Proceedings of the General Assembly 2003*.

The Presbyterian Record. Toronto. Various issues, 2002–2003.

Root, Andrew. *Evangelism in an Age of Despair: Hope Beyond the Failed Promise of Happiness*. Grand Rapids: Baker, 2005.

34. Osmer, *The Invitation*, 12.
35. Pope-Levison, *Models of Evangelism*, 181.
36. Root, *Evangelism in an Age of Despair*, 25.

12

Ishmael as Insult

Presbyterians, Quakers, and Scriptural Polemics in 1650s England

Amanda Pullan

INTRODUCTION

When I first began researching the Expulsion of Hagar and Ishmael story, it was due to its surprising popularity as the subject of seventeenth-century domestic embroidery. It seemed to me a bizarre choice out of all possible biblical stories. Seeing it as belonging within the larger story of Abraham's household and covenant of faith was clearly one reason for its importance. The Protestant Reformers encouraged using stories from Genesis for household instruction. Old Testament stories, in the eyes of the Reformers, were a far safer choice compared to stories from the Life of Christ, which could lead one into the sin of idolatry.[1] But even so, this was not a satisfying explanation for why the expulsion of Hagar and Ishmael with its dubious moral message seemed more popular than other Genesis stories. I set off to investigate further what it was about this story that resonated with people in the seventeenth century. One of the research tools that was newly available was corpus analysis using a digitized corpus of *Early English Books Online*, a

1. For how Biblical stories were to be historical exemplars and not aids to devotion see Perkins, *Reformed Catholike*, 172.

digital collection containing over 146,000 titles from the first printed book in English in 1475 to the texts printed in 1700.

Using this digital tool, I noticed some trends in printing that coincided with what I was finding in material culture. Tracing mentions of Hagar and Ishmael, I found evidence pointing to the mid seventeenth-century, and particularly to the 1650s as a significant decade. Mentions of "Ishmael" surpassed any other decade in the whole seventeenth century. Closer analysis of these texts and their contents revealed that Ishamel was being used as an insult solely by the Quakers to refer to the Presbyterians and other Independent ministers under Cromwell's national church. The insult was based on specific qualities in the ministers that were analogous to the qualities in the biblical Ishmael, attesting to considerable knowledge of the text and its associations. This article attempts to explain this finding and argues that this very use of "Ishmael" as an insult was indicative of a battle between the Presbyterians and the Quakers for superiority and skill in handling the Scriptures that was heightened the 1650s, an extraordinary time.

Recent work by Margaret Anne Johnston also focused on the conflicts in the 1650s between the Puritan clergy and the early Quakers. Johnston argued that these "pamphlet wars"[2] represented an absolute stand-off between both groups with no possibility of compromise apparent.[3] For the Puritan clergy, a mix of Presbyterians and Independents, this stand-off was evidence of a persisting struggle to reform the Church within a national Church-like structure to which the Quakers were obstacles. Kate Peters also highlights the important role of print as media in the early formation of the Quakers and how the skill of a select group in publishing their work was key to making the movement visible.[4] Catie Gill also looks at this early period of Quaker writing finding women's participation in the movement and in pamphlet writing to be significant.[5]

This article with its focus on Ishmael and its appearance in printed text speaks to these perspectives while providing new evidence. I argue that this new sect, the Quakers, by using biblical allegory, were signaling their religious authority over the Presbyterians and other clergy in their fight against accusations of being the false church. I also argue that the figure of Ishmael resonated at a time when the idea of discerning a true church from a false church was a public concern. The article begins with a short overview

2. I use "pamphlet wars" as Johnston does to explain to a "discrete exchange of pamphlets"; see Johnston, "Confrontation Between Quakers and Clergy," 210.

3. Johnston, "Confrontation Between Quakers and Clergy."

4. Peters, *Print Culture.*

5. Gill, *Women in the Quaker Community.*

of the allegorical meaning of Hagar and Ishmael drawing on the work of John Thompson.[6] This is followed by a discussion of the findings from my analysis of trends in print, using digitized corpus and a closer examination of the texts containing references to Ishmael. Lastly, I show how the Quaker, John Whitehead used "Ishmael" to convey a sophisticated critique of the Presbyterian minister John Kaye, and how Kaye battled back in print.

THE EXPULSION OF HAGAR AND ISHMAEL: THE ALLEGORICAL TRADITION

The Expulsion of Hagar and Ishmael in Genesis is unique amongst other biblical stories for having an allegorical reading that was both ancient and canonical. The story is first recorded in Genesis 21:

> And the child grew and was weaned: and Abraham made a great feast, the same day that Isaac was weaned. And Sarah saw the sonne of Hagar the Egyptian, which shee had born unto Abraham, mocking. Wherefore she said unto Abraham, "Cast out this bond woman, and her sonne: for the sonne of this bond woman shall not be heire with my sonne, even with Isaac.[7]

The story's significance for Christians comes from it being referenced in the New Testament by the Apostle Paul who explains its allegorical meaning in his letter to the Galatians. According to Paul, the two women in the Genesis story illustrated God's two covenants. Hagar represented Mount Sinai, where the Israelites had received the law while Sarah represented the heavenly Jerusalem "which is above is free."[8] The Galatian Christians, Paul wrote, were being persecuted by those who wanted them to keep the Jewish laws and thus they were like Abraham's son Isaac, who had been persecuted by Abraham's other son Ishmael:

> Now wee brethren, as Isaac was, are the children of promise. But as then hee that was borne after the flesh, persecuted him that was borne after the Spirit, even so it is now. Neverthelesse, what saith the Scripture: Cast out the bondwoman and her sonne: for the sone of the bondwoman shall not bee heire with the son of

6. Thompson, *Writing the Wrongs*.

7. Gen 21:8–10, *The Holy Bible, Conteyning the Old Testament, and the New* (London: Robert Barker, 1611), STC 2216; hereafter cited as Authorized Version, (AV).

8. Gal 4:26 (AV).

> the freewoman. So then brethren, we are children of the bondwoman but of the free.[9]

Both Hagar and Ishmael therefore symbolized the antagonists of God's promises to Abraham and persecutors of the true church.

This allegorical interpretation has been manifest in text and visual imagery through the centuries. In the early Christian period, the story was used to justify the separating of Christianity from its Jewish roots, and scholars have pointed to how the allegory persisted.[10] In the medieval period these characters and their symbolism continued to be conveyed through the two contrasting female figures, the icons of *Synagoga* and *Ecclesia*, visible in the portal carvings in cathedrals across Western Europe.[11]

John L Thompson traced historical responses to the figure of Hagar in biblical exegesis and found that the allegorical interpretation sanctioned by the Apostle Paul, was the traditional way of reading the story. He suggested that in biblical exegesis, allegory was a common device to avoid explaining something that appeared morally dubious.[12] The commentators would not deny that the event happened but just that it had not occurred in the literal way described. The importance of the allegorical reading is especially pertinent for the expulsion story with all its moral ambiguities, and because it was unique amongst other biblical stories by having an allegorical reading that was both ancient and canonical.[13]

Thompson traced the discourse back to Philo and ended with Martin Luther and John Calvin, describing how the allegorical reading of the story that focused on persecution resurfaced in many of these writings. Origen's seventh homily on Genesis focused on Paul's discussion of persecution as evidence of why the story should be understood allegorically to represent a spiritual struggle.[14] St. Augustine, Bishop of Hippo discussed the Expulsion story in the context of persecution and applied it to his contemporary struggle with the Donatists. Pope Urban III also used the story of Hagar and Ishmael in Genesis 21 as a justification for casting out oppressors, in his eyes, the Saracens were the persecutors of Christendom.[15]

9. Gal 4:28–30 (AV).

10. Thompson, *Writing the Wrongs*; Sellin, *Fractured Families*, 12, n.3.

11. Sellin mentions Chartres, see *Fractured Families,* 12, but similar sculptures can be seen at Cathedrals including Paris's Notre-Dame, Strasbourg Cathedral, Reims, and Bamberg.

12. Thompson, *Writing the Wrongs*, 25.

13. Thompson, *Writing the Wrongs*, 94.

14. Origen, *Homilies*, Gen. 7:3–6, quoted in Thompson, *Writing the Wrongs*, 30.

15. Sellin, *Fractured Families*, 18.

With the Reformation, and the revived interest in the Abrahamic cycle of stories in Genesis, a more compassionate reading of Hagar and sometimes Ishmael is found in works by artists[16] and by theologians. Martin Luther's commentary on Genesis 21 even declared Ishmael a "true son of promise" and Hagar a "mother of the church."[17] Nevertheless, other Reformers like John Calvin continued to cast both Hagar and Ishmael in negative light.[18] Thompson concluded that even with the Reformers paying more attention to the literal reading, and being less interested in allegory than the medieval church, the traditional allegorical reading of this story remained present.[19]

The sixteenth-century biblical commentators representing a range of translations from the Geneva Bible to the Douai-Rheims, also maintained the traditional allegorical meaning of the Genesis story. In the Authorized Version, the allegorical interpretation was indicated by simply providing the cross-reference of Galatians 4:30 in the margin.[20] The Geneva Bible provided more directed commentary on the passage by noting in the margin: "He [Ishmael] derided God's promise made to Izhak, which the Apostle calleth persecution, Gal. 4:29, 4:30."[21] The commentary found in the Catholic Douai translation even more strongly reinforced the allegorical interpretation. The commentator draws on the allegorical interpretation of Ishmael's persecution to justify the 'persecuting' of heretics and thereby defending the Catholic church as the true church. The commentator identifies Ishmael's 'playing' with Isaac as persecution and explained that "Heretikes and other infidels do persecute when either by word, or sword the impugne the truth."[22] Furthermore, according to the commentator, who quoted St. Jerome, only the carnal were capable of persecuting others: "S. Hierom teacheth that the spiritual never persecuteth the carnal: but spareth him as his rustical brother, knowing that he may in time be profitable."[23]

16. Sellin, *Fractured Families.*

17. Thompson, *Writing the Wrongs,* 89–92; Sellin also describes how some Protestant Reformers including Zwingli, Pellikan, Musculus, and Vermigli commended Hagar for her repentance in *Fractured Families,* 17–18.

18. Thompson, *Writing the Wrongs,* 83–88.

19. Thompson, *Writing the Wrongs,* 99.

20. Gen 21 (AV).

21. Gen 21, *The Bible Translated According to the Hebrew and the Greek and Conferred with the Best Translations in Diverse Languages* (London: Deputies of Christopher Barker, 1599), STC 2173; hereafter cited as Geneva Bible, (GV).

22. Gen 21, *The Holie Bible Faithfully Translated into English, Out of the Authentical Latin* (English College of Doway: Laurence Kellam, 1609), STC 2207; hereafter cited as Douai-Rheims (DR).

23. Gen 21 (DR).

The Douai commentator's view of persecution, as a sign of false belief and something done by heretics, is context for understanding the significance of the Expulsion story in the 1650s. All of these biblical commentators indicate that during the Reformation, the prevalent way of reading the Expulsion story in Genesis was allegorically. Ishmael's persecution of Isaac was understood as an example of how the true church could be preserved by casting out the false. The false church could likewise be identified by its persecution of the true church. Thus, the long-rooted symbolism of the expulsion story could be read to promote orthodoxy in an age where the uniformity of Christian doctrine was under attack.

TRACING "ISHMAEL" IN THE TEXTS: HITS AND FREQUENCIES

One of the primary methods from the digital humanities available to scholars interested in studying printed texts is calculating word frequencies. This is done by searching a large, digitized body of printed texts. These words are counted by the number of times they appear in printed texts and in the number of printed texts that the word appears.

It is by calculating word frequencies that one can identify that printed texts published during a certain time indicate a particular word occurred in greater numbers than at other times. I used the word frequency method to discover that it was the decade of the 1650s when the word, "Ishmael", appeared most often in printed texts, at frequency that was higher than in all the other decades of the seventeenth-century.

Using the Early English Books Online Corpus[24], we can search this digitized collection of the early English printed works 1475–1700 for mentions of "Hagar" and "Ishmael." A basic search for "Hagar" pulls up 1578 hits in 611 texts, and a basic search for Ishmael pulls up 1997 hits in 577 texts.[25]

Word	No. of Hits	No. of Texts
Hagar	1,578	611
Ishmael	1,997	577

Table 1.1 "Hagar" and "Ishmael" in the Early English Books Online Corpus

24. Mark Davies, "Early English Books Online Corpus," 2017, https://www.english-corpora.org/eebo/; hereafter cited as EEBO.

25. EEBO.

There are two ways to apply statistical analysis to gauge the popularity of the subject in text: by counting the number of references (hits) and the number of texts (distribution), and by measuring word frequency.[26]

Without taking the frequence ratios into account, numbers of hits can be misleading. In Table 1.2, the number of hits for "Hagar" by decade is greatest in the 1650s with 344, but the word frequency of 3.46 is lower than 1630s when it is 4.11.

Dates	No. Hits	No. Texts containing hits	No. Total Words (Million)	Frequency Rate
1600–609	49	26	40	1.22
1610–19	82	40	42.9	1.91
1620–29	99	43	38.6	2.57
1630–39	176	42	42.8	4.11
1640–49	170	68	47.1	3.61
1650–59	344	131	99.5	3.46
1660–69	124	68	63.4	1.95
1670–79	97	59	74.6	1.30
1680–89	150	47	92.6	1.62
1690–99	152	51	79.7	1.91

Table 1.2 Word Frequencies for Hagar

Fluctuations in number of hits and word frequencies during the seventeenth century are expected due to the significant increase of print output from the 1640s onwards, with the abolition of the Star Chamber in July 1641, and the absence of the bishops' censorship. Indeed, for both Ishmael and Hagar, one can see the total number of hits is greatest in the 1650s, but the number of texts printed in the 1650s is higher than, and in fact nearly double, the preceding decades. This is why the frequency rates are so important, because they account for the total number of texts printed during a certain year. In the table below, one can see that the word frequency for Ishmael of 6.38 indicates that despite the overall spike in publication activity, there is still a higher ratio of mentions of Ishmael than in the other decades.

26. A word frequency test measures the number of hits against the sum of total words printed and is counted in millions. It is useful for weighing other findings against the general printing trends at the time.

Dates	No. Hits	No. Texts containing hits	No. Total Words (Million)	Frequency Rate
1600–609	12	10	40	0.30
1610–19	36	16	42.9	0.84
1620–29	28	15	38.6	0.73
1630–39	55	25	42.8	1.28
1640–49	231	68	47.1	4.90
1650–59	631	118	99.5	6.30
1660–69	198	70	63.4	3.12
1670–79	189	74	74.6	2.53
1680–89	340	72	92.6	3.67
1690–99	231	83	79.7	2.90

Table 1.3 Word Frequencies for Ishmael

Among several possible statistical insights, the key point for this article from the study of word frequencies is that both distribution and word frequency are higher for Ishmael in the 1650s than any other decade. Meaning even with the large number of texts printed, the frequency of the word "Ishmael" in these texts is highest in this decade. For Hagar, this is not quite the case, since her name appears most frequently in print in the 1630s indicating another resonance with her story, that would be another exploration.

These statistics are useful for drawing our attention to the1650s, when Ishmael's name surged in print. When investigating the reason for this, we should first acknowledge that in 1650s England, biblical currency was strong. Therefore, we must consider, is Ishmael unique among other biblical characters for this increase in mentions in printed texts?

By searching the digital corpus for mentions of other biblical characters, some other characters also experience a peak in hits during the 1650s including: Rebecca and Bathsheba. However, this is not the case for all biblical characters: Esther, Judith, and Susannah appear more often in different decades: 1640s, 1680s, and 1690s respectively. Against a general backdrop of biblical interest, it does seem that the increased number of references to Hagar and Ishmael in the 1650s should be considered indicative of a specific interest in the story that resonated with the time.

SEVENTEENTH-CENTURY HETERODOXY AND ORTHODOXY

The decade of the 1650s in England was a critical period. Scholars have aptly characterized the 1650s as "a riot of conflicting sects"[27], a "religious marketplace"[28], and a "unique challenge for historians"[29]. Often positioned as a strange chapter in the history of the Reformation in England, it has also been argued that it should not been seen as *that* strange. Instead, the 1650s represented the logical progression of a Reforming church and reforming clergy attempting to create a national Reformed church.[30] Amidst these efforts, the 1650s represented a considerable challenge to the orthodox beliefs outlined in the Elizabethan settlement, which had been articulated in the most general way as to include as many radical and conservative clergy as possible. By the 1650s, the Westminster Assembly and the Solemn League and Covenant had moved England further towards reform. Never in the history of Christianity in England had there been such a diverse variety of churches, many of which became known as the sectaries or sects.[31]

The English Civil Wars occurred throughout 1642–1651, with the execution of King Charles I in 1649, and the period of the Interregnum from 1649–1660. The political turmoil of the country and the lifting of previous restrictions on print, worship, and speech, allowed for new possibilities and the flourishing of the sects.

One of the new churches, or sects, birthed at this chaotic time were the Quakers. There are no early records of the first Quakers until the prominent Quaker George Fox recorded the history in 1670s, but they have been characterized as "seekers" those longing for an "authentic faith experience."[32] Part of this faith experience was an emphasis on personal revelation otherwise known as the inward light. George Fox recounted his own story and how it was hearing an inward voice that convinced him that an experience of revelation was key to faith. The movement was political since they preached spiritual and social equality and were concerned with the need for change.

27. Hill, *Century of Revolution*, 169.

28. Capp "Religious Marketplace."

29. Capp, "Stability and Flux."

30. Milton, *England's Second Reformation*.

31. Some of these included the Levellers, Fifth Monarchists, Diggers, Ranters, Muggletonians, etc.

32. D. Gwyn, "Seventeenth-Century Context and Quaker Beginnings," in *Early Quakers and Their Theological Thought, 1647–1723*, edited by Stephen W. Angell and Pink Dandelion, Cambridge University Press, 2015, quoted in Healey, "History of Quaker Faith," 13–30.

Armed with inward light, many saw no need for priests or magistrates. They immediately ran into trouble with the authorities. Early Quakerism has been explained as charismatic in expression and apocalyptic in theology.[33]

A closer look at the texts that discuss the Expulsion of Hagar and Ishmael suggests that one key reason for this story's currency in print was the identity of Ishmael as a persecutor of Isaac, the son of promise. While the discourse of persecution was not new it seems to have become especially charged during periods when religious uniformity was under attack. It is not until the 1650s when accusations of heterodoxy raged, that a more pejorative use of "Ishmael" drawn from the allegorical interpretation to signify those who persecuted true believers, emerged. As Laura Gowing found in her work on court depositions from this period, insults can be a way into studying persisting ideologies.[34] Hence, by looking at pejorative use of "Ishmael" we can discern that the allegorical reading was being perpetuated because it was a framework for explaining persecution.

"ISHMAEL" AS A PEJORATIVE

The first indication that 'Ishmael' was an insult with a meaning specific to the 1650s, is found by searching titles of printed works. In the whole Early English Books Online corpus, the biblical 'Ishmael' appears in four titles.[35] While it seems most mentions of Ishmael came from within the text of the work, some authors (or printers) chose to include it in the title. It is telling that all these works with "Ishmael" in the title were written by Quakers, and all can be dated to the 1650s. One of these four titles, *Ishamel and his mother cast out into the wilderness among the wild beasts of the same nature* (1655) makes direct reference to the expulsion story.

At first glance, the description "cast out" appears to be most fitting for the sects fighting for recognition within the church. This was especially true for the Quakers. One can imagine how seeing this pamphlet title from a printer's shop or vendor's cart might entice a passer-by to take a second look only to find that it was the Presbyterians and Independents, those who were part of Cromwell's state Church, who were to be "cast out". This title, *Ishmael and his mother,* a thirteen-page pamphlet, was printed on low-quality paper and written by a group of four Quakers while in prison.

33. Healey, "History of Quaker Faith," 13–30.

34. Gowing, *Domestic Dangers,* 2.

35. These include works by Christopher Atkinson, Francis Bugg, James Naylor, and James Parnell.

ISHMAEL.
And his
MOTHER,
Cast out into the
WILDERNESS,
Amongst the Wild Beasts of the same
NATURE:
OR,
A Reply to a Book entituled, The

Ishmael and his mother is one of the Thomason Tracts, a surviving collection, which belonged to bookseller George Thomason, of approximately 22,000 broadsheets and pamphlets that dealt with contentious religious and political issues of the mid-seventeenth century. Authorship of this particular tract is attributed to Christopher Atkinson, but textual evidence suggests others including George Whitehead were involved.[36] Their tract cleverly took the allegorical interpretation of the expulsion where Hagar and Ishmael represented the law, carnal believers, and the old covenant, and turned these associations onto their opponents. In the longer version of the title, it is explained that Samuel Townsend, a conforming minister of a parish in Norwich was the "Ishmael" in their eyes because he mocked them (in their work as ministers) and caused them to suffer in jail:

> A reply to a Book entitled, *The Scriptures proved to be the word of God*, put forth by one of Ishmael's children, who calls himself a Minister of the gospel, and a pastor of S. Austen's and Saviour's parish in Norwich; but is clearly made manifest by the light of God in his servants to be a scoffer, and an enemy to the gospel, which the saints of God are ministers of, and sufferers for, by such as he is, who Ishmael-like, hath laid his folly open, and is

36. EEBO records Christopher Atkinson as the author for *Ishmael and His Mother*, but it is attributed to George Whitehead in other works, including Francis Bugg's *A Modest Defence of My Book Entituled, Quakerism* (1700); Whitehead is asked if he wrote it and answers that "I and four more writ it between us," according to Thomas Smith, *Quaker Disarm'd*, sig. A2; a broadsheet, *Of the Quakers Despising the Holy Scriptures*, printed in 1700, also lists George Whitehead as the author of *Ishmael and His Mother*.

> discovered to the faithful, who are of Abraham and of the seed of promise.[37]

This description of conforming minister[38] Samuel Townsend, contains some of the traits that had come to be associated with Ishmael in exegetical commentary since the third century.[39] That Townsend was a "scoffer" was particular interesting because it was a reference to the behavior of "mocking or playing" that, according to the Genesis account, so angered Sarah that she demanded Abraham expel Ishmael along with Hagar. "Scoffing" is also one of the main collocates of "Ishmael" that can be identified using the *Early English Books Online* Corpus.[40] It is the seventh most common collocate with 55 mentions. It is also the first descriptive word in this list. That the software has detected a proximity and relationship between these two words in the corpus, suggests that it was a core characteristic associated with Ishmael and the story itself. The fact that Atkinson carefully chose this adjective for Townsend is indicative of his knowledge of the story and its common interpretations.

Like others interpreting the expulsion story before them, Atkinson and his fellow Quakers were applying the allegory to their personal circumstances, and by doing so legitimizing their vision of the church. Anybody who persecuted them, for example, another minister who spoke against them, was by direct application "persecuting" the true church and could be considered an "Ishmael". Atkinson re-emphasized this binary by explaining how he was making a "cleer distinction between the Ministers of Christ who are the seed of Abraham and the priests of this generation who are Ishmael's root"[41] and by setting up this insult, invited others to sling it around. It was a particularly apt insult for the more Laudian or conforming type of Protestant, who by keeping ordinances like infant baptism and following set prayers and services could be doubly accused, not only for their "persecution" or the Quakers but also for "living the law". In contrast, Samuel Townsend's retort to Atkinson of "sauce-box" was decidedly less sophisticated."

Importantly, Atkinson's tract was published in 1654/55, the same year that the *Early English Books Online* corpus shows a peak in hits for

37. Atkinson et al., *Ishmael and His Mother*, frontispiece.

38. It is unknown whether Townsend was Presbyterian, Independent in this time of flux.

39. Thompson, *Writing the Wrongs*, 43, 78, 84, 89, 92.

40. Collocates are the words most frequently associated with the subject; see "Ishamel" and "collocates" in EEBO.

41. Atkinson et al., *Ishmael and His Mother*, frontispiece.

"Ishmael". This was precisely the period when the numbers of imprisoned Quakers increased and consequently early works defending Quakerism penned from prison erupted from the presses.[42] Around the time that Atkinson was imprisoned in Norwich[43], another Quaker, John Whitehead had entered into a debate in print with William Kaye, Presbyterian minister of Stokesley, Yorkshire. Kaye received his BA in 1637 from Sidney Sussex, Cambridge and became curate at Stokesley in 1640.[44] When Thomas Pennyman, Rector of Stokesley, was ejected in 1644, it seems that Kaye stayed on as a minister. By 1652, Kaye had taken the living and the parish records name him as parson.[45]

Kaye's pamphlet is insightful because it lists out, as set of queries, many of the contentious issues between the Presbyterians (and other Puritan clergy) and the early Quakers in the early phase of their society's emergence during the 1650s.[46] According to Kaye, the positions he outlined, rightly represented "the Reformed Protestant religion." This was a religion that was skeptical of the idea of infallibility.[47] It was on guard against popery.[48] It defended unction, the anointing of priests as both a calling and from biblical precedent.[49] As Kaye himself put it, "And yet to answer thee more fully whether I own the unction or ne, I say in the name of Christ, though I do discover the false applications which are made of it, I do confesse that the Unction is the seed of my Soul, my Joy and Crown, so much I own it."[50]

The "Reformed Protestant religion" that Kaye defends, also upheld the practice of collecting tithes for the ministers maintenance: "tithes freely given by the Magistrates, are lawfully received by the Gospel."[51] Or as Kaye further explains, he accepted tithes, since he could not find in scripture any example to show that he "being not persecuted, should notwithstanding so voluntarily persecute myself and deny God's free mercy."[52]

42. Peters, *Print Culture*, 21–22.

43. Apparently 1654/55 was also when Atkinson was under suspicion for sexual impropriety, and was later formerly ejected from the Quaker; see Peters, *Print Culture*, 146–47.

44. Matthews, *Calamy Revised*, 303.

45. Stephen Copson, "Advocate of the reformed protestant religion," *Baptist Quarterly*, 1994, http://hdl.handle.net/20.500.12424/153115.

46. Kaye, *Plain Answer*, 11–12.

47. Kaye, *Plain Answer*, 2.

48. Kaye, *Plain Answer*, 2.

49. Kaye, *Plain Answer*, 3–4.

50. Kaye, *Plain Answer*, 4.

51. Kaye, *Plain Answer*, 11.

52. Kaye, *Plain Answer*, 11.

Notably missing from all of Kaye's response is any mention of the Expulsion of Hagar and Ishmael. Kaye refers to other biblical figures, King David, King Hezekiah, the Apostle Paul, but Ishmael is not a figure that holds resonance in this debate for him.

For John Whitehead, his Quaker opponent, Ishmael looms large. When Whitehead is imprisoned in Northamptonshire, he publishes a pamphlet entitled, *The Enmitie Between the Two Seeds*. In this he declares himself and his fellow imprisoned Quakers to be "*the righteous seed* whom the world in scorn calls Quakers, whose bodies are in outward bands, in the common goal in Northamptonshire."[53] The righteous seed stands in contrast to those ministers like Kaye who oppose him and who are the "serpent's seed" whom Whitehead warns against. Whitehead states on the frontispiece of his work: "Herein is discovered, the subtilty and envie of the Serpents seed: who rules in the man of sin, that is born after the flesh, and persecutes him that is born after the Spirit".[54]

Strikingly, Whitehead draws on the ancient allegory of Hagar and Ishmael as expounded by the Apostle Paul to build his case against the ministers of God who oppose him. Few could deny that his writing from the setting of prison spoke powerfully of persecution. While throughout the 33-page work, many different allegories and scriptural passages are cited, Whitehead concludes his appeal by making another reference to Ishmael. He directly addresses the clergy who speak against the Quakers, i.e., William Kaye. Whitehead preaches:

> we do again declare, in the presence of the Lord God of Heaven and Earth, and it shall be answered with the light in all Consciences, that you that do imprison, falsely accuse, persecute, and scorn those that declare against sin in your streets, and in your Steeple-houses (under the names before mentioned,) are shut out from amongst all the Saints and Children of God, that believe in the Lord Jesus, and you are found in Cains way, who slew his Brother, and in Ishmaels nature born after the flesh, which birth is the same that crucified Christ, stoned Stephen, and put to death his faithful Ministers and witnesses in all ages.[55]

And so, Whitehead made the allegory explicit, those who imprisoned him were persecutors and should be understood to be sons of the flesh—like Cain and like Ishmael.

53. Whitehead, *Enmitie*, frontispiece, 33.
54. Whitehead, *Enmitie*, frontispiece.
55. Whitehead, *Enmitie*, 31–32.

These exchanges captured in pamphlet form encouraged outpouring from other Quakers. After Whitehead and Kaye, in 1655, several more pamphlets (now also part of the Thomason collection) were printed that invoked the symbolic associations of "Ishmael" to criticize the clergy. George Fox, the founder of the Quakers, or the Religious Society of Friends, pointed out the parallels he saw in Ishmael and the clergy: "the same seed is mocked now by you Ishmaelites, who are children of the bond-woman, who are cast out and are found without mocking and scoffing at the righteous seed."[56] Frances Howgill replied directly to William Kaye that he was " in his sins, in stature of Cain and Ishmael."[57] James Pain addressed his audience as "ye persecuters, ye scoffers and scorners, ye sons of Ishmael who scoffs the righteous."[58] James Parnell followed Christopher Atkinson and John Whitehead and also used "Ishmael" to draw a distinction between true and false believers. On the frontispiece to Parnell's work, he has identified himself with Christ and his accusers with Ishmael: "Written from the Spirit of the Lord by one who suffers amongst the little flock of Christ who go under the name of Quakers, so called by the stock of Ishmael."[59]

In addition to Atkinson and Parnell, another Quaker, the infamous James Naylor, also drew on the understanding of Ishmael as a persecutor to attack his accusers. In October 1656, Naylor re-enacted Christ's Triumphal Entry by riding a donkey into Bristol and was later prosecuted for blasphemy and convicted. While Parliament tried to inflict the death penalty, Oliver Cromwell intervened, and Naylor was flogged and imprisoned for life. As David Smith has suggested, Naylor's case highlighted how Cromwell was worried about the precedents for violence against sectarian religion, which shows the strength of opposition against perceived heterodoxy at this time.[60] Given Naylor's experience, it is not surprising to find him describing his opposition as "Ismaels seed" in the long title for his short book, *Love to the Lost* (1656). Furthermore, it is only Naylor's second edition printed in 1665, which includes the reference to Ishmael in the title, which was evidently after his indictment.[61]

These debates in printed pamphlets reveal how the biblical figure of Ishmael was used as an insult to launch a deep criticism of the national

56. Fox, *To All the Ignorant People*, 10.

57. Howgill, *Common Salvation*, 9.

58. Pain, *Discovery of the Priests*, 18.

59. Parnell, *Shield of Truth*, frontispiece.

60. Smith, *History of the Modern British Isles*, 190.

61. Naylor, *Love to the Lost* (1665); for first edition see Naylor, *Love to the Lost* (London, 1656), Wing N294.

church under the Cromwellian government. To the Quakers, the Presbyterian and Independent ministers were "living by the law", like Ishmael, when they led prayers or collected tithes. When these ministers spoke out against Quaker practices or even worse, worked with a magistrate to imprison them, the ministers showed themselves to be the false church and persecutors of the true church like Ishmael.

One of the early historians of the Quaker movement, John Gough, described in his *History of Friends* the significance of the Steeple-house debates. He says it was "not infrequent for friends to enter places of public worship under a sense of religious duty and declaring to the priests and people the burden of the word on their minds".[62] Gough also notes that the people at this time were receptive to such a display since they did not have singularity of thought concerning prophesy. During the civil war and thereafter, it was "no unusual practice for laymen, soldiers, and others to speak or preach in public places of worship and elsewhere with the connivance if not with the approbation of the ruling powers.[63] Moreover, it seems that people attended these happenings with great interest. They liked to see, as Whitehead describes, "human learning ill-matched against the learning in the school of the prophets and of the spiritual generation of men".[64] Apparently on one occasion when John Whitehead asked the priest Thomas Andrews to prove his doctrine and practice by scripture, Andrews initially refused and then agreed but was "mortified" by the result and challenged him to a rematch. The rematch took place as a public lecture that turned into a launch of invectives and verbal attack.[65] It was the aftermath of one of these public lectures that apparently led to Whitehouse's first arrest and imprisonment when the priest at Torrington "laid violent hands on John and dragged him by force out of the steeple-house."[66] Afterwards, a warrant was procured and Whitehead was taken before the magistrate and later imprisoned.

Going back to Kaye and Whitehead's exchange, it seems that Kaye avoided the public disgrace of a steeple-house meeting, by being delivered Whitehead's queries in writing by a friend. He was able to engage in debate through writing alone and even that he was reluctant to do as Kaye himself

62. Chalk, *Life and Writings*, quotes John Gough, *History of the People Called Quakers: From Their First Rise to the Present Time. Compiled from Authentic Records, and from the Writings of that People*, vol. 1. Dublin: Robert Jackson, Meath-Street, 1790, 86.

63. Chalk, *Life and Writings*, 14–15.

64. Chalk, *Life and Writings*, 17.

65. Chalk, *Life and Writings*, 17; admittedly this is the perspective of John Whitehead as written in his autobiography recounted by Chalk.

66. Chalk, *Life and Writings*, 17.

recounts: "Though at the first I was unwilling to answer thee, yet shortly after I was also moved to discharge my Conscience to bear witnesse to the truth, for the information of the Election . . . writing first thy words which thou sent unto me by an Acquaintance of mine, I thus, as required, in the strength of Christ, faithfully make this plain Answer."[67]

One can imagine how disagreeable it must have been for a minister at a local parish to be called to defend one's knowledge publicly to a group of people who had no formal training. It would have been even more galling to find that one's opponent was skillful. The Quakers' challenge of the clergy's biblical knowledge as well as their right to tithes, appears to have raised a remarkable ire. Even Fox commented on it: "But oh, the rage that then was in the priests, magistrates, professors and people of all sorts, but especially in the priests and professors."[68] It is perhaps even better captured in the famous criticism attributed to Francis Bugg (1640–1727) who wrote against the Quakers: "Who hath writ more than a Quaker? Whoever exposed the professors of Christianity more than they?"[69]

CONCLUSION

I began this research to explain the popularity of the Genesis story, the Expulsion of Hagar and Ishmael, in seventeenth-century needlework. I found by studying word frequencies that "Ishmael" is mentioned in printed English texts in the 1650s more frequently than any other decade of the seventeenth-century. A closer look at the texts containing the mentions, revealed that the use of "Ishmael" was pejorative, an insult exclusively (as far as I have been able to tell) used by the Quakers for the Presbyterians and Independent ministers who were part of Cromwell's national church.

Like others before and after them, the Quakers in the 1650s were drawing on the biblical story and ancient allegory because they envisioned themselves as persecuted for their true faith in the same way that Isaac had been persecuted by Ishmael. Their struggles were a significant part of their experience as Quakers[70], and by drawing on what they saw as parallels from the biblical story, they could defend their position and justify their sufferings. The Quakers' verbal railings at their opponents were not random, and their invectives used biblical language pointedly. Moreover, it is noteworthy

67. Kaye, *Plain Answer*, 1.

68. George Fox, *The Journal of George Fox*, edited by John L. Nickalls, Religious Society of Friends, 1997, 36, cited by Johnston, "Confrontation Between Quakers," 219.

69. Gill, *Women in the Quaker Community*, 1.

70. Gill, *Women in the Quaker Community*.

that while both Quakers and the Presbyterian ministers were so opposed to each other, they were both wrangling with the same scripture.[71]

However, the kind of insult that Ishmael represented, a richly allegorical one suggests that this conflict between the Quakers and the Presbyterians and other Puritan clergy, was about more than different theology. This was also about a display of knowledge. The Quaker arguments demonstrate sophistication with the biblical text and as in the case of their use of Ishmael, rely on theological interpretations passed down through the church fathers. In fact, they clearly are all part of the church tradition that they are attacking. And thus, the desire to show the other group the errors of their ways through biblical metaphor suggests this was a battle for supremacy in the church classroom. The elongated theological debate in pamphlets could be viewed as a battle for who was the worthiest teacher of scripture and the top choice in the crowded religious marketplace of the 1650s. As illustrated by the Quakers' steeple-house meetings, the laity were captivated by the freedom of public debate and the freedom to gather, free of restrictions. In this environment, the biblical story of Hagar and Ishmael with its canonical warnings about the true believers and the false had strong resonance for people living through the enormous ecclesial changes. Observing the imprisonment of ministers could easily be interpreted as persecution, but with so many new sects to choose from, the challenge of discerning the true church was real.

Many of these freedoms as well as the controversies of the 1650s were short-lived after the Restoration of the Monarchy and the re-establishment of the Church of England under the 1662 Act of Uniformity and the Clarendon Code. The Quakers were suppressed by this legislation and so were many Presbyterians and other non-conforming ministers. Nevertheless, the decade of the 1650s and its display of biblical acrobatics tells us that English Protestants' (Presbyterians and Quakers) regard for biblical learning was so pronounced as to make it visible in domestic embroidery and contested publicly in the steeple-houses. This would continue to have an impact on the decades to follow as biblical literacy continued to be a key factor behind the immense growth in the consumption of print. One could therefore argue that the Reformed church of the 1650s was a church where knowledge was king.

71. Johnston also finds their choice of language not random; see Johnston, "Confrontation Between Quakers," 211, 221–22.

BIBLIOGRAPHY

Atkinson, Christopher, et al. *Ishmael and His Mother Cast Out into the Wilderness Amongst the Wild Beasts of the Same Nature*. London: For Giles Calvert, at the Black Spread-Eagle, at the west end of Pauls, 1655.

Augustine. *The City of God*. Translated by Henry Bettenson. London: Penguin, 2003.

The Bible Translated According to the Hebrew and the Greek and Conferred with the Best Translations in Diverse Languages. London: Deputies of Christopher Barker, 1599.

Capp, Bernard. "Introduction: Stability and Flux: The Church in the Interregnum." In *Church and People in Interregnum Britain*, edited by Fiona McCall. London: University of London Press, 2021.

———. "The Religious Marketplace: Public Disputations in Civil War and Interregnum England." *English Historical Review* 129.536 (2014) 47–78.

Chalk, Thomas, ed. *The Life and Writings of John Whitehead, an Early and Eminent Minister of the Gospel in the Society of Friends*. London: Gilpin, 1852.

Fox, George. *To All the Ignorant People, the Word of the Lord, Who Are Under the Blind Guides the Priests*. London: [s.n.], 1655.

Gill, Catie. *Women in the Seventeenth-Century Quaker Community: A Literary Guide of Polemic Identities, 1650–1700*. Aldershot, UK: Ashgate, 2005.

Gowing, Laura. *Domestic Dangers: Women, Words, and Sex in Early Modern London*. Oxford: Oxford University Press, 1996.

Healey, Robynne Rogers. "History of Quaker Faith and Practice: 1650–1808." In *The Cambridge Companion to Quakerism*, edited by Stephen W. Angell and Pink Dandelion, 13–30. Cambridge Companions to Religion. Cambridge: Cambridge University Press, 2018.

Hill, Christopher. *The Century of Revolution 1603–1714*. New York: Norton, 1966.

Howgill, Frances. *Common Salvation Contended For, and the Faith Which Was Once Delivered to the Saints*. London: For Giles Calvert, 1655.

The Holie Bible Faithfully Translated into English, out of the Authentical Latin. Diligently Conferred with the Hebrew, Greeke, and Other Editions in Divers Languages. English College of Doway: Laurence Kellam, 1609.

The Holy Bible, Conteyning the Old Testament, and the New: Newly Translated Out of the Originall Tongues, and with the Former Translations Diligently Compared and Revised, by His Maiesties Speciall Comandement; Appointed to be Read in Churches. London: Barker, 1611.

Johnston, Margaret Anne. "The Confrontation Between Quakers and Clergy 1652–1656: Theology and Practice." *Quaker Studies* 26.2 (2021) 209–40.

Kaye, William. *A Plain Answer to the Eighteen Quaeries of John Whitehead, Commonly Called Quaker*. London: printed for N.E., 1654; Wing K38.

———. *Heterodoxy and the English Reformation*. London: Routledge, 2016.

Luther, Martin. *Lectures on Genesis: Chapters 21–25*. Translated by Jaroslav Pelikan. St. Louis: Concordia, 1964.

Matthews, A. G., ed. *Calamy Revised. Being a Revision of Edmund Calamy's Account of the Ministers and Others Ejected and Silenced, 1660–2*. Oxford: Clarendon, 1934, 1988.

———. *Queries Propounded to the Quakers*. London, 1653.

Milton, Anthony. *England's Second Reformation: The Battle for the Church of England 1625–1662*. Cambridge, 2021.

Naylor, James. *Love to the Lost and a Hand Held Forth to the Helpless, to Lead Out of the Dark Wherein Is Plainly Held Out Divers Particular Things As They Are Learned of Christ, and Are Most Needful to be Known of All, Who Profess Godliness: Set Forth Chiefly for the Directing by One That Sought the Redemption of Zions Seed, and a Lover of the Creation of God, Who Was Called in Derision by Ismael Seed a Quaker.* London, [s.n.], 1665.

———. *Love to the Lost.* London: 1656; Wing N294.

Of the Quakers Despising the Holy Scriptures. Broadsheet. [n.p.], 1700.

Origen. *Homilies on Genesis and Exodus.* Translated by Ronald E. Heine. Washington, DC: Catholic University of America, 1982.

Pain, John. *A Discovery of the Priests.* London: Jo. Streater for Giles Calvert, 1655.

Parnell, James. *A Shield of Truth or, The Truth of God Cleared from Scandals and Reproaches Cast Upon It.* London: Jo. Streater for Giles Calvert, 1655.

Perkins, William. *A Reformed Catholike.* Cambridge: Legat, 1598.

Peters, Kate. *Print Culture and the Early Quakers.* Cambridge: Cambridge University Press, 2005.

Sellin, Christine Petra. *Fractured Families and Rebel Maidservants: The Biblical Hagar in Seventeenth-Century Dutch Art and Literature.* T&T Clark International, 2006.

Smith, David. *A History of the Modern British Isles, 1603–1707: The Double Crown.* Blackwell, 1998.

———. *James Nayler and the English Revolution.* Oxford: Oxford University Press, 2012.

Smith, Thomas. *The Quaker Disarm'd, or, A True Relation of a Late Publick Dispute Held at Cambridge by Three Eminent Quakers Against One Scholar of Cambridge; with a Letter in Defence of the Ministry and Against Lay-preachers; Also Several Quaeries Proposed to the Quakers to be Answered if They Can.* London: J. C., 1659.

Thomason, George. *The Thomason Tracts.* British Library, London.

Thompson, John L. *Reading the Bible with the Dead: What You Can Learn from the History of Exegesis That You Cannot Learn from Exegesis Alone.* Grand Rapids: Eerdmans, 2007.

———. *Writing the Wrongs: Women of the Old Testament among Biblical Commentators from Philo through the Reformation.* Oxford: Oxford University Press, 2001.

Whitehead, John. *The Enmitie Between the Two Seeds: Wherein Is Discovered, the Subtilty and Envie of the Serpents Seed: Who Rules in the Man of Sin, That is Born After the Flesh, and Persecutes Him That Is Born After the Spirit.* London: [s.n.], 1654; Thomason E.848[19]; Wing (2nd ed.) W1975.

13

Death of Christian Canada?

Does Arthur Leonard Griffith's Testimony Support Stuart Macdonald and Brian Clarke's Theory of Canadian Church Decline in the 1960s?

Robert Revington

In his 2007 review of Callum G. Brown's book *Religion and Society in Twentieth-Century Britain*, Stuart Macdonald observed: "If there is one thing the book illustrates, perhaps unintentionally, it is the incredible unreliability of the clergy's insights into the faith of the average person."[1] He adds later: "Clergy always seem to have been convinced that people were falling away from the church and to have complained about this, and in the late twentieth century it actually happened."[2] Even so, Macdonald praised Brown's use of "oral testimony" to show "the continuing importance of religion to lay people throughout most of the twentieth century and when this changed."[3]

Ironically, the present essay ignores Macdonald's caution about accepting the testimony of the clergy, but does so to support the findings of some of Macdonald's own work. A unique exception can be made for

1. Macdonald, review of *Religion and Society*, 155.
2. Macdonald, review of *Religion and Society*, 155.
3. Macdonald, review of *Religion and Society*, 155.

Arthur Leonard Griffith—a Canadian minister (and later professor) who served both the United Church of Canada and the Anglican Church of Canada. Griffith was a remarkably long-lived clergyman; he was born on March 19, 1920, and lived nearly a century, until April 7, 2019.[4] He was ordained in 1945. This makes Griffith one of the few clergymen whose ordained ministry career *began* the same year Stuart Macdonald and Brian Clarke's book *Leaving Christianity: Changing Allegiances in Canada since 1945* starts its story—and who was *still alive* when the book was published in 2017.[5] Griffith was a unique and articulate first-hand witness for the cultural changes that Macdonald and Clarke cover in their book. Griffith had the perspective to recognize the Canadian churches' failures after the 1960s, but also—and this is crucial—their growth and success from 1945 until the early 1960s. Scholars have not always given the church credit for their triumphs in the postwar era, but—following the secularization thesis—sometimes inaccurately assumed that religious decline must have been a gradual phenomenon throughout the twentieth century.

Now, I first met Stuart Macdonald in 2009 when he was a workshop leader at "Canada Youth"—the former name of The Presbyterian Church in Canada's national youth conference. Young people who attended Stuart's workshops that year learned two things that are characteristic of him: first, that Presbyterians and other Reformed Christians do not give enough credit to Ulrich Zwingli, and second, that the 1960s were a crucial decade in the history of the Canadian churches. The present essay fits with the latter insight. In this essay, I demonstrate that Griffith's autobiographical account corroborates the trajectory of religious change in Canada that Clarke and Macdonald chart with their statistical research. In other words, Griffith provides valuable anecdotal support for Clarke and Macdonald's work. His testimony gives a human face to the numbers Clarke and Macdonald chart so meticulously and gives us a clear picture of how these changes were perceived by someone on the ground.

GRIFFITH'S LIFE

Before proceeding to the story of church decline, it is necessary to give a brief outline of Griffith's life. Though born in Preston, England, his family moved to Brockville, Ontario, when he was nine years old in 1929.[6] His family

4. "Arthur Leonard Griffith."
5. Clarke and Macdonald, *Leaving Christianity.*
6. Griffith, *From Sunday to Sunday*, 1–12; "Arthur Leonard Griffith."

background was Welsh.[7] After completing a BA at McGill in 1942, he then earned his degree at the United Theological College (also in Montreal) three years later and was ordained in the United Church of Canada.[8] He started at two smaller Ontario churches in Arden and then Grimsby, before switching to the much larger congregation of Chalmers United Church in Ottawa in 1950—where he stayed for just over a decade.[9] One memorable Easter Sunday in 1955, he preached on "the transience of all material things," and told his congregation, "'Even this pulpit will not last forever.'"[10] As if to prove his point, the church caught fire that afternoon.[11] During his years in Ottawa, while on a sabbatical, he also completed a doctoral degree on Karl Barth at Mansfield College, Oxford.[12] Griffith left Ottawa in 1960 and moved to London, England, to begin a six-year ministry at the famous nonconformist church known as the City Temple.[13] In 1966, Griffith came back to Canada to become the minister at Toronto's Deer Park United Church, but his time ended nine years later under stressful and bitter circumstances, when he felt his authority was being undermined by church members.[14] After his negative experience at Deer Park, in 1975, he switched from the United Church to the more hierarchical Anglican Church and became the minister at St. Paul's Bloor Street (also in Toronto).[15] While he was there, Stephen Neill observed to him that St. Paul's may have been the world's biggest Anglican church—outside of the great cathedrals in England.[16] In addition, in 1977, Griffith began teaching preaching courses at Wycliffe College (one of the two Anglican seminaries in the Toronto School of Theology at the University of Toronto); Wycliffe also awarded him an honorary doctorate in 1985.[17] He officially retired from both St. Paul's and Wycliffe in 1986—and was also diagnosed with cancer that year, though he recovered.[18] His autobiography was published not long after. After his official retirement, Griffith nonetheless continued preaching regularly—serving as an interim

7. Griffith, *From Sunday to Sunday*, 5.
8. Griffith, *From Sunday to Sunday*, 13–34; "Arthur Leonard Griffith."
9. Griffith, *From Sunday to Sunday*, 35–96; "Arthur Leonard Griffith."
10. Griffith, *From Sunday to Sunday*, 71.
11. Griffith, *From Sunday to Sunday*, 71.
12. Griffith, *From Sunday to Sunday*, 85–96; "Arthur Leonard Griffith."
13. Griffith, *From Sunday to Sunday*, 97–133; "Arthur Leonard Griffith."
14. Griffith, *From Sunday to Sunday*, 147–159; "Arthur Leonard Griffith."
15. Griffith, *From Sunday to Sunday*, 173–184; "Arthur Leonard Griffith."
16. Griffith, *From Sunday to Sunday*, 178.
17. Griffith, *From Sunday to Sunday*, 183–84; "Arthur Leonard Griffith."
18. Griffith, *From Sunday to Sunday*, 195–201; "Arthur Leonard Griffith."

minister several times—and maintained the title of Honorary Assistant at St. Paul's.[19] Griffith's former Wycliffe colleague Alan Hayes describes him as "a powerhouse in the pulpit."[20] Having said this, Hayes also believes that "his preaching style probably wouldn't be so popular today, though; it was pretty formal and polished, in the manner of the day."[21]

In any event, Griffith may have preached more sermons than any Canadian of the last century. Even though he was not ordained until 1945, he preached his first sermon as early as 1939—as a pre-theology student.[22] He recalled that after this first sermon, an elderly church member praised it as "a fine sermon" albeit only because "I heard every word."[23] By the time he wrote his 1987 autobiography, he observed: "I realize with a kind of shock that I have been preaching for almost fifty years. That's 2, 600 Sundays, and with few exceptions I have preached at least one on nearly all of them."[24] Then we can add a few more decades of preaching after those words were written! Even around his ninetieth birthday in 2010, he preached fifteen sermons that were then compiled on a DVD titled "Questions Christians Ask."[25] Again, given his remarkably long career, he had a front-row seat to the massive changes in the Canadian churches in the twentieth century that Clarke and Macdonald covered in *Leaving Christianity*, and thus, his autobiography provides useful anecdotal corroboration of their findings. Yet to contextualize Griffith's testimony here, it is necessary to understand what Macdonald, Clarke, and Callum G. Brown have written on church decline.

STUART MACDONALD, BRIAN CLARKE, CALLUM G. BROWN, AND CHURCH DECLINE

Stuart Macdonald's scholarship on Canadian church decline (sometimes co-written with Clarke) did not happen in a vacuum. Up to the early 1990s at least, many books took the "secularization thesis" for granted in places such as Canada and Britain.[26] The secularization thesis is a theoretical model

19. "Arthur Leonard Griffith."

20. Alan Hayes, email message to author, 28 May 2025.

21. Alan Hayes, email message to author, 28 May 2025.

22. Griffith, *From Sunday to Sunday*, 1.

23. Griffith, *From Sunday to Sunday*, 1.

24. Griffith, *From Sunday to Sunday*, 1.

25. "Arthur Leonard Griffith."

26. For example, in the Canadian context, see Marshall, *Secularizing the Faith*; Cook, *Regenerators*. For British examples, see Gilbert, *Making of Post-Christian Britain*; Green, *Passing of Protestant England;* Green, *Religion in the Age of Decline*.

that explains "the diminishing social significance of religion"[27] It tends to represent the declining significance of religion as a gradual process, tied to the industrialization and modernization of societies. Consequently, some scholars have emphasized the presence of secularization in Canada in the late nineteenth and early twentieth centuries—including David B. Marshall, Ramsay Cook, and A. B. McKillop.[28] The problem is that this model does not necessarily align with the statistical evidence.

One of the most important books to challenge the secularization thesis was Callum G. Brown's book *The Death of Christian Britain*—which was first published in 2001 and then re-released in a second edition eight years later.[29] It is one of the most important books to have been published in the field of church history in the past twenty-five years. Although this book is about Britain, its insights have proven to be applicable in other places as well. As the book's back cover summary puts it: "Brown challenges the generally-held view that secularisation was a long and gradual process dating from the industrial revolution. Instead, he argues that it has been a catastrophic and abrupt cultural revolution starting in the 1960s." In other words, Brown claims that the decline of Christianity in Britain is a story specifically related to the *1960s*, in his words, because of Britain's "short and sharp cultural revolution of the late twentieth century."[30] Brown repudiates secularization theorists by calling the 1960s the *beginning* rather than the end of British secularization.[31] In fact, Brown identifies the period from 1945 until the late 1950s as a period of church *growth* and even a "Return to Piety."[32] Brown believes that there "was not the long, inevitable religious decline of the conventional secularisation story, but a remarkably sudden and culturally violent event" in the 1960s.[33] He links this change to rapid changes in laws on censorship, abortion, homosexuality, and divorce, and finally, the rise of new rebellious youth cultures.[34]

In his related book *Religion and Society in Twentieth-Century Britain*, Brown again questions the inevitability of secularization—or at least sees it as more of a *Eurocentric* progression (though also affecting Japan, Canada,

27. Wallis and Bruce, "Secularization," 11.

28. See Marshall, *Secularizing the Faith*; Cook, *Regenerators*; McKillop, *Matters of Mind*.

29. Brown, *Death of Christian Britain*.

30. Brown, *Death of Christian Britain*, 2.

31. Brown, *Death of Christian Britain*, 15.

32. Brown, *Death of Christian Britain*, 170–75.

33. Brown, *Death of Christian Britain*, 175–76.

34. Brown, *Death of Christian Britain*, 176.

Australia, and New Zealand).[35] He reiterates that in Britain, in the latter part of the 1940s and into the 1950s, the churches actually grew, "but after 1963, this was then dramatically reversed into a *negative* correlation."[36] Even so, Brown believes that the 1950s featured many successful evangelistic efforts—including the Billy Graham crusades.[37]

Similar to Brown, Hugh McLeod's book *The Religious Crisis of the 1960s* examines why in Britain (and other places), the church's numbers and clergy declined around the 1960s, and he cites a range of factors, including: the new range of conflicting worldviews, the change from Christianity to pluralism, the Vietnam War, the increasing *affluence* of the population, the "radicalization" of certain theologians, and the sexual revolution.[38] McLeod also argues that the 1960s included the rise of a new youth counterculture that was at odds with traditional Christianity.[39] The 1960s were the decade of the "sexual revolution" as well, and this "revolution" led to challenges to religious orthodoxy with increasing premarital sex, and the rise of feminism and gay rights.[40] The year 1968 was a significant turning point because it saw the rise of new religious radicals, student protests about Vietnam, and Catholic disillusionment with the *Humanae Vitae* document (which forbade Catholics from using contraception).[41] Brown and McLeod agree that the 1960s were a crucial decade for the decline of religion, although they disagree on when the most important year of decline was.

Brown in particular greatly influenced Macdonald's research on Canada, but Brown would be grateful for Macdonald's work in turn. In fact, in the acknowledgments to the second edition of *The Death of Christian Britain*, Brown thanks Macdonald for his work in the years between the first and second edition of his own book.[42] He credits Macdonald with demonstrating that the mainline Protestant churches in Canada followed a similar negative trajectory in the 1960s to what Brown charted in his work on Britain.[43] In other words, Macdonald's work enhanced Brown's case because Macdonald applied Brown's analysis of the British situation to Canadian church statistics in parallel.

35. Brown, *Religion and Society*, 11.
36. Brown, *Religion and Society*, 36.
37. Brown, *Religion and Society*, 188–202.
38. McLeod, *Religious Crisis of the 1960s*, 1–29.
39. McLeod, *Religious Crisis of the 1960s*, 124–40.
40. McLeod, *Religious Crisis of the 1960s*, 161–87.
41. McLeod, *Religious Crisis of the 1960s*, 141–60; 192–93.
42. Brown, *Death of Christian Britain*, xi.
43. Brown, *Death of Christian Britain*, 216.

Brown highlighted Macdonald's work because of a paper Macdonald gave to the Canadian Society of Church History in 2006.[44] Macdonald's paper played on Brown's book in its title, as it was called: "Death of Christian Canada? Do Canadian Church Statistics Support Callum Brown's Theory of Church Decline?"[45] Obviously, the title of my present essay in turn references the title of Macdonald's 2006 essay. In any event, in 2006, the short answer to the second question in Macdonald's second question was . . . yes.

Macdonald starts this article by noting a Presbyterian Church in Canada magazine article from 1967 that picked up on the fact that the church had seen some decline in recent years.[46] Macdonald summarized Brown's arguments about the British case: how religion grew in Britain after the Second World War and throughout the 1950s, only to rapidly decline in the 1960s.[47] He asks: "Could similar arguments also hold true for Canada?"[48] Then, Macdonald lays out his basic argument and says:

> Influenced by Callum Brown's findings for Britain, this paper examines indicators of religious decline among Anglicans, Presbyterians and the United Church of Canada and argues that the 1960s were the crucial decade in their declension. It was in the late 1950s or early 1960s that decades of uninterrupted growth suddenly shifted for these denominations, a trend that has continued to the present.[49]

Macdonald gathers statistics from both census data and the churches themselves to "triangulate" them; in other words, to see if all of the data from different sources point in the same direction.[50] He starts with the United Church, noting that from its creation in 1925 to the first half of the 1960s, its membership and other statistics such as Sunday School steadily grew—but things changed around 1965.[51] Similarly, he demonstrates similar growth in the Anglican and Presbyterian churches in the 1950s and into the 1960s—at which point this growth stopped.[52] Macdonald discusses the decline in the 1960s, but observes that other scholarship had a tendency to overlook the Canadian churches' impressive growth during the 1950s and

44. Macdonald, "Death of Christian Canada?," 135–56.
45. Macdonald, "Death of Christian Canada?," 135–56.
46. Macdonald, "Death of Christian Canada?," 135.
47. Macdonald, "Death of Christian Canada?," 136.
48. Macdonald, "Death of Christian Canada?," 137.
49. Macdonald, "Death of Christian Canada?," 136.
50. Macdonald, "Death of Christian Canada?," 137–38.
51. Macdonald, "Death of Christian Canada?," 139–40.
52. Macdonald, "Death of Christian Canada?," 140–41.

see the decline in the 1960s as just part of a longer-term decline.[53] Macdonald summarizes: "The data we have looked at so far from these three Protestant denominations tells a similar story of growth through the 1950s followed by decline."[54] In addition to census data, Macdonald finds similar trends in statistics about the number of baptisms these churches were doing: growth in the 1950s and decline in the 1960s.[55] Unlike census data, baptismal data also gives us yearly numbers—instead of every ten years—so there are advantages to it.[56] Macdonald notes:

> The number of baptisms performed in denominations that practice infant and child baptism is clearly related to the number of children born. In the years of the baby boom the growth of baptisms is not surprising. What is worth noting is that while both the number of baptisms after 1960 and the number of children born after 1959 declines, the number of baptisms falls much faster.[57]

To paraphrase, the percentage of children being baptized went down; it was not just that the number of baptisms decreased when the baby boom started leveling off. In addition, since young people typically joined the church around the age of 14 or 15, given that baptisms were their highest in 1958, confirmations *should have* peaked around 1972, but the number of professions of faith instead peaked much earlier.[58] Macdonald reiterates: "The data presented is consistent with the findings of Callum Brown in relation to Great Britain, namely that church growth in the 1950s was followed by a sudden, sharp decline."[59] Near the end of his paper, Macdonald says that the decline of the Anglican, United, and Presbyterian churches is "a decline from which there is currently no evidence of recovery."[60] Macdonald also states: "While we continue to hear stories about mega-churches and a general interest in spirituality, Canada strikes me as a less religious and far different culture now than it was in 1960."[61] Again, in both Canada and Britain, if the churches grew after 1945 before declining in the 1960s, this

53. Macdonald, "Death of Christian Canada?," 141–43.
54. Macdonald, "Death of Christian Canada?," 147.
55. Macdonald, "Death of Christian Canada?," 148–49.
56. Macdonald, "Death of Christian Canada?," 148.
57. Macdonald, "Death of Christian Canada?," 148–49.
58. Macdonald, "Death of Christian Canada?," 150.
59. Macdonald, "Death of Christian Canada?," 150.
60. Macdonald, "Death of Christian Canada?," 151.
61. Macdonald, "Death of Christian Canada?," 156 n. 43.

should indicate that a gradual model of religion's diminishing significance (such as the secularization thesis) does not fit the evidence.

Macdonald subsequently combined with Brian Clarke to explore these issues further. The two of them partnered together on an article that explored the details on religious decline in Canada in the 2001 Canadian census and how it differed from past censuses.[62] They looked at the broader statistical changes in Canadian Christianity since 1945 in more detail in their aforementioned book *Leaving Christianity*.[63] Here, they note that from 1961 to 2011, the percentage of Christians in Canada declined from 96% to 67% in the census data, while the number of people with "No Religion" kept rising.[64] Clarke and Macdonald reiterate: "Decline in Christian affiliation, membership, and participation started in the 1960s and has picked up pace rapidly since then."[65] Again, they describe the years immediately after the Second World War as a time where the churches "experienced exceptional growth."[66] *Leaving Christianity* also demonstrates that those who remain in the traditional Protestant churches tend to be older now.[67] The book finds statistical decline in Sunday School numbers, membership, and baptism statistics.[68] They conclude: "The contrast between the immediate postwar period and today in terms of the vibrancy of mainstream Canadian Protestant denominations could not be starker."[69] Moreover, the declining number of children makes it hard to imagine these churches reversing the trends.[70] In their third chapter, they look at statistical changes among Roman Catholics—which have been greatly affected by the increasing secularization of Quebec in recent decades; unsurprisingly, Catholic church attendance in Canada has also dropped.[71] Chapter Four explores the growth of "No Religion" in Canada even further.[72] According to the census, the number of people with "No Religion" went from less than 1% in 1961, to 4% in 1971, 7% in 1981, 12% in 1991, 16% in 2001, and 23.6% in 2011.[73] Chapter Five

62. Clarke and Macdonald, "Five Largest Protestant Denominations," 511–34.
63. Clarke and Macdonald, *Leaving Christianity*.
64. Clarke and Macdonald, *Leaving Christianity*, 6.
65. Clarke and Macdonald, *Leaving Christianity*, 11.
66. Clarke and Macdonald, *Leaving Christianity*, 37.
67. Clarke and Macdonald, *Leaving Christianity*, 37–38.
68. Clarke and Macdonald, *Leaving Christianity*, 41–52.
69. Clarke and Macdonald, *Leaving Christianity*, 69.
70. Clarke and Macdonald, *Leaving Christianity*, 70.
71. Clarke and Macdonald, *Leaving Christianity*, 122–62.
72. Clarke and Macdonald, *Leaving Christianity*, 163–96.
73. Clarke and Macdonald, *Leaving Christianity*, 163.

of the book reiterates the importance of the 1960s to this trajectory of religious decline.[74] Significantly, they observe that this decline in the churches would not have been predicted at the beginning of the 1960s.[75] The book's findings show again that for Canada, "theories of long-term decline of religion simply do not fit the facts," since the change did not really start until the 1960s.[76] At the same time, they note that it "is not always recognized . . . just how recently Christendom in Canada was a reality."[77] Their book has the numbers to back up its case.

HOW GRIFFITH'S TESTIMONY SUPPORTS MACDONALD AND CLARKE'S FINDINGS

Griffith lived through—and preached through—the changes that Clarke and Macdonald covered in their statistical analysis of the Canadian churches after 1945. Unlike the types of unreliable clergymen Macdonald highlighted in his already-discussed review of Brown, Griffith was in a position to take the long view and give a reasonably balanced account of both the churches' successes and failures, instead of pessimistically always assuming that people were leaving the faith and things were always getting worse. That means having the perspective to recognize the churches' growth during the 1950s—not just the later decline. Though it does not have the statistical data in Clarke and Macdonald's book, in broad strokes, it is striking how reading Griffith's autobiography gives us a similar narrative of the fate of the churches in Canada.

As has been mentioned, Griffith was the minister of Chalmers United Church in Ottawa from 1950 to 1960. As we have seen, this period was a time of significant *growth* for the Canadian churches before the decline in the 1960s. Consequently, in his 1987 autobiography, Griffith shares a story from "the late 1960s," where, although by then in Toronto, he bumped into a former attendee of his Ottawa church.[78] They saw each other "in the sauna room of a health club," and, upon recognizing each other, fondly talked about their years back in Ottawa.[79] Griffith recalls: "He summed up our happy reminiscences by saying, 'Leonard, those were great years for both

74. Clarke and Macdonald, *Leaving Christianity*, 197–231.

75. Clarke and Macdonald, *Leaving Christianity*, 197.

76. Clarke and Macdonald, *Leaving Christianity*, 229.

77. Clarke and Macdonald, *Leaving Christianity*, 234.

78. Griffith, *From Sunday to Sunday*, 60.

79. Griffith, *From Sunday to Sunday*, 60.

of us.'"[80] Griffith adds: "For me those were indeed great years, the best in my ministry, and I recognized it even then."[81] In his Ottawa days, he could recall one Sunday where he preached to at least a thousand people in both his evening service and his even larger morning service, and saying to his wife when he got home: "These are our best years. We had better make the most of them."[82] In short, by his own personal account (albeit written much later) Griffith recognized that the 1950s were a time of impressive growth for the churches, and already he saw a significant difference even by the late 1960s by the time he saw his old congregant in that Toronto sauna. Obviously, this fits with Brown, Macdonald, and Clarke's depiction of religious decline as a *sudden cultural change* in the early 1960s.

Griffith corroborates this portrayal in other passages. For instance, he writes:

> In the 1950s, it was estimated that the various church bodies in Canada were building new places of worship or Christian education centres or manses or rectories at a rate of one every five days. That was a period of phenomenal expansion for the church and an exhilarating time to be a pastor. Seminarians today cannot imagine the popular appeal of the church in those post-war years.

Memberships were soaring, budgets skyrocketing, and buildings bursting at the seams.[83]

Griffith wrote these words in his 1987 autobiography, but these same words could have easily been cut and pasted into Clarke and Macdonald's book without incident. In fact, they wrote some rather similar things in the opening pages of *Leaving Christianity*; after discussing the healthy state of the Canadian churches at the 1961 census, Clarke and Macdonald record:

> Canada's Protestant denominations were expanding in other ways as well. They had successfully planted new churches in the growing suburbs, and everyone expected this growth to continue. More churches would need to be built. More ministers would need to be trained. Indeed, some were concerned that the number of ministerial candidates would not keep pace with church growth.[84]

80. Griffith, *From Sunday to Sunday*, 60.
81. Griffith, *From Sunday to Sunday*, 60.
82. Griffith, *From Sunday to Sunday*, 60.
83. Griffith, *From Sunday to Sunday*, 52.
84. Clarke and Macdonald, *Leaving Christianity*, 5.

The similarities are clear. Griffith thus avoids a common failing for people writing about Canadian churches after 1970; writing after the beginning of the churches' religious decline, he does not overlook the churches' accomplishments in the 1950s. Notably, the book *Enduring Witness*—John S. Moir's official history of The Presbyterian Church in Canada—fell into this trap when it was first published in 1974.[85]

Griffith's autobiography shares other reflections on these issues. Griffith had his own theories on why the churches thrived in the 1950s specifically. Among other things, he believed that the aftermath of the Second World War, coupled with "the reality of the atomic bomb" and "threat of Soviet Russia" may have "turned people to the church with renewed expectation and loyalty."[86] In another chapter, he also affirms that the churches had more cultural authority in the 1950s.[87] As Griffith explains, in that era, "people in high places took the church seriously and paid attention to its pronouncements. Nor did the preacher need to be a heretic or stand on the street corner to command a hearing. If he had something to say, people came to church and listened to him, and the newspapers reported his sermons."[88] Of special note, Griffith states: "Beyond any doubt the 1950s were a time of religious revival in North America."[89] Historians have not always recognized that this was the case in Canada, but the fact that such a revival took place is a key point in Clarke and Macdonald's book.[90] Though their case stands without it, Griffith's testimony as a pastor in that era nonetheless offers corroboration from someone who was in ministry at the time. Griffith uses his own congregation in Ottawa as a case study for these trends and writes:

> During my years in Ottawa the communicant membership of Chalmers rose to 2, 100, the church school enrolment reached 500, and twelve young men presented themselves as candidates for the ministry. That was not unusual then, because the 1950s were a time of phenomenal growth in churches of all communions, but it might be unusual now except in the southern United States. The truth is that North American churches never had it so good. As one of my friends in the ministry said almost

85. Moir, *Enduring Witness.*

86. Griffith, *From Sunday to Sunday*, 52.

87. Griffith, *From Sunday to Sunday*, 64.

88. Griffith, *From Sunday to Sunday*, 64.

89. Griffith, *From Sunday to Sunday*, 64.

90. Admittedly, Griffith does not seem to recognize that such a revival was also taking place in Britain in this same era to some extent. See Griffith, *From Sunday to Sunday*, 64.

> with embarrassment, "If things were any better they would be sinful."[91]

In words we have already alluded to, Clarke and Macdonald said of the Canadian decline of the 1960s that "few observers or churchgoers in the early 1960s would have predicted or imagined this occurring."[92] Griffith independently made exactly the same point in his autobiography. Looking back at his time at Chalmers, he writes of the Canadian churches in that era:

> We were too drunk with our own achievements. We believed that God in his purpose had brought the church to its position of strength, we felt sure that it would last forever, and we did not see the dangers inherent in the situation. We never foresaw a time when the religious revival would peak, church statistics decline, and many congregations become like an old man climbing a hill who suddenly loses his footing and tumbles to the bottom. *Certainly I could not have predicted it when I left Chalmers in 1960* (emphasis mine).[93]

Again, Griffith's personal testimony fits perfectly with Clarke and Macdonald's depiction of the churches in that era and it is striking how closely both books independently parallel each other with their words about how this change would not have been predicted before 1960. The opening pages of *Leaving Christianity* capture the churches' heady confidence at the beginning of the 1960s in a similar way to Griffith's words quoted above.[94]

Given that Griffith was at the City Temple in London in the crucial years from 1960 to 1966, it is also interesting to compare his time there with Brown's conclusions in books such as *The Death of Christian Britain*. Griffith remembers that when he was there, "the British churches were not dead, but they certainly seemed to be dying."[95] He compares his experiences to those of John A. T. Robinson, the controversial Bishop of Woolwich, who published the controversial book *Honest to God* in 1963.[96] Both Griffith and Robinson were clergymen in London in this era and saw evidence of irreligion in the city. Furthermore, Griffith recalls a significant conversation he had with another minister in Britain not long before he left the country

91. Griffith, *From Sunday to Sunday*, 64.
92. Clarke and Macdonald, *Leaving Christianity*, 197.
93. Griffith, *From Sunday to Sunday*, 65.
94. Clarke and Macdonald, *Leaving Christianity*, 3–5.
95. Griffith, *From Sunday to Sunday*, 124.
96. Griffith, *From Sunday to Sunday*, 124. See Robinson, *Honest to God*.

in 1966.[97] This clergyman told Griffith that he wished Griffith's ministry in London had started a decade earlier than it did.[98] He explained: "'Even then you would have felt a measure of public response and a sense of personal fulfilment that would have given you a different view of the whole situation. The fact is, however, that you came at the worst possible time.'"[99] Griffith's English clergyman friend continued:

> I have been in the ministry twenty years and I can honestly tell you that the past five have been difficult to a degree that I never anticipated. The whole spiritual climate of this country seems to have become cold and cynical and almost atheistic. Once people were simply critical of the church. Now they have become hostile or indifferent to it."[100]

Though we should acknowledge the fact that Griffith wrote these words much later, if this nonetheless reflects a real conversation from 1965 or 1966, it is worth pondering. Those clergyman's words do not perfectly align with Brown's emphasis on the year 1963 specifically, but they show that at least some clergy in England recognized a significant difference in the religiosity of the country in the mid 1960s in contrast with the not-too-distant 1950s. This supports Brown's contention that a significant cultural change occurred in the 1960s, even if the precise details do not perfectly line up. Granted, Griffith reflects that not long after arriving in London, he found people there to be noticeably less religious than those he had just left behind in Canada—and so he did not see evidence of the revival in Britain that Brown described.[101] That being said, Griffith arrived in Britain at the end of the religious wave, and Clarke and Macdonald themselves observed of that general era: "If one can speak of a Christian Britain, as Brown and McLeod do, there are many ways in which Canada was even more markedly a Christian society."[102]

The timing of Griffith's time in England means that he was in a unique position to comment on the changes in Canada in the 1960s. Since he left Ottawa in 1960 but returned to Canada to Deer Park United in Toronto in 1966, based on Clarke and Macdonald's analysis, this indicates that he left when the Canadian churches were at their peak but returned when their

97. Griffith, *From Sunday to Sunday*, 124.
98. Griffith, *From Sunday to Sunday*, 124.
99. Griffith, *From Sunday to Sunday*, 124.
100. Griffith, *From Sunday to Sunday*, 124.
101. Griffith, *From Sunday to Sunday*, 123–24.
102. Clarke and Macdonald, *Leaving Christianity*, 214.

rapid decline had begun. Is this reality reflected in his autobiography? Indeed it is. Griffith recalled:

> During the difficult years in Britain I often looked back nostalgically at the period of phenomenal church growth in Canada during the 1950s. When I returned to Canada I did not realize that the religious boom had peaked and that Canadian churches had entered a period of rapid decline. Memberships were dropping everywhere, Sunday school enrolments plummeting, and new churches in the suburbs had to close even before they had paid off their mortgages.[103]

Again, these words fit perfectly with Clarke and Macdonald's evidence in *Leaving Christianity*. Griffith was only gone from Canada for six years, so the fact that he saw such a significant difference in the Canadian churches of 1960 compared with 1966 obviously fits with the conclusion that there was a *sudden* drop in the churches in these years. Consequently, he elaborates further on his return to Canada and says: "Friends warned me that the situation had changed during my absence, but I was not prepared for the extent to which the church had lost popular support and had been pushed from the centre to the fringe of people's lives."[104] It is striking to see such a change reflected in a span of just six years, but this is consistent with *Leaving Christianity*. For his part, Griffith attributed the churches' decline in the 1960s to the Canadian population's increasing affluence and leisure time.[105] He adds: "The change expressed itself in a phrase heard on people's lips as early as Thursday evening, 'Have a nice weekend.' Sunday had ceased to be a day of worship—the first day of the week—and had become part of a long, pleasurable weekend."[106] In these years, he also recalls regularly hearing the members of a service club he attended "telling one another about their plans for the weekend, plans that rarely included anything to do with the church."[107] He notes that by 1968, the United Church of Canada's Toronto presbyteries already saw evidence of church decline; they commissioned surveys of congregations and clergy to investigate further.[108] Griffith says that the firm that compiled the data "charged $100,000 to tell us what we already knew."[109] The survey data officially showed that Toronto United

103. Griffith, *From Sunday to Sunday*, 150.
104. Griffith, *From Sunday to Sunday*, 150.
105. Griffith, *From Sunday to Sunday*, 150.
106. Griffith, *From Sunday to Sunday*, 150.
107. Griffith, *From Sunday to Sunday*, 150.
108. Griffith, *From Sunday to Sunday*, 150.
109. Griffith, *From Sunday to Sunday*, 150.

Church membership was declining, and "average attendance at worship services was forty-two percent of the membership, and the average church was half-full at the largest service, half the worshippers being over fifty years of age."[110] The report also showed that United Church Sunday School enrolment had rapidly dropped over the previous six years and suggested that some churches could close and some congregations should merge.[111] Given that he was in the United Church, it is possible that the decline in Sunday School enrolment may owe something to that denomination's controversial new Sunday School curriculum from the 1960s.[112] Even so, Griffith adds that he saw similar things happening "in all the mainline denominations" in these years.[113] Clearly, everything he reports here is consistent with Clarke and Macdonald's findings.

Griffith also records how these trends played out at his own congregation in Deer Park, Toronto.[114] He remembers: "In fifteen years the communicant membership had decreased by one-third, Sunday-school enrolment had been cut in half, and mid-week programs for children and youth had almost ceased to exist. Our sanctuary, which seated 1,000 was little better than half-filled on Sunday mornings, while the evening congregations disappeared altogether."[115] To reach more people, Griffith experimented by offering extra services on Wednesday nights and Thursdays in the lunch hour, but despite heavily advertising these services, "there were never more than thirty worshippers and usually less than half that number."[116] He gave up on these services after two years.[117] Once again, Griffith's testimony gives us a boots-on-the-ground account of the changes that Clarke and Macdonald cover in their book.

Finally, like Clarke and Macdonald, Griffith had a grimly realistic view of the challenge the church faced—and whether the Canadian churches could continue to function as they always had. We can start with Clarke and Macdonald. In the closing pages of *Leaving Christianity*, they wrote that too many authors "assume that by tweaking a program, churches can improve their fortunes or even return to the golden days of the past," but they say instead:

110. Griffith, *From Sunday to Sunday*, 150–51.

111. Griffith, *From Sunday to Sunday*, 151.

112. Cf. Flatt, *After Evangelicalism*.

113. Griffith, *From Sunday to Sunday*, 151.

114. Griffith, *From Sunday to Sunday*, 151.

115. Griffith, *From Sunday to Sunday*, 151.

116. Griffith, *From Sunday to Sunday*, 151.

117. Griffith, *From Sunday to Sunday*, 151.

> We do not believe this is possible. Our evidence suggests that changes in Canadian culture have been so dramatic that the first step churches across the theological spectrum of Protestantism, Catholicism, and other Christian traditions need to take is to accept that Canada is a de-Christianized, post-Christian society.[118]

Then, the last words of *Leaving Christianity* state bluntly: "We are now in a post-Christian Canada."[119]

Even in 1987, Griffith had a similar view of the situation. In the last chapter of his autobiography, he wrote a letter addressed to his former ministry students.[120] It intentionally mimics the greetings, closing, and structure of Paul's epistles in the New Testaments. Griffith tells the next generation of Canadian ministers that "you can expect to live and work amid change."[121] He continues: "The church, like every other institution in society, is inevitable involved in the process of rapid social change. Dietrich Bonhoeffer predicted that by the close of this century . . . the form of the church will have changed beyond recognition."[122] Griffith adds that pastors must be ready for these changes, "and I hope you will be ready for them and come to terms with them."[123] He notes that in the churches people respond to change differently because "some make it happen, some watch it happen, others do not know that it is happening, and still others do know that it is happening but try to ignore and resist it."[124] Griffith writes that this last group of people—both clergy and laypeople—"are the people who assume that the church can stand still while the world around it is changing."[125] Yet he believes: "They are like a small dog I once saw on an ocean beach barking furiously at the waves and rushing at them savagely, as though by his puny strength he could hold back their encroachment on the seashore."[126] Although Griffith reminds his readers that "Christ does not change," he nonetheless wants the churches to be realistic about where they are.[127] His book did not minimize the decline of Christianity in Canada, so his words

118. Clarke and Macdonald, *Leaving Christianity*, 239.

119. Clarke and Macdonald, *Leaving Christianity*, 245.

120. Griffith, *From Sunday to Sunday*, 202–10.

121. Griffith, *From Sunday to Sunday*, 205.

122. Griffith, *From Sunday to Sunday*, 205.

123. Griffith, *From Sunday to Sunday*, 205.

124. Griffith, *From Sunday to Sunday*, 205.

125. Griffith, *From Sunday to Sunday*, 205.

126. Griffith, *From Sunday to Sunday*, 205.

127. Griffith, *From Sunday to Sunday*, 205.

about change can also be read—like Clarke and Macdonald—as a warning to the churches to acknowledge that Canada has changed.

CONCLUSION

In the end, although Griffith did not have all the statistical data on the churches that Clarke and Macdonald compiled in their work, he was a perceptive observer of the significant changes in the Canadian churches in the twentieth century. His unusually long ministry career gave him the perspective to recognize both that the churches quickly declined starting in the 1960s *and* that they nonetheless grew and made great achievements between 1945 and the early 1960s. Following Brown's example, Macdonald correctly seized on the fact that the churches in Canada followed this trajectory—rather than a more gradual decline—and he and Clarke tracked that progression into the early decades of the twenty-first century. Griffith was an unusually good witness of these changes because his ministry career lines up so well with the span of the years they covered. Even so, using the thoroughly-researched framework Clarke and Macdonald provide, there may be more room to interpret and contextualize how other Canadian observers perceived these changes as they happened—just as Macdonald praised Brown for using people's personal stories to support his claims about the changing nature of Christianity in Britain.[128] In other words, there is room for future scholarship in Canadian church history to write accounts of twentieth-century religion and society *in Canada*, using people's personal stories but thoroughly informed by the data in *Leaving Christianity*. Finally, although Griffith's autobiography helps us understand the decline of Christianity in Canada during the 1960s, his testimony about the Canadian churches' impressive growth in the 1950s also cannot be overlooked. This is because—as Macdonald said when writing about Brown's work—we must be aware of how important religion was in past eras, "because the culture in which we now function sees it more as an exotic relic, than as something that once was a central part of culture."[129] We are fortunate to have had church historians like Stuart Macdonald to help us understand these things but there is more work that can be done to build on his work, so the churches can make sense of their current situation by understanding how we got here.

128. Macdonald, review of *Religion and Society*, 155.

129. Macdonald, review of *Religion and Society in Twentieth-Century Britain*, 155.

BIBLIOGRAPHY

"Arthur Leonard Griffith: March 19, 1920–April 7, 2019." Humphrey Funeral Home. https://www.humphreymiles.com/obituaries/Arthur-Leonard-Griffith?obId=27111473.

Brown, Callum G. *The Death of Christian Britain: Understanding Secularisation, 1800–2000*. 2nd ed. New York: Routledge, 2009.

———. *Religion and Society in Twentieth-Century Britain*. New York: Longman, 2006.

Clarke, Brian, and Stuart Macdonald. "How Are Canada's Five Largest Protestant Denominations Faring? A Look at the 2001 Census." *Studies in Religion/Sciences Religieuses* 40.4 (2011) 511–34.

———. *Leaving Christianity: Changing Allegiances in Canada since 1945*. Montreal and Kingston: McGill-Queen's University Press, 2017.

Cook, Ramsay. *The Regenerators: Social Criticism in Late Victorian English Canada*. 2nd ed. Toronto: University of Toronto Press, 2016 [1985].

Flatt, Kevin N. *After Evangelicalism: The Sixties and the United Church of Canada*. Montreal and Kingston: McGill-Queen's University Press, 2013.

Gilbert, Alan D. *The Making of Post-Christian Britain: A History of the Secularization of Modern Society*. London: Longman, 1980.

Green, S. J. D. *The Passing of Protestant England: Secularisation and Social Change, c. 1920–1960*. Cambridge: Cambridge University Press, 2011.

———. *Religion in the Age of Decline: Organisation and Experience in Industrial Yorkshire, 1870–1920*. Cambridge: Cambridge University Press, 2002.

Griffith, Leonard. *From Sunday to Sunday: Fifty Years in the Pulpit*. Toronto: Irwin, 1987.

Macdonald, Stuart. "Death of Christian Canada? Do Canadian Church Statistics Support Callum Brown's Theory of Church Decline?" *Historical Papers 2006: Canadian Society of Church History*, 135–56.

———. Review of *Religion and Society in Twentieth-Century Britain*, by Callum G. Brown. *International Review of Scottish Studies* 32.1 (2007) 153–55.

Marshall, David B. *Secularizing the Faith: Canadian Protestant Clergy and the Crisis of Belief, 1850–1940*. Toronto: University of Toronto Press, 1992.

McKillop, A. B. *Matters of Mind: The University in Ontario, 1791–1951*. Ontario Historical Studies Series. Toronto: University of Toronto Press, 1994.

McLeod, Hugh. *The Religious Crisis of the 1960s*. Oxford: Oxford University Press, 2007.

Moir, John S. *Enduring Witness: A History of the Presbyterian Church in Canada*. 3rd ed. Burlington, ON: Eagle, 2004 [1974].

Robinson, John A. T. *Honest to God*. London: SCM, 1963.

Wallis, Roy, and Steve Bruce. "Secularization: The Orthodox Model." In *Religion and Modernization: Sociologists and Historians Debate the Secularization Thesis*, edited by Steve Bruce, 8–30. Oxford: Oxford University Press, 1992.

14

"Reformulating the Faith"

An Initial Inquiry into the Nature and Development of Doctrine in The Presbyterian Church in Canada

John A. Vissers

The Presbyterian Church in Canada is bound only to Jesus Christ, the Church's King and Head. The Scriptures of the Old and New Testaments, as the written Word of God, testifying to Christ the living Word, are the canon of all doctrine, by which Christ rules our faith and life. We acknowledge our historic continuity with the Holy Catholic Church and our doctrinal heritage in the ecumenical creeds, and the confessions of the Reformation. Our subordinate standards are the Westminster Confession of Faith as adopted in 1875 and 1889, the Declaration of Faith concerning Church and Nation of 1954, Living Faith (*Foi Vivante*) as adopted in 1998, *and such doctrine as the church, in obedience to Scripture and under the promised guidance of the Holy Spirit, may yet confess in the church's continuing function of reformulating the faith.*

(Preamble to the Ordination Questions, 1970; emphasis added)

INTRODUCTION

Doctrine: what is it, and how does it change? In the past, Canadian Presbyterians believed that doctrine was a set of eternal truths set down once for all time, taught in the Bible, and articulated in the ecumenical creeds and the Reformation confessions. There was a time, not so very long ago, when every minister and elder owned a copy of *The Westminster Confession of Faith* and carried it to worship on the Sabbath along with a Bible. They knew what the Presbyterian Church believed and why. Christian doctrine seemed settled. However, it is also true that since its formation in 1875 through the union of four Presbyterian bodies, the Presbyterian Church in Canada has, from time to time, amended or modified its doctrine. In general, these changes have been shaped by ongoing theological reflection on the church's historic doctrine and the church's desire to accommodate its lived experience in Canada. How were such changes in doctrine understood? It's a complicated story.

Stuart Macdonald's recent book, *Tradition and Tension: The Presbyterian Church in Canada, 1945–1985*, provides a new denominational history during a period when questions concerning the nature and development of doctrine were paramount. I am pleased that this essay appears in a festschrift honoring my good friend and colleague for his lifelong contributions as a Presbyterian minister, church historian, and theological educator. In *Tradition and Tension*, Macdonald describes several changes in Presbyterian doctrine that occurred over a forty year period from 1945 to 1985: the adoption of "The Declaration of Faith Concerning Church and Nation" in 1955; the recognition in 1962 of the Belgic Confession, Heidelberg Catechism, Second Helvetic Confession, and the Confession of La Rochelle, as Reformed confessions parallel to the subordinate standards; the decision to ordain women to the role of ruling and teaching elders (ministers of Word and Sacraments) in 1966; the adoption of the new preamble and ordination questions in 1970; and the approval of *Living Faith* as a statement of Christian belief in 1984.[1]

If we take these as examples of "reformulating the faith," what did the Presbyterian Church in Canada think it was doing when it took these steps? Were they correcting existing doctrine? Were they re-stating old doctrine in a new way? Were they creating a new doctrine? My conclusions are much like Macdonald's: at the time, Presbyterians didn't always know, and often it didn't matter; until it did. But when it did, it really did, because it exposed significantly different understandings of the function and authority of

1. *Living Faith* was subsequently adopted as a subordinate standard by the General Assembly in 1998 and 1999.

doctrine among them. This essay, then, is an initial inquiry into the nature of doctrine at the time the Presbyterian Church in Canada was formed in 1875 and Church Union in 1925, and what that meant for the development of doctrine during the period documented in Macdonald's book, 1945–1985.

WHAT IS DOCTRINE IN THE PRESBYTERIAN CHURCH IN CANADA?

The most precise and straightforward description of Canadian Presbyterian doctrine is set out in the 1970 Preamble to the Ordination Questions. As noted above, it states that "The Presbyterian Church in Canada is bound only to Jesus Christ, the Church's King and Head. The Scriptures of the Old and New Testaments, as the written Word of God, testifying to Christ the living Word, are the canon of all doctrine, by which Christ rules our faith and life. We acknowledge our historic continuity with the Holy Catholic Church and our doctrinal heritage in the ecumenical creeds and the confessions of the Reformation. Our subordinate standards are the *Westminster Confession of Faith* as adopted in 1875 and 1889, the *Declaration of Faith concerning Church and Nation* of 1954, *Living Faith* (*Foi Vivante*) as adopted in 1998, and such doctrine as the church, in obedience to Scripture and under the promised guidance of the Holy Spirit, may yet confess in the church's continuing function of reformulating the faith."[2]

This paragraph describes several ways in which Canadian Presbyterians understand the meaning of doctrine. First, the Presbyterian Church in Canada is bound only to Jesus Christ as the Church's King and Head. Christ is the living Word who rules the church by the written Word. Doctrine is the way the church articulates what it believes Christ is saying through the Holy Spirit speaking in the Scriptures of the Old and New Testaments. For Canadian Presbyterians, doctrinal authority is Christological: Christ is the Prophet, Priest, and King who teaches and rules. The ultimate authority for doctrine is Jesus Christ as he is attested in Holy Scripture.

Second, the Scriptures of the Old and New Testaments are "the canon of all doctrine." Canon means measure, regulation, or rule. For Presbyterians, the Bible is the canon of all doctrine in the sense that it contains the essential teachings of the Christian faith and is the norm against which all doctrine of the church is to be measured. Holy Scripture is the primary standard of doctrine. As Calvin taught, Christ comes to his church clothed in the words of the Bible. Doctrinal authority is, in this sense, biblical.

2. PCC, "Preamble and Ordination Questions," Standards and Subscription, para. 447, in *The Book of Forms*.

Third, doctrine in the Presbyterian Church is understood to stand in historic continuity with the ecumenical creeds (e.g., the Apostles' Creed, the Nicene-Constantinopolitan Creed, and the Council of Chalcedon) and the confessions of the sixteenth-century Reformation. Doctrine stands within the tradition of the holy catholic church (reformed).

Fourth, three confessional documents are identified as "subordinate standards" (The Westminster Confession of Faith, The Declaration of Faith Concerning Church and Nation, and Living Faith). These documents, Presbyterians believe, represent the church's best efforts to say what the Bible teaches. They have a special degree of authority, but this authority is subordinate to Holy Scripture.[3] The subordinate standards are to be read and interpreted under the Lordship of Jesus Christ and in the light of the Bible.

It is the final line of the preamble, however, that has been decisive in determining the nature and development of doctrine for Canadian Presbyterians since 1970. The subordinate standards include "such doctrine as the church, in obedience to Scripture and under the promised guidance of the Holy Spirit, may yet confess in the church's continuing function of reformulating the faith."[4] In this rendering, the confessional position of the Presbyterian Church in Canada is open, not closed.[5] The church has a continuing task, it seems, of reformulating the faith, and thus may confess in the future doctrine which it does not now confess; or alternatively, it may cease confessing doctrine that it once confessed. At least three questions emerge. First, what does it mean to "reformulate" the faith? Second, was the Presbyterian Church in Canada an "open-ended" confessional church before 1970? Third, how does the church "reformulate" the faith?

To take the third question first, since its formation in 1875, the Presbyterian Church in Canada has had an authorized process for amending its doctrine and polity called the Barrier Act. Originating in the ecclesiastical law of the Church of Scotland, the Barrier Act was created in 1697 to require the General Assembly to consult with the wider Church before making changes to doctrine, polity, or worship. In its current form in the Presbyterian Church in Canada, any such proposal for change (remit) must be adopted by a General Assembly and then sent down to all presbyteries, where the vote can be only yes or no. If most presbyteries approve, and if

3. In the Presbyterian tradition, the authority of doctrine is grounded in the authority of the church to discipline its ministers and elders in accordance with the Bible and the subordinate standards.

4. PCC, "Preamble and Ordination Questions," Standards and Subscription, para. 447, in *The Book of Forms*.

5. On the distinction between an "open" confessional system and a "closed" confessional position, see Church Doctrine Committee, *Confessing the Faith Today*, 17–30.

these presbyteries represent most of the ministers and elders of all presbyteries (i.e., a double majority), the remit is put to a vote at a second (usually the next) General Assembly, where, when adopted, it becomes the doctrine of the Church. This process seems quite straightforward. The first two questions, however, are less so.

What does it mean when the Barrier Act is deployed to "reformulate" the faith? In its most basic sense, to reformulate something means to formulate something again in a different way. To formulate something is to create or devise it. It is to express an idea in a concise or systematic manner. To formulate doctrine, then, is to state or articulate it clearly and succinctly in a formulaic form. Presumably, to reformulate doctrine is to restate it or to state it again, more clearly, and in ways that are more meaningful and comprehensible. Both the formulation of doctrine and the reformulation of doctrine are expressions of second-order discourse. The church believes that Jesus teaches something in the Bible. The formulation and reformulation of doctrine is the church's attempt to distill biblical teaching. The reformulation of doctrine is best understood in relation to the church as a confessing church, i.e., a church with an ongoing vocation to bear witness to Christ by confessing the faith. It should also be set in the context of how Canadian Presbyterians use the phrase "reformed and reforming." Some use this phrase in its historic sense, meaning that a reformed church is always in the process of sanctification in its faith and practice, i.e., becoming more like Christ and conforming to what Christ teaches in the Bible as the Word of God. Others, however, use it to signal a "changing" church in a changing context. So, what does "reformulate" mean in the Preamble? Is it formulating again, reforming, confessing, or changing; all of these, or none?

This raises the more basic question: Did the 1970 Preamble change the understanding of the nature and development of doctrine in the Presbyterian Church? Does the Preamble shift the force of the Barrier Act from a "closed confessional' position to an "open confessional" position? Was this commitment to an open confessional position already implicit and at work in 1875? Or did a shift in understanding occur sometime between 1875 and 1970? If so, how and why did that happen? To answer these questions, we must begin at the beginning, in 1875.

THE BASIS OF UNION, 1875

At its formation on June 15, 1875, The Presbyterian Church in Canada adopted "A Basis of Union" consisting of two principles; all ministers and elders were required to subscribe to the standards of the new church:

> 441.2 The Westminster Confession of Faith shall form the subordinate standard of this church; the Larger and Shorter Catechisms shall be adopted by the church and appointed to be used for the instruction of the people; it being distinctly understood that nothing contained in the aforesaid Confession or Catechisms, regarding the power and duty of the civil magistrate, shall be held to sanction any principles or views inconsistent with full liberty of conscience in matters of religion.
>
> 441.3 The government and worship of this church shall be in accordance with the recognized principles and practice of Presbyterian Churches, as laid down generally in the "Form of Presbyterian Church Government" and in "The Directory for the Public Worship of God."

The whole historical and confessional base of The Presbyterian Church in Canada stands at the forefront of the denomination's *Book of Forms.* It states that the Presbyterian Church in Canada is in historical continuity with the Church of Scotland, reformed in 1560. The four Presbyterian churches that reunited in Canada in 1875 consisted of presbyteries and synods that had their origin in the Church of Scotland, or in one or other of the branches of the Secessionist church in Scotland. As the Basis of Union, the Presbyterian Church in Canada received the Scriptures of the Old and New Testaments as the Word of God and the only infallible rule of faith and manners (practice). It also adopted the Westminster Confession of Faith as its principal subordinate standard, approved by the General Assembly of the Church of Scotland in 1647. The government and worship of the Church were to be in accordance with the recognized principles and practice of Presbyterian Churches as laid down in "The Form of Presbyterial Church Government" and in "The Directory for the Public Worship of God." Finally, the "principles and practice of Presbyterian Churches" as set forth particularly in the Second Book of Discipline, 1578, acknowledge that Christ Jesus . . . "as the Head of his Church, has appointed its constitution, laws, ordinances and offices; that its government and discipline are to be administered according to his will as revealed in Holy Scripture, by officers chosen for their fitness, and duly set apart to their office; that these officers meet for deliberation and united action in sessions, presbyteries, synods, and General Assemblies, and in such order that the organic unity of the church is maintained in a hierarchy of courts (in contra-distinction to a hierarchy of persons); the authority of which courts is ministerial and declarative, announcing what Christ has revealed, and applying his law according to his direction."[6]

At least four observations should be made about the reception and adoption of The Westminster Standards as the Basis of Church union in 1875 and their significance for doctrine. First, the Basis of Union adopted the Westminster Confession of Faith as the Church's subordinate standard. Holy Scripture was the primary standard. It also adopted the Westminster Larger and Shorter Catechisms as the basis for the instruction (i.e., teaching doctrine) of the people. Presbyterians believed that the biblical doctrine of the church as contained in the approved catechisms was to be taught to the people. It had a catechetical purpose.

Second, the Basis of Union inserts a qualifying interpretive clause when it states that "it being distinctly understood that nothing contained in the aforesaid Confession or Catechisms, regarding the power and duty of the civil magistrate, shall be held to sanction any principles or views inconsistent with full liberty of conscience in matters of religion." This statement effectively appeals to Chapter XX, "Of Christian Liberty, and Liberty of Conscience," in the interpretation and application of Chapter XXIII, "Of the Civil Magistrate." As Stuart Macdonald notes, "Disagreements over the relationship between church and state had splintered Presbyterians into various competing denominations."[7] Since at least the seventeenth century, Presbyterians had divided into three prominent positions on this issue: (1) the Free Church tradition expected to receive financial support from the civil magistrate, but denied that the civil magistrate had any authority to interfere in the church; (2) the Established Church of Scotland tradition expected the civil magistrate to pay for the church and in exchange the church accepted that the civil magistrate had jurisdiction in the life of the church; (3) The Voluntarist or Antiestablishment tradition, believed that the church should rely solely on member's monetary contributions. Thus, the civil magistrate had no authority over the church's faith and life, nor any financial obligation to the church.[8] The four churches that joined to create the Presbyterian Church in Canada in 1875 represented denominations that each, in its own way, held one of these interpretations, with the Free Church tradition being the largest. The only way forward was an agreed-upon qualifying clause that made it clear that the Church of Scotland's establishment view (which was the way WCF XXIII was commonly interpreted) could not be imposed on the new Church. This resulted in three questions that have

6. PCC, *The Book of Forms*, 2025 Edition, 01, 02, 03.

7. Macdonald, *Tradition and Tension*, 116.

8. Macdonald, *Tradition and Tension*, 116.

vexed Presbyterians in Canada since: (1) Can the Westminster Confession of Faith be changed? (2) Did the new Presbyterian Church in Canada have a confessional statement on the "church and civil magistrate"? (3) What is "liberty of conscience," and must it be explicitly permitted by the church to be invoked by parties within the church?

Third, the Basis of Union was a "basis of union." The purpose of these statements was to create a *united* Presbyterian church in Canada, and the new church's purpose was primarily to establish a Christian Canada. There is no evidence to suggest that the Presbyterians of 1875 saw it as their right and responsibility to "reformulate the faith." They wanted to create a strong Protestant church in the "Dominion of Canada." This was a "Basis of Union" that agreed upon the Westminster Confession, but it was not in and of itself a confessional statement. The confessional status of the Westminster Confession of Faith existed for all the Presbyterian churches that created the union. That was a given. It was also agreed that a Presbyterian church could enter a union with other Presbyterian churches in accordance with Presbyterian polity, and that interpretive compromise clauses on the confessional standards could be employed in such unions. But did they think the new church had the power to make significant doctrinal changes?

Finally, and this happened fourteen years later in 1889, the General Assembly adopted a statement that gave "liberty of conscience" or "liberty of opinion" on Chapter XXIV.4, "Of Marriage and Divorce." This is the paragraph on consanguinity in marriage that states the WCF's teaching that "The man may not marry any of his wife's kindred, nearer in blood than he may of his own: nor the woman of her husband's kindred, nearer in blood than of her own." It would be one hundred and thirty years (2019) before a General Assembly again invoked "liberty of conscience" on the doctrine of marriage, this time on the definition of marriage as the union between one man and one woman.[9] But in 1889, this was an agreement on a libertarian interpretation of a particular chapter of the Westminster Confession of Faith. It was considered neither an amendment to the Westminster Confession nor a reformulation of doctrine.

However, things were not as theologically and ecclesiastically settled as they might have appeared. Until the 1870s in English Canada, Scottish Common-Sense realism in philosophy undergirded Presbyterian Reformed theology. By the time the Presbyterian Church in Canada was formed in 1875, however, Hegelian evolutionary views of Christian doctrine lurked in Canadian Protestant theological schools. Talk of another church union

9. Acts and Proceedings, 2019, Remits B and C.

lay just ahead. The nature of doctrine—its authority, and its development—bubbled just underneath the established social ecclesial surface.

CHURCH UNION, 1925

Macdonald's lucid account of the church union debates in the Presbyterian Church in Canada provides important background concerning how the United Church of Canada came to exist and how a minority of Presbyterians successfully resisted the Presbyterian decisions that created the United Church and voted the Presbyterian Church in Canada out of existence. Why "continuing Presbyterians" resisted remains unclear. As Macdonald notes, "The answers were not clear at the time, nor have they become clearer with time."[10] For this initial inquiry into the nature and development of doctrine, however, those reasons are not as important as how the decisions were made. The events that unfolded between 1910 and 1925 demonstrate that not all Presbyterians were willing to follow their own polity, at least not when it came to whether the Presbyterian Church should exist as an explicitly Presbyterian denomination. At the same time, those who opposed church union had a strong case for recognition by the courts as standing in doctrinal continuity with the Westminster Confession of Faith.

As Macdonald notes, the 1910 General Assembly approved church union by a majority. Following Presbyterian polity, this was sent down under the Barrier Act, where a majority of presbyteries representing a majority of the denomination voted in favor.[11] It should have been straightforward. In 1911, the General Assembly should have voted again and, if the motion had been adopted, the Presbyterian Church should have moved forward with the proposed union. That's not what happened. The 1911 General Assembly decided instead to hold a plebiscite among the church's membership to determine the percentage of Presbyterians who supported church union. The report was received by the General Assembly in 1912: 70 percent in favor. In 1916, the vote that should have been held in 1911 happened: the General Assembly voted (406/90) for church union. It took nine more years

10. Macdonald, *Tradition and Tension,* 13.

11. Macdonald's describes the process under the Barrier Act, stating that a majority of the denomination's members is required for approval, but cites no basis for this description in the historical record. At the time of the first church union in 1910, the Barrier Act required a majority of presbyteries to pass legislation. In 1946, this was amended to include a majority of presbyteries and a majority of the ministers and elders within presbyteries. Unless there is evidence to the contrary, the majority was to consist of presbyteries, not of members of the denomination. The exception was the 1911 plebiscite.

of ecclesiastical, political, and legal wrangling before the United Church of Canada was created on June 10, 1925. The "continuing Presbyterians" fought to continue. According to their own polity, they had no justification for doing so. But they won the right to continue. How and why?

As John S. Moir, N. Keith Clifford—and now Stuart Macdonald—demonstrate, the Presbyterians who resisted church union won the right to continue as Presbyterians in the courts and the legislatures. In civil law, as Macdonald notes, a decision made in the British House of Lords that is known commonly as the Overtoun decision awarded the property and legal rights to a minority within the Free Church of Scotland when, in 1900, the United Presbyterians and the Free Church of Scotland joined to become the United Presbyterian Church. This decision had implications for Canada and provided the resistance to church union with a basis for their opposition. What is essential for our study is this: the decision emphasized that doctrine is critical to the identity of a Church. As reported in the *Presbyterian Record,* the British decision had direct relevance for church union in Canada. The "identity of a religious community described as a Church must consist in the unity of its doctrine. Its creeds, confessions, formularies, tests, and so forth are apparently intended to ensure the unity of the faith which its adherents profess, and certainly among all Christian Churches the essential idea of a creed or confession of faith appears to be a public acknowledgment of such and such religious views as the bond of union which binds them together as one Christian community."[12]

On April 12, 1924, "An Act respecting the Union of certain Churches," known as *The United Church of Canada Act,* received royal assent. The Basis of Union had been agreed to by the Methodist, Congregationalist, and Presbyterian Churches in Canada, and on June 10, 1925, the United Church of Canada was born. The Basis of the Union should have been enough on its own. Still, the three Churches had petitioned the Parliament of Canada to secure legal recognition of the new United Church and a mechanism to settle ownership and the transfer of assets and properties, especially across the provinces. It was also believed that the parliamentary act would settle the complex juridical issues of church unions and the civil magistrate, as well as legitimating the United Church of Canada amid public controversy, once and for all. It did not. Fourteen years later, the "continuing" or "non-concurring" Presbyterians legally regained the name "The Presbyterian Church in Canada" by the Supreme Court in a decision that held that while it was true that institutionally the Presbyterian Church in Canada ceased to exist legally in the Basis of Union as approved in 1924, it was also true that

12. E. Scott, *Church Union,* 81, in Macdonald, *Tradition and Tension,* 18.

the United Church had effectively vacated the name, leaving it available to the continuing Presbyterians.

The non-concurring commissioners met on June 9 at 11:45 p.m. at Knox Presbyterian Church in Toronto to reconstitute the General Assembly of The Presbyterian Church in Canada and ensure that it met over the midnight hour. According to the United Church of Canada Act, the Presbyterian Church in Canada was to cease to exist at 12:00 am on June 10, 1925, when the United Church of Canada came into existence. The Presbyterians continued with another sederunt of the Presbyterian General Assembly, and the Presbyterian Church in Canada did not cease to exist.

Several observations may be made about the meaning of these events for the nature and development of doctrine within the Presbyterian Church in Canada after 1925. First, the continuing Presbyterians maintained their doctrinal heritage as Presbyterians by refusing to accept the decision for church union through the Barrier Act. This was ironic. The historic tool employed by Presbyterians to effect changes in doctrine and polity, including church unions, was not, on this occasion, accepted by the minority (30 percent) as the outcome. The irony was deepened by the continuing Presbyterians when they later added a phrase to the ordination vows requiring that all ministers and elders accept the government of the church by sessions, presbyteries, synods and General Assemblies, promising to share in and submit to all lawful oversight therein, and *to follow no divisive course* but to seek the peace and unity of Christ throughout the Holy Catholic Church.[13] Whose lawful authority did they mean? Had they not followed a divisive course? Which church government was to be obeyed? Whose church is the Holy Catholic Church—United or Presbyterian?

Second, the 1925 Basis of Union contained a statement of faith as the agreed-upon doctrinal basis of the new church. This statement of faith was rejected by continuing Presbyterians for several different reasons. Some believed it was too conservative and traditional. Others saw it as too liberal. A third group argued that it was not properly a confession at all, but merely a basis for union. The 1875 Basis of Union was not a confession, to be sure, but, as noted above, it adopted the Westminster Confession as the church's theological standard. Not so the 1925 Basis of Union, they argued. The continuing Presbyterians were able to make their case in public and in the courts by arguing that the United Church had departed from the historic Westminster tradition and had 'reformulated' the Protestant faith.

Third, immediately following the establishment of the United Church in 1925, the non-concurring commissioners who met to continue the

13. PCC, *The Book of Forms*, 447.3.

General Assembly of the Presbyterian Church in Canada "unanimously affirmed adherence to the Westminster Confession of Faith and the Larger and Shorter Catechisms."[14] At the time, this was clearly intended to situate the continuing Presbyterians in continuity with the Presbyterian Church in Canada that had existed since 1875. But did they really believe it? Was this intended to affirm a "fixed" or "closed" confessional tradition for the continuing church? In sum, the Presbyterian understanding of doctrine in 1925 was inconsistent. This does not mean that Presbyterians did not know what they believed as Reformed Christians. They did. It means, rather, that they were confused about how what they believed established their identity as a denomination. That's the confusion about the nature and development of doctrine, which helps explain the unresolved theological tensions during the next period of the denomination's history.

TRADITION AND TENSION, 1945–1985

Macdonald's account of the theological developments from 1945 to 1985 within the Presbyterian Church in Canada lays bare how this period was marked at one and the same time by a deep theological engagement with the tradition of the church in its lived experience, and a profound theological confusion about its identity and the place of doctrine in it. The questions of church and state, liberty of conscience, the authority of the Bible, the status of the Westminster Standards, and the ordination of women were among the presenting issues. Beneath it all, however, lay the question of the theological identity of the Presbyterian Church in Canada after 1925. Was it a confessional church? If so, what did that mean? Was there an urgent need, as some argued, for Presbyterians to reformulate their faith as continuing Presbyterians?

Macdonald begins his chapter on theology and worship in the Presbyterian Church during this period (Chapter 5, "Preserving the Past") by noting that in the years immediately after 1925, the denomination was more closely tied to the Westminster Standards than had been "the case prior to the disruption."[15] This is true. Ephraim Scott argued that there was no need for a General Assembly committee on doctrine because nothing needed to be changed.[16] Scott was a staunch conservative Calvinist. Doctrine was a settled matter; Presbyterians believed what the Westminster Confession of Faith taught (except when they didn't have to, as in 1875 and 1889). The

14. Church Doctrine Committee, *Confessing the Faith Today*, 20.
15. Macdonald, *Tradition and Tension*, 117.
16. Scott, *Church Union*, 132, cited in Macdonald, *Tradition and Tension*, 117.

Reformed faith was the faith reformed once for all time in the sixteenth century, handed down through the church since then. Presbyterians had a closed confessional position. After all, that's what they had been fighting for in 1925. There were other voices, however. More liberal Calvinists, like Stuart C. Parker of St. Andrew's Church, Toronto, argued for an open and malleable interpretation of doctrine. Doctrine was intended to set forth the substance of what was believed, not provide a rule for faith. The problem with church union, as he and his colleagues saw it, was not that it was based on a new statement of faith; rather, the Basis of Union was too traditional as a creed. From 1925 until 1939, these so-called "fundamentalists" and "modernists" within the continuing Presbyterian Church had to make common cause against the United Church of Canada to secure their future in law and public perception. Once that was settled, however, a new crisis emerged, triggered by the German Church and the Second World War. So it was, Presbyterians moved from the crisis of Church Union to the crisis of the Confessing Church, and they began the process of "reformulating the faith" in earnest.

The "Paris Deliverance" triggered the first major development in April 1939. This was a statement made by the Presbytery of Paris in Ontario in support of the "Confessing Church" in Germany and in opposition to German National Socialism's attack against the Gospel. The statement was forwarded as a memorial to both the synod and the General Assembly, and it has become, as Stuart Macdonald notes, "central to the way Canadian Presbyterians have told the story of how they began to rethink church and state relations during World War II."[17] What was behind this statement?

During the 1930s, Walter W. Bryden of Knox College and his students began to give voice to the teachings of the Swiss Reformed theologian Karl Barth and to neo-orthodoxy, which sought to find a way past the divide between fundamentalism and modernism. In Europe, Conservative and liberal Protestant as well as Roman Catholic churches had failed to stand against Hitler. The Barmen Declaration of 1934, shaped by Karl Barth, became the foundational statement of the "Confessing Church." Bryden and his students believed that confessions were more than historic doctrinal statements; they were public declarations of the Lordship of Jesus Christ.[18] The need for such a public confessional statement by Presbyterians in Canada, it was argued, was exacerbated by the fact that in 1875 the Basis of Union had neutralized Chapter XXIII of the Westminster Confession of Faith (with its interpretive clause), thereby leaving the Presbyterian Church in Canada in

17. Macdonald, *Tradition and Tension*, 117–18.

18. Vissers, *Neo-Orthodox Theology*.

effect without a statement concerning church and nation. The special committee that was struck at the 1942 General Assembly to look into this, and other matters of church and state that emerged during the war, concluded that the way forward was to re-examine "our whole confessional position as a church, with a view to eventually stating what we believe, as a Reformed Church, in language and concepts relevant to our own day and situation."[19] This was a major turning point for doctrinal development among Canadian Presbyterians.

It took twelve years until the next major step was taken. The Declaration of Faith Concerning Church and Nation was adopted by the General Assembly in 1954 and sent down under the Barrier Act, where it received the required approvals and was adopted as the doctrine of the Presbyterian Church in Canada in 1955. There were false-starts in the reports that finally led to this step. In the "Articles of Faith Committee," some argued for an entirely new statement of faith to replace the Westminster Confession of Faith; some for a Barmen-like statement on church and state; and some for nothing at all. As a result, when, in 1955, the Presbyterian Church in Canada adopted the Declaration of Faith Concerning Church and Nation, the denomination was unsure what it had done. Did the Declaration of Faith Concerning Church and Nation replace Chapter XXIII of the Westminster Confession of Faith? As Macdonald notes, that was what the Committee intended. Was it to be read alongside the Westminster Confession? Did the Declaration of Faith Concerning Church and Nation have the authority of a subordinate standard? And, importantly, did the Declaration of Faith Concerning Church and Nation truly reflect the position of the Presbyterian Church in Canada in relation to the Canadian nation in the way the Church acted and experienced itself in the 1950s? The General Assembly of the Presbyterian Church in Canada was not unaware of some of these issues in 1955, and it asked the 'Articles of Faith Committee' to report on what it meant that the denomination now had two confessional documents: The Westminster Confession of Faith and the Declaration of Faith Concerning Church and Nation. It took fifteen years to sort this out, but in the meantime, the Church was overtaken by several other doctrinal developments.

In 1962, the General Assembly took the significant, but largely noncontroversial step of adopting several historic Reformed confessions as parallel standards:

> That our church recognize the Second Helvetic Confession, the Belgic Confession, the Gallican Confession (Confession of La

19. Acts and Proceedings, 1943, 131, cited in Macdonald, *Tradition and Tension*, 122.

> Rochelle), and the Heidelburg Catechism, as standards parallel to ours, and direct that, as we recognize these as parallel, ministers, members of the Order of Diaconal Ministries and ruling elders of these standards coming to us recognize our standards as parallel to theirs, and for the sake of uniformity of law within our church that these ministers and ruling elders in ordinations and inductions subscribe to our subordinate standards as we do, it being permitted to these persons, where so desiring, to teach from these Confessions, (Second Helvetic, Belgic and Gallican) and the Heidelburg Catechism. (A&P 1962, p. 288–89)[20]

For the most part, this represented an act of hospitality and accommodation toward ministers and elders entering the Presbyterian Church in Canada from other Reformed denominations. By doing this, the Presbyterian Church in Canada acknowledged that other Reformed and Presbyterian churches had confessions that played the same role as the Westminster Confession of Faith for Canadian Presbyterians. What this meant, however, is unclear. It appears that the parallel standards could be appealed to by a minister or elder if they wished to take issue with the doctrine of the Westminster Confession. The Presbyterian Church in Canada also approved these parallel standards as acceptable statements of faith for teaching. Beyond that, however, their status as parallel standards have been, for the most part, left untested and underdeveloped.

As Stuart Macdonald notes, the decision of the Presbyterian Church in Canada to approve the ordination of women as ministers and elders in 1966, and the contesting of that decision by some Presbyterians in the late 1970s, proved to be a decisive factor in how the Church came to understand the nature and development of doctrine. "Despite reservations and some opposition, the denomination changed its doctrine and polity in 1966 when it approved the ordination of women as both elders and ministers . . . . While there was opposition at the time, it did not cause the major divisions that would happen later for the simple reason that those who disagreed believed they could simply ignore the decision."[21] This is true. Those who disagreed with the decision, including significant numbers who registered their dissent at the General Assembly in 1966, did not consider that this change in doctrine and practice would have immediate, widespread implications for the life of Canadian Presbyterians. They were not wrong. It took more than a decade before the denomination began to see women serving in the offices of minister and elder in significant numbers. Until then, those who

20. PCC, *The Book of Forms*, Appendix F.

21. Macdonald, *Tradition and Tension*, 91.

opposed the ordination of women, as well as those who affirmed it, simply acted as if not much had changed, in doctrine or practice. Few within the Presbyterian Church in Canada treated this doctrinal decision as having the same authority as the denomination's subordinate standards. Macdonald summarizes it nicely: "And this largely worked. Until it didn't."[22] The new Preamble in 1970 and the debates around "Liberty of Conscience" in the late 1970s clarified and confirmed the changes in the nature and development of doctrine that had been underway in the Presbyterian Church in Canada since 1943.

The significance of the new Preamble and the revised ordination questions, adopted by the General Assembly in 1970, has been underexplored in the way the Presbyterian Church in Canada tells the story of its theological history. It was, I argue, a major decision with implications not only for how Canadian Presbyterians understood Reformed doctrine at the time and going forward, but, perhaps more importantly, for how they interpreted doctrinal changes within the denomination since 1875. From 1970, candidates for ordination were required to subscribe not only to the subordinate standards, but also to "such doctrine as the church, in obedience to Scripture and under the promised guidance of the Holy Spirit, may yet confess in the church's continuing function of reformulating the faith."[23] This was an open-ended commitment. Ordinands were now asked whether they accepted "the subordinate standards of this Church, promising to uphold its doctrine under the continual illumination and correction of the Holy Spirit speaking in the Scriptures."[24] This was not a change in doctrine per se; it was a change in the nature and development of doctrine, thereby altering how Presbyterians understood their theological identity as a denomination. That change played out in subsequent theological developments in the 1970s and 1980s.

First, it enabled the Presbyterian Church in Canada to be clear about the status of the ordination of women as doctrine. As Macdonald notes, at the beginning of the 1970 *Book of Forms*, "the section outlining the doctrine of the church included the decisions related to the ordination of women as elders and ministers."[25] That the ordination of women to the eldership and ministry was a change in doctrine was now clear in a way that it had not been for everyone in 1966. The 1970 Book of Forms included what the General

22. Macdonald, *Tradition and Tension*, 115

23. PCC, "Preamble and Ordination Questions," Standards and Subscription, para. 447, *The Book of Forms*.

24. PCC, "Preamble and Ordination Questions," Standards and Subscription, para. 447, *The Book of Forms*.

25. Macdonald, *Tradition and Tension*, 215.

Assembly had enacted in the new preamble and ordination questions with reference to the 1966 decision on the ordination of women. Macdonald notes that "The Presbyterian Church in Canada was also not always good at updating what it believed in terms of doctrine."[26] This is true. But in this case, it updated its beliefs about the ordination of women, the Declaration of Faith Concerning Church and Nation, and the Parallel Standards. In 1970, this was the church's doctrine. The Book of Forms said so. This was a change in the understanding of the nature and development of doctrine regarding the ordination of women that had not been clear in 1966.

It also became unclear again when this was challenged in the late 1970s by those who opposed the ordination of women. Those who argued for "Liberty of Conscience" believed (wrongly, as it turned out) that the ordination of women—or that ordination in general, for that matter—was not a matter of doctrine in the same sense that Canadian Presbyterians meant doctrine when they spoke of the subordinate standards. Before 1970, they had a case, and those ordained before 1970 might have legitimately made that appeal. Those ordained after 1970 really had no case. The Presbyterian Church in Canada had made it clear in the new Preamble and ordination questions that ministers and elders were now required to subscribe to the subordinate standards and to such doctrine as the church may yet confess in its continuing function of reformulating the faith. That there was confusion about this is evident by the fact that, as Macdonald nicely observes, later editions of the Book of Forms in the 1970s omitted the ordination of women to the eldership and the ministry from the section on doctrine. Put simply, those who contested the ordination of women helped the Presbyterian Church in Canada clarify what it thought it had done in 1966 and 1970. But between 1966 and 1981, Canadian Presbyterians were confused and divided. The confusion and division were not just about the ordination of women; it was about the nature and development of doctrine.

Finally, the 1970 preamble and ordination questions clarified the status of the Declaration of Faith Concerning Church and Nation as a subordinate standard, and it prepared the way for the writing and adoption of a new statement of faith, which had been the intent of the General Assembly in 1943. *Living Faith* was accepted as a statement of belief acceptable for instruction in 1984 and has since achieved wide acceptance across the Church. In 1998, it was adopted as a subordinate standard. If this is what Presbyterians thought 'reformulating the faith' meant, there was a consensus that this document represented a confessional statement that stood in continuity with the historic Westminster Confession of Faith and, at the same time,

26. Macdonald, *Tradition and Tension*, 214.

fulfilled the church's call to confess its faith anew in every generation.[27] In 1875, Presbyterian doctrine was defined by the Westminster Confession of Faith and the Larger and Shorter Catechisms. In 1985, it was defined by the Westminster Confession, the Declaration of Faith Concerning Church and Nation, Living Faith (Foi Vivante), and such doctrine as the Presbyterian Church in Canada confessed in its continuing function of reformulating the faith. Doctrine had developed, and its nature, function, and authority had changed, and with it the identity of The Presbyterian Church in Canada.

CONCLUSION

As an initial inquiry into the nature and development of doctrine within The Presbyterian Church in Canada, based primarily on Stuart Macdonald's *Tradition and Tension*, this study suggests that there were two major turning points that led to changes in the way the Church understood its own doctrinal history: the 1943 decision to strike the Articles of Faith Committee, and the 1970 adoption of the Preamble and Ordination Questions. These two decisions were not changes in doctrine; they were changes in what The Presbyterian Church in Canada believed doctrine to be and in how they thought they should conduct themselves as a confessional church in the Reformed tradition.

This study also suggests that some of the nuances, ambiguities, and outright inconsistencies surrounding the decisions of 1875 and 1925 regarding the status and interpretation of the Westminster Confession of Faith indicate an open-ended confessionalism that was nascent from the very beginning in the formation of the Presbyterian Church in Canada. Understanding this on its own terms and within the broader tradition of Reformed and Presbyterian churches will be important for further study.

Finally, in the essay, I suggest that in the study of Canadian Protestantism, the meaning, function, authority, and development of doctrine remain underexplored. Canadian historians have tended to situate doctrinal change in Protestantism almost entirely within the narrative of secularization and the church's relationship to Canadian society and culture. I agree with Macdonald when he rightly pushes back against such simplistic narratives. Canadian theologians, on the other hand, have tended to situate doctrinal change in Protestantism almost entirely within the narratives of tension between conservative confessionalism, progressive idealism, and a mediating neo-orthodoxy. I think Macdonald agrees with me when I argue that the development of Presbyterian doctrine in Canada is much more complicated

27. Macdonald, *Tradition and Tension*, 233. See Introduction, *Living Faith*, 3.

than that. So, this article is written not only to honor Stuart Macdonald's career and his important new book. It is also an invitation to my colleague and friend to work together in the years ahead on a robust historical-theological account of the development of doctrine within the Presbyterian Church in Canada. After 150 years, the entire story deserves to be told, and there are few who can tell it as ably as he can.

BIBLIOGRAPHY

Church Doctrine Committee (CDC). "Confessing the Faith Today: The Nature and Function of Subordinate Standards." Acts and Proceedings, Presbyterian Church in Canada, 2003, 247–72.

Clifford, N. Keith. *The Resistance to Church Union in Canada 1904–1939*. Vancouver: University of British Columbia Press, 1985.

Living Faith: A Statement of Christian Belief. The Presbyterian Church in Canada, 1984.

Macdonald, Stuart. *Tradition and Tension: The Presbyterian Church in Canada, 1945–1985*. McGill-Queen's University Press, 2025.

Moir, John S. *Enduring Witness: A History of The Presbyterian Church in Canada.* Toronto: Bryant, 1974.

Presbyterian Church in Canada (PCC). *The Book of Forms.* 2025.

Scott, Ephraim. *"Church Union" and The Presbyterian Church in Canada.* Montreal: Lovell, 1928.

Vissers, John. *The Neo-Orthodox Theology of W.W. Bryden.* Princeton Theological Monograph Series 56. Eugene, OR: Pickwick Publications, 2011.